# The
# Lord
# Cornbury
# Scandal

The
Politics of
Reputation
in British
America

# The
# Lord
# Cornbury
# Scandal

## Patricia U. Bonomi

*Published for the*
Omohundro Institute of
Early American History
and Culture,
*Williamsburg, Virginia,*
*by the* University of
North Carolina Press,
*Chapel Hill and London*

*The Omohundro Institute of Early American History and Culture is sponsored jointly by the College of William and Mary and the Colonial Williamsburg Foundation. On November 15, 1996, the Institute adopted the present name in honor of a bequest from Malvern H. Omohundro, Jr.*

Library of Congress Cataloging-in-Publication Data

Bonomi, Patricia U.

   The Lord Cornbury scandal : the politics of reputation in British America / Patricia U. Bonomi.

     p.   cm.

   Includes bibliographical references (p.   ) and index.

   ISBN 0-8078-2413-5 (cloth : alk. paper)

   1. Clarendon, Edward Hyde, Earl of, 1661–1723.   2. Political corruption—New York (State)—History—18th century. 3. Political corruption—New Jersey—History—18th century. 4. Great Britain—Colonies—America—Administration—Case studies.   5. New York (State)—Politics and government—To 1775.   6. New Jersey—Politics and government—To 1775. 7. Political culture—New York (State)—History—18th century. 8. Political culture—New Jersey—History—18th century. I. Omohundro Institute of Early American History & Culture. II. Title.

F122.B655   1998

974.7′02—dc21                                                97-40318

                                                                                     CIP

The paper in this book meets the guidelines for permanence and durability of the Committee on Production Guidelines for Book Longevity of the Council on Library Resources.

This volume received indirect support from an unrestricted book publication grant awarded to the Institute by the L. J. Skaggs Foundation of Oakland, California.

02   01   00   99   98      5   4   3   2   1

For Lydia

Calomniez! Calomniez!

Il en restera toujours quelque chose

("Go ahead and slander!

Some of it always sticks").

— Beaumarchais, *The Barber of Seville*

# Acknowledgments

Many individuals and institutions contributed to the development of this book. A fellowship from the National Endowment for the Humanities and a grant from the New Jersey Historical Commission provided funds for research and writing. The staff of the New-York Historical Society, which owns the portrait that first prompted my interest in Lord Cornbury, has been generous in its support; I owe particular thanks to Stewart Desmond, Betsy Gotbaum, Margaret Heilbrun, Margaret Hofer, Holly Hotchner, Richard Kowall, John Kuss, and May Stone.

I am also grateful to the staffs of the Albany Institute of History and Art; the Ashmolean Museum, Oxford; the Bodleian Library, Oxford; the British Library; the British Museum; the Brooklyn Museum; the William Andrews Clark Memorial Library, University of California, Los Angeles; the Courtauld Institute of Art, London; the Fine Arts Library of Harvard University; the Guildhall Library, London; Historic Hudson Valley, Tarrytown, N.Y.; the Colonial Williamsburg Foundation; the Historical Society of Pennsylvania, Philadelphia; the Huntington Library, San Marino, Calif.; the John Carter Brown Library, Providence, R.I.; the Manuscripts Departments of the Library of Congress and the Folger Shakespeare Library, both of Washington, D.C.; the Pierpont Morgan Library, New York City; the Musée de l'Horlogerie, Geneva; the National Portrait Gallery, London; the New York Public Library; the New York State Library, Albany; the Rare Book Room, Firestone Library, Princeton University; the Public Record Office, London; the Worcestershire Records Office, Worcester, England; the Lewis Walpole Library, the Beinecke Library, and the Yale University Library, all of Yale University; and the Yale Center for British Art.

Specific queries were answered and expertise generously shared by Simon Adams, Phyllis Barr, Kathryn Bonomi, Antonio Feros, Robin Gibson, Barbara Graymont, Martha Hodes, Craig W. Horle, Richard R. Johnson, Gary Kates, Darline Levy, Leslie Lindenauer, Ellen G. Miles, Alison Gilbert Olson, Deborah Rosen, the late Eugene R. Sheridan, David S. Shields, Stewart Stehlin, David Steinberg, George Thompson, and Lotte C. van de Pol. Bert Hansen offered invaluable advice in the early stages of the research.

For special assistance with the illustrations, I wish to thank David Alexander, Martha Hamilton-Phillips, Josie Joyce, James Kilvington, Robert Maccubbin, Sheila O'Connell, Kate Ohno, Mme. Fabienne X. Sturm, Joan Hall Sussler, and Sarah Wimbush.

I appreciate the interest of colleagues in early American history who voluntarily sent materials pertinent to the project: Jon Butler, Edward Countryman, Richard Godbeer, J. Jefferson Looney, Dennis Maika, Brendan McConville, Eric Nooter, Robert C. Ritchie, Peter Thompson, and David Voorhees. Important support was given by Joyce Appleby, John Bonomi, Jr., Jacob Judd, Michael McGiffert, and Judith Van Buskirk. The Earl of Clarendon has been generous in responding to my queries. Frances Pingeon and Carolyn Stifel provided a sounding board for Cornbury stories, seemingly with unflagging interest, over a number of years.

I wish to thank the *William and Mary Quarterly* for permission to reprint material that first appeared there in my article "Lord Cornbury Redressed: The Governor and the Problem Portrait."

Laura Jones Dooley and Gil Kelly supplied expert copy editing and management of the project. My editor at the Institute, Fredrika Teute, put her powerful critical skills at my service. For their detailed critiques of the manuscript I am indebted to Bernard Bailyn, Kathryn Bonomi, Jack Bonomi, Ronald Hoffman, W. A. Speck, and Sam Tanenhaus. Each of them helped make this a better book.

Patricia Updegraff Bonomi

# Contents

# Illustrations

# Introduction : Under History's Carpet

Edward Hyde, Viscount Cornbury, royal governor of the English colonies of New York and New Jersey from 1702 to 1708, is ritually set down in the history books as a man of corrupt, venal, and bigoted character. He is also depicted as a transvestite who scandalized colonial American society by appearing publicly in women's clothes. It is a rare historical consensus, one that has stood unchallenged for more than two centuries. Contemporary rumors of cross dressing and vague charges of financial misconduct form the base of evidence on which Cornbury's image has been constructed. Yet all the charges against him come from heavily self-interested sources — from political enemies who resisted his program to consolidate British imperial controls, and from religious Dissenters who feared his effectiveness in strengthening the Church of England in the colonies.

My own interest in Lord Cornbury, and the gradual erosion of my confidence in the conventional story, came about somewhat accidentally. While doing research in England, I kept running across contemporary assessments of Cornbury's governorship, and even of his character, that were distinctly at odds with his subsequently assigned role as everyone's favorite villain. Any number of English officials, it turns out, applauded his administrative competence. In much of the official correspondence he is depicted as an aggressively shrewd and effective governor who devoted his considerable talents to placing the recently royalized colonies of New York and New Jersey on a solid imperial footing, all the while warding off the spiteful slanders of self-interested locals.

The disjunctive nature of these two versions of Cornbury's reputation piqued my curiosity. Following the trail of evidence into the thicket of British politics, I found myself in a world steamy with intrigue, gossip, and rumormongering — all part of an early modern political style with implications going far beyond Cornbury's case. In the decades between the Restoration in 1660 and the death of Queen Anne in 1714 — with succession to the throne under repeated challenge — political reputations were more susceptible to attack than in perhaps any other period of modern English history. That age was renowned for cabals and backstairs conspiracies, both imagined and real, as the English state sought to establish stability in the wake of the Civil War and the Glorious Revolution.[1] Political life was hazardous and unsteady at a time when, in the absence of a sanctioned party system that could channel and manage conflict, no legitimate outlet for criticism of government yet existed. Politics were further inflamed by the goadings of an emergent Grub Street press, as print was released from prior restraint by the expiration of the Licensing Act in 1695. The transatlantic setting, moreover, within which colonial governors functioned was especially likely to breed suspicion and rumor, with communications extending across vast stretches of space and time subject to all manner of mischief. In short, a climate of conspiracy, slander, and general foul play pervaded the public life of the Anglo-American world.

This dark underside of late Stuart politics has seldom been explored, historians having focused primarily on the composition of political factions or on the administrative machinery of the British state and empire. Most recently, attention has centered on the culture of civility and "polite moralism" promoted by social commentators like Addison and Steele and the third earl of Shaftesbury, who sought to counteract the vulgar rough-and-tumble of English life with a program of politeness.[2] But, if a concern for manners and refinement was on the rise in Anglophone culture generally, the public square was still a place where gutter politics prevailed. Gossip, calumny, prurient satire, and a muckraking press were active instruments of partisan conflict, at times deliberately employed to attack the character and integrity of those in power.

This seamier aspect of early modern, preparty political history is no-where better seen than in the Lord Cornbury episode, which inadver-tently throws light on all sorts of otherwise hidden facets of Anglo-American culture, especially on the mentality, motives, and behavior of certain prominent political actors in England and North America around the turn of the eighteenth century. That episode and its subsequent retelling also reveal much about the way early American historians con-structed a very particular "Whig" interpretation of provincial politics — one that looked benignly on our colonial forebears as progressive pa-triots while portraying the English as reactionary monarchists. This Whig perspective proved so routinely acceptable to later generations of Americans that it has retained much of its persuasiveness.

A word about each of these themes might set the stage for another look at the political ethos of our imperial age.

### THE CORNBURY LEGEND

Edward Hyde, Lord Cornbury, is notorious in the historical literature as a moral profligate, sunk in corruption, and perhaps the worst governor Britain ever imposed on an American colony. Cornbury first acquired his unwholesome reputation in histories written from the mid-eighteenth to the late nineteenth century, a period during which American nationalism came to take for granted that the struggle against England had been an epic contest between darkness and light. The earliest accounts assert that Cornbury took bribes and plundered the public treasury. One describes him simply as "this worthless person." Soon historians were portraying him as the embodiment of all that was wrong with the empire; some drew a line directly from Cornbury's administration in the first decade of the eighteenth century to the coming of the Revolution in 1776.[3]

The nineteenth-century historian George Bancroft declared that Corn-bury, though a member of the English aristocracy, "illustrated the worst form of its arrogance, joined to intellectual imbecility." Indeed, a later and less restrained historian saw Cornbury as a "degenerate and pervert who is said to have spent half of his time dressed in women's clothes." As early as the end of the nineteenth century, the mere mention of Cornbury in a history book was enough to evoke something unsavory and odious. "In passing from Lord Bellomont [Cornbury's predecessor] to Lord

Cornbury," one author wrote, "we feel at once that we are breathing a lower moral air."[4]

This early version of the Cornbury legend has even caught the fancy of popular writers in our own day. Under the title "His Most Detestable High Mightiness," *American Heritage* in 1976 published a story depicting Cornbury as "a fop and a wastrel." At a banquet welcoming him to New York City in 1702, Cornbury supposedly delivered a "flowery panegyric on his wife's ears," after which he invited every gentleman present "to file past Lady Cornbury and feel for himself the shell-like conformation of those ears." He misappropriated fifteen hundred pounds intended for New York's harbor defenses; he viciously persecuted Dissenters from his own Church of England; and, most scandalous of all, Governor Cornbury would deck himself out in women's clothes and then delight in "lurking behind trees to pounce, shrieking with laughter, on his victims." In 1988 the *New York Daily News Magazine* ran a five-column spread, repeating all of the above and more, under the title "The Trouble with Cornbury: His High Mightiness Was a Real Drag."[5]

Accounts of Cornbury's governorship by modern professional historians are not much different. They, too, assert that Cornbury dressed as a woman, engaged in "peculations from the treasury of New York," accepted bribes, and generally degraded his office. One leading authority declared that Cornbury has "a very strong claim to be considered as the worst governor in the history of the empire."[6] Yet in presenting Cornbury to their readers, most scholars simply recycle hand-me-down tales of cross dressing and corruption without venturing to check whatever the original sources might have told them. It is as if Cornbury's reputation were so beyond redemption that normal standards of historical proof need not apply.

Of what does the evidence for Cornbury's presumed derelictions consist? Surprisingly little, once it is sifted and isolated for scrutiny. Three colonials, all members of an opposition faction that rose against Cornbury's imperial program in New York and New Jersey, wrote four letters between 1707 and 1709 relaying a rumor that Governor Cornbury frequently wore women's clothes. In addition, a few early documents include vague and contradictory charges that he took bribes and misapplied government funds. There the contemporary evidence trails off. The eighteenth-century New York historian William Smith, Jr., no contemporary of Cornbury's but heir to the political gossip of the time, incorporated all these allegations in his *History of the Province of New York*, published in 1757. Committed to print, the charges took on an authority not easily erased. The power of print is further illustrated by the publication of a memoir from 1820 that became the basis for many of the more picturesque details of the Cornbury legend. Gertrude Van Cortlandt Beekman, a teenager during Cornbury's administration, seems to have recounted in her dotage a number of tales about the governor to her step-granddaughter, Janet Livingston Montgomery. When Janet Montgomery herself at age seventy-six included them in a family memoir, she was recording a fifty-year-old impression of a version of events that had supposedly occurred some one hundred years earlier, a recollection full of errors in both chronology and identity. Actually Janet Montgomery did not have a very high opinion of her grandam's character or of her trustworthiness. But these reservations were blurred over by prurient readers, and a new chapter of the Cornbury legend fell into place. As Janet Montgomery remembered the old lady telling her, Governor Cornbury had vowed to wear women's clothes one month a year and was frequently seen at night, so garbed, on the ramparts of the fort. The memoir is also the source of the story about Cornbury's supposed infatuation with his wife's ears, though it says nothing about gentlemen filing past to inspect them. It also includes a hostile portrayal of Lady Cornbury.[7]

If the evidence had simply stopped there, we might have considerable ground for skepticism. Gertrude Beekman did not claim to have been a direct witness to any of the scenes featuring Governor Cornbury that she recounted to her step-granddaughter. Nor, indeed, did any of the three whose stories William Smith, Jr., wove into his *History*. Such tales might well be seen as having their origin in the malicious gossip of political enemies.[8] Yet there exists a further piece of evidence, an extraordinary material artifact that has over the years imparted an almost palpable reality to the legend. A portrait of Lord Cornbury dressed in women's clothes hangs today in the New-York Historical Society. For well over a century, the identification of the figure in the portrait as Cornbury has to all intents and purposes been authenticated by a label attached to the frame. To be sure, portraits can be mislabeled, a particularly relevant issue here because the label was not added until 1867, more than 140 years after Cornbury's death. Moreover, the painting dissolves in mystery in the face of any effort to discover who painted it or where it came from. Nonetheless, considering the number of times over the years that comment about Cornbury has been illustrated with a reproduction of the portrait, there can be little doubt that the attribution of Cornbury as its subject has, perhaps more than anything else, given weight to the legend.

Sometimes large meanings are concealed in small events. In the present case, scrutiny of the old tale about Lord Cornbury discloses much not only about the politics of Anglo-America but also about the subjective nature of history itself.

### THE UNDERSIDE OF OPPOSITION POLITICS

The modern reader — though no stranger to rough political practices — is scarcely equipped to grasp the intense ardor, the unbounded ferocity of politics in the time of Cornbury. The talk of Civility and Reason in that dawning Age of Enlightenment might even be seen as a reaction to the raw passion that often drove the struggle for power and interest. Yet the notion that rival elites might compete for political authority within some embryonic kind of party system was unimaginable in a regime based on hierarchy and royal prerogative. That an Aristotelian mechanics of civic virtue kept such a regime in balance was mostly theory. Competition there was — bitter, irrepressible competition; and in that preparty age there was as yet no accepted vocabulary with which to explain or justify it. Hence such activity could only be seen by anyone, even those engaged in it, as conspiratorial and sinister in intent.[9]

This politics without rules called forth the most extravagant rhetoric when an opposition rose against those in power. Distrust and suspicion were heightened when power appeared to operate through connections and personal preferment. Doubting a rival's character or judgment, his opponents did not hesitate to accuse him of taking bribes or plundering the treasury he was pledged to defend. Suspect officials were repeatedly depicted as pandering to an ignorant rabble, as incapable of discerning good men for appointment to office, or as given to violent fits of rage. Nor was the opposition loath to insinuate that they were prone to sordid personal vices. Such charges were hurled so frequently in partisan rhetoric aimed at the royal governors, from New England to the Chesapeake, as to suggest a common source in English opposition, or "Country," thought — a mentality emerging by the later seventeenth century in both England and the colonies, and characteristic among those shut out from the "Court," or ruling circle. "Court" and "Country" constituted for an entire era a primary polarity in English politics.

The so-called Glorious Revolution of 1688–1689 had abruptly thrust England onto the largely unexplored terrain of constitutional monarchy. The reorganization of power that would in any case have had to accompany the new political arrangement was accelerated by William III's resolve to commit the nation to war against France. The war required a professional army far larger than any that had been at the disposal of William's predecessors; it also required an expanded navy and, most critical, a financial system capable of supporting enlarged undertakings in both the foreign and domestic spheres. In the 1690s the government negotiated huge loans from wealthy merchants and London financiers, who in turn were granted special privileges in the institution set up to fund the debt, the newly chartered Bank of England. The debt would be repaid from excise taxes (collected by "an army of excise officers, who were all dependent on the Crown") and, especially, from a heavy land tax of four shillings to the pound. To implement these initiatives administrative bureaus proliferated, as did placemen to fill them.[10]

This bewildering array of new financial arrangements and administrative forms excited the widest variety of fears among Country opponents — that sector of the political nation not at the center of things and thus sensing itself somehow left out of account in the new order. The Country persuasion, originating in the landed gentry during the last quarter of the seventeenth century, subsequently attached to itself a variety of elements in English political society, reactionary as well as radical, often Tory and sometimes Whig. What they principally had in common was an "outsider" state of mind. They professed to discern an increasingly swollen executive establishment in unholy alliance with the emergent forces of high finance, surrounded by placemen and Court hangers-on. Here were new mechanisms of power; how did outsiders gain credibility and influence in such a setting? The Revolution of 1688 had supposedly come about to restrict a rampant executive, to protect property, to reaffirm the independence of the landed gentry, and in sum to uphold the nation's virtue. Yet to the increasingly alienated opposition it now appeared that patronage, "stock-jobbery," corruption, and immorality had joined in a conspiracy to blow it all away.[11]

The acerbic partisanship of the post-Revolution years was magnified by a second late-seventeenth-century development: the emergence after 1695 of the Grub Street press. Together they promoted the vulgarization of political rhetoric. Grub Street provided a newly efficient way for opposition leaders to communicate their fears, suspicions, and insinuations to a wider audience. A bumptious tribe of hack writers eagerly put their talents at the disposal of the opposition, developing a scurrilous, defamatory style that reveled in gossip and did not flinch at slandering reputations. The scandalmongers attacked crowned heads, ministers of state, and imperial officials at home and abroad. Charges of financial corruption, blasphemy, and drunkenness — to say nothing of adultery, incest, and sodomy — became almost commonplace. Thus were early politics tinctured, as one colonial complained, with "False and Villanous Storyes . . . hatcht and Contrived . . . by Scandalous men."[12]

This combination of post-Revolutionary partisanship with vitriolic print fostered the growth, in its initial rough form, of the opposition, or Country, attitude. In fact, it cannot yet be called a Country ideology; this was before the Age of Walpole, before a Court-Country polarity had taken settled shape, before Country rhetoric would become, in the Hanoverian years, the lingua franca of opposition.[13] At this earlier point the Country persuasion was little more than a vast, vague umbrella for any kind of gross political attack. It was a politics of impulse and asperity, directed mainly to demolishing an opponent's reputation.

This tawdry underside of civic discourse influenced political life in both England and America in the late seventeenth and early eighteenth centuries.[14] Indeed, so familiar did it become that most people took it at something of a discount when judging the character of others, especially those in positions of public authority. If the critic of a public figure were out of favor, this "ma[de] his Information the less certain."[15] Did he now belong to a competing faction? Was he settling an old score? Was he trustworthy or a known gossip? Only after weighing the source and tone of what one heard or read could an observer of the public scene decide whether it was worth taking seriously.

Yet with time and shifting political conventions, this intuitive understanding of the excesses of early opposition rhetoric faded, leaving only the text itself — replete with slurs and calumnies now shorn of their context, and thus increasingly liable to be read as actual descriptions of past events and persons. This was particularly true when the surface text coincided with the readers' predispositions. Such was the case for Americans of whiggish inclination regarding attacks on the royal governors, who as surrogates of the British crown were for many years almost reflexively villainized by those sympathetic to the American colonies.

And given the particular conjuncture of time and place, who better to symbolize the sublime wickedness of the royal governors than Lord Cornbury?

### MOVING BEYOND WHIG HISTORY

This book takes a fresh look at the political culture of the First British Empire. The subject does not naturally lend itself to a neutral survey, because the processes of Anglo-American politics in that era culminated in the American Revolution, an event for which Americans in general, understandably, can seldom imagine more than one outcome. Though the "patriots" who favored independence did not at first compose a majority of the colonial population, the patriot, or Whig, version of the Revolution's political antecedents has for practical purposes taken its place in the nation's historical memory as the only version. The colonists, according to this view, defended liberal values and individual freedom, whereas the British upheld aristocratic privilege and control. Yet in many respects this conventional Whig understanding of our imperial past constitutes an imperfect foundation. For example, the "bad" royal governor is an image that persists to this day in the sinister light historians frequently cast not only on Cornbury but on a sequence of strong imperial governors from William Berkeley of Virginia and Edmund Andros of New England in the seventeenth century to, among others, Francis Nicholson of Virginia, John Seymour of Maryland, John Dudley of Massachusetts, and William Cosby of New York in the eighteenth century. These officials, while undoubtedly wielding power and patronage with a firm hand, might nonetheless look somewhat different if liberated from the partisan and anachronistic context in which they are usually judged. Considerable evidence suggests that the royal governors often responsibly administered their colonies to serve what they reasonably believed was the greater good of the empire.

And how, it might be asked, did things appear to that body of colonials who saw the rising power of the British Empire, at the dawn of a triumphantly imperial age, as a source of political, economic, and even moral strength? What about the support that many royal governors received from these provincial "courtiers," colonials who cast their lot with the empire and who in a number of places and times amounted to a majority? How did such imperial-minded provincials (who included among their number Benjamin Franklin) influence thinking on both sides of the Atlantic as British leaders sought to meet their responsibilities, respond to provincial needs, and resist or redirect colonial demands? [16]

These questions came up time and again as I read more deeply in the public and private records of that time and as I weighed the evidence from a broader Atlantic-world perspective. Having already acquired doubts about the Cornbury legend, I soon found myself questioning much that has been written on the whole subject of royal government and on the colonies' relation with England. Imperial politics could not fully be understood, I concluded, unless set in an Anglophone political culture rarely glimpsed in most histories of the period, a culture pervaded by gossip, satire, slander, and sexual innuendo, and within which words and meanings took on new and unexpected colorations.

If the familiar depiction of Lord Cornbury, in all his supposed depravity, affords a striking example of the politics of scurrility, it also raises knotty questions about how to deal with the past when records are incomplete and historical biases ingrained. A good deal of evidence is available regarding Cornbury's administrative career, as would be true of any colonial governor who served for six and a half years. We also know something of his experiences in England as an army officer and member of a prominent family. Nonetheless, there are significant gaps in both the public and private records, especially in private materials with regard to Cornbury's personal life and habits. This is not the first time that historical imagination has supplied the connective tissue for a fragmentary past, though in Cornbury's case it seems to have run amok. How, then, might we come to a more considered view of Lord Cornbury and his imperial world?

That Cornbury lived in a time when public figures were beset by charges of venality and moral turpitude suggests that context — social, political, cultural, even linguistic — has been the ingredient missing from his story. By exploring a number of different contexts pertinent to the Cornbury episode, this study aims to add shading and depth to a tale that has been peculiarly one-dimensional. It will examine the effects of gossip and of a rising Grub Street press on eighteenth-century Anglo-American politics. It will weigh conceptions of corruption and latent aspects of imperial discourse. It will seek a broader frame in which to set Cornbury's financial and religious programs, his military leadership and dealings with the Indians, his political views, and what is known of his personal and family relationships. It will attempt to gauge the aspirations and outcomes of the first era of imperial reform, especially as they affected Anglo-American political practice during the reigns of William and Mary and Queen Anne. And, given the nature of the specific charges against Cornbury, it will also look into the sexual culture of England and North America at the turn of the eighteenth century as well as explore gender symbolism, the modern clinical understanding of transvestism, and fraud in art history. After these variant contexts have been laid out and Cornbury's conduct appraised within them, we can return to the cross-dressing issue and to questions about Cornbury's character, evaluating them against the fuller landscape of his times.

The Lord Cornbury that emerges in these pages looks different — and I believe *was* different — from the version I encountered when I began. Yet if the resolution of some questions should continue to elude us, given the private nature of the "proofs," the exploration itself, it is hoped, will open new terrain. The larger assumption of this study is that by re-examining the conventional view of Cornbury (and by inference that of other royal governors) we might actually learn something new about the complex balance of loyalties, the contending ideals and emotions, that animated the politics of the First British Empire, perhaps even about the causes of the American Revolution.

Lord Cornbury's intriguing story in this way serves as a kind of foil, a device for exploring the underside of an intensely partisan age that provided an idiom, and eventually an ideology, for all who resisted political authority in early modern times.

# { 1 }   Lord Cornbury Redressed

## *The Governor and the Problem Portrait*

One of the most curious artifacts of the eighteenth-century British Empire is a painting, hanging in the New-York Historical Society, that is said to be a portrait of Edward Hyde, Viscount Cornbury, in women's clothes. At least that is what viewers have been told — that Cornbury is indeed the subject — ever since his lordship's name became associated with the painting in the late eighteenth century (fig. 1). At first glance the portrait seems to offer prima facie evidence for the long-accepted view that Cornbury was a cross dresser. But is the person in the portrait Lord Cornbury? Or might the painting simply constitute a particularly exuberant, if compelling, legacy of the rumors spread by Cornbury's political foes in the early eighteenth century? These questions suggest some intriguing possibilities concerning the portrait's history, which might be considered as a prelude to exploring the larger political culture of Cornbury's time.

### EARLY HISTORY OF THE PORTRAIT

Lord Cornbury died in 1723. Throughout the sixty-two years of his life and for three-quarters of a century thereafter, not a word seems to have been recorded in the colonies or England about a painting of him in women's clothes. His name was first associated with the portrait in England in 1796, the occasion being a visit by Horace Walpole and George

Figure 1. Putative Portrait of Edward Hyde, Viscount Cornbury, in Women's Clothes. Artist unknown; date unknown. Oil. © *Collection of The New-York Historical Society*

James ("Gilly") Williams, one of Walpole's Strawberry Hill circle of literary gentlemen, to the country estate of a friend, Sylvester Douglas, Lord Glenbervie. The three men were recalling stories about Katherine Hyde, duchess of Queensberry, a famous eighteenth-century beauty. This reminded Walpole, son of Robert Walpole and thus heir to old Whig tales, of a story about her cousin Lord Cornbury, "the mad Earl (as he [Walpole] called him)," which Glenbervie recorded in his diary as follows: "He was a clever man. His great insanity was dressing himself as a woman. Lord Orford [Walpole] says that when Governor in America he opened the Assembly dressed in that fashion. When some of those about him remonstrated, his reply was, 'You are very stupid not to see the propriety of it. In this place and particularly on this occasion I represent a woman (Queen Anne) and ought in all respects to represent her as faithfully as I can.'" At this point Williams volunteered that his father "told him that he has done business with him [Cornbury] in woman's clothes. He used to sit at the open window so dressed, to the great amusement of the neighbours. He employed always the most fashionable milliner, shoemaker, staymaker, etc. Mr. Williams has seen a picture of him at Sir Herbert Packington's in Worcestershire, in a gown, stays, tucker, long ruffles, cap, etc." [1]

A saucy story indeed, and one that points to a transvestite Cornbury not only in the colonies but also in England. The portrait mentioned by Williams is undoubtedly the one on view today at the New-York Historical Society; the description of the clothing matches, and it was from the Pakington family that the painting, purchased at auction by the society in 1952, descended. Yet the closest we can come to a source specifically attaching Cornbury's name to this painting is a thread spun by three merry gentlemen on a bibulous evening seven decades after Cornbury's death.

All three were well-known gossips. William Hazlitt called Walpole the "very prince of gossips," whose "mind, as well as his house, was piled up with Dresden china." Glenbervie, for his part, is said by the editor of his diaries to have "loved gossip" and to have recorded it with such abandon that his stories should be viewed with "a reservation of judgment." Williams is described as "one of the gayest and wittiest of his set in London society," qualities borne out by his droll, gossipy correspondence with George Selwyn. [2]

Williams could have been no more than seventeen when his father, a law reporter and member of Gray's Inn, told him the cross-dressing story some sixty years earlier. Gray's Inn is adjacent to Holborn, a street in London where transvestites publicly exhibited themselves in the early decades of the eighteenth century; a number of them, in full regalia, were hauled from Holborn through the streets to the workhouse in 1714 and perhaps again in the 1720s to the Old Bailey. That Lord Cornbury — a peer of the realm and first cousin to Queen Anne — could have been among their number or had displayed himself in women's clothes at open windows, and the fact gone unrecorded in any public or private document until three-quarters of a century after his death, is extremely unlikely.[3] It is more likely that Williams, or perhaps Glenbervie, conflated Williams's sixty-year-old transvestite story with Walpole's even older one about Cornbury in the colonies.

Williams could possibly have been told during his visit to Pakington's Worcestershire seat that the figure in the portrait was Cornbury. A letter from the son of Lord Sandys of Worcestershire, dated September 16, 1796, reported to the art cataloguer Sir William Musgrave on three paintings owned by Pakington, including one described as "The Second E. of Clarendon in Women's cloaths." Cornbury was in fact the third earl of Clarendon, having acceded to the title in 1709. Though we cannot know for certain whether Sandys, Williams, or some third party first linked Cornbury to the portrait, what information we do have points to a date circa 1796.[4]

Why was the attribution made at that time? Again, we must guess. But it does happen that the date coincides with a period in which English society had become inordinately absorbed with the issue of cross dressing. This was owing to the presence in their midst of the famous Chevalier d'Eon de Beaumont (1728–1810) of ambiguous gender. The chevalier's story is somewhat elusive. Toward the end of the Seven Years' War, d'Eon — after performing valorous service for France as a captain of the elite corps of Dragoons — had been dispatched to England to help negotiate a peace treaty, after which he remained in London supposedly to spy for Louis XV. By the mid-1770s London was aflutter with rumors that d'Eon was in fact a biological woman, news to this effect, including stories of cross dressing, having issued from the Continent. Soon a debate was raging in the English press over whether d'Eon was man, woman, or hermaphrodite, and thousands of pounds were wagered on the question.[5]

The chevalier, after losing his patrons in France, took up permanent residence in England in 1783. Never able to shake off the transvestite gossip, and increasingly destitute, he staged public fencing matches, allegedly dressed on occasion in women's clothes. Between 1794 and 1796, such exhibitions, according to the newspapers, drew large crowds at Bath, Brighton, Southampton, Oxford, Birmingham, and Worcester — the last being but a short distance from the Pakington estate (fig. 2).[6]

The English fascination with cross dressing in the late eighteenth century may well have given new life to the old story about Cornbury, contributing to his association with the Pakington portrait in a way we may never fully trace.

Cornbury's name was attached to the portrait more or less officially in 1867, when the painting was publicly displayed in an exhibition of national portraits at London's South Kensington Museum. By that time, and probably for that occasion, a label had been affixed to the frame identifying the sitter as Cornbury. Still there today, the label bears, not a curator's authoritative description, but a quotation from British historian Agnes Strickland's *Lives of the Queens of England*, published in 1847: "Among other apish tricks, Lord Cornbury [the "half-witted son" of "Henry, Earl of Clarendon"] is said to have held his state levees at New York, and received the principal Colonists dressed up in complete female court costume, because, truly, he represented the person of a female Sovereign, his cousin-german queen Anne."[7] Strickland offered only one specific source, a letter written to Hanover in 1714 by the German diplomat Baron von Bothmer relaying the rumor that when in "the Indies" Cornbury "thought that it was necessary for him, in order to represent her Majesty, to dress himself as a woman." The exhibition catalogue noted that the portrait was on loan from Sir J. S. Pakington and added, on cue from Strickland, that Cornbury "is said to have dressed himself in woman's clothes in order to represent her Majesty Q. Anne at New York."[8]

On July 18, 1867, the *New-York Daily Tribune* carried a special correspondent's report on the exhibition, including a brief discussion of the portrait. The correspondent noted that Cornbury was depicted "in female low-necked evening dress, it being his idea of loyalty to his Queen to dress like her!" He went on to quote the same picturesque passage

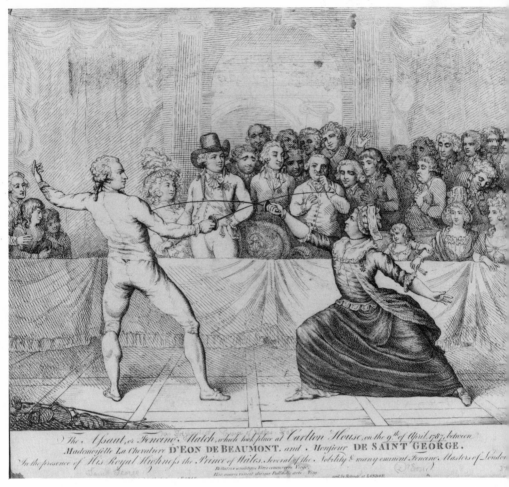

Figure 2. *The Assaut, or Fencing Match, Which Took Place at Carlton House.* Engraving by Victor Marie Picot. 1789. *Chevalier d'Eon de Beaumont versus Monsieur de St. George, 1787. Courtesy of the Print Collection, Lewis Walpole Library, Yale University*

from Strickland that appeared on the label. The *Tribune* story constitutes the first mention of the portrait in any known American source, printed or manuscript. Once the story appeared, the way was open for a luxuriant expansion of the Cornbury legend in the United States.[9]

### SPECULATIONS: EXPERT AND OTHERWISE

One reason Americans knew nothing about the portrait before 1867 is that it was very likely painted not in the colonies, as has sometimes been assumed, but in England. Most American specialists I consulted on this point agree that in the early eighteenth century no artist sufficiently skilled to produce a painting of this sort — even one modeled on a figure in an English mezzotint engraving, as was common in colonial portraiture — was working in North America.[10] A survey of portraits by such provincial artists as Gerret Duyckinck, Evert Duyckinck III, Nehemiah Partridge, John Watson, and Peter Vanderlyn — all painting in New York or New Jersey during or shortly after Cornbury's tenure as governor — seems to support that opinion. Their naive rendering of their sitters' features and their inexperience in dealing with light make it probable that the portraitist, though not an artist of the first rank, was working in England.[11] It seems a fair guess, too, that if a colonial had been taking a satirical poke at the governor — or, to put the most extreme case, if Cornbury had actually posed for the artist — word of the portrait would have got around.

Robin Gibson of the National Portrait Gallery in London, the leading expert on the Hyde family paintings known as the Clarendon Collection, commented on the New-York Historical Society portrait: "I feel certain that the so-called portrait of Lord Cornbury is a perfectly straightforward British provincial portrait of a rather plain woman c. 1710." Gibson thinks it unlikely that the portrait was painted in the colonies: "Although I do not think it would be possible to positively identify either the artist or the sitter of the portrait in question, it seems to me the sort of portrait which might have been painted of a well-to-do woman living well outside London society, perhaps in the north of England. It is not necessarily of a member of the aristocracy." But might the portrait be an English caricature of Cornbury, as some have suggested? Gibson thinks not. "Caricature portrait paintings (certainly in Britain at this date) are unknown to me and extremely rare at any time. Any caricature would have taken the form of an engraving or drawing."[12] This seems to rule out the possibility of a prank specifically aimed at Cornbury: a caricature, intended for circulation, would not have been done in oils. Further, if the portrait were of English origin, it could not have been produced during Cornbury's tenure as governor in North America — unless the subject happened to be someone else.

Might Cornbury have sat for the portrait after returning to England in 1710? This seems unlikely, given the absence during his lifetime of the

*Edward Hyde, third*
*Earl of Clarendon,*
*A Drawing by Silvr. Harding*
*from a Carving in Ivory —*
*At The Grove, The Seat of*
*The Earl of Clarendon,*

Figure 3. Sketch, Said to Be of Edward Hyde, Viscount Cornbury. By Silvester Harding (from an ivory carving). Before 1809. *Courtesy of the Ashmolean Museum, Oxford. Photograph Courtauld Institute of Art, London*

notice such a portrait would have occasioned. For all their love of scandal in the eighteenth century, English gossips and political diarists seem never to have identified Cornbury as a transvestite or imputed to him any other kind of androgynous peculiarity. Of the eighteenth-century connoisseurs who examined the famous Clarendon Collection, not one remarked that it included unusual portraits, much less one of Cornbury in women's clothes. George Vertue, tireless visitor to country seats and preeminent commentator on eighteenth-century painting, described the pictures at Cornbury Hall, Oxfordshire, which he saw in 1729, as "that Noble Collection of portraits." [13]

If there existed other authenticated likenesses of Cornbury, standards of comparison against which the portrait likeness could be measured, some of the mystery might be dispelled. A few candidates have turned up. One is an early-nineteenth-century sketch made from an ivory carving — apparently a kind of cameo — that is said to represent the third earl of Clarendon (Cornbury). But the sketch artist, Silvester Harding, did not say why he believed the ivory, now lost, depicted the third earl (fig. 3). The figure is attired in armor with a lace cravat at the throat and a swag of cloth over the right shoulder, a costume in which gentlemen were often portrayed from the 1680s to the 1720s. [14]

Supposing for the moment that Harding was right, how do the features in his sketch compare with those in the New-York Historical Society painting? The heavy eyes and full mouth are not incompatible with those of the New York portrait, though the pendulous lower lip is absent. The rather weak chin of the sketch does not match the long chin of the painting. Nor does the low forehead in the sketch resemble the unusually high one in the portrait. The noses are not at all alike, turning up in Harding's drawing and down in the portrait. [15]

Another ostensible likeness of Cornbury is an engraving that illustrates a history of New Jersey published in 1902. When copied to illustrate subsequent writings about Cornbury, the engraving was retouched and darkened, making it appear increasingly sensuous. Actually, the person in the engraving is not Cornbury at all. The author of the New Jersey history, Francis Bazley Lee, seems to have been rather a rascal. To illustrate his florid account of Cornbury's governorship, Lee used a portrait from James Grant Wilson's *Memorial History of the City of New York* (1892), where the subject is clearly identified as the duke of Marlbor-

Figure 4. Portrait in Miniature, Said to Be of Edward Hyde, Viscount Cornbury, Age Nineteen. By Jean-Louis Durant. 1681. Oil on vellum. *The inscription (added later) records that Cornbury participated in the civic festival Tirage de l'arc at Geneva in 1680.* ©-*Musée de l'Horlogerie, Ville de Genève. Photograph by Maurice Aeschimann*

ough. Lee removed Marlborough's name from beneath the picture, re-placed it with Cornbury's signature from a different page in Wilson's history, added a sketch of the family estate, Cornbury Hall, from yet an-other page, and passed off the composite as authentic Cornburiana.[16] Such knavery in our own century raises fresh fancies about the scruples of more interested parties in previous centuries.

Another supposed likeness of Cornbury, one never published or dis-cussed in previous writings about him, turned up in Geneva, Switzer-land. This portrait, a miniature painted on vellum, is in the collection of the Geneva Museum of Art and History (fig. 4). The only identifying mark on the portrait itself is an inscription on the reverse side, "J. L. Durant fecit anno 1681." On the right side of the oval case in which the picture rests is a second inscription, in a different hand and of unknown date. It identifies the sitter as "Milord Edouard Hide, Comte de Corn-bury" and notes that the portrait was deposited in Geneva's Bibliothèque Publique by order of the city council. At some point the miniature apparently fell into private hands. It was included in a gift to the city in 1846 and transferred permanently to the museum in 1870.[17]

As it happens, Geneva is not an entirely unexpected place to find traces of Cornbury. The young viscount lived in the city from early 1680 until May 1682 while a student at l'Académie de Calvin, an institution known in the seventeenth century for educating young European gentlemen of rank. Moreover, he received a singular honor in 1680 when at eighteen he was chosen for a leading role in the city's premier civic festival, l'Exercice de l'Arc — a day given over to military drills, shooting contests, and lavish banquets featuring multiple toasts. In ancient times, the best marksman among the citizens of the town had customarily been acclaimed "king" of the Arquebuse Drill, or troop of musketeers, and it may have been for his skill in musketry that Cornbury received the extraordinary honor of being chosen king in 1680 and perhaps again in 1681. It is quite possible that the Genevan artist Jean-Louis Durant (1654– 1718) painted a miniature of Cornbury to mark the occasion.[18]

The figure in the portrait is draped in blue cloth with orange fringe, the same colors used by the drill in 1680 when Cornbury was made king, and the unusual blue bow suggests some kind of costume or "club tie." The sitter appears to be about the right age (in 1681 Cornbury was nineteen); the luminous blue eyes and fair skin might be expected in a young man whose grandfather, the earl of Clarendon, was still quite blond in his forties and whose mother was once described as having "a complexion of dazzling fairness" (see figs. 6 and 9).[19] Further, the person represented in the miniature could be seen to bear some resemblance to Harding's sketch, most notably in the full mouth, fleshy chin, and round face. (At the least, the miniature and the cameo sketch look more like each other than either looks like the figure in the New-York Historical Society portrait.) Still, one cannot be certain that the miniature depicts the young viscount, because the artist did not identify his sitter and nothing is known about the circumstances in which Cornbury's name was subsequently assigned to the portrait. The most we can say, in view of the considerable evidence for Cornbury's connection to the miniature, is that we may now have a notion of what one artist thought he looked like as a young man. In any event, neither the Harding sketch nor the miniature is likely to put an end to speculation about the New-York Historical Society portrait, given the necessarily subjective quality of any effort to compare them.

One of the most challenging questions concerning the society's painting is why a portrait of Cornbury, if such it was, should turn up at the Worcestershire estate of the Pakington family. There was no blood tie or even close marital connection between the Hyde and Pakington families, nor did they, so far as can be determined, ever own property in the same counties. That the portrait might have been passed to, or become mixed with, the Pakington collection thus seems improbable. The Pakington family papers include many items from the eighteenth century. One is a 1786 "Inventory of Household Furniture Belonging To the Honorable Sir Herbert Pakington Baronet, at His House At Westwood Near Worcester." A number of portraits of unidentified women (possibly including the later-titled "Cornbury" portrait) were among the items inventoried a mere ten years before Cornbury's name was associated with the famous painting, yet none was described as "curious," the common designation for anything out of the ordinary.[20]

One English historian has suggested that Pakington might have bought the painting for the amusement of his guests. Perhaps so. Yet it may also be that Lady Theresa Lewis, a Hyde descendant who in the mid-nineteenth century also tried without success to trace the portrait's provenance, spoke more wisely than she knew when she observed that as portraits moved from estate to estate and family to family the names of their sitters were often forgotten, sometimes to "live again with fresh names in the hands of fresh owners."[21]

At my request, the New-York Historical Society agreed in 1990 to undertake a full scientific investigation of the painting. Examination showed that the picture carries no signature or other markings that would help to date it or to identify the artist.[22] The canvas is linen of a type used during the seventeenth and eighteenth centuries in both England and North America; the frame dates from the nineteenth century. Radiography revealed no underdrawing, no tampering with an original figure, and no clues to the portrait's provenance. Pigment analysis, it was thought, held out the best hope, for had the sitter's dress been painted with Prussian blue, the portrait could have been dated to post-1730–1735, after Cornbury's death. Analysis of cross-sections of pigment by a specialist at the Los Angeles County Museum showed, however, that the

Figure 5. *Mrs. General Washington Bestowing Thirteen Stripes on Britania.* In *Rambler's Magazine*, London, March 1783. *Two months earlier a London newspaper had reported that Washington was in fact a woman. Permission, Beinecke Rare Book and Manuscript Library, Yale University*

paint was smalt and indigo of types used in both the colonies and England well before and long after Cornbury's time.[23]

So: contemporary evidence for Cornbury's cross dressing is elusive; no scientific findings or evidence of the portrait's provenance point to Cornbury; the information on the label attached to the frame is spurious by modern standards; the picture was probably painted in England. It would appear that one of the most influential pieces of evidence for the charge that Cornbury was a transvestite must be declared factitious.

It is significant, moreover, that Cornbury's name became associated with the portrait at a time when cross dressing, owing to the Chevalier d'Eon, was much in the news. At the close of the American Revolution, George Washington himself was accused in an English newspaper of being "of the female sex" and was grouped with other military cross dressers — Joan of Arc, Hannah Snell, and the Chevalier d'Eon. It was perhaps fortunate for the Americans, the journalist concluded, that General Washington's "Circumstance was not known at a more early Period of the Contest."[24] Within two months of the appearance of this story, Washington was caricatured in a British magazine dressed in women's clothes (fig. 5).

Thus were Cornbury and Washington both mocked as cross dressers in a century notable for political satire and gossip, whose practitioners wantonly employed sexual innuendo.[25] That Cornbury was in such good company suggests the fresh possibilities in a scrutiny of the man and the political climate of his time.

# { 2 }    Lord Cornbury in England

Edward Hyde, Viscount Cornbury, later third earl of Clarendon, lived from 1661 to 1723 — from the Restoration of the monarchy following the English Civil War to the overthrow of James II in the Glorious Revolution, to the reigns of William and Mary and Queen Anne, to the accession of the House of Hanover and the rise of Robert Walpole — a critical and turbulent era in English history. Throughout these years divisions over religion and the succession to the throne split political leaders into warring factions. Relative stability was achieved only after 1715 with the advent of the long-lived Protestant Hanoverian kings, the defeat of the Stuart Pretender, and the diminution of party strife. Cornbury witnessed or participated in many pivotal episodes of this fractious age.

In 1660, a year before Cornbury's birth, the English, having had second thoughts about their decade-long adventure with republicanism, restored the Stuarts to the throne in the person of Charles II (1660–1685). Charles appointed his companion in exile, Cornbury's grandfather Edward Hyde, as lord high chancellor of England, perhaps the most powerful office in the realm (fig. 6). Hyde — member of a respectable Protestant family of jurists, magistrates, and clerics — was soon elevated to the peerage as baron of Hindon, which title might have served well enough under ordinary circumstances. The circumstances, however, were anything but ordinary. During the dark days of the Interregnum, Hyde's

Figure 6. Edward Hyde, Lord High Chancellor and First Earl of Clarendon. By Sir Peter Lely. Engraving by J. Cochran, 1829. *Courtesy of the Print Collection, Lewis Walpole Library, Yale University*

Figure 7. The Duke and Duchess of York. By Sir Peter Lely. Oil. 1669. *The future James II with Anne Hyde, his first wife, who holds his helmet in her lap. By courtesy of the National Portrait Gallery, London*

daughter Anne, a commoner, had caught the eye of Charles's brother, James, duke of York, a possible heir to the throne. The couple entered into a contract of betrothal in November 1659, and by the time they returned to England in the summer of 1660, Anne was several months pregnant.[1]

The chancellor, accused by sharp-elbowed political rivals of plotting to connect himself to the royal family, was in fact humiliated by his daughter's indiscretion. (He told Anne he would rather see her dead than disgrace the crown.) Nonetheless, James and Anne were secretly married on September 3, 1660, conferring legitimacy on the son born seven weeks later. Even so, Anne was not publicly recognized as duchess of

York until February 1661 (fig. 7). Charles II, fixing on his chancellor as the father-in-law and grandfather of potential future kings, resolved to elevate him to a more fitting rank. Apparently Hyde refused a proffered dukedom "as likely to incite envy"; instead, in April 1661, he accepted the title first earl of Clarendon.[2]

Clarendon's rapid rise might seem to contradict the current notion that early modern England was controlled by a small, closed aristocracy. But as early as the Renaissance membership in the elite was defined not simply by bloodlines but also by "social determinants of honor and wealth." Such rewards often fell to leaders from the prosperous landed gentry, into which status Hyde was born as a consequence of his father's marriage to the heiress of a wealthy Wiltshire gentleman. In a sense, then, the first earl typifies the still limited pool from which the aristocracy was likely to refresh itself.[3]

Clarendon was chancellor for seven vital years before a characteristically English change in the political weather brought him down — his fall owing in part to a certain political brusqueness and moral inflexibility (his refusal to recognize Charles's principal mistress, Barbara Villiers, made her a venomous enemy). In 1667 the late chancellor, so recently elevated to an earldom, was impeached, saw his beloved London residence, Clarendon House, attainted, and was exiled to France, where he died in 1674.[4]

In spite of Clarendon's rough treatment at the hands of Charles II, including a burden of debt that left his descendants financially straitened for years to come, the Hyde family remained intimately bound to the House of Stuart (fig. 8). For when Charles died in 1685, the duke of York succeeded him as James II. Though Anne Hyde was by then long dead, she had borne for England two future Protestant queens. Each would ascend the throne after the Catholic James was expelled in the Revolution of 1688, first Queen Mary, wife of William III of Orange, in 1689, and then Queen Anne in 1702. Both monarchs were first cousins to Edward Hyde, Viscount Cornbury.

When Henry Hyde succeeded his father as second earl of Clarendon in 1674, his only son and heir, the young viscount, was twelve. The royalist Henry, brother-in-law and intimate of James II, was appointed lord privy seal and then lord lieutenant of Ireland in 1685. A second pillar of

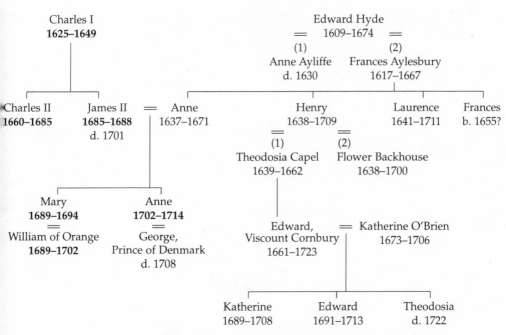

Figure 8. A Genealogy of the Stuart and Hyde Families. *Based on Vicary Gibbs, ed.,* The Complete Peerage . . . , *new ed. (London, 1913), VIII; Richard Ollard,* Clarendon and His Friends *(New York, 1988), app. 2. Drawn by Stinely Associates*

the Hydes' rebuilding political edifice was Henry's brother, Laurence, created earl of Rochester in 1683 and named James II's first lord treasurer. Nor was this loyalty to the Stuart monarchs confined to Cornbury's paternal side. His mother, Theodosia, was also from a royalist family, being the daughter of Sir Arthur Capel, baronet, a devoted supporter of Charles I executed by Oliver Cromwell in 1648 (fig. 9). Theodosia was only twenty-two when Edward was born, yet he never knew her. She had died of the smallpox three months after his arrival.[5]

The infant Edward was named after his famous grandfather, no doubt in expectation that he would carry on the family tradition of service to the crown. Given the scurrilous anecdotal history that later grew up around his term as governor of New York and New Jersey, one should logically look for further clues to Cornbury's character in what is known about his early years in England.

Figure 9. Henry Hyde, Viscount Cornbury (Later Second Earl of Clarendon) with Theodosia Capel, Viscomtess Cornbury (His First Wife). By Sir Peter Lely. Oil. Circa 1661. *Courtesy of the earl of Clarendon. Photograph by courtesy of the National Portrait Gallery, London*

### YOUTH AND MARRIAGE

If indeed it took three generations for families new to the peerage to feel secure in their social superiority,[6] Cornbury's aristocratic upbringing is testimony to the Hydes' belief that they had arrived. The young viscount's earliest years were apparently divided between his father's London establishment and Cornbury Park, the family's six-hundred-acre Oxfordshire seat. In January 1675, two months after turning thirteen, Cornbury was entered a matriculant at Christ Church, Oxford — an early start even for a precocious lad, though how long he remained at the college is not clear.[7] By 1680, at age eighteen, he was enrolled at l'Académie de

Calvin in Geneva, where he studied for nearly three years. At that time the institution, which later became the University of Geneva, housed faculties in theology, letters, jurisprudence, medicine, and philosophy. It was known as a refuge for French Protestants and for educating sons from some of the most distinguished Danish, Swedish, Polish, Hungarian, and English families. Cornbury — whose Anglican family apparently did not fear exposing him to nonconformist ideas — probably undertook a broad liberal education; perhaps there he learned the French that would later serve him well in a diplomatic post.

We have seen that the young viscount was esteemed by the citizens of Geneva, who facilitated his participation in their civic festival, l'Exercice de l'Arc, by granting him the freedom of the town, or *lettres de bourgeoisie* — making him perhaps the first foreigner so honored. When Cornbury departed Geneva in 1682, the brotherhood of musketeers saw him off with a parade and speeches, followed by four musket volleys to wish him a happy journey. En route home he visited Paris, where an acquaintance of his father's deemed him at age twenty "a very accomplished gentleman upon all accounts" and presented him to Louis XIV.[8]

Restricted by traditions of rank to a position in the military or the church, Cornbury's skill as a marksman may have tipped the scales toward an army career. In 1683 he was commissioned lieutenant colonel of the Royal Regiment of Dragoons under the command of John Churchill, later the great duke of Marlborough; 1685 found him at Vienna defending that city against the Turks. Later that year Churchill's dragoons distinguished themselves during Monmouth's Rebellion, most notably at the Battle of Sedgemoor, where the duke of Monmouth's army was defeated. At a critical point, a "squadron commanded by Cornbury charged the rebel guns, killed their Dutch crews, and relieved the royalists from their murderous fire." When Churchill was rewarded with the colonelcy of the Third Troop of Horse Guards, the twenty-three-year-old Cornbury was elevated to full colonel and commanding officer of the dragoons. He is prominently listed among the leading officers at the king's summer encampments at Hounslow Heath (fig. 10). Cornbury's father wrote with pride to his brother about "the King's being so well pleased with the account . . . of my son's regiment."[9]

Cornbury acquired further marks of his rank in 1685, being chosen

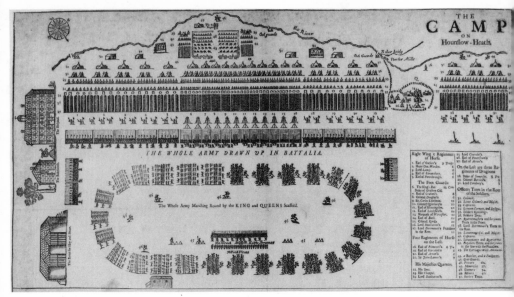

Figure 10. The Royal Encampment at Hounslow Heath, 1686. *Lord Cornbury's regiment is no. 30 (right, above legend). From the Sutherland Collection, courtesy of the Ashmolean Museum, Oxford*

member of Parliament from Wiltshire (1685–1687, 1690–1695) and later from Christchurch (1695–1701), as well as master of the Horse (1685–1690) to Prince George of Denmark, husband of Cornbury's cousin Princess Anne. A brief but intriguing glimpse of young Edward's political views has been preserved by the diarist and family friend Sir John Evelyn, who dined with the viscount and his father at Cornbury Park in August 1687. Edward, then twenty-five, had just returned from accompanying Prince George to Denmark, where, he told the assembled company, he discovered that the Danes lived under a "miserable tyranny." [10]

These years were possibly the happiest the family would know; they were certainly the most financially secure. Henry Hyde had in 1670 taken as his second wife Flower Backhouse, a "most religious and vertuous Lady" of solid standing and substance who became genuinely attached to her young stepson. As Henry later observed, "My wife . . . had always been as fond of my son, as if he had been her own." In 1685, Clarendon was named high steward of New Sarum, a lucrative post. Also that year he was awarded the same position for Reading, Berkshire, and on James II's accession was appointed lord privy seal and lord lieutenant of Ireland. Savoring the elegant setting and appurtenances of Cornbury Park, Henry took his place as one of the great lords of the shire around whom both the local gentry and the haut monde revolved. Perhaps to gain a further purchase on what Clarendon knew was the slippery slope of aristocratic eminence, Henry lavishly entertained the locals and visiting nobility, including the duke and duchess of York shortly before James became king.[11]

Clarendon was unusually dependent on James's patronage, largely because he insisted on carrying out his father's plans to refurbish and enlarge the great house at Cornbury Park — that estate being a striking example of the way new peers often "left their posterity overhoused for daily needs" and burdened by debt.[12] Shortly before his death, the first earl had admonished his son to spend at least one month a year there. Henry faithfully supervised the completion of the chapel begun by his father in 1666; he then improved the park and surrounding forest (fig. 11). He spent additional sums to rebuild Swallowfield, his second wife's estate in Berkshire, also restoring its park and gardens. All this was done in the face of multiple debts, including a fifteen-thousand-pound lien on family properties at Blunsden and Christchurch, which Henry held in trust for Edward.[13] It would seem that by remaining loyal to his father's vision of how an aristocrat should live, Henry, if inadvertently, impoverished his son.

The second earl chose a time-honored path out of his fiscal predicament. Beginning in late 1685, Henry turned his energies to finding for his son a wife of sufficient fortune to shore up the family's financial base. Like many longer-standing peers of that time, Henry was prepared to barter the Hyde and Clarendon names for a wealthy bride (even if from the commercial class) whose family sought a more elevated social position. He first entered negotiations for the hand of the young widow Whitmore. Henry, who "would do all I can to establish my family," believed that the widow's fortune would "make us as happy as we need to be." Cornbury, his heart "extremely set upon this lady," continued to court her even after his father learned that her parents were "startled at my miserable condition." To facilitate the match desired by her stepson, Lady Clarendon arranged to lend her husband some twenty thousand pounds. But negotiations over the marriage portion remained stalled and in March 1686 came to an end.[14]

Nonetheless, Clarendon wanted his son married, "and the sooner the

DEVS · NOBIS · HÆC · OTIA · FECIT.

*Cornbury Park, Oxfordshire; The Seat of the Right Hon^ble Lord Churchill.* July 27^th 1826.

Figure 11. Cornbury Hall, Oxfordshire, East Front. Drawn by J. C. Buckler, 1826. Reproduced from Vernon J. Watney, *Cornbury and the Forest of Wychwood* (London, 1910). *Photo Courtesy of Yale University Library. By permission of the British Library*

better, whilst I am in some seeming credit." He next cast his match-maker's eye on the daughter of Sir Stephen Fox, since giving Fox "a little honour might, I believe, go far." This time it was Cornbury who balked, leading his father to complain about his "temper and proceedings."[15] Henry next essayed Sir John Bankes's daughter, "with great advantage of portion" though "there is objection enough to the birth," as well as a Mrs. Cabell, worth "£2000 . . . besides money." But these schemes also came to naught, and as 1687 drew to a close young Cornbury was still a bachelor.[16]

Lord Clarendon was an indulgent if somewhat overbearing father, fretful when his son came down with a fever, and bemoaning his negligence in paying court to Princess Anne and her husband. Nonetheless, when Rochester proposed the twenty-four-year-old Cornbury for an important task in 1686, Henry warmly endorsed his son's abilities: "I think him fully of weight enough; and I am sure he will do it both heartily and faithfully, just in the method you direct him." On another occasion he offered perhaps the highest accolade a father can give a son: "I am sure he promises as much as I can desire." Still, "passionate" was a word Henry often used to describe his son, a characteristic that was sometimes attributed to Henry himself, as well as to his brother and father.[17] A certain intensity of feeling, especially about political and religious principles, evidently ran in the family. In these years, however, Cornbury's passion seems most often to have been sparked by his father's many schemes for marrying him off. Yet in that era it was incumbent on the scion of a great family to be sensible of its interests.

By early 1688 a happy resolution was in prospect, for Clarendon was "at my son's desire" in treaty for the hand of fifteen-year-old Katherine O'Brien, descendant of the Irish earls of Thomond and potential heiress of Charles, duke of Richmond and Lennox. But Clarendon soon drew back as it became evident that any estate Katherine might inherit would be heavily encumbered by debt. Not only would she bring no dowry to ease Henry's financial woes, but she would become "an unavoidable charge, [making it] the most inconvenient match that could have been for me." Thus Henry "broke very fairly off." Yet Cornbury and Katherine had other ideas, and on July 10, 1688, they eloped. News of this filial betrayal staggered Clarendon. "O Lord," he grieved, "make me able to bear this irrecoverable blow. Good God! that my poor family should be brought into utter misery by him who was the only hope of raising it." Lady Clarendon, however, believed the match a good one and in fact assisted the young couple in their plans. At first Henry refused to see the newlyweds.[18] But his affection for his son soon overcame his disappointment; as he confided to his diary, because Edward was "his son and only child . . . I ought to make the best of a bad market." Yielding to the entreaties of his wife and brother, he dined with Cornbury and his bride; then capitulating fully, he took them home with him to Cornbury Park.[19]

## CORNBURY AND THE GLORIOUS REVOLUTION

The most eventful year in Cornbury's life was without question 1688. Four months after his marriage he would play a signal part in the Glorious Revolution when he became the first English officer to defect from James II to the invading Prince William of Orange. This radical act once again left his father reeling, for Clarendon's loyalty to King James was absolute. This was true less because James was his brother-in-law than because Henry embraced the High Church belief that hereditary monarchs were divinely ordained to rule, even if support of this doctrine kept a Catholic on the throne. As Henry observed in his diary, the Anglican religion "did not allow of the deposing of Kings." This hallowed principle of divine right had survived a break with James the previous year when Henry and his brother, Laurence — undoubted Tory royalists but also devout Church of England men — had rebuffed James's effort to have them convert to Catholicism, leading to the brothers' abrupt dismissal from office.[20]

But if Clarendon's loyalty to James cannot be questioned, Cornbury's sentiments were more divided, very likely influenced by his association with the court of Princess Anne. Suspicion of Orangist sympathy certainly fell on the Protestant circle around Anne, to whom Cornbury was connected both as cousin and as her husband's master of the Horse. It is even possible that the earl of Rochester, the more political brother, though loyal to James, was maneuvering to position the Hyde family favorably in the event of an Orangist victory.[21] Cornbury's defection to William dramatically accomplished this end, at least for a time. In spite of efforts by some nineteenth-century Whig historians to minimize Cornbury's role in initiating the army's shift to William, it now seems beyond doubt that he was a prime leader in this first defection, an act spectacular in the eyes of James's court.[22]

When the prince of Orange landed at Torbay on November 5, 1688, an advance contingent of King James's army, including Cornbury's dragoons and several regiments of horse, was already deployed at Salisbury, where the twenty-seven-year-old Cornbury was commanding officer. A remarkably detailed eyewitness account, somewhat tainted by Jacobite sympathies, tells what happened next. Shortly before the defection, "a private Cabal was held at Salisbury to agree of the time and manner of doing it." Leading the "cabal" were Cornbury, Sir Francis Compton, commander of the duke of Berwick's Royal Horse Guards, Thomas Langston, colonel of the duke of St. Albans's regiment, and some few other trusted officers. Colonel Langston contrived to hand Cornbury counterfeit orders from the War Office instructing the troops to march toward the enemy, whom they met near Honiton on Sunday, November 11. At that point the majors of both Cornbury's and Compton's regiments, excluded from the scheme owing to their known royalist sympathies, grew suspicious over the rapid advance and demanded to see their colonels' orders. Compton quailed at this challenge and wheeled about — or, in the more earthy language of the eyewitness: "Sir Francis Compton hung an arse, and sneaked away back again to Salisbury, with almost his whole Regiment." Cornbury, by contrast, with his lieutenant colonel and some fifty to one hundred of his men rode into the camp of Prince William. Colonel Langston's men (many of whom, as in all the regiments, were loyal to King James) were at a distance and "knew nothing of what had happened in the other Regiments." Thus Langston was able to lead his troops on November 12 into William's camp at Honiton, "to the great Surprize of all that were not entrusted with the Business."[23]

Thereafter, an anonymous observer at the scene could report, "the Country dayly and hourly flocks into" the prince of Orange. Six hundred "of my Lord Cornbury's Regiment and the Duke of Barwicks came into Towne about two of the Clock this morning and is going to Joyne the Prince[.] My Lord Cornbury with my Lord Colchester and other Gentlemen went to every man this day and asked them if they would fight for the Church of England, very few deny'd them and those as did had their Horses and Armes taken from them." Given the confusion and the whirl of rumors whipped up by the defection, it is not surprising that witnesses differ over the timing of events and the number of troops involved. Defector estimates usually fell in the range of fifty to one hundred dragoons (Cornbury's troop), about one hundred men from St. Albans's (Langston's) regiment, and twenty-seven to thirty from Berwick's (Compton's) regiment. Yet the effect was immense, because the early rumor that three regiments had gone over did not distinguish between wholes and parts. Nonetheless, all accounts fasten on Cornbury's action as a turning point in the fortunes of the Orangist invasion. One contemporary even believed that William, whose horses were sick from a rough channel crossing, was ready to give up the fight when Cornbury's timely shift gave the invaders fresh heart.[24]

Cornbury's defection made him quite a hero to the Orangists.[25] He was also lionized by the local Wiltshire gentry, some thirty of whom promptly agreed to support him for member of Parliament from the county. But news of his action could not have been more unwelcome to his father. "O God, that my son should be a rebel!" wailed Clarendon to

his diary. Yet when Henry visited Princess Anne to express his mortifi-
cation over Cornbury's "villany," Anne coolly replied that "people were
so apprehensive of Popery . . . many more of the army would do the
same." By December 3, Henry was at Salisbury attempting to conciliate
matters between James and William, with William at this point still asserting that he did not seek the throne. The plan apparently was to retain
the Catholic James as king but to make his Protestant daughters next in
succession. There he found his son, as well as Churchill, Bishop Gilbert
Burnet, and many other gentlemen at the prince's side. A number of the
courtiers told Henry that the prince was "very sensible" of Cornbury's
part in initiating the defection. Next William himself assured Clarendon
"that my son's coming over to him was a seasonable service, and he would
always remember it." [26]

Yet when the parliamentary convention called in 1689 to settle the
succession voted to make William king of England, Henry could not accept him as legitimate monarch, even paired with his niece Mary — a
seeming betrayal of Hyde family interests that angered both Mary and
William. Perhaps more surprising is that Cornbury, too, was having second thoughts, in February of that year voting against the convention bill
that would place William and Mary on the throne. Pressure from his
father and uncle — Rochester at this point also opposing William and
Mary's succession — no doubt took a toll. But a more plausible explanation for Cornbury's vote is his association with Princess Anne, who initially saw William more as consort than king, with the legal succession
flowing directly from Mary to herself in the event that a childless Mary
predeceased her husband (fig. 12).[27] That Cornbury's vote was less anti-
William than pro-Anne is suggested by his subsequent introduction of a
bill to grant Anne an annual allowance of seventy thousand pounds, an
extraordinary sum. Squabbles over the allowance, later reduced to fifty
thousand, and over Anne's position in the succession, as well as other
disagreements between the princess and her sister, Mary, led to the
growing estrangement of Anne's court from that of William and Mary.[28]

Meanwhile Anne reluctantly bowed to the convention's insistence that
she follow William in the order of succession (possibly on the very day
Cornbury had voted to support her claim above William's), thereby
stranding Cornbury, to say nothing of his father, who had organized the
Tory faction supporting Anne. On February 16, Mary refused her uncle

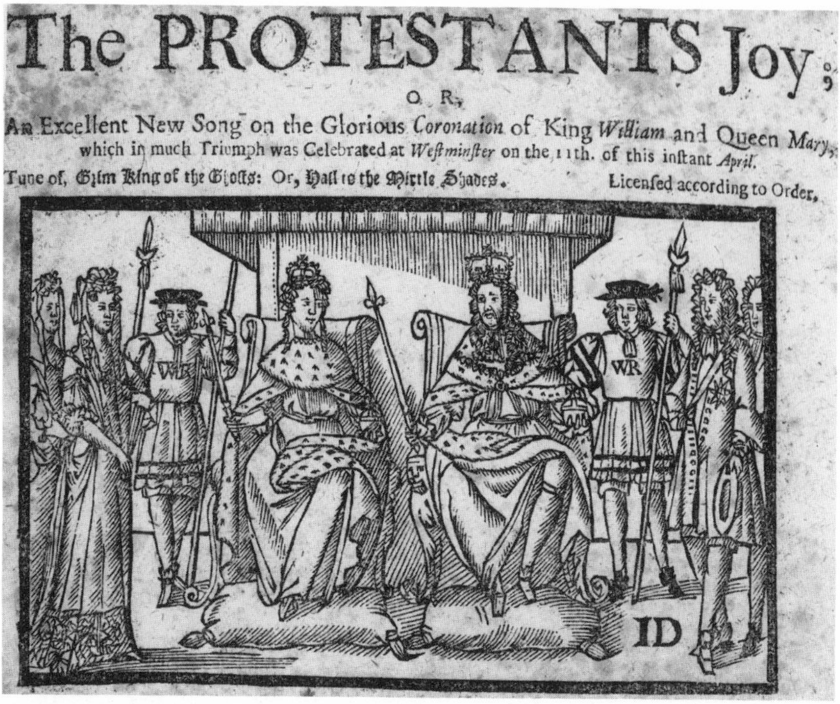

# The PROTESTANTS Joy;

## O R,

An Excellent New Song on the Glorious *Coronation* of King *William* and Queen *Mary*,
which in much Triumph was Celebrated at *Weftminfter* on the 11th. of this inftant *April.*
Tune of, 𝕺jm 𝕶ing of the 𝕮jotts: Or, 𝕳all to the 𝕸irtle 𝕾hades.     Licenfed according to Order,

Figure 12. *The Protestants Joy.* Broadside. 1689. *In celebration of the coronation of William and Mary. Note the licensing order at upper right. Courtesy of the British Library*

an audience; in March, Henry still could not bring himself to take the oath of loyalty to William and Mary, a decision he confirmed at the end of May, thereby entering the ranks of the nonjurors.[29]

## FINANCIAL DOLDRUMS

William now apparently graded Cornbury's loyalty at about the same level as Clarendon's and Rochester's, for in spite of his battlefield vow never to forget the young viscount's timely support, on July 17, 1689, William abruptly took Cornbury's regiment from him.[30] So much for the promises of kings. More trouble awaited when, in May 1690, Cornbury refused to accompany Prince George as he joined King William's army in Ireland, where Cornbury's former regiment was deployed. To go would have been inconsistent with his honor, the king having "put such a mark of disgrace upon him, as to take away his regiment, after what he had done upon the first invasion." Rochester, who believed that his nephew had "great reason" for his refusal, interceded with Princess

Anne, but Cornbury was nonetheless dismissed as George's master of the Horse.[31]

The family's slide continued the next month when Clarendon found himself briefly confined in the Tower of London after again declining the oath of fealty to William and Mary. In early 1691, Henry was accused of supporting the Jacobite Preston Plot, arrested on a charge of high treason, imprisoned in the tower for more than six months, and finally discharged on a twenty-thousand-pound bond only after Queen Mary's intercession (fig. 13).[32] Mary's death in 1694 stilled the one voice that might have spoken for Clarendon at court. William, beset by cabals and defections, seems to have reacted with particular spleen against disaffected members of his family. Clearly he did not trust Clarendon, and without trust there would be no offices — a deprivation that could spell financial ruin for an impoverished peer. If Henry had briefly gained a degree of financial security under the smiles of James II, his rigid resistance to the outcome of the Glorious Revolution — in his mind a point of honor — doomed the Clarendon line to hard times. Now holding no major office, Henry faced the bleakest prospects of his life. Yet as a member of the aristocracy he still had to keep up appearances. Bishop Gilbert Burnet once characterized him as "naturally sincere" with regard to everything but his debts, where he displayed "a particular art [in devising] a plausible excuse and a new promise" to pay.[33]

Meanwhile, Clarendon's son and heir, Viscount Cornbury, also had no remunerative position. Nor was Cornbury's station in life such that he could simply go out and seek employment. It must have been some comfort that the local electors again chose him M.P. for Wiltshire and then for Christchurch, but that office was paid in honor, not silver.[34] Cornbury's most pressing business now became the struggle to maintain an establishment befitting his dignity as heir to an earldom and head of a growing family. Early in 1690, he engaged in a "very loud and hot" dispute with his wife's stepfather about some accounts; he later sued to obtain one of Katherine's properties, though he could not press the case "for want of a fee to give a lawyer." In 1696 he petitioned the crown for grants of land in Kent and Surrey that he had "discovered," that is, whose titles had lapsed. He also had dealings with a London goldsmith at the Three Cups in Lombard Street, presumably to pawn or sell valuables. In the

Figure 13. *The Nine Conspirators Executed for the Assassination Plot.* Circa 1697. *Woodblock portraits of leading gentlemen implicated in the Jacobite Preston Plot. Courtesy of The Pierpont Morgan Library, New York. English engraved portraits, vol.II, f.21*

summer of 1697, with his father, Lord Rochester, and his goldsmith out of town, Cornbury had feared exposure "to the greatest affront imaginable [presumably arrest] for so small a sum as £7," and by the end of the year it was reported that he and his lady were "starving."[35]

That their situation was painful is surely true; in October, Cornbury had written his father that he had "not a shilling to help myself with, nor to get dinner for my Wife and myself." After trying unsuccessfully to borrow money from a family lawyer, he "by great good luck met with a friend who lent me forty shillings." Even if Cornbury overstated the case to gain Clarendon's sympathy, there is no mistaking his desperation. He begs his father to make security on a mortgage he had taken on family properties at Christchurch — "the only thing my poor Grandfather had secured for me to give me bread" and the only means "to support me for all this winter." He swears vengeance against a family lawyer who had advised him to cut off the entail in order to obtain the mortgage, which he now saw as erroneous counsel that could lead to his utter ruin. But if ruined he was to be, Cornbury would take the lawyer down with him by publishing his villainy "at large, and post it up in Westminster Hall, and all the publick places I can think of." "If I had lost my life either in my travells, or in the Army it had been happy," he writes his father, "but now that I have a Wife and Children, I can not forgive any man that endeavours the ruin of them and me[.] Mr. Longueville is that man, and my Curses shall attend him most heartily." Cornbury then adds: "I hope your Lordshippe will not take this to be the effects of passion."[36]

His financial condition had not improved much by the following February, when it was reported, "Lord Cornbury hath lockt his lady up for some time past and suffers her not to stir out." One overly imaginative writer has interpreted this conventional seventeenth-century usage to mean that Cornbury had literally "in an outburst of temper . . . shut [Lady Cornbury] up in her room," but it surely means only that Lord and Lady Cornbury were by force of circumstance retired from society during this low point in their fortunes.[37]

Was Cornbury himself responsible for these humiliations? It is difficult to say. The impoverished aristocrat scrambling to maintain a front while dodging creditors, staving off importunate tradesmen, and cadging loans is a familiar type in English history. But it is not at all clear that Cornbury lived extravagantly. His position was inevitably linked to that of his father, and the nonjuring earl's lot continued to deteriorate throughout William III's reign. To settle some of his debts, Clarendon sold a number of paintings inherited from the first earl. In 1696 his heavily encumbered estate, Cornbury Park, passed to Lord Rochester in discharge of a five-thousand-pound debt, though title passed secretly in order to preserve Henry's reputation. The next year even Lady Clarendon's Swallowfield was apparently in jeopardy. In short, Lord Clarendon's fortunes, caught in the doldrums of his nonjuring principles, sank to a new low by the end of the seventeenth century.[38] His son and heir, Viscount Cornbury, inevitably partook of his father's fate.

But if Cornbury's financial troubles were in many respects beyond his control, his politics — in a time of shifting alignments when both Whigs and Tories could be found supporting William — might reasonably be expected to respond to changing conditions. Two family members had already made a kind of peace with William: Princess Anne was partially reconciled to her brother-in-law following Mary's death; and Rochester, having taken the oath in the early 1690s, returned to the government, though William remained suspicious of him.[39] In the House of Commons, Cornbury moved away from his high Tory stance of 1689 toward more moderate positions, voting in 1696 for the act of attainder against Sir John Fenwick, a Jacobite accused of plotting to assassinate William; he also opposed a bill to disband William's standing army. Whether in recognition of Cornbury's political support, at the instigation of family members, or from personal proddings of conscience, William in August 1698 offered relief to a financially embarrassed relative, being "pleased to order £10 per week, to be paid every Monday morning by way of subsistence, to the lord Cornbury" — a somewhat churlish meting out of royal charity that bespoke *oblige* at the expense of *noblesse* (fig. 14).[40]

## CORNBURY APPOINTED GOVERNOR GENERAL

Nonetheless, things were looking up, especially as the Whig Junto in Parliament lost power to the Rochester-Nottingham Tories in the last years of William's reign. In the spring of 1701, William appointed Cornbury, now thirty-nine, governor general of the colony of New York. Some historians — captive to the Cornbury legend or inclined to a skeptical

Figure 14. William III. Studio of Sir Godfrey Kneller. Oil. *Courtesy, Leeds Museums and Galleries (Temple Newsam House): photograph Courtauld Institute of Art*

view of imperial patronage — have asserted that the king did so either to be rid of his troublesome cousin or to provide him an opportunity to repair his fortune at the expense of the provincials, thereby inferring that competence was not an important qualification for that particular post.[41] Yet such assessments betray an outmoded understanding of England's perception of its growing North American empire and also misconstrue the later Stuarts' interest in imperial reform, especially during times of war. William, and later Anne, knew the difference between venality and patronage. As John Brewer has observed: "Private connection and public duty were not necessarily incompatible and it behoved both patron and client to ensure they were consonant."[42]

Cornbury was no doubt relieved to obtain gainful employment at last; at the same time, the governorship of New York was too important a post to throw away on an incompetent. "Esteemed as the center of your Majesty's Plantations on that Continent," as a Board of Trade memorandum to the king noted in 1702,[43] New York was militarily and diplomatically the most strategically situated colony on the North American mainland and the only one where English soldiers were permanently stationed. Its governor was responsible for defending the Hudson River–Lake Champlain corridor to French Canada; he also was charged with conducting delicate negotiations with the Iroquois Nations in the effort to bind them to the crown. Not only is there no evidence, either in England or North America, that Cornbury was considered unqualified for this significant post, but there is reason to think he was chosen because of specific strengths he would bring to it, notably his military experience and the prestige inherent in his close relationship to the royal family.

Appointed in May or June 1701, Cornbury did not embark for America for several months, in part because of his determined lobbying with government departments for supplies to bolster New York's defenses.[44] He also had to settle a vexing lawsuit. Some time before August 22, 1701, Cornbury was arrested for a sum of six hundred pounds owed to a mercer. This large debt most likely resulted from the government's decision to buy new uniforms for the soldiers stationed in New York. It was customary for commanding officers (Cornbury having been appointed colonel of the New York regiment) to assume such costs, to be reimbursed later from the "respites," a percentage of the men's pay reserved for their colonel. Cornbury of course was in no position to advance six hundred

Figure 15. *Arrested for Debt*. By William Hogarth. Engraving. 1735. *A gentleman emerging from a sedan chair is taken up by the bailiff. Courtesy, Colonial Williamsburg Foundation*

pounds, and when the mercer's suit threatened to delay his departure, he immediately sought a writ of supersedeas granting him immunity, as a member of Parliament, from arrest (fig. 15). But Parliament, which alone could act on the request, was not in session. Therefore, to the discomfort of one observer, the matter was "hushed up some other way," namely by reaching a private settlement with the mercer, who "was under a terror that hee shall be called to account when the parliament meets for a breach of privilege in arresting the person of a Member." Cornbury, like many other gentlemen of his day, was not above pulling rank on a creditor. In this instance, he also had the clandestine support of the king: William ordered the Treasury to pay Cornbury's debt from the secret service fund "to enable him to proceed on his voyage."[45]

The mercer's suit and other delays in winding up his affairs meant that Cornbury and his family did not board their ship, the *Jersey*, until November 5. Their voyage to New York so typically reflects the early modern experience with time and distance that it serves as a reminder of the pace of life in the early eighteenth century. At first confined to the roadways of Spithead by contrary winds, the *Jersey* slowly felt its way west along the southern coast of England to Falmouth by late December. A stormy winter prevented further progress until March 13, when the ship finally unfurled its sails and set course for North America. Only after a stop in Boston did Governor Cornbury at last reach New York on May 2, 1702, almost six months from the day he and his family first took ship in England.[46]

### RETURN TO ENGLAND, 1710–1723

This discussion is restricted for the moment to the contours of Lord Cornbury's career in England; thus his eight years in the colonies, from 1702 to 1710, are considered in later chapters. At the end of his governorship Cornbury returned to England in the fall of 1710, living another thirteen years until his death in 1723. As prologue to a review of his postcolonial years, it might be noted that along with any number of favorable reports on Cornbury's performance as governor of New York and New Jersey, certain complaints about his fiscal integrity and moral conduct had been communicated to England from about 1707 onward. Therefore the way he was received by the queen and other British officials on his return may serve as a barometer of their response to such complaints as well as a measure of Cornbury's reputation among his peers.

Cornbury arrived home in October 1710 as the third earl of Clarendon, his father having died the previous October. Before taking up his new role in English society, however, Cornbury — as I shall continue to call him for convenience, though Clarendon would be more correct — set out to clear his name of aspersions cast on it by a number of "wicked liars" in America. As he had written his father and uncle from New York: "An honest Man's Reputation is dearer to him than either" life or estates; yet it was almost impossible to answer charges, which he knew himself

Figure 16. Queen Anne. By Sir Godfrey Kneller. 1703. Oil. *Courtesy, The Honourable Society of the Inner Temple: photograph Courtauld Institute of Art*

"not to be guilty of," from three thousand miles away. In London he gathered evidence, possibly in preparation for suing his critics for libel. He obtained extracts of letters sent to officials of the Church of England as well as sworn depositions from colonial officials, British officers of New York's regiment, and private citizens. At the same time he attempted to clarify his accounts in New York and New Jersey to show that money was due him from both governments and to discharge debts left behind, especially money owed to the soldiers stationed at New York. To these ends he gathered letters and affidavits from provincial revenue officers, all of which he submitted to the Board of Trade.[47]

It was not unusual for returning governors to defend their administrations in this manner.[48] And though it was some years before the extremely complicated financial issues were resolved, the verdict in England on Governor Cornbury's overall performance and personal integrity was clearly positive. The queen's response is especially telling, for Anne was known to hold her servants to a high moral standard. As Lord Chesterfield put it: "Queen Anne had always been devout, chaste, and formal; in short, a prude. She discouraged as much as she could, the usual and even the most pardonable vices of Courts" (fig. 16). Cornbury had of course known Anne all his life and had moved within her orbit in the 1680s, though it is unclear how close their relationship was in those early years. After 1710, however, he seems to have gained a marked favor with his royal cousin. The loss of both cousins' spouses — Lady Cornbury having died in New York in 1706, Prince George in 1708 — may have drawn Cornbury and Anne together. Within a few weeks of his return from America, it was reported that "her majestie has given the earl of Clarendon lodgings in Somerset house," a royal palace on the Strand used for visiting dignitaries and members of the nobility who did not have, or could not afford, London establishments. Then on December 13, 1711, Cornbury was appointed to the Privy Council, serving until Anne's death in 1714; in January 1712 he was also named first commissioner of the Admiralty.[49] Commencing in December 1713, Cornbury was granted a pension of two thousand pounds per year, a clear sign of appreciation for his imperial service. Moreover, when Queen Anne in 1714 lifted certain restrictions on the use of the pension, she addressed her relative with unusual affection as "Right Trusty and Right Entirely Beloved Cousin and Councellor."[50]

All these actions and appointments signaled Cornbury's acceptance not only by the queen but by leaders of his own Tory party, which had experienced a resurgence at the polls in 1710. When tension mounted between the moderates of Robert Harley, Lord Oxford, and the high Tories of Henry St. John, Viscount Bolingbroke, Cornbury tended to support Bolingbroke's policies from his seat in the House of Lords. By May 1714, with the queen's health failing, attention focused on the issue of Anne's successor. (Following the death of her only surviving child, the duke of Gloucester, at age eleven, Queen Anne — whose sorrowful lot was to see all eighteen of her children die — became the last of the Stuart monarchs.) The Regency Act of 1706 had provided for a stable transfer of power to the Protestant House of Hanover. Though all parties supported the Protestant Succession, rumors that Bolingbroke was a closet Jacobite were soon being whispered about, possibly by Harleyites, certainly by Whigs. Thus Anne decided to send a personal representative to reassure her cousin and heir apparent, Prince George, elector of Hanover. On May 26 she turned abruptly from Oxford's nominee to appoint as envoy extraordinary to the court at Hanover "Bolingbroke's nominee, her own first cousin the Earl of Clarendon." By this astute choice Anne not only certified her faith in Bolingbroke's loyalty but reiterated her support for the Hanoverian line, since no one could question Cornbury's devotion to the Protestant Succession. The appointment achieved one other objective as well, for, as a contemporary noted, her cousin Edward was "a person the Queen has always desired should be in some employment."[51]

Such a delicate mission, given the many currents swirling about the succession, would only have been entrusted to a person of some weight. As a friend of Cornbury's wrote him from New York, the appointment was a "peculiar mark and distinction of Royall Favour" and one of the "Rewards of Meritt." The queen herself wrote to the elector that she had chosen Cornbury because of her knowledge of his ability (*"la Capacite"*); he carried the sentiments of her heart, and she was sure George would soon perceive his merit. Secretary of State William Bromley also considered Cornbury "a very proper . . . Instrument for settling the friendship [between Anne and the elector] upon a firm and lasting Foundation." As the queen's condition worsened and concern about Jacobite intrigues launched from France escalated, Bromley wrote to Cornbury, now at

Hanover, that should the queen die, ships of war would be sent to escort the elector from the Dutch coast to England.[52]

The court at Hanover seethed with gossip that Anne secretly favored the Stuart line; apparently to signal his displeasure with such rumors, Prince George forced Cornbury to cool his heels in antechambers for several days before granting him an audience. During that interval Cornbury was visited by one of the elector's chamberlains, a schoolmate from his days at Geneva (where they were "truly Comrades"); the acquaintance, Cornbury wrote Bromley, "may be usefull." Being experienced in the ways of courts and diplomacy, Cornbury sent meticulously detailed reports about his reception, for he knew that in such minutiae the government at home would discern Hanover's attitude toward the British crown and ministry. Finally on August 7, Cornbury could report:

> I had my first Audience of the Elector at Noon at Herenhausen. . . . a Gentleman of the Court came to my Lodgings here, with two of the Electors Coaches and carried me to Herenhausen, I was met at my alighting out of the Coach . . . [by the] Marshall of the Court, and at the top of the Stairs by the Chevalier Redem[,] Second Chamberlain (The Count de Plaaten Great Chamberlain being Sick). [H]e conducted me through three Rooms, to the Room where the Elector was, who met [me] at the Door of that Room, and being returned three or four Steps into that Room he stopped and the Door was shut. I then delivered my Credentials to him, and made him a Compliment from the Queen, to which he answered, that he had always had the greatest Veneration imaginable for the Queen.[53]

With such detail did Cornbury convey not only the substance but the mood of his first meeting with the elector.

Unlike some of his predecessors, Cornbury was warmly received at Hanover. After presenting his credentials he spent an hour alone with Prince George, was introduced to the electoral prince and other members of the royal family, and then "had the Honour to dine with them all." In an evening marked by good humor, Prince George asked him many questions about England, betraying in the process, as Cornbury wrote Bromley, his ignorance of the English constitution. Thereafter Cornbury could report that he had been at court every night, had dealt plainly with the ministers of state, and was entertained by all. The warmth of his welcome was confirmed by his secretary, John Gay: "My Lord Clarendon is very much approved of at Court, and I believe is not dissatisfied with his reception." [54]

The only sour note regarding Cornbury's mission had been sounded on June 16, 1714, by the Hanoverian diplomat Hans Caspar von Bothmer, a man disliked by Bolingbroke and other high Tory ministers as a tool of the Whigs. On hearing of Cornbury's appointment, Bothmer wrote the elector's adviser on English affairs to express his distaste both for Cornbury and for Gay, his "Jacobitish secretary." Bothmer was at that point envoy to the Hague, and he may or may not have been acquainted with either man. But this did not stop him from passing along a bit of gossip picked up no doubt from his Whig friends: Cornbury was "a selfish and presumptuous fool . . . to such a degree, that [when in America] he thought that it was necessary for him, in order to represent her Majesty, to dress himself as a woman, which he actually did." [55] Because Bothmer's letter must have arrived by the time Cornbury reached Hanover at the end of July, we can surmise from Cornbury's favorable reception that direct acquaintance with him forestalled whatever bad effects such gossip might have had.

In the midst of Cornbury's diplomatic conversations, Queen Anne died on August 1. Hearing the news some days later, as Cornbury wrote a friend, it "struck me dumb"; it was "the only misfortune I had to fear, it being not only the loss of the best Queen, the best Mistresse, and the best friend, but the only friend I had in the World." His chief comfort lay in forcing his grief to yield to "the Service of my Country." [56]

In spite of the hope of Cornbury's friend, the earl of Strafford, that the new monarch, George I, would seek the aid of "honest men" (that is, Tories), "and then Your Lordship cant fail of being distinguished with the King's favour as you deserve," the death of Anne signaled the decline of Cornbury's government career. Though there is some evidence that King George was initially well disposed toward the Tories and hoped to include some of them in his ministry, the Whigs soon gained the upper hand. [57] Cornbury's membership in the House of Lords was thus his only public role in the last decade of his life. As earl of Clarendon, he had taken his seat for the first time on December 5, 1710. His service in the House of Lords, whether under Anne or George, was conservative yet supportive of the crown. He voted most often, though not blindly, with the Tory party, and as a major leader in the Lords he chaired the important Committee of the Whole House 124 times between 1710 and 1718, far more than anyone else in those years (fig. 17). After 1720 his participation apparently declined, for his name rarely appears in notes about the debates.[58]

Death stalked Lord Cornbury in his later years, gradually contracting his family circle until he alone remained. His thirty-three-year-old wife had died at New York in 1706. Of seven children born to that marriage, three had survived. The eldest, Katherine, died in 1708 at age eighteen.[59] The death in 1709 of Cornbury's father was followed in 1711 by that of his uncle, the earl of Rochester. The next year he was dealt a crushing blow when his only son, twenty-two-year-old Edward, a promising student at Christ Church, Oxford, died of a "high feaver."[60] This left only Cornbury's younger daughter, Theodosia, who had been with him in New York and on returning to England had in 1713 married John Bligh, later earl of Darnley. Having inherited her mother's title of Baroness Clifton as well as her apparently solvent Cobham Hall estate, Theodosia seemed to promise, at last, a recovery from the financial anxieties that had tormented the Hyde family for decades. But it was not to be, for in 1722, Theodosia, while giving birth to her seventh child, also died.[61]

Following Theodosia's death, Cornbury's name disappears from the records altogether. Whether he was ill, in body or in spirit, during his last months is not known, but in early April 1723, "Hearne's Newsletter" reported that "on Sunday, March 31st last, died at Chelsea the Rt. Honble Edward Hyde, Earl of Clarendon, Viscount Cornbury, and Baron of Hindon." Then followed a standard obituary, Hearne adding no gratuitous comment on Cornbury's character or reputation as he often did in the gossipy newsletters. On April 5, Cornbury was interred in the family crypt at the foot of the stairs leading to the Henry VII chapel in Westminster Abbey, where he rests to this day.

The straightforward way Cornbury's death was reported as well as the offices and respect bestowed on him after his return from America seem to contradict the scandalous reports about his behavior in New York and New Jersey. Nor is there anything from contemporary English gossips

Figure 17. *Queen Anne in the House of Lords.* By Peter Tillemans (1684–1734). Oil. *The queen is attended by her ladies; the peers spiritual and temporal are seated left and right; in the foreground are members of the House of Commons and officers of the royal household. Permission, The Royal Collection © Her Majesty Queen Elizabeth II*

suggesting that Cornbury was a man of other than good character. Still, there is a curious final note. Lady Frances Keightly, Cornbury's aunt and one of the few family members to survive him, made the following entry on the flyleaf of her Bible: "My dear nephew the Earl of Clarendon died the 31st March; it was Passion Sunday; by the blessed passion sweet Jesu I beseech thee to look on the sincerity of his heart and his great charity. Lay not his follies to his charge, but have mercy on his poor soul."[62] The word "follies" fairly jumps off the page at a reader familiar with the Cornbury legend. Are we being tricked again by the eighteenth-century idiom?[63] Or did Lady Frances know something we should know?

Getting to Know Governor Cornbury

As Cornbury's ship hove into view off Sandy Hook on May 2, 1702, New Yorkers awaited their new governor's arrival with edgy anticipation. New York had emerged from the upheavals of the Glorious Revolution more passionately divided than any other colony in North America. Only in New York were the political leaders of that furious time tried and convicted of treason, then hanged and beheaded before a howling public. Jacob Leisler, the martyred pro-Orangist leader whose name became fixed to New York's near–civil war of 1689–1691, also left his mark on its politics, as the colony split into Leislerian and anti-Leislerian factions in the relentlessly bitter aftermath of Leisler's Rebellion. Each royal governor thereafter appointed to New York confronted a dilemma: to befriend one colonial faction guaranteed a ready-made opposition from the other.

The Tory imperialist governor Benjamin Fletcher (1692–1698) nonetheless cast his lot with the group he found most congenial, the Anglicizing anti-Leislerians, thereby earning the fierce enmity of the more broadly based, often Calvinist Leislerians. His liberal Whig successor, Richard Coote, earl of Bellomont (1698–1701), while first trying to even the political scales, soon tilted into the eager arms of the Leislerians. The now-stranded anti-Leislerians rejoiced when Bellomont died suddenly in March 1701, though as it turned out his temporary successor, Lieutenant

Governor John Nanfan (1701–1702), became an even firmer ally of the Leislerians. Nanfan's government arrested the man many New Yorkers still blamed for Leisler's demise, Nicholas Bayard, who was promptly convicted on trumped-up charges of high treason and condemned to death. Bayard's life hung in the balance for two weeks, until Governor Nanfan granted him a reprieve on March 30, 1702.[1] Such was the tangled political scene that greeted Cornbury when he stepped ashore in New York City, the colony's capital, five weeks later (fig. 18).

New York's melancholy history was well known to imperial officials at Whitehall. But ever hopeful of stabilizing politics in the strategically important colony — especially as another war with France loomed — the Board of Trade had instructed Cornbury to deal evenhandedly with the two parties. One of Cornbury's achievements, often overlooked, is that he actually managed to lower the temperature in politically feverish New York.

On his arrival in May 1702, Governor Cornbury immediately reached out to a number of different interests. The entrepreneurial upriver politician Robert Livingston, who rarely had a kind word for any imperial official, observed that Cornbury had obviously made an effort to inform himself about New York's troubles. "My Lord is Extream hearty to redresse all grevances," Livingston noted; "we must reckon it a duble mercy that God has been pleased to send him at this juncture." Attorney General Samuel Broughton, likewise impressed, praised Cornbury's "great wisedome and justice, which adapt him for Government and are conspicuous in H[is] E[xcellency]." Leading merchants and gentlemen of New York, in a petition to the queen, thanked her for "the Blessing we have in being under the administration of the Lord Cornbury." And formal addresses to the new governor from a broader segment of some 375 inhabitants of New York, Richmond, Kings, Westchester, and Albany Counties, as well as about half of the freeholders — though "the cheifest and Greatest Part" — of Ulster County, voiced "entire confidence in your Lordship's great prudence, justice, courage and conduct," while praying that "the name of Party and Faction may henceforth vanish."[2]

True, many of these flattering words came from men either attached by political or economic interest to imperial government or aspiring to become so attached. Yet the sanguine tone and relatively broad base of

Figure 18. *New York City—View of the Fort and Town.* Circa 1708. *The fort where Governor Cornbury took up residence, the chapel, and the secretary's office are designated* A, B, *and* C *at far left.* © *Collection of the New-York Historical Society*

Cornbury's support suggests that many New Yorkers looked forward to a respite from the political storms of the past decade and a half. Governor Cornbury himself wrote the Board of Trade shortly after his arrival that New Yorkers seemed peaceful except for a few "troublesome spirits," whom he chose not to name. "For as I came a stranger hither, soe I am sure I have noe spleen to noe man, but I shall always think it my duty to give your Lordships a true representation both of persons and things."[3]

As a Boston newsletter reported a year later, "The proceedings of The Lord Cornburry here, are well approved by her Majesty and Council, and the Lords of Trade."[4] Further evidence of that approval came when Cornbury was appointed the first governor of the newly royalized colony of New Jersey, a post he would assume concurrently with the governorship of New York, initially to general approbation, in August 1703. On the whole, given the time and place, Governor Cornbury had made an auspicious beginning. Yet within two years grumblings against his policies would become audible, and by 1707 a ferocious opposition — focused in New Jersey — would demand his recall. Was such opposition more or less inherent in the reformist turn imperial relations were taking? Or was there perhaps some further aspect of Cornbury's personality that provoked it?

In Cornbury's case the difficulty in answering such questions has been compounded by more than two and a half centuries' overlay of myth and innuendo. One way to search for the man beneath this deposit would be to cut directly to certain critical incidents in Cornbury's administration, times of stress that might reveal his character in unguarded moments. He left behind a voluminous public record as well as a more limited private one; in each can be found gleams of anger, hurt, bewilderment, supplication, distress, and pride. And running through it all are traces of an imperious temperament. An effort to correlate such traces might add up to a better understanding of the way Cornbury pictured himself in the post of provincial governor.

MODELING THE ROLE OF IMPERIAL GOVERNOR

A regard for principled public service had been instilled in Cornbury as a youth, perhaps because his family's recent elevation to the peerage made its members unusually attentive to the conventions of rank, its responsibilities as well as its privileges. Cornbury's grandfather, father, and uncle had each given up high public office rather than compromise political or religious principles. And each had responded in a manner that can be described only as exceedingly prickly on questions of family honor.[5] Though there can be no doubt that as governor Cornbury expected to be deferred to and obeyed, it also seems that he wished to govern well.

An opportunity to set the tone of his administration presented itself shortly after his arrival in New York. By July 1702, Cornbury was at Albany to parley with the Indians; during his sojourn four black men — probably slaves — were accused of killing an Indian sachem, Minichque, for which they were tried and condemned to die. A few days before the scheduled executions, a delegation of sachems asked Cornbury to grant reprieves to the condemned, since Minichque "upon his death bed desired that no revenge should be taken of the 4 negroes, that killed him [and] he forgave them." In response, Cornbury invited the Indians to attend the executions to "see how farr I would goe towards the gratifying of them." What the Indians found on execution day was that "his Lordship had caused one of the 4 negroes to be executed (who was the principle Ringleader)," whereas the other three were reprieved until the queen's pleasure should be known, for which "the Sachims returned his Excellency thanks for his justice and Paternall care over them."[6]

This Solomon-like resolution was followed by other instances that displayed Cornbury's conception of justice, as when he released a number of jailed slaves to the custody of their masters or interceded on behalf of two New Jersey women — one accused of murdering her child, the other charged with killing her husband — because he thought their trial and condemnation too swift.[7] And imperialist though he was, Cornbury was not blind to the occasions when officers of the crown overreached their authority, as, for example, in impressing seamen. When Captain George Fane, senior naval officer at New York, "pressed some Country People who were going out a fishing," Cornbury reported to Whitehall that the locals from Long Island and New Jersey now feared the same treatment if they came to market in New York, which was bad for business. Another officer impressed more sailors than he needed and then sold them to other captains. This was "very hard usage," Cornbury protested to the Admiralty, considering that New Yorkers had shown they were willing to do their duty.[8]

But however much Governor Cornbury may have prided himself on dispensing evenhanded justice, he was a Tory royalist who viewed the authority vested in him as legitimate and plenary. He never doubted that the British imperial system benefited the colonists and deserved their unqualified allegiance. Trained as a soldier, and with a lifelong absorption in military affairs, he was the sort of outspoken imperialist approved by the duke of Marlborough, who believed that "no one but soldiers should have the government of a plantation." In other words, Cornbury was the very model of a modern governor general.[9] Indeed, Cornbury's perception of himself as a military man may go far to explain his behavior as a colonial official. And Whitehall, in recognition of his soldierly prowess, granted him a large measure of military responsibility. New York by the eighteenth century was increasingly seen as the pivotal colony in organizing both defensive and offensive action against the French in Canada. Cornbury was appointed governor during a pause in Anglo-French hostilities following King William's War. But with tensions rising again by 1702, he arrived in New York as a kind of commander-in-chief invested with wide authority to improve the mainland colonies' military posture. William III's instructions authorized him to collect specific sums of money from the other colonies — ranging from £150 (Rhode Island) to £900 (Virginia) — to be expended on strengthening the northern frontier. He was also to notify the colonies from Virginia northward as to the number of militiamen they should offer for the common defense, to "call for the same" should the frontier be invaded, and to aid other provinces if attacked. He was to speed repairs on the forts at Albany and New York City and to report on all fortifications in the colonies of New York, Connecticut, and the Jerseys, over which he was appointed "Captain-General of all forces by sea and land." [10]

While still in England Cornbury had taken pains to inform himself about his new post, especially the status of "the poor souldiers," that is, the four independent companies of foot stationed at New York City and Albany. He knew the companies were under strength and ill clothed and their pay thousands of pounds in arrears. These conditions were bad for morale, and he set about redressing them before departing for America. He got the government to order 120 men to fill out the companies' ranks; in addition, three half-pay officers — a lieutenant, a cornet, and a quartermaster, probably from Cornbury's old regiment — asked to accompany him to New York. Cornbury also realized while in England that New Yorkers had been overtaxed to defend the frontiers. Drawing up a list of needed supplies, including cannon, muskets, barrels of powder, flints, and grenade shells, he badgered the Board of Trade, Privy Council, and Parliament until they agreed to provide a good portion of the additional ordnance. [11] As we have seen, Cornbury also carried to America new uniforms for the troops. His reaction when the packages were opened in New York is of some interest. The uniforms, which, though placed against his account, had actually been ordered by the previous governor's London agent, were made from appallingly shoddy cloth — "the worst cloathing ever was put upon soldiers backs." Rather than go along with this classic species of military graft, Cornbury had the agent, John Champante, brought up on charges before the Board of Trade, which found some of the cloth "defective." (He thereby earned a bitter enemy, as Champante schemed for the next six years to have Cornbury ousted from his governorship.) [12]

Governor Cornbury's first act on reaching New York was to deliver what one auditor called "an heroick millitary speech," in which he told the assembled government officials that "his education had been in for- eigne Courts and Armys, that he came to regulate Abuses and see that the laws had their intended course." [13] Next Cornbury set to work com- piling an inventory of stores at New York and Albany and repairing the fort at New York City, which he found in "miserable condition," the para- pet fallen down and the gun carriages rotting. On his first trip to Albany in July, he also undertook to replace the town's stockaded fort with a new one of stone. He informed the Board of Trade that he had made more progress on the fort in a few weeks than Colonel Wolfgang Romer, the king's military engineer, had done in a year and a half. Nor did he hesitate to redesign the fort and relocate it to higher ground in order to provide better defense at lower cost. Cornbury then demanded an audit of Col- onel Romer's accounts, which he found to be delinquent, Romer having, among other things, appointed his sixteen-year-old son overseer of the works. Romer was furious, telling Cornbury he thought such treatment "a very hard thing for a man of his quality and station." But, as Cornbury replied, it was the custom "for all persons who received any of the Queen's money to account for the same let their quality or station be what it would." In a letter to the Board of Trade, Cornbury predicted that Romer "will complaine of some hardship done to him. But I can assure your Lordships he has received none, unless it is a hardship to hinder a man from defrauding the Queen." [14]

However peremptory Cornbury's action regarding the fort may have been, it gained the support of Albany's magistrates. In a formal address the town's leaders thanked Cornbury for visiting the frontiers and for his "so long stay amongst us," reciting that whereas their previous requests for protection against the French had gone unanswered, Cornbury had actually begun construction of a new stone fort large enough to shelter them and their Indian allies. Having appraised the northern frontier's exposure to assaults from French Canada, Cornbury also proposed, in what one military historian has called "an unusually well presented ar- gument," the construction of four other forts or stone redoubts on the frontier, and in time of war a force of six hundred soldiers to man them. [15]

He also laid plans for protecting New York's harbor against incursions by French men-of-war, which could, given the city's weakened defenses, "Bombard the City as they please." The solution, he informed London, was to erect two stone batteries at the Narrows, as the channel between Staten Island and the western tip of Long Island was called. Cornbury's various proposals garnered the support of many local leaders, several of whom expressed appreciation for the care he had taken to inform himself about the colony's needs.[16] More important, the New York Assembly appropriated eighteen hundred pounds to strengthen frontier defenses and fifteen hundred to fortify the Narrows, as well as additional money in support of government. The other colonies, however, with the partial exception of Virginia and Maryland, failed to comply with their quotas of money for defense, leaving New Yorkers saddled once again with a disproportionate share of the costs, a situation the new governor thought outrageous and in need of remedy. The conclusion Cornbury drew from these experiences suggests that he increasingly saw himself as an instrument of imperial power in an era of reform: "This vast continent, which might be made very usefull to England if right measures were taken, will never be so till all the Proprietary and Charter Governments are brought under the Crowne."[17]

Nor was Cornbury's military strategy cast only in defensive terms. His trained soldier's eye quickly saw the potential for so exploiting war fever as to expel the French from Canada altogether, thereby securing the entire continent. Cornbury may even have seen himself as the Marlborough of North America. He proposed that "fifteen hundred well disciplined men from England well officered, and eight fourth Rate Frigots" aided by some one thousand colonials attack Quebec by sea, while another twenty-five hundred colonials should march from Albany against Montreal. The expedition would soon pay for itself, he reasoned, by opening new sources of furs and eliminating the need for gifts to the Indians. Cornbury hoped his plan would be approved at Whitehall; if not, he asked the Lords of Trade to "pardon my Zeal for the service of my Country" — a zeal that in 1704, with a French invasion imminent, included his vow "to go in person against the enemy for the security of the province."[18] The governor general, charged with defending an important frontier of the empire, was in high feather.

### A NAVAL ENGAGEMENT

Lord Cornbury's military flair and sense of command, his self-image as a man of justice, his determined assertion of imperial might and expectation of obedience, and his brusque manner of dealing with those whose competence or honesty he questioned were aspects of his administrative style much on display as he took up the office of governor. These same qualities would be in evidence throughout his career in North America. Nor were they such as to endear him to independent-minded provincials or, for that matter, to fellow servants of the crown whose attitudes or ambitions might take a different course from his own. One episode in particular shows each of these traits at work, and may serve as one set of cues to an evaluation of Cornbury's governorship as a whole, whatever the final estimate might be.

The episode occurred in 1706 and involved a conflict of jurisdiction between the governor and two naval officers whose ships, the *Lowestoffe* and *Triton's Prize*, were assigned to patrol New York waters (fig. 19).[19] That October, Cornbury was informed by a Lieutenant Thomas Wilcox, second in command of *Triton's Prize*, that his captain had suddenly died. Cornbury immediately issued an oral order for Wilcox to "take care of the Ship" pending further instructions from the lord high admiral, Queen Anne's husband, Prince George. But before Wilcox could return to his ship, Captain Fane of the *Lowestoffe*, the senior naval officer in port, who believed his authority over the vessels under his command was superior to that of the governor, issued to his own first officer, one Richard Davis, a commission as captain of *Triton's Prize*.[20]

Cornbury, who had been appointed vice admiral as well as governor general of New York, had since his arrival in the colony frequently requested clarification of his power over the naval officers stationed there, the lines of imperial authority being still ambiguous, though in process of reform, and with Royal Navy influence on the rise.[21] But, as he told Captain Fane, "unless he could shew me a Power from His Royal Highness . . . to grant Commissions, the command of that Ship [*Triton's Prize*] should go according to the Queen's Instructions to me, and his Royall Highness' Printed orders." Fane's response was to place his man, Davis, in possession of *Triton's Prize*, to confine Cornbury's man, Wilcox, on board the *Lowestoffe*, and then, in defiance of Cornbury's order that Fane appear before him, to hoist anchor and head out to sea.[22]

Cornbury was incensed. As he later wrote the Board of Trade, he could have compelled Fane's obedience by "firing upon the Queen's ship which I did not think proper to do" — adding, "tho' it is certain I could have

Figure 19. *A South Prospect of New York* (detail). From *Burgis View of New York* (1719–1721). *British men-of-war in New York Harbor, those on the left possibly of the same rate as the frigates* Lowestoffe *and* Triton's Prize. © *Collection of the New-York Historical Society*

sunck the Ship, for I have from the Fort and the Batteries of the Town Eight and Thirty Guns that bear upon one point at the same time, so that indeed no Ship can go out or come into the Harbour but must be tore to pieces." The grim relish with which Cornbury unfolds this scene hints that he played it over in his head more than once. But because Fane had managed to elude him, Cornbury turned his wrath on Captain Davis. First he ordered Davis to surrender *Triton's Prize* to Lieutenant Wilcox, "whereof you are not to fail." When Davis responded that he was "obliged to perform the duty of Command according to the Tennor of the Comission" given him by Fane, Cornbury sent a new order that "Required and Commanded [Davis] to Appear before me at Fort Anne," which order would be ignored "at your perrill." When Davis again refused, this time with growing insolence — because "the Service requires me on board her Majesty's Shipp *Triton Prize* which I command; I humbly desire your Lordship will pardon my not appearing at Fort Anne" — Cornbury decided the time for halfway measures was at an end.[23]

Cornbury called out the troops. He ordered John Riggs, captain of the garrison at Fort Anne, two lieutenants, one sergeant, sixty men, and one drummer to march double time to Kip's Bay, where *Triton's Prize* was anchored. Riggs was instructed to board the ship and require Davis, whom Cornbury now charged with "Endeavour[ing] to Levy warr against the Queen," to surrender himself. So that the order would be clear to all, Riggs was to read it "publickly on the Deck" to the entire ship's company. If Davis responded by shutting himself in his cabin, its door was to be broken open and Riggs was to seize him by force of arms "Dead or Alive." Furthermore, any officers or members of the crew who resisted the order were to be dealt with as "Enemys to the Queen and Rebells."[24]

Confronted with this show of force majeure, Davis elected to surrender himself to Riggs, after which, in his own version of the story, he was "carried Like a Traytor" to Fort Anne. There Cornbury demanded "how I durst take the Command [of *Triton's Prize*] knowing him to be Vice Admiral"; he then confined Davis to an apartment in the barracks. "Being unaccustomed to Such Usage I writ a Submissive Letter to his Lordshipp, Cl[e]aring my Self of the Bad manners he was pleased to Charge me with; not paying the respects due to her Majesty's Governour."[25]

There are at least three ways to interpret this episode, of which the simplest — and the one most in accord with historical tradition — would be to set it down as one more instance of Cornbury's arrogance, vindictiveness, and perverse talent for antagonizing everyone he dealt with, including his fellow imperial officers. Subsequent events, however, tell a different story. After Davis wrote his submissive letter, he and the governor apparently reached an accommodation, for Cornbury himself then appointed Davis captain of *Triton's Prize* pending confirmation by the Admiralty. A few months later Davis acquitted himself brilliantly in a fierce encounter with a French privateer ten leagues off the New York coast. *Triton's Prize* destroyed the French ship's spritsail, yard, and main topgallant, and Davis would have boarded the disabled privateer had his crew — no doubt many of them impressed locally — not been so inexperienced. *Triton's Prize* suffered "four Men killed on the spot" and five mortally wounded, with Davis himself taking some small shot in the neck. The French ship managed to escape only by sawing its gunnels and dumping its heavy cannon overboard. As Cornbury glowingly wrote Whitehall, "Captain Davis behaved himself as bravely . . . as any man in the world could do." [26]

A second interpretation might note the intensifying struggle for power between administrative departments during these years, in this case the Admiralty versus the Board of Trade, as the governments of both William and Mary and Queen Anne sought to place the empire on a more efficient footing. Cornbury was uneasy about the confused signals emanating from Whitehall regarding naval officers assigned to New York, and as late as October 1706 he had once again asked the Board of Trade to clarify his authority over them. Meanwhile, the officers, restive about encroachments on their professional terrain, wrote to the Admiralty protesting that colonial officials interfered with their duties. The previous captain of *Triton's Prize* had been informed by the Admiralty that in refusing to obey Governor Cornbury's orders on impressment he had "misconstrued his instructions," for "although they directed him to follow the orders of Captain Fane of the *Lowestoffe*, yet both ships being put under the immediate directions of the Government he ought to have obeyed the commands of His Lordship." [27] Such an ambiguous pronouncement did little to clear the air.

But the officers' complaints, combined with the *Triton's Prize* incident, may have been the catalyst that led the Admiralty to clarify its relations with the colonial governors. In April 1707, the secretary of the Admiralty informed the Board of Trade that whereas naval officers were required to obey the governors in most matters, the captains had full power from the Admiralty to appoint officers to ships under their command. The same letter also conveyed the lord high admiral's personal dissatisfaction with Captain Fane's behavior toward Lord Cornbury. That Queen Anne's husband, in whose entourage Cornbury had once served, was lord high admiral may have been a complicating factor. Yet there is much in this episode to suggest that what shaped responses on all sides was more a matter of departmental rivalry and the processes of bureaucratic self-definition than of the personal qualities of any of the actors.[28]

Yet a third interpretation of the *Triton's Prize* incident might simply rest on Cornbury's sense of his own duty as a military commander. Once having decided to assert his authority over the naval officers in his jurisdiction, Cornbury did so with military flourish in a swift preemptive strike that settled the issue firmly in his favor.

### CORNBURY AND THE CHURCH OF ENGLAND

A second occasion that affords glimpses of Cornbury's temperament and administrative style took place about this same time. Here one sees Cornbury in another favorite role, that of patron and advocate for the colonial Church of England.[29] Some background will help to set the scene for this episode.

We have already encountered the Hyde family tradition of dedicated Anglicanism. Cornbury's conservative understanding of church and state as entwined institutions that supported hierarchy and civic stability was fortified by his experiences in New York and New Jersey, where Anglicans formed but an island in a sea of Dissenters. As governor, Cornbury vowed to the Society for the Propagation of the Gospel in Foreign Parts (SPG), founded in 1701 as the missionary arm of the Church of England, "Nothing shall be wanting on my part to promote the Interest of the Church." Building on the efforts of his Anglican predecessor, Governor Benjamin Fletcher, to settle the New York church on a stable foundation, Cornbury granted a charter of incorporation to New York City's Trinity Parish and persuaded the SPG to send six of its first missionaries to New York and New Jersey. He further obtained from Queen Anne confirmation of Fletcher's patent for a large glebe, thereafter called the Queen's Farm, to provide a permanent income for Trinity's clergy, and turned over to the church his own right to part of its rents.[30]

He also contributed to the building of the French Reformed Church, where following the death of its minister he sought to place an Anglican cleric. Alive to the critical role of religious institutions in the dissemination of national cultures, Cornbury supported Anglican educational endeavors as a means of raising a new generation of New Yorkers in English ways. He obtained assembly support for founding a Latin free school and took the lead in establishing two other schools, all to be under the direction of the church. He also supported Anglican catechist Elias Neau's efforts to "Catechize the Negroes and Indians and the Children of the Town of York."[31] Everyone was to be Anglicized, and as much as possible Anglicanized, in Cornbury's New York.

One of the charges most commonly lodged against Cornbury is that he persecuted Dissenters. When Increase Mather made such a complaint in a letter to Sir Henry Ashurst, London agent for Massachusetts and a staunch Dissenter, Ashurst dismissed it out of hand: "As to my Lord Cornbury, he was bred at Geneva, and would no more have attempted upon your religious interest than I would." Nonetheless, Cornbury no doubt would have agreed with Henry Fielding's Parson Thwackum that real Christianity meant "not only the Protestant religion, but the Church of England." As governor he was aware of the alarms he would raise in promoting Anglicanism at the expense of the locally predominant Dissenting interest. The best tactic, he confided to the SPG, was to recommend Anglican ministers for Dissenting churches when their own clergy died or left the colony. This would "with schools be a means to make this Colony an English Colony." Cornbury expected that Dissenting ministers would seek his approval before taking up pulpits in his domain, and when they did so with an appropriate show of deference, he "licensed" them to preach.[32]

At the same time, any Dissenting clergyman who caused trouble or failed to show proper respect to Cornbury's authority was not likely to get away with it. When John Hubbard, a Presbyterian minister at Jamaica in Queens County, violated the custom that denominations share churches built with public funds by countenancing an assault on Anglicans worshiping at the town church, Cornbury ejected Hubbard from the premises as well as from the glebe. (Dissenters later magnified the incident into a premier example of Cornbury's intolerance.) Yet after Hubbard presumably made his peace, Cornbury granted him a license to preach over the objections of a number of Anglican clergymen.[33] Another challenge to Cornbury's authority may have prompted his decision in 1707 to prosecute Francis Makemie, a visiting Presbyterian minister, for preaching without a license. The governor had actually entertained Makemie and a young colleague at his table on their arrival in the colony, "being willing to shew what Civillity I cou'd to men of that character." But how was Cornbury's hospitality repaid? "They pretended they were going towards Boston; they did not say one syllable to me of preaching here . . . , nor did they offer to qualify themselves as the Law directs." The famous Makemie trial need not detain us here except to note that historical accounts of it, which cast Cornbury in the role of Anglican persecutor and Makemie as a martyr of Dissent, rely exclusively on a Presbyterian *Narrative* of the proceedings written by Makemie himself.[34]

Against this background, we may now turn to the lively events of Governor Cornbury's encounter with the Reverend Thoroughgood Moore. Following his first visit to Albany in 1702, Cornbury had urged the Society for the Propagation of the Gospel to assign an Anglican missionary to the Iroquois, fearing their alienation by French Jesuits, who had already converted some members of the tribes to Catholicism. In the fall of 1704 the society complied, sending newly ordained Thoroughgood Moore, a thirty-two-year-old graduate of Magdalene College, Cambridge. Moore was welcomed and entertained by Cornbury on arriving in New York City, afterward reporting to London that the governor was "very kind to me and all of the Clergy in general." Cornbury in turn thought Moore "a very good Man," advised him to learn the Indians' language and customs, provided him with an interpreter, and gave him the names of those Albany residents most likely to assist his work. After several months' stay at Albany, which yielded little progress among the Indians, Moore, discouraged and restless, removed to a recently vacated church in Burlington, New Jersey — apparently without Cornbury's leave, though accounts differ on this point. Cornbury "reproached" Moore but did not give up on what he saw as an important mission to the Iroquois, notifying SPG authorities that he hoped to persuade the Indians to accept Moore the following summer. He still considered Moore a good man and by his own account "readily agreed" to the Burlington plan, since it was dangerous to leave an Anglican church vacant in Quaker West Jersey. The SPG subsequently approved Moore's relocation, though the secretary urged Cornbury to keep a watchful eye on the missionaries, not allowing them "to Remove from Place to Place without leave."[35]

With no resident bishop in the colonies to deal promptly with ecclesiastical irregularities, Cornbury had been instructed by the crown to oversee the Anglican clergy in his jurisdiction, to remove from their pulpits any who gave offense or scandal, and to supply vacancies.[36] The SPG, which provided initial monetary support for all missions in New York and New Jersey, shared responsibility for the colonial church with the bishop of London, within whose diocese all the North American colonies fell. Though lines of authority to the provincial clergy were less tangled than those to the naval establishment, the entire enterprise of overseas missions was new and replete with unexamined ambiguities and potential difficulties.

And the Reverend Thoroughgood Moore, a passionate High Anglican and man of action, seems to have had a taste for trouble. The first hint of this comes from a report about Moore's dealings with the English officers garrisoned at Albany. Moore, possibly influenced by an Anglican movement that opposed dueling as an expression of masculine honor, had apparently asked the officers whether on "being insulted, and their Reputation Stained by some Enemy . . . They should think Themselves obliged to fight that Man." As professional soldiers and gentlemen the officers had stoutly answered that they should, whereupon Moore "took an opportunity to refuse to admit Them to Receive the Sacrament the next Communion Day." A similar scene unfolded after Moore settled at Burlington, where he struck up an acquaintance with New Jersey's lieutenant governor, Richard Ingoldsby, a seasoned English army officer whose stalwart services had earned him the civilian post. The two men were out riding one early spring day in 1706 when Moore, seemingly determined to curb the martial spirit, asked Ingoldsby if he had "so much patience and Christian temper as to take a Box on the Ear without resentment or returning the Injury." Ingoldsby replied "with some Warmth that he neither would nor could take such an effront." To at least one of his contemporaries this seemed fair enough, Ingoldsby being "a soldier and got his Living by his Sword." But Moore thought otherwise. When Ingoldsby, his wife, and daughter attended Moore's church on Easter Sunday and rose to take Communion, Moore intercepted the lieutenant governor at his seat and, after ascertaining that his views on vengeance had not changed, publicly "forbid him to approach the Holy Table." At that point the stunned and embarrassed Ingoldsby and his family withdrew from the church.[37]

Such a public and seemingly gratuitous humiliation of the lieutenant governor made "a very great noise in the Country." Cornbury, who had reason to be angered by this insult to his government, nonetheless initially attempted to conciliate. First he heard Ingoldsby's complaint, after which he wrote to Moore and others to get "the whole truth of it." At his urging Moore and Ingoldsby exchanged letters, but to little avail. Cornbury next called both men to meet with him at Perth Amboy, where his secretary heard Moore confess his error and promise to give Ingoldsby "Satisfaction . . . as publick as the affront had been" if Ingoldsby required it. Ingoldsby did so require, demanding stiffly that the apology be delivered before the entire congregation at Burlington. When Moore refused to go that far, matters "grew worse and worse every day" until Ingoldsby asked Cornbury to remove either Moore or himself out of the colony.[38]

Cornbury was already irritated with Moore for taking up with Lewis Morris, a New Jersey land magnate and officeholder whose circle of entrenched local gentry was obstructing policies promulgated by the new — and first — royal government of the colony. Seeing the rise of "Factions in both Church and State," Cornbury decided that the best solution was to speed Moore's return to Albany. Yet when he directed Moore to attend him in New York, the clergyman refused, asserting that a governor had no power over the clergy in America. This at last was too much. Cornbury suspended Moore from preaching at Burlington and ordered the sheriff to take him into custody, which he did on August 15, 1707.[39]

One account of how events unfolded thereafter is that of Moore himself. Shortly after the arrest Governor Cornbury came in person to Perth Amboy, where in a private conference with Moore and Ingoldsby he condemned Moore for his rebellious behavior and charged that he had sided with the government's enemies. Cornbury then suspended Moore from all preaching. When Moore declared that the suspension was illegal, Cornbury retorted that "he would be obeyed and that if I did not, he would use me like other Rebels." Cornbury then placed Moore in the custody of the sheriff, who was ordered to escort him to the governor's barge for the trip back to New York. During the trip to New York, as Cornbury's secretary reported, the governor invited Moore to dine with him, which Moore "obstinately refused" to do; nonetheless, Cornbury sent him dinner and a bottle of wine. Moore was taken to Fort Anne, where he was confined to Chaplain John Sharpe's room but was provided with the best victuals and drink.[40]

Moore wrote from the fort that he was comfortable, Cornbury having said he should "want nothing" while awaiting transport to England. In a second letter, however, Moore described his confinement as "arbitrary and illegal," declared that his friends in New Jersey and New York were all disliked by Cornbury, and observed that once officials at home were "acquainted with his Lordship's Character I am sure they will cease inquiring [about the reason for Moore's imprisonment] and be satisfied I could not . . . have his Friendship."[41]

Still more drama was in store, complete with a tragic ending. It seems that Moore — with the connivance of Lewis Morris, the Anglican catechist Elias Neau, and Moore's fellow New Jersey missionary the Reverend John Brooke — had hatched a plan to free Moore from the fort. He and Brooke would then take ship for England and lay their dispute with Governor Cornbury before the bishop of London.[42] Cornbury was at Albany on the day of the planned escape. Brooke and Morris dined with Moore, and at four o'clock Brooke returned to the fort and asked the guard on duty if he had orders to stop anyone from leaving. When told he had not, Brooke walked out the gate with Moore. The officers of the fort, discovering Moore was gone, tried to arrest Brooke. As Neau tells it, "They placed two Centinals before my door; but Mr. Brook was not in my house. I caused him to be hid by one of my friends." The mayor of New York completes the story. Brooke escaped with Moore "and went to Coll. Lewis Morris his house, a most Inveterate and bitter Enemy to his Lordship and Government."[43]

From Morris's Westchester estate Moore and Brooke fled to Boston, where a fellow missionary returning from England encountered them in late November and urged them to return to New York. He warned them of the dangers of an ocean crossing in that season, but "poor Thorogood said he had rather be taken into France than into the Fort at New York, and if they were sunk in the Sea, they did not doubt but God would receive them." Moore's premonition proved all too accurate. On the voyage home, his ship "foundered at Sea; [and] neither he, or any of the Crew, or any Wreck of the Ship, were ever heard of after."[44]

Clearly Cornbury relished wielding power, was impatient of insolence, and was not loath to intervene in the chain of command. He might well be seen by rival officials and Dissenters as somewhat high-handed while viewing himself as an efficient and fair-minded administrator. His capacity for handling bureaucratic strife or sensitive political incidents is not easily judged from the variant readings of it by his contemporaries, though his actions against both Captain Davis and the Reverend Mr. Moore were, at least initially, measured rather than precipitate. In his dealings with the colonials, Cornbury was not much disposed to the kind of balancing and bargaining that would come to characterize the subsequent Age of Walpole. Indeed, such a notion as "salutary neglect" would have seemed to him an appalling abdication of duty.

Cornbury served at a time when the crown sought to put its imperial house in order by promoting greater centralization, administrative efficiency, and orderly trade. As a proponent of empire and a surrogate of the crown, Cornbury would do everything in his power to support that effort. From the provincials' perspective, however, the first decade of the eighteenth century was in many ways an extension of the seventeenth century. New Yorkers, still feeling the aftershocks of Leisler's Rebellion, and New Jerseyans, full of second thoughts about having agreed to put themselves under a royal charter, were beset with factions and discontents. Without an understood mechanism through which to express their domestic grievances, those who opposed the royal government seem to have concluded they had no alternative but, as some observers put it, "to blacken Lord Cornbury's administration" by "heap[ing] up Complaints against his Lordship to remove him from his Government."[45]

One time-proven way to cast opprobrium on a governor's reputation was to charge him with misapplying the crown's revenue.

"Money's the Leading Card"

*Governor Cornbury and Imperial Finance*

The notion that Governor Cornbury's administration was corrupt depends heavily on his handling — rather his alleged mishandling — of money. Charges that Cornbury accepted bribes in New Jersey, diverted public funds to private uses in New York, and fell deeply into debt from extravagant and licentious living have appeared routinely over the years in writings about his administration.[1] Because fiscal corruption is one of the two main pillars on which the Cornbury legend rests, it may be useful to have another look at this part of the story.

The somewhat hazy notion of "corruption" was itself subject to sharpening definition around the turn of the eighteenth century as the impulse to reform domestic and imperial administration, especially regarding finance, reached a peak under the reigns of William and Mary and Queen Anne. The government's previously desultory efforts to regulate trade and its often slack oversight of administrative and military affairs would no longer do in the face of growing overseas commerce and the start in 1689 of a series of wars against France. Rules of navigation and trade were tightened; piracy was suppressed, the navy enlarged, and vice admiralty courts expanded. Accounting procedures at all levels of government were subject to scrutiny and reform from an increasingly active Treasury department. In 1696 a full-time professional Board of Trade was established to oversee colonial administration, appoint officials, gather data, and report to the Privy Council.[2]

Stated this way, the reformers' program sounds trim and efficient. The missing ingredient, of course, is politics, for politics was the cement of the new edifice as it had been of the old. Crown, Parliament, heads of departments, and Whitehall bureaucracies all continued to operate in a political environment. Appointments were weighed and policies measured within a calculus of Whigs and Tories, Court and Country. Yet if patronage and preferment based on personal acquaintance or family connection did not disappear (as indeed they could not in an oligarchic system), experience and demonstrated competence were increasingly esteemed. As the bureaucracies of high finance and state officialdom expanded, they introduced new, recondite sources of political power, unsettling the expectations of traditional oligarchies.[3] As in any period of transition, elements of the old coexisted with the new, raising anxieties and suspicions on all sides.

In the colonies, the executive's power over appointments and land patents provided important leverage in enlisting support for imperial policies. Nor was the granting of offices and lands to the governors' political supporters seen as "corrupt," though a number of ambiguities in the system created opportunities for unscrupulous dealings. Further temptations lurked in the modest level of the governors' salaries, which were expected to be supplemented by local perquisites — notably, fees for patenting land and the governors' "thirds," the one-third value of ships and cargos from vessels confiscated for violating the acts of trade. Given the makeshift nature of this system over the seventeenth century, the intermittent attention of those regulating it, and the potential for bribery and other financial thimblerigging, it is surprising that abuses were relatively limited. But this did not stop critics of the royal governors from assuming the worst, especially in the decades on either side of 1700, when anyone not educated in the mysteries of the new financial order could see corruption all around, sometimes with good cause.[4] The result was an explosion of charge and countercharge in which political opponents operating in the twilight of a changing system regularly vilified each other as swindlers and bribe-takers.

Though Governor Cornbury was but one of many officials accused of such misdeeds, historians — especially those of whiggish cast susceptible to negative readings of Cornbury's character — have never compared his experience with that of other royal governors or set it in the transatlantic context of imperial reform. Also overlooked are Cornbury's systematic efforts to refute the opposition's charges in legislative debate and courts of law as well as the support his policies found among the royalist, or Court, faction in the colonies and from imperial authorities at home.[5] When these elements are added to the story, it becomes less a morality tale than an account of human and political forces in contention.

## CHARGES OF FINANCIAL CORRUPTION IN
## NEW JERSEY AND NEW YORK

On May 8, 1707, the New Jersey Assembly publicly accused Governor Cornbury of taking bribes some four years earlier, shortly after being appointed royal governor of the colony in 1703. In a published *Remonstrance*, the assembly asserted that it was "notoriously known, that many considerable Sums of Mony have been raised" to further certain private interests in New Jersey, the members having "great reason to believe, the Money so gathered was given to Lord Cornbury." In his formal written response, Cornbury declared that the assembly's "scandalous Reflections" were fabricated by Speaker Samuel Jennings and the wealthy landowner Lewis Morris, "Men always possest with passionate Heats and the transports of most vindictive Tempers." Contending that he knew nothing about any such sum, Cornbury added, "But this I know, that if any Money was raised, it was not given to me, nor was ever any Money offered to me." To strengthen its case the assembly collected depositions from at least twenty-two men, a number of them sworn before an assembly committee chaired by Lewis Morris (fig. 20). (Morris's presence becomes more and more insistent in this story.)[6]

The bribes Cornbury was alleged to have received were of two sorts. In the first instance, Dr. John Johnston, a leader of the proprietary group that ruled East Jersey before it was converted to a royal colony, deposed that in 1703 he had visited New York to call on Lord Cornbury. At that time he offered to make Cornbury "a present of a piece of [silver] Plate to the value of two hundred pounds," a fairly standard practice in welcoming new governors before 1703.[7] The disallowance of presents was, however, one of the reforms instituted under Queen Anne in an effort to regularize assembly appropriations for the support of colonial governors.[8] Cornbury thus told Johnston, according to Johnston's deposition, that "he was commanded by Her Majestie to receive no presents," and

Figure 20. Lewis Morris. By John Watson. Oil. Circa 1726. *Courtesy, The Brooklyn Museum, 43.196, Dick S. Ramsay Fund and John Hill Morgan, Brooklyn, New York*

refused the offer. Cornbury also directed that the queen's order regarding presents be "entered at large in the council books, and the books of the general assembly." Johnston tried again some months later, this time offering one hundred pounds. But "his Lordship refused to take it saying her Maj[es]ty had for bid him and he would not touch with it." At that point "this Deponent left it in his Lordships chamber and came away." Later Johnston visited Cornbury with another hundred pounds, "which his Lordship with seeming earnestness refused." Advising that the queen had not forbidden presents of plate, Johnston assured the governor that the gift was "not given as a Bribe but a mark of favour and regard to his Lordship," upon which he left the money on a table.[9] Johnston's language itself suggests how blurred was the line in these years between presents and bribes.

Four years would pass before anyone accused Cornbury of impropriety in this matter. By 1707, when Johnston's deposition was sworn, he was second only to Lewis Morris as leader of a New Jersey opposition determined to oust Cornbury from his governorship. Yet even Johnston's statement makes clear that Cornbury did not have his hand out but repeatedly refused the money. These aspects of the episode as well as the subsequent enlargement to a bribe of what Johnston himself had earlier called a customary gift suggest that a strong political current was charging the air by 1707. But no definitive verdict is possible, because the question of whether money passed hands comes down to Johnston's word against Cornbury's. Moreover, each man, working from different assumptions in a time of shifting rules, might have believed that he had given or refused a bribe.

The other allegation of bribery, also raised for the first time in 1707, involved money collected by two New Jersey men in 1703–1704 "for the good of the Country." This fund of several hundred pounds was, according to the assembly *Remonstrance*, given to Cornbury by seekers of favor opposed to land policies of the proprietors who had ruled New Jersey before it became a royal colony. Most witnesses said the amount collected was seven to eight hundred pounds; Lewis Morris claimed that it was fifteen hundred; and one man, hauled before the New Jersey Supreme Court for defaming Governor Cornbury, charged that the amount of the "present" was thirty-five hundred pounds.[10] Sworn depositions describing the episode vary considerably about the facts. Though all deponents agree that the money was collected by Richard Salter and Captain John Bowne, supposed minions of Cornbury, what happened thereafter is disputed.

Several contributors thought that the fund had been gathered to defray lawyers' fees, others that it would be offered to Cornbury's chief justice in New York, and still others that the contributors were to be reimbursed by the assembly. Some who gave money said they were told that it was for Governor Cornbury; some did not know for whom the money was intended but "believe[d] 'twas for his Ldship"; and one man declared, "I cannot tell what use this money was converted to . . . [but] I have as much reason to think his Lordship has part of it as anybody because he is the most able to oblige us." [11] Yet others, "perceiving the Fallacie and Deceit" of Salter and Bowne, concluded that the money had been "craftily Extorted . . . [by] specious Promises of the Publick Good." In other words, Salter and Bowne, while promising to cross the palms of high officials, had pocketed the money. Even Lewis Morris, though he believed that the fund was given to Cornbury, finally had to acknowledge that "it cannot be well knowne how these persons dispos'd of that money." With the depositions painting such a murky picture, the assembly backed off in its response to Cornbury's answer, hinting weakly rather than asserting that "in all probability" the money was given to him. [12]

Cornbury was so angry about the accusations that he asked permission from the Board of Trade to sue the assemblymen for "the extravagant Injury they have done me." The lieutenant governor and council of New Jersey sprang to his defense by addressing the queen directly, avowing that the colony's confusions were "wholly owing to the Turbulent, Factious, uneasy and Disloyal Principles of two men in that assembly Mr. Lewis Morris and Mr. Samuel Jennings, a Quaker." Where their facts carried any truth at all, "they have been malitious and unjust in not mentioning the whole Truth, which would have fully justified my Lord Cornbury's just conduct." Thus the councilmen branded the assembly's charges a "Scandalous and Infamous Libell" cooked up by "wicked designing men." [13]

In the colony of New York, rumors of corruption focused on a single episode, a fifteen-hundred-pound tax authorized by the assembly in 1703 to erect a pair of batteries at the Narrows, the entry to New York's harbor. This was Cornbury's pet project (see above), and though he foresaw the difficulty of obtaining such a large sum from New Yorkers already squeezed by trade losses and high wartime taxes, he wrote the Board of Trade in June 1703 that, when collected, the money "shall be laid out forthwith, to the uses for which it was given. I hope to get one of the Batteries up this summer." In fact, though stonework for the batteries was apparently started, the cannon — supposed to be supplied by England — never were mounted at the Narrows during Cornbury's regime.[14] No voice was raised about this, however, until 1706, when rumors suddenly began to fly that the fifteen hundred pounds had been diverted to build a "pleasure house" for Cornbury on Nutten Island.

The term "pleasure house" falls seductively on the modern ear, yet in the eighteenth century it described nothing more voluptuous than a weekend retreat or country house. As one New York official recorded some years later, Cornbury built "a pleasure house on Nutten Island for himself and succeeding governors to retire to when he inclined to free himself from business." (Thus it was that Nutten Island was renamed Governors' Island [fig. 21].) Cornbury did indeed build the house in 1703, though the extant bill for timber, nails, labor, and other costs amounted to less than a hundred pounds, suggesting that it was far from sumptuous.[15] What, then, happened to the fifteen hundred pounds?

It turns out that only about a fourth of the fifteen hundred pounds assessed by the assembly for the cannon mounts was ever collected from the taxpayers. Cornbury noted this fact in May 1706, when on his own initiative he addressed the New York Assembly about the rumors. Nonetheless, he was "sensible that some Malicious ill minded People have reported that I had taken that Money into my Hands." To determine the truth of this charge, once again served up three years after the event, he confronted the rumors by demanding that the assembly make "a strict Enquiry into that Tax." A committee appointed by the house to investigate the matter reported one month later that it "could not come to any certain Resolution in that Affair." They agreed that no more than £398 of the £1,500 was ever raised. When the customary fees for collecting the tax were subtracted, the balance was reduced to £356, which, the committee found, was now in the custody of two men, the colonial receiver of revenues and a member of the council. There is thus no evidence

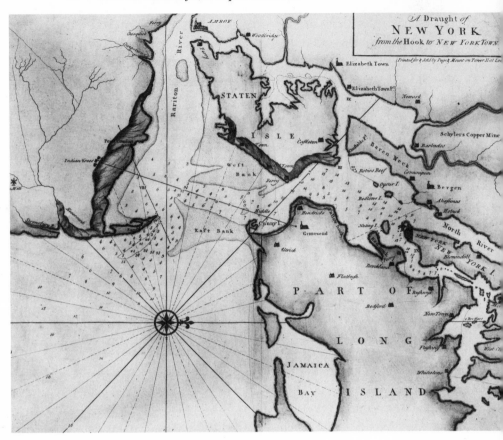

Figure 21. *A Draught of New York from the Hook to New York Town, 1732. Sandy Hook is at the left; the Narrows is at the center between Staten Island and Long Island; Nutten, or Governors' Island, lies off the tip of Manhattan at right; New Jersey is at the upper right. This chart, apparently drawn for mariners, indicates depths and shallows.*
© *Collection of the New-York Historical Society*

that Cornbury himself ever handled the money, which in any case was fully accounted for in 1706.[16]

There the assembly let the matter rest. Governor Cornbury, not surprisingly, was dissatisfied with this result, considering it "hard Usage to me that you did not think fit to examine that Matter thoroughly"; they had time to do it and should have, in view of the "scandalous Report" that he had misapplied the money. Clearly, Cornbury thought the legislature should have exonerated him explicitly and perhaps have ferreted out the author of the rumor. Yet by 1706 his initial honeymoon with the New

York Assembly was increasingly burdened by the accumulation of grievances that in time beset all royal governors. Besides, a small opposition faction — in part stirred up by none other than his New Jersey nemesis, Lewis Morris — was about to launch a concerted effort to obtain his recall to England.[17]

## GOVERNOR CORNBURY'S EXPENSE ACCOUNT

If the case against Cornbury for taking bribes and diverting public funds tends to dwindle on close inspection, there remain the more general charges that he lived extravagantly, spent government funds with a lavish hand, and ineptly managed both his public and private finances — alleged trespasses that caused him to be arrested for debt and detained in New York for seventeen months after his replacement as governor in December 1708. Treasury records contain a great deal of information about colonial expenses, and it is true that Cornbury's accounts for his first months in office were audited and returned to New York to be "Rectifyed." Specifically questioned was the cost of supplying candles and firewood to the forts at Albany and New York City, where the four companies of British soldiers and a number of English officials, including Cornbury, resided, that item being "So Excessive, that the same will not be allowed by the Lord Treasurer." Also judged excessive was a £677 charge for Cornbury's trip to Albany in 1702 to parley with the Indians, which "will not be allowed by my Lord Treasurer, unless more particular and Satisfactory Account be given of it, the same far Exceeding all former Disbursements on the Like Occasion."[18]

On their face these audits would seem to incriminate Cornbury, yet to pluck such comments from the full record out of context is misleading. For it was during Cornbury's governorship that England's attempt to tighten imperial controls and improve administrative efficiency, especially regarding finance, reached full pitch. Queen Anne gave unprecedented power to her treasurers, and in Sydney Earl Godolphin (1702–1710) she found a man of great vigor who would be the first to turn a clear eye on the auditing of colonial accounts. "For fifty years after the close of Queen Anne's reign there was never quite the same emphasis on the audit."[19] At the same time, in a period of fierce infighting among government departments and political factions, the Treasury increasingly clashed with the Board of Trade over imperial expenditures.

One consequence of this reformist climate was the rise in New York, as in England, of two competing centers of financial authority. At one pole were the governor, councilmen, and crown-appointed receiver, who, under supervision of the Board of Trade, had traditionally taken primary responsibility for verifying provincial expenditures. At the other pole was the Treasury's appointed local representative, the deputy auditor, who inspected the colony's accounts — including the civil list, administrative expenses, customs receipts, and revenue from confiscated ships' cargoes — with an eye toward implementing the fiscal reforms of Godolphin. If the solitary figure of a deputy auditor seems a poor match against the combined authority of the colonial governor and council, it is important to note that the growing power of Lord Treasurer Godolphin stood behind that deputy and that Godolphin had the final say on approving funds for provincial governments.[20]

William Blathwayt, longtime servant of the crown and now Godolphin's auditor general, functioned at first as a bridge between these competing camps. Blathwayt was an old acquaintance of Cornbury's and had everything to gain by remaining on good terms with the queen's cousin, who also had powerful friends in the ministry. When Blathwayt's relative George Clarke was sent to New York as the Treasury's resident deputy auditor early in Cornbury's administration, Blathwayt urged Clarke to cooperate with local officials and to "endeavour by Doing your duty to please his Excellency and get his good will."[21] But as the Treasury under Godolphin gained power at the expense of the Board of Trade, its provincial auditors — in New York's case, Clarke — came to exercise enlarged authority over local accounts. At the same time, Godolphin was steadily eroding Blathwayt's position, leaving him no choice but to press Deputy Auditor Clarke to a close questioning of all New York expenditures.[22] Thus did imperial government in New York, as at home, harbor discord within its ranks.

Clarke supported Cornbury at first, noting that "in my Lord Bellomonts and [Lieutenant Governor] Nanfans time the Creditt of the Government sunk so low and the Revenue so much decayed that no body has any faith left." Yet Cornbury, he observed, was attempting to disentangle the accounts and restore trust in the government. On April 17, 1705, however, the governor suspended from office Clarke's friend Thomas Byerly, the receiver of New York. The main bone of contention between them was Byerly's seizure of the merchant ship *Eagle Galley*, which Cornbury subsequently ruled had not violated the laws of trade (though had the ship's cargo been condemned Cornbury stood to receive one-third of its value). The suspension of a receiver was not unusual in New York, given the tangled nature of such disputes, and Clarke forbore to comment on the merits of the case; still, he was "sorry it has fallen on my friend, and acquaintance."[23]

The next step in the deterioration of Cornbury's relationship with Clarke resulted from a typical eighteenth-century misunderstanding, one concocted of distance, time, and rumor, to say nothing of suspicion, fear, and private interest — factors that were forever inciting mischief in the early modern political world. In the late spring of 1705, Clarke made a trip to Virginia. When he was detained longer than expected, a rumor began to circulate in New York that he had sailed for England, leading some New Yorkers to urge the governor to suspend him as auditor. Though Clarke returned from Virginia by late summer and resumed his office, he now sensed that Cornbury's confidence in him had been diminished. Fearing that his suspension was imminent, Clarke began to cast Cornbury in a less favorable light.[24]

With his nerves on edge, Clarke's responses were subject to wide swings: at one moment he saw Cornbury as consumed by money concerns — "in short money's the leading Card"; at the next he exonerated the governor, blaming his troubles instead on Lady Cornbury, who "never fails to lessen my Reputation with my Lord."[25] Cornbury in turn, already uneasy about Clarke's power over the colony's accounts, began to withhold information and to delay responding to Clarke's requests about expenditures, thereby increasing Clarke's suspicions.

Thus when Clarke, in response to Godolphin's order, told Cornbury's secretary that the governor's accounts from the Albany trip of 1702 would have to be rectified, the secretary "flew into a passion and told me that the accounts were never thus comptrolled before, and that it must be upon some complaint sent home against my Lord." At this point Clarke challenged Cornbury's bills for candles and firewood by refusing to reimburse suppliers, or doing so only after long delay. Clarke then turned petty as he also balked at paying for such items as flags and awnings, asserting that these were personal rather than public expenses—

a distinction that Cornbury, raised under an aristocratic system, must have found puzzling. When the governor at about this same time advanced money for the burial of two "frozen sailors," Clarke refused to reimburse him, declaring that the deceased were not navy men but only poor provincial seamen and thus a local charge.[26]

Concerned that the government's credit would be damaged, and short of funds for important initiatives, Cornbury, like governors before and after him, sometimes dug into his own pocket to pay for such items as firewood, sloop hire, certain minor officials' salaries, and gifts for the Indians. When his own ever-limited funds ran short, he reached for the familiar but risky expedient of accepting credit from local merchants, securing the debts with government warrants.[27] Given the experience of his predecessors, Cornbury must have known that he might be held responsible by local creditors for any warrants still unredeemed when he left office.

George Clarke, for all his questioning of Cornbury's lesser expenses, tended to support the governor on big items. He justified the cost of building a new powder vault at Fort Anne, and he unequivocally defended Cornbury against the charge of "excessive" expense during the Albany trip — which accounts still had not been paid by the Treasury in November 1705. As Clarke explained to Blathwayt, Governor Cornbury could not return to New York City following negotiations with the Indians at Albany in 1702 owing to a virulent epidemic. "No man can suppose his Lordship would have staid in Towne during such a Pestilence, which hurryd Twenty or Thirty a day sometimes to their Graves." Cornbury instead governed the colony from Jamaica, in Queens County, where he convened the legislative assembly and council. And since "no man I'm sure can think he lives by Air," observed Clarke, "these must be expences of the same kind as tho' he was att his owne Table in the Fort at New York." Clarke then urged "the solid Service and real necessity of this Expence." He did think that with good management the consumption of candles and firewood might be reduced by a third, though, he added, "the truth on't is, Wood is growne very dear."[28]

Nonetheless, by the fall of 1705, Clarke and Cornbury were often at loggerheads, the inevitable bureaucratic tensions being exacerbated, according to Clarke, by the governor's tendency to "groundless pique." In a series of remarkably candid letters, Clarke complained bitterly to Blathwayt that Cornbury "brow beated" him. The governor had called him on the carpet and "demanded why I did not pass his accounts . . . at which he flew into a passion." Cornbury further expostulated that if the auditor controlled provincial expenses, then "he [Cornbury] would be no longer Governor." "This money," wrote Clarke, "is the Devill." Meanwhile he continued to suffer "insulting or reviling usage of a Governour"; indeed, under Cornbury's contemptible treatment he was dealt with "like a footman, or a Slave." [29] As gentlemen, both Cornbury and Clarke obviously felt debased by the very medium in which their relationship was rooted, as squabbles over money threatened to reduce Cornbury to impotence and Clarke to the abject lot of slave. Yet in the new era of imperial finance, money was the coin not only of exchange but of power.

By late 1705, Clarke and Byerly formed a core of opposition within the royal government of New York, joining their voices to those of Lewis Morris and other disgruntled New Jerseyans to agitate for Cornbury's removal. "I find many things are whispered against me," Cornbury wrote his father, but "assure your self that I will answer every point fully, and to the confusion of those that have spread them." [30] Cornbury, supported by his council and the Board of Trade, was still more than a match for Deputy Auditor Clarke. Yet with the rise of the Marlborough-Godolphin ministry in 1706, the Treasury's reform faction, into which Clarke had now been fully drawn, was gaining ascendancy in England.

The struggle between Cornbury and Clarke sheds light on both the strains produced by imperial reform and the internal dynamics of Cornbury's administration. Equally illuminating is a comparison of Cornbury's experience in colonial finance with that of the governors who preceded and followed him.

## CORNBURY'S ADMINISTRATION IN
## COMPARATIVE PERSPECTIVE

Every New York governor in these years entered office complaining about the malfeasance of his predecessor and left office being complained about by his successor. One cause was the alternation of Whigs and Tories in the governorship, a consequence of the shifting sands of metro-politan politics. The Tory royalist Benjamin Fletcher (1692–1698) was charged with running up a provincial debt of £1,391 and conniving in every sort of public and private graft. Under the alleged "ill manage-ment" of his whiggish successor, Richard Coote, earl of Bellomont (1698–1701), the debt reached £10,000, £12,000, or £24,000, depend-ing on whom you read. The conservative squire of Westchester County, Caleb Heathcote, wrote his brother in England that Governor Bello-mont's "memory will stink in the nostrils of all good men for Severall ages." Never had he known "soo much Wickednesse to be in one man."[31] Lieutenant Governor John Nanfan took over the administration on Bel-lomont's death in 1701. Though only fourteen months in office, he, too, was charged with misapplication of the revenue, having become so caught up in New York's web of debt that he was arrested and prevented from returning to England for more than a year. About this same time Lady Bellomont, the governor's widow, was restrained from departing New York by the newly arrived Governor Cornbury pending settlement of her late husband's accounts. Her ladyship nonetheless managed to slip on board the HMS *Advice* and escape to England, leaving her husband's debtors no alternative but to sue her from afar.[32]

Cornbury no doubt thought it necessary to use harsh measures against his predecessors, given that on arriving in New York he found, according to Robert Livingston, "an Empty Treasury . . . [and] a greater Debt than It had ever been." When Robert Hunter took over as governor in 1710, he did not fail in his turn to charge Cornbury with "misapplica-tions" and "Misgovernment." Yet four years later Hunter himself stood in fear of debtor's prison because of the twenty thousand pounds he owed a number of merchants, from whom he had borrowed money to subsist New York's government-sponsored Palatine refugees.[33]

This frenzy of charge and countercharge by successive administra-tions came about primarily because of three circumstances: the relent-lessly bitter factional aftermath of Leisler's Rebellion; the still unresolved ambiguities of metropolitan politics and bureaucracy; and the chaotic state of imperial finance — the last being the very problem Godolphin's program of reform was designed to correct. The debt that shadowed New York affairs from 1689 to 1717, when it was finally paid off, became the flash point of a series of power struggles, putting at risk the reputation for honesty and fiscal competence of every governor bold enough to assume the helm in these troubled years.

A further complication was the presence in New York of the only garrison of English soldiers permanently stationed on the North American mainland: the four independent companies of foot (see above). Undermanned and perpetually in arrears of pay, the New York troops were a constant drain on the funds of governors committed to a strong defense against French Canada. Given "the ghastly confusion of army finance in England," which made chief executives hostage to the soldiers' salary and subsistence demands, it is little wonder that each newly arrived governor hounded his predecessor to discharge his debt to the troops before departing the colony. (By Cornbury's reckoning, Lord Bellomont at the time of his death owed the four companies almost nineteen thousand pounds.)[34]

By the turn of the eighteenth century, company officers were resorting to the New York courts to sue governors for the soldiers' back pay. Captain James Weemes's lawsuits, for example, contributed to the arrest and detention in New York of both Lieutenant Governor John Nanfan in 1702 and Cornbury in 1709, and would no doubt have vexed Governor Bellomont had not his death made the issue moot. That paying the soldiers became embroiled in politics was almost inevitable in an era of ferocious party rivalries in both province and metropolis. "So entangled were the accounts and so vehement the accusations and counter-accusations," according to one historian, "that the comptrollers of the army accounts, when they came to audit, could not be sure who was innocent and who was guilty."[35] Such a verdict could perhaps be rendered about all provincial finances in these years.

The conditions just described created a pernicious environment in which backbiting and slanderous gossip thrived. Every governor, every high official — no matter how responsibly he tried to do his job — was subject to charges by someone who believed himself the victim of the sly evasions and nefarious bargains of those in power. And in a world in flux, who was right or what was true was not always evident. The presence of such charges in the record, moreover, later played into the prejudices of Whig historians, who have tended to set down Tory loyalists like Fletcher and Cornbury as corrupt while portraying such Whig governors as Bellomont and Hunter in benignly sympathetic terms.

## PATRICIANS IN THE PROVINCES

For all these reasons, an accurate picture of Cornbury's governorship has been difficult to come by. Nonetheless, a more balanced assessment of Cornbury's administration should provide a clearer sense of how royal government was received in a provincial society undergoing rapid change and social maturation. Cornbury was one of a number of highborn Englishmen sent to the colonies as royal influence grew in America, and as a matter of course he, or a Lord Bellomont, brought with him metropolitan manners and aristocratic refinements. No doubt any number of aspiring gentlemen in New York and New Jersey took their cues about English taste and decorum from encounters with such officials, as did their wives and daughters from the courtly style introduced by these governors and their ladies. Other colonials, however, may have interpreted such displays as evidence of prodigality and corruption. Governor Cornbury would have made an especially strong impression, considering that he was initially received as near-royalty owing to his close relationship to the queen. That Lord and Lady Cornbury intended to maintain as much as possible the trappings of English aristocracy is apparent from hints about their domestic arrangements and from glimpses into their public style. Such glimpses, in turn, bear on questions relating to Cornbury's financial practices and on charges by his enemies of extravagant and voluptuous living.

From England, Governor Cornbury brought some 130 tons of goods and equipage to New York. In addition to new uniforms for the four companies of foot and other military supplies, the cargo included such personal items as fine clothing, paintings, books, furniture, linens, and tableware. Lord and Lady Cornbury obviously considered it a mark of their station to entertain well, and many were the honored colonials, British officials, and gentlemen sojourners from England who acknowledged the gracious hospitality they received at the governor's table. George Keith, the Quaker turned Anglican, found during a preaching tour that "my Lord Cornbury . . . was very kind to us, and at his Invitation, we did eat at his table both Sundays and other Times." An English gentleman passing through New York wrote home that Cornbury had received him "in a manner far beyond my deserts." The list of goods the governor sold at auction before departing New York leaves little doubt about the activity of his table, including as it does nine damask tablecloths with two dozen napkins, three fringed tablecloths with four dozen matching napkins, one dozen new garlic (linen) napkins, bolts of cloth from which to make additional napery, as well as pewter dishes and French doilies. We also learn from the items auctioned that the family slept on Holland or Irish linen sheets, had a "Counterpaine Wrought with Worsted," an India satin coverlet, suites of curtains at the windows, and such fine furniture as a wood inlaid writing desk, "an Imbroidered Squat" (footstool), a large looking glass, and an oval tea table.[36]

Pictures and books added a further note of refinement to the governor's residence, their subjects and titles reflecting not only Cornbury's English taste but something of his personal qualities as well. Among the more than fifty pictures and prints he eventually sold at auction, religious subjects prevailed, including depictions of Joseph and his brothers, Jesus and his disciples, the woman of Samaria, Saint Jerome, the temple of Jerusalem, and a painting on glass of the Virgin Mary. On the secular side were representations of Charles I, Charles II, the duke of Buckhurst, a number of India prints, a picture of a sea fight, and one of Venus and Cupid. The preponderance of religious themes is even more pronounced among the books sold, which included one Bible, several paraphrases of the Psalms, *A Discourse against the Fear of Death, Closet Devotions, The Daily Communicant, The Great Duty of Self Regulation,* John Milton's *Paradise Lost,* Robert Barclay's *Apology,* John Tillotson's *Sermons, The Parable of the Pilgrim, The Whole Duty of Man,* John Flavell's *Works* in two volumes, and "Josephus in folio," which last sold for three pounds. Other volumes included histories of Europe, *The Republic of Venice,* "The Impeachment of the Earl of Clarendon," "Prince Arthur a Poem," John Dryden's *Plays,* three volumes of Tacitus, Lord Coke's *Detections,* "A Dancing Book," and such novels as *The Unfortunate Duchess* and *Arnolda and the Injured Lover,* which may have been Lady Cornbury's.[37]

That Cornbury would live like the patrician he was is suggested not only by these lists of goods but by other glimpses into his household accounts. The governor traveled throughout his domain in style, on land by coach and on water by the barge *Cornbury,* often accompanied by a considerable train of local gentry. He built a country house, as we know, and with the chaplain from the fort went "a shooting" in the wilds of New Jersey. Family purchases included such items as black serge, 3½ dozen red vest buttons, six pairs of men's fine stockings, five packs of cards, and two pistols for milord, as well as many yards of black silk, lace, gold gallcone, fine white fustian, India camblet, and two pairs of women's black silk stockings, presumably for his wife and daughter.[38]

Lord Cornbury was also punctilious about observing the English custom of "treating," the supplying of liquor to those who served under or worked for him. Thus was a "Pipe of Brandy given to the workmen at several times when [Fort Anne] was repairing," liquor provided for the "Gunners . . . to drink the queens health," rum and beer dispensed to the barge crew, and wine supplied to the soldiers at Albany. All of this alcoholic largesse was in the tradition of the English upper class, and it no doubt furnished a model for colonials who aspired to a comparable eminence on their side of the water. Even the governor's most intractable enemy, Lewis Morris, had to acknowledge — though perhaps with an ironic edge — that Cornbury was a man of breeding who possessed "a great Deal of good Manners."[39]

Furthermore, when it came to behaving in a "condescending" manner to the locals — using that word in the eighteenth-century sense of mingling unpretentiously with all levels of society — Cornbury was something of a master. The Philadelphia Quaker James Logan left a memorable description of Cornbury's first visit (one is tempted to call it a progress) to Pennsylvania in June 1702. Shortly after his arrival, Governor Cornbury dined at Logan's house, telling his host afterward that the hospitality extended to him was "Really Equal . . . to any thing he had seen in America." That night he and his accompanying party of thirty lodged at Colonel Shippen's house, where he let it be known that he was impressed with "the Decency of his Entertainment in all its parts." As he proceeded through the colony, Cornbury attracted additional Pennsylvanians to his train, for when Logan met him again a few days later, following the governor's trip down the river to Pennsbury, he was attended by four boats beside his own and a company of fifty. During the visit, Cornbury made a point of expressing to Logan his "great Regard" for William Penn. Logan reported all this to Penn in a tone that shows he was not immune to Cornbury's flattering attentions.[40]

Perhaps the best look into Cornbury's style as well as his seeming delight in an assignment that combined important functions with a good deal of personal prestige can be gained from the accounts pertaining to his trip to Albany in 1702, the same bills the Treasury office would later question and Clarke justify. This diplomatic mission had a number of objectives. It was designed to shore up the crown's alliance with the Iroquois, which had been weakened under previous administrations; it gave Cornbury an opportunity to meet with the "River Indians" of the Hudson Valley; and it introduced him to a number of "Far Indians" from the Great Lakes region, whose trade he hoped to divert from Montreal to Albany. Because the Indians gathered slowly, perhaps to signal their disgruntlement with English policy, Governor Cornbury remained at Albany throughout most of July and August. When the sachems at last arrived, however, he did not stint in entertaining them. He seems to have been well briefed on the Indian tradition of hospitality and was prepared to demonstrate that an English gentleman understood the symbolic as well as the material benefits of gift-giving, feasting, and conviviality. The governor, accompanied by Lady Cornbury, occupied housing sufficiently capacious to permit of both indoor entertainment and outdoor treaty sessions on the grounds. That Cornbury fed and lodged a number of the sachems is shown by an entry in the accounts for "30 Indians constantly being in my [hou]se during the Treaty" — a juxtaposition of nobleman and "noble savage" that whets the appetite for more news about this extraordinary encounter (fig. 22).[41]

The partial list of victuals supplied for what must have been a festival of tremendous repasts included two lambs, two wild turkeys, six geese, two pigs, three sheep, and numberless deer, lobster, pigeons, fish, chickens, and ducks. All of which was washed down with barrels of beer, pipes of wine and brandy, and gallons of rum.[42]

The meetings between Cornbury and the Indians were exceptionally cordial. When the thirty-six sachems of the Five Iroquois Nations had finally gathered, they opened the conference by singing "a sorrowful Song, which they had made upon the death of his late Majesty King William the third," after which they congratulated Cornbury on the accession of Queen Anne. They were "extreamly glad that the Crown of England has been pleased to send one to be our Governor who is nearly related to that great Woman." This was followed by the customary diplomatic give-and-take and exchange of gifts. Delegates from the Far Indians gave their "Father" Cornbury a beaver coat; the River Indians, "glad that we have now got a mother as well as a father," gave Lady Cornbury an otter muff. The governor in turn provided each tribe with

Figure 22. Indian Council at Johnson Hall. By Edward Lamson Henry. 1903. Oil. *Though the council depicted in this history painting took place around the middle of the eighteenth century at the British official Sir William Johnson's residence near Albany, the scene is similar to that described by Governor Cornbury during the Albany council of 1702. Collection of the Albany Institute of History and Art, Albany, New York*

gifts of wampum, guns, cloth, hatchets, tobacco, fans, looking glasses, "Lace for 3 coats the far Indians had," and of course rum — though a Mohawk sachem requested that the Five Nations' rum be held until the conference ended, because "if their People should fall a drinking they would be unfitt for businesse." Accordingly, the rum was lodged temporarily in Robert Livingston's cellar.[43]

That Lord and Lady Cornbury entertained not only the Indians but the local gentry is attested by a laundry bill for thirty-five tablecloths, more than eight dozen napkins, and twenty-eight dozen small linen. They also stood godparents to several infants baptized in the Albany Dutch Reformed Church, including at least two Edwards, probably named after Cornbury. Much as their presence seems to have been appreciated by the locals, the main objective of Cornbury's long and costly stay at Albany was to mend relations with the Iroquois. He must have been gratified when the Five Nations expressed their pleasure that "things runn in the right Channell again."[44]

This look at the financial side of Governor Cornbury's administration suggests the difficulties encountered by royal governors caught in a web of political factions — both provincial and metropolitan — and squeezed between colonial and imperial expectations in a time of reform. From about 1707 on, Cornbury's policies and integrity were subject to periodic attack, especially in New Jersey, from a vitriolic opposition faction. In New York his aristocratic style was fodder for such as Robert Livingston, now alienated from Cornbury because of differences over money. "'Tis said he is wholly addicted to his pleasure," Livingston wrote a friend, "and enriching himself with Strange and unheard of methods . . . after dinner till 12 a Clok at night is spent at the Botle."[45] At the same time Cornbury had the support of a number of interests in both colonies: a royalist faction that advocated a strong, coherent imperial policy; a New York merchant group that saw both political and commercial advantage in making Albany rather than Montreal the primary center of trade in furs and European goods for the northern Indians; an Anglican interest eager to expand its presence; and a New Jersey proprietary faction that opposed the programs of Lewis Morris and his circle as well as the West Jersey Quakers. A number of these groups, like those in the opposition, enlisted related interests in England to support their policies in America.

Considering the volatility of the times, Governor Cornbury achieved a number of administrative successes, especially in the early years. When later attacked for corruption and misapplication of funds, he like governors before and after him made a spirited defense. One area particularly open to gubernatorial cupidity was the granting of land — a long-recognized means of binding colonials to royal government. Yet few contemporaries complained about Cornbury's policies, which were generally responsive to Queen Anne's reforms.[46]

As for Cornbury's debts, the comparative frame offered here indicates that he was responsible for no more, and perhaps less, than his proportionate share of the public debt. His arrest for personal debt was in large part a consequence of the Morris-controlled New Jersey Assembly's refusal after 1706 to pay his salary — a political stratagem increasingly employed by colonial assemblies in the years ahead. And in another tactic soon to become familiar, Thomas Byerly, New York's dissident receiver of customs, had by 1707 slowed payment of the governor's salary and expenses in that colony: "I must send ten times before I can get one Warrant paid," complained Cornbury, "and that three or four months after it is due." Meanwhile, Byerly "tells every body over his Cups, that I and the Councill have nothing to doe with him, nor his accounts." Cornbury apparently believed he had no alternative but to borrow money in New York to pay administrative expenses in New Jersey.[47] On the private side, Lord Cornbury and his family lived well, as patricians were expected to do in the eighteenth century, but not necessarily beyond their means as understood at the time.

Little that happened in New York and New Jersey in these years makes sense outside a political context. Appointments, salaries, land grants, personal debts — all were subject to political manipulation. Nor could those in the public eye escape the climate of rumor, gossip, and suspicion that colored most political, and many personal, transactions in early modern life, a climate further poisoned by bitter party animosities during Queen Anne's reign when the Tories briefly regained power in England. Some attention to that larger Anglophone political culture, particularly the scurrilous underside of the Country opposition, may make the charges against Cornbury more comprehensible.

"One Tale Is Good Till
Another Is Told"

*Gossip and Satire in Anglo-American Politics*

Rising concern about civility and the reform of manners in
English public culture around the turn of the eighteenth
century was in good part a reaction against the increasingly corrosive tone of political disputation.[1] Gossip, backbiting, and defamation permeated the vocabulary of English politics from the Restoration through the reign of Queen Anne.
The sharpest peaks of political invective were scaled between 1695 and
1714, owing to the convergence of the new moneyed state with two especially pungent elements in English public life — party rage and the
Grub Street press. Personal slurs against public figures reached a wider
audience after press licensing laws lapsed in 1695, with most such attacks
emphasizing sexual or pecuniary misadventures, often both, much in the
manner of the assault on Lord Cornbury. A look at the forces that contributed to this high age of calumny and at the forms such gossip and
satire took will provide a context for measuring what was done to
Cornbury.

THE POLITICS OF CONSPIRACY

English political life underwent extraordinary strains over the seventeenth century, as one Stuart king lost his head in the Civil War and
another his throne in the Glorious Revolution. If historians once cast the
Revolution of 1688–1689 as the terminal point of a chaotic political age
and the dawn of a stable constitutional monarchy, scholars have now rec-

ognized that even "glorious" revolutions do not bring peace and stability all at once. Clashes between the defenders of royal prerogative and the champions of parliamentary power continued after the Revolution as the power relationships of a new constitutional era were painfully adjusted. Nor did the struggle fall into a neat pattern of Whigs versus Tories. A tract published in 1701 listed "State Whigs and Church Whigs, State Tories and Church Tories, King William's Tories and King James's Tories, Court Whigs and Country Whigs."[2] Party rage was also manifest in the ten general elections called between 1694 and 1714, a record still unequaled today.[3]

The first post-Revolutionary monarchs, William and Mary, demonstrated sound political instincts, vigorously safeguarding the ancient powers reserved to them under the Bill of Rights by reaching out to Whigs and Tories alike. Nonetheless, in 1702 the Tories gained manifest ascendancy with the accession of Queen Anne, chilling the hearts of all good Whigs. Having been the target of Tory muckrakers in the 1690s, the Whigs now sought revenge. "The most extraordinary feature of the age of Anne was the unprecedented extent to which party strife . . . invaded and finally took possession of the very lives of the politically-conscious" (fig. 23).[4]

Early-eighteenth-century politicians had no tradition of bipartisanship to ease them through this troubled time. Indeed, the few "Mod'rate Statesmen," as one satirist tagged them, who attempted to mediate between the variant factions were vilified as unprincipled trimmers:

> Then in their stead let *Mod'rate* Statesmen Reign,
> Practice their new pretended Golden Mean.
> A Notion undefin'd in Virtues Schools,
> Unrecommended by her sacred Rules.
> A Modern Coward Principle, design'd
> To stifle Justice, and unnerve the Mind.
> A Trick by Knaves contriv'd, impos'd on Fools,
> But Scorn'd by Patriot and Exalted Souls.[5]

Moderates, lacking the heroic virtues, compromised high principles and opened the door to subversion.

True Whigs, by contrast, with the treason trials and Jacobite assassination plots of the 1690s fresh in memory, saw Tories as a pernicious

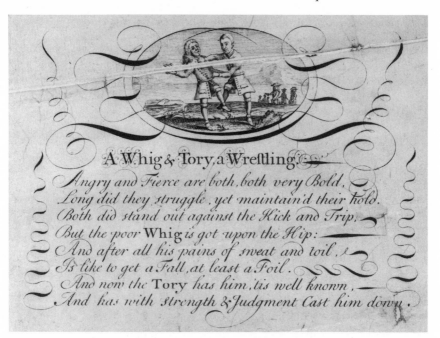

Figure 23. *A Whig and Tory, a Wrestling.* Montage engraving from *The Whig's Medly* (1711). *From the Bowditch Collection, Courtesy of the Print Collection, Lewis Walpole Library, Yale University*

force bent on undermining the still fragile Revolution Settlement. Even that proponent of polite civic discourse, the third earl of Shaftesbury, described the Tories as a "malignant party" with "poysonous Principles." Tories, in turn, perceived Whigs as mere panderers to commercial and Dissenting interests, sapping the traditional structure of English society. Neither characterization was true, Whigs and Tories of all stripes being drawn from the elite echelons of society with every reason to promote the well-being of the state. But the notion that any political group, when out of power, might function positively as a loyal opposition simply lay beyond the mental horizon of these premodern leaders.[6] The other side could not be seen as equals in a legitimate contest of party politics; it was a disloyal presence that threatened the very existence of the nation, a wicked faction of conspirators that must be put down by good and faithful statesmen. "For that different, distant world the question asked of an event was not 'how did it happen?' but 'who did it?'"[7]

That most politicians of Queen Anne's reign could picture the struggle for office and power in such Manichean terms gave a kind of license to whatever weapons came to hand in the battle to exterminate the opposition. And it was in this charged climate, abetted by a newly liberated press, that gossip and satire, much of it seasoned with sexual innuendo, pervaded the political life of the realm.

### THE RISE OF GRUB STREET

Ribald slander was not new to English life. The rough wit of Juvenal provided the prime model for satirists from Elizabethan times to the era of Dryden, as society's vices were exposed and its follies derided in caustic lampoons. And though such writings usually had a didactic, moralistic intent, with the Restoration they became more political, "more obscene and less obscure," as persons still living were aspersed by name in both privately circulated manuscript satires and in print.[8] Nor were kings and queens excepted. Indeed, assaults on the monarchy are of special interest, given the metaphorical structure of Restoration satire, which can now be seen as considerably more than a post-Puritan explosion of gamy pornography. To show the great either as unable to govern their lusts or as impotent to consummate them was to exhibit them as unequal to governing the state. Thus Charles II was lampooned for both his supposed appetites and his imagined inadequacies. The contradiction lessens when the innuendoes are read as an attack on his thirst for power and, power once gained, his incapacity for wielding it.[9]

Charles's satyriasis, as mocked by John Lacy:

> The seaman's needle points always to the pole,
> But thine still points to ev'ry craving hole,
> Which wolf-like in your breast raw flesh devours,
> And must be fed all seasons and all hours.

But at least one of the king's mistresses, the duchess of Cleveland, seems to have required a great deal more than he could provide:

> Cleveland, I say, was much to be admir'd,
> For she was never satisfi'd or tir'd.
> Full forty men a day have swiv'd the whore,
> Yet like a bitch she wags her tail for more.[10]

Attacks on the king's leading ministers were equally marked by salacious metaphor, as in this verse mocking the second duke of Buckingham and his mistress:

> She knew his ways and could comply
> With all decays of lechery;
> Had often lick'd his am'rous scepter
> Until the jaded stallion leapt her.[11]

Crowned heads who failed to produce an heir made easy targets for their political enemies, who were sure to charge them with impotence or "sins against nature." William III, for example:

> Lets pray for the good of our State and his Soul
> That He'd put his Roger into the Right Hold.
>
> .  .  .  .  .  .  .  .  .  .  .  .
>
> Ah who wou'd have thought that a low Country Stallion,
> And a Protestant Prince shou'd prove an Italian.[12]

To skirt the libel laws, most Restoration satire was handed about in manuscript. Only in the later reign of William and, especially, that of Queen Anne did printed lampoons come to dominate. This shift brought a significant broadening of the political audience, as gossip and scandal laid the basis for a new development in English cultural life: the emergence of the Grub Street press. In 1695 the law that required all printing presses to be licensed by Parliament, increasingly observed in the breach, was finally allowed to lapse. This opened new commercial opportunities and led to a spectacular rise in the volume of printed matter (London alone had twelve newspapers in 1705). A freer press combined with the strident politics of the time to produce a tribe of hack writers who actually managed to eke out a meager living with their pens, scratching out coarse verse, novels, newspapers, broadsides, and pamphlets steaming with political gossip and prurient tattle. The Grub Street writer was not immune from legal action; as Sir William Blackstone later wrote, he had to "take the consequences of his own temerity" if convicted of civil or criminal libel.[13] Yet the lifting of prior restraint on print was sufficiently liberating to release a torrent of sensational journalism after 1695, notably in the City of London. As one observer put it in 1711: "You may go

Figure 24. *The Coffeehous Mob.* Frontispiece to [Ned Ward], *Vulgus Britannicus: or The British Hudibras,* Part IV [1710]. *Permission, Beinecke Rare Book and Manuscript Library, Yale University*

into a coffee house and see a table of half an acre's length covered with nothing but tobacco, pipes and pamphlets, and all the seats full of mortals leaning on their elbows, licking in tobacco, lies and laced coffee, and studying for arguments to revile one another with" (fig. 24). At about this same time Jonathan Swift wrote a friend in New York: "I could send you a great deal of news from the *Republica Grubstreetaria*, which was never in greater altitude." [14]

Thanks to the work of Robert Darnton and others, we know a good deal about the effect of Grub Street writing on late-eighteenth-century French politics. Yet the original Grub Street was of course in London. [15] And although most of its denizens never rose above their squalid beginnings to gain recognition in the polite world of letters, Defoe got his start there, and even Swift was known to make occasional appearances in the neighborhood (fig. 25). But being primarily Tories with no place at court, Grub Street's larger geniuses like Edward "Ned" Ward and Tom Brown proceeded to fashion "a literature of the impolite." That so little has been written about the political dimensions of this first full-scale era of English yellow journalism may in part be owing to its very excesses. Besides churning out the usual tales of adultery in high places, cuckoldry at all levels, and sodomites at play in the "mollyhouses" of London, hack writers festooned it all with endless scatology, flatulence being among the milder themes (fig. 26). [16] This material, though piquant and hilarious to an eighteenth-century public meeting it for the first time in print, does not inspire the jaded modern reader to trace any sort of pattern in it. Nonetheless, the larger body of satire and gossip that issued from this corps of professional defamers merits attention. Without it, the political language of late-Stuart times would not have been what it was.

William III was attacked by both Whig and Tory writers, depending on which way he leaned. In *The Foreigners: A Poem* (1700), the Whig John Tutchin scorned the king and his Dutch courtiers as alien to English ways. William "rob[bed] our Treasure, to augment his State," while one of his favorites rose by "Whoring, Pimping, or a Crime that's worse." The Tory Tom Brown was rebuked in 1700 for writing lampoons that "affronted kings, libelled princes, [and] scandalized the court and city." He explicitly attacked William in *An Essay on the Late Politics; or, The Government out of Joynt* (ca. 1701) and with robust indiscrimination denounced corrupt officials, cuckolds, women, displays of learning, fops,

Figure 25. A Scene in Grub Street. *Domestic Architecture: North East View of an Old House Lately Standing in Sweedon's Passage, Grub Street.* By J. T. Smith. 1791. Etching. *Courtesy of the Yale Center for British Art, Paul Mellon Collection*

specific clergymen, and politicians generally (fig. 27). When Ned Ward, a firm churchman, thought Queen Anne had betrayed the church to favor Whigs and Dissenters, he was so indiscreet as to avow in *Hudibras Redivivus* that "woman's words are only wind," for which he was arrested on June 13, 1706. John Tutchin was also arrested for a seditious paper that, the government charged, attacked Anne's councillors: "that the

THE MAIDEN GRANADEERE

FRANCE had her Pucelle; for her Charles who fought
And great defeats upon our English brought
Now to quitt Scores with them I thus appeare
In the new mode of arms a Granadeere,
Dare they peep forth at Sea? Ile Soon their Pride
Pluck down, with one discharge of my broad side

And if their Stomacks be so high at Land;
As they a Battle or a Seige will stand,
The Shell I from my Morter-peice let Fly,
In feild or Town; shall make all Quarter Cry,
S.t George for England, then and next to whom
For thee great Brittain I a Champion come

Figure 26. *The Maiden Granadeere.* Circa 1700. Engraving. *The cross-dressed female grenadier discharges a grenade at a French fort. Harleian 5944-f319, by permission of the British Library*

Figure 27. Frontispiece to the *Works of Mr. Thomas Brown, in Prose and Verse,* I (London, 1707). *By Permission of the Folger Shakespeare Library*

Figure 28. Queen Anne. Circa 1711. From *Playing Cards of Various Ages and Countries, Selected from the Collection of Lady Charlotte Schreiber*, 3 vols. (London, 1892), I, plate 35. *One of many prints glorifying the reign of Queen Anne. Photo courtesy of the Print Collection, Lewis Walpole Library, Yale University. Courtesy, the British Museum*

Ministry was corrupted with French gold, and that great men in offices took bribes (as it were) to betray the nation, and several other scandalous expressions."[17]

On the whole, Queen Anne, unlike her predecessors, was largely exempt. That ponderous lady, whose life was blameless, might have given an example comparable to that of Queen Victoria for the morals of the English nation had she lived longer and in a different age. As it was, she gave the hacks of her own day little to work on. Anne's self-image as "a nursing mother" to her people was reinforced by her serial pregnancies, her willingness to bestow the "royal touch" on victims of scrofula, and the domesticity of her rather dull court. Yet for all these maternal traits, Anne was no cipher in politics. She could be forceful in dealing with her ministers and as a female sovereign had their respect. Anne's right to rule was never seriously challenged on the ground of her sex (fig. 28).[18]

This does not mean, however, that Anne's court was devoid of sexual tension. With party strife at full pitch, both Whig and Tory leaders were suspicious of backstairs intrigue and anxious about the possible manipu-

Figure 29. Queen Anne's
Bedchamber Favorites. Circa 1711.
From *Playing Cards of Various Ages and
Countries, Selected from the Collection of
Lady Charlotte Schreiber*, 3 vols. (London,
1892), I, plate 39. *A comment on the
dismissal of the duchess of Marlborough
from Queen Anne's court and her
replacement by the duchess of Somerset.
Photo courtesy of the Print Collection,
Lewis Walpole Library, Yale University.
Courtesy, the British Museum*

lation of Anne's political affections by her bedchamber attendants. Sarah Marlborough was Anne's closest female confidant from the 1680s into the early years of her reign, and Sarah was not only first lady of the bedchamber and wife of a powerful duke but a woman of pronounced opinions. By the time Anne became queen, Sarah was a dedicated Whig, and she aggressively strove to turn Anne from her Tory councillors, repeatedly painting them as treacherous Jacobites. But Anne, who questioned Sarah's political acumen and ignored her advice, would have none of it. With rising impatience she rebuffed Sarah's political meddling and, finally, in January 1711 dismissed the duchess from court (fig. 29). Meanwhile Abigail Hill, Lady Masham, cousin of the moderate Tory leader Robert Harley, had become the queen's new favorite, an elevation that outraged the wounded Sarah. It mattered little to court gossips that Anne did not in fact consult these women on matters of state. Their mere proximity to the throne, and their occasional role as messengers or conduits for politicians seeking access to the queen, was enough to imply sinister doings.[19]

Throughout English history the sovereign's favorites had been seized upon as choice targets of opposition invective. Now, deprived of a crowned head to assault, the scribblers of Anne's time set to work on her court with unprecedented gusto. That a number of the queen's favorites were women suggested a ready-made line of attack. Sarah, duchess of Marlborough, attracted by far the most comment, being depicted in a cascade of ballads, pamphlets, and novels as a prostitute and a devotee of adultery, incest, and witchcraft. Her imagined assignations with such figures as Lord Treasurer Godolphin and the earl of Kent were of course portrayed as schemes to further her position at court. In one especially reeky bit of doggerel, the duchess was cast as having a corrupting influence on her supposed lover Godolphin (Volpone):

> So closely they united lay
> That really 'twere uncivill
> For any, to distinctly say
> Ones Witch or t'other Devil
>
> .    .    .    .    .    .    .    .
>
> Oh were the sage Volpone bound
> His head her Thighs betwixt Sir
> To suck from thence his Notions sound
> And Savr'y Politicks Sir [20]

When Sarah Marlborough was displaced from the queen's side by Abigail Masham, and when Masham helped Robert Harley gain access to the queen, the occasion was too good to miss:

> *Harley* and She each Night do meet,
> And drink to the Pretender,
> And hug and kiss, and are as great,
> As the Devil and Witch of *Endor.*
>
> .    .    .    .    .    .    .    .
>
> Oh! that some truly zealous Friend
> Would give the Bitch a Potion,
> While *Harley's* Mouth at lower End
> Were set to meet the Motion. [21]

The closest any lampoon came to striking directly at the queen was *A New Ballad* (1708), probably written by the Whig hack Arthur Mainwaring, an ally of Sarah Marlborough, who very likely aided in its produc-

Kept from insulting a too bountious Queen,
She on the faithfull Mas—m sheds her Spleen.

Figure 30. The Rivalry between the Duchess of Marlborough and Abigail Hill, Lady Masham. Circa 1711. From *Playing Cards of Various Ages and Countries, Selected from the Collection of Lady Charlotte Schreiber*, 3 vols. (London, 1892), I, plate 40. *Photo courtesy of the Print Collection, Lewis Walpole Library, Yale University. Courtesy, the British Museum*

tion. Though it skirted dangerously near the throne, its primary target was Abigail Masham (fig. 30):

> Whenas Queen *Anne* of great Renown
> *Great Britain*'s Scepter sway'd
> Besides the Church, she dearly lov'd
> A Dirty Chamber-Maid.
>
> O! *Abigail* that was her Name,
> She starch'd and stitch'd full well,
> But how she pierc'd this Royal Heart,
> No mortal Man can tell.
>
> However, for sweet Service done
> And Causes of great Weight,
> Her Royal Mistress made her, Oh!
> A Minister of State.
>
> Her Secretary she was not
> Because she could not write
> But had the Conduct and the Care
> Of some dark Deeds at Night.[22]

A later favorite of Queen Anne, the duchess of Shrewsbury, was depicted in one pasquinade as "bauding for whores" and in another as being led by her husband into the bed of an amorous Louis XIV:

> The Duke o'erjoy'd, that his *Italian* Dame
> Could in so Old an Hero raise a Flame,
> With an ambitious Pleasure, as 'tis said,
> Led her himself unto the Royal Bed.[23]

The political satirists of Queen Anne's time also took on the leading ministers of state. Mary de la Rivière Manley, a Tory writer, published *Secret Memoirs and Manners of Several Persons of Quality, of Both Sexes: From the New Atalantis* (1709), lewd tales about the highborn featuring seduction, rape, incest, and homosexuality, male and female. Her targets, unnamed but easily identified, included the earl of Portland, the duchess of Cleveland, and, of course, John Churchill, duke of Marlborough. Though one of the most illustrious and envied men of the age, Marlborough was held up as a prevaricator, a skimmer of public funds, and an adulterer. He greatly resented "the villanous way of printing which stabs me to the heart" (fig. 31). Harley was also depicted as a schemer and a bribe-taker. And when Robert Walpole lost his parliamentary seat in the election of 1713, he blamed it on the hacks' depictions of him as a debauched office seeker who made a prostitute of his sister to gain preferment.[24]

Thus did a new era of press freedom after 1695 combine with the rancorous parties of Queen Anne's time to foster not only a literature of high satire but one of muckraking defamation. From 1702 on Parliament tried without success to legislate against the spread of libels and lurid tales, while Anne's speeches "deplored the licentiousness of the press." The Tory Charles Davenant warned in 1703 that "the liberty of the press will be the ruin of the nation"; others bemoaned the "Reams of Scandalous and impious Lies" propagated by party hacks. In 1712 the ministry and Parliament, horrified by the torrent of scandalous writings, placed a tax on newspapers, pamphlets, and broadsides in the vain hope that it would spell the death of Grub Street. But nothing could slow the presses at a time when the intense struggle for power and office meant that "just about every prominent politician was the victim of a savage attack in the public prints."[25] The smut and scandal of Grub

Figure 31. The Alleged Peculations of the Duke of Marlborough. Circa 1711. From *Playing Cards of Various Ages and Countries, Selected from the Collection of Lady Charlotte Schreiber*, 3 vols. (London, 1892), I, plate 35. *The Duke counts his ill-gotten gains. Photo courtesy of the Print Collection, Lewis Walpole Library, Yale University. Courtesy, the British Museum*

Street had become indispensable as each side strove to smear and discredit the other.

### THE ENGLISH GOSSIPS

Spoken gossip and common rumor drove the wheels of politics with a force at least equal to that of the printed satires, as is evident from the correspondence of some of the leading political families of the time. Their letters abound with conjectures about who was in or out of favor, along with rumors of courtship and marriage, of dalliance and seduction. These stories tended to be governed by certain conventions of their own. They moved via indirection; they were conditional; their truth could seldom be certain, and their purveyor knew this well. But once the whisper had reached the ear, it was hardly thinkable that the hearer should simply leave it there. The device for keeping it going was one that allowed the gossip to have it both ways, "'Tis said . . . tho' I doubt how truly . . ."[26]

John, Lord Berkeley, one of the most engaging gossips of his day, passed along the latest scraps to everyone he wrote to. He did not give full credence to it all. He graded and qualified the authenticity of each item. But Berkeley left little out; whatever he heard offered some kind of interest. The queen went to church three times a week; the duke of Ormond was in deep mourning at the death of his daughter; there were rumors of great changes at court. Berkeley could not be sure whether the duke of Marlborough was up to mischief abroad; he did not have it "upon any good ground." Was Queen Anne making changes in the ministry from her deathbed? He had been out of town when the rumors began and could provide "no certain account of anything," though doubtless "a great deal more being said then is true." Of a rumored visit to the Stuart Pretender by Lord Sussex and his son, Berkeley was becomingly cautious. "There is a story goes about, which tho I believe nothing of, yet I cannot help sending you." But a scandal that was on everyone's lips could allow him to cast caution aside, as with "an odd story of Mrs. Dormer, whom you may better know by the name of Die Kirk[,] that a footman of hers pretending to have had great familiarities, being refus'd money beat her very unmercifully. The story is so publickly told that there needs noe great scruple in repeating it." Berkeley's consort seems to have followed a similar principle. In a letter filled with the gossip from London, Lady Berkeley observed, "You desire scandall and this town at present will suply you, for Lady Linsey is with child and the town says if she knows the fathere 'tis Lord Lumley."[27] "The town says" and a story "soe publickly told" may have been something short of the full warrant of truth but were enough to keep the tale going.

Another prime source of gossip was manuscript newsletters. These were weekly series composed in London and sent to subscribers in the city and the country. Over the later seventeenth and early eighteenth centuries, newsletters grew in number as rising party competition excited a hunger for political news. They also could be more efficiently distributed with the founding of the Penny Post, which delivered them to individuals and the newly popular coffeehouses approximately three times a week. The various series of newsletters totaled many thousands of pages and were intended primarily as reports on diplomatic and military happenings in Europe. But bits of trivia and gossip were often tacked on to fill whatever blank space remained. A death, a woman with child, duels, brigands executed, a duchess suing for divorce, a rumor of incest, or what must have been a very old tale naming one of the supposed lovers of Queen Elizabeth — all were typical entries. These newsletters, because handwritten, were less often subject to libel action than printed newspapers and so flourished as a fairly systematic means for satisfying the public appetite for the latest coffeehouse gossip.[28]

How, then, did the reputation of the Hyde family, and of Cornbury in particular, fare in this culture of calumny and scandal? Remarkably well. Some abuse was inevitable, considering the family's prominence during the years Cornbury's grandfather was chancellor to Charles II and his father and uncle were politically active. But there was strikingly little in the way of sexual innuendo or attacks on character. The first earl was himself a ready critic of the licentiousness of Charles's court, and the worst he or his sons were accused of was a certain stiffness in political and religious principles and a tardiness when it came to repaying personal debts. The single exception concerned the chancellor's daughter, Anne Hyde, who allowed the duke of York to get her pregnant before their marriage. Her severest critic was her father.[29]

As for Cornbury, Jacobites naturally went after him following his defection from James II in 1688. In their satirical doggerel, he was the second earl's "pocky son" (a common slur of the time), and he and Marlborough were paired as "cowardly villains." But no such insults appear in the many subsequent reports of his appointments to office or of his ordinary comings and goings (though from 1689 to 1702 when he was out of favor and pinched for money he would have been an unlikely target). And to date not one English newsletter or bit of Grub Street doggerel has been found to contain any reference to Cornbury as effeminate, a fop, or a cross dresser, even after rumors of his supposed transvestism in North America were received at home.[30] As Queen Anne's first cousin, and especially had he shown any peculiarities of behavior, Cornbury would have offered an obvious mark for the ridicule of Grub Streeters and the Whig opposition. But gossip gathers real momentum only if it corresponds in some way with the reputation of the person being gossiped about. Could it be that, like most other members of that straitlaced High Church family, Cornbury failed to provide any ground for those attacks?

### GOSSIP AND SATIRE IN AMERICA

Americans visiting England during these years professed astonishment at the climate of slander and gossip they encountered there. Isaac Norris of Pennsylvania wrote from London in 1707: "Every Coxcomb,

Either from Envy, Malice or the Vanity to be thought Somebody . . . takes the Liberty of telling and Improveing[,] and I perceive by Some Companies I've been in, nobody's Reputations Valued over a pott."[31] Yet back in America things were not so very different. In the colonies, too, an embryonic Grub Street press was developing and with it a politics of slander nearly as inflamed as that of England. Two sorts of public figures were the principal targets: government officials, notably the imperial-minded crown appointees in the royal colonies, and, in that contested religious terrain, clergy of all denominations — especially the Anglican, who were considered part of the imperial state.

Massachusetts, Virginia, and New York — all royal colonies of strategic importance in King William's and Queen Anne's Wars — attracted the most attention among otherwise preoccupied officials in England. To those colonies were posted men accustomed to command and with appropriate military experience: Joseph Dudley to Massachusetts, Sir Francis Nicholson to Virginia, and Lord Cornbury to New York. All were strong imperialists and hence prime targets for the gossip and calumny of American Whigs or of any faction that supposed its interests imperiled by the rod of state. Governor Dudley, though Massachusetts-born, was not spared the malice of his provincial enemies. They excoriated him in print for trading with the enemy in wartime, appointing avaricious men to government, and nepotism; he was a covetous and treacherous "Criminal Governour" under whose administration "without Money, there is no Justice to be had."[32] Nicholson's opponents diligently forwarded vicious reports to London charging him with acts of "Lewdness and rudeness to Gentlewomen" in Virginia. They also held him up first as a tyrant and then as a laughingstock for his supposed infatuation with "a hansome young lady of this country" who spurned him.[33]

Certain members of Cornbury's opposition in New York, and especially New Jersey, were equally abusive. Given his zeal both for the empire and for the Anglican church, he was a marked man. So, too, was Peter Fauconnier, the governor's secretary and receiver of revenues (and of French descent, which did not help), who was execrated for his ostensible mishandling of public funds. Powerless to strike back, Fauconnier finally vented his frustration in an emotional petition to Governor Cornbury himself — six closely written pages — accusing the opposition of engaging in a slanderous conspiracy against him. A secret "combination

between the Deputy Auditor [George Clarke] and other complainants"
had been devised to cover their own neglect of duty. With no proof of
any misconduct by Fauconnier, they had proceeded "to publish it as true,
in most Taverns, and such other like Publik places in Town." This proceeded from an "Inveterat hatred against Him, and Tend but to the entire
Ruine of your Petitioners Credit and Reputation" — crucial assets for an
ambitious placeman making his way in the new world of finance. Most
galling was his enemies' "Barbarity and filthy Baseness" in spreading the
rumor that he had bought a fine plantation in South Carolina, to which
he planned to abscond with his family. Swearing before God and men
that it was all "Base, malicious and false," Fauconnier promised to sue in
court if the slanders were not withdrawn.[34] The impassioned language of
Fauconnier's petition was typical of an age that possessed few resources
for a graded management of political conflict.

The experience of Peter Sonmans of New Jersey, agent for the East
Jersey proprietors and Cornbury's ally on the colonial council, offers another example of how gossip and rumor poisoned provincial politics.
Once Cornbury was safely out of office, the New Jersey Assembly publicly turned on Sonmans, charging him with corrupting the administration of law and attempting to pack juries. The assembly further accused
him, in an unprecedented public remonstrance, of adultery: "He openly
Cohabits with a Scandalous Woman [and] has had one Bastard by her,"
setting an "evil Example" for her majesty's subjects. This last was apparently in extenuation of the assembly's decision to make Sonmans's
private behavior a public issue. Sonmans prepared a detailed response
to the charges (the modern printed version covers twenty-eight pages),
examining and refuting each item in turn. The allegations that he had
abused his authority were deliberate misrepresentations by a party of
men "known to be my professed Enemies." The adultery charge was
"False, Scandalous, and Malitious, invented for a handle to fling dirt." If
provincial assemblies were permitted to proceed in this manner, Sonmans
declared, "any Gentleman who has the honour of Serving the Queen,
or any other Officer of the Government, shall be Turned out, Ruined
in his Reputation (which ought to be dearer to him than his Life) and
treated as a high Criminal, Convicted with out being heard, or any Proof
against him."[35]

Sonmans's alarm about colonial officials' being exposed to ruin by mere gossip was fervently seconded by another of Cornbury's men in New Jersey, Councilman Daniel Coxe. As Coxe and probably every other politician in the region knew, the attack on Cornbury's supporters in New Jersey was being managed by Lewis Morris, leader of the local opposition. In January 1709, Coxe reported to an acquaintance in London that the latest "masterpiece of Mr. Morris, and that Confederate Gang" was to pack a grand jury at Perth Amboy and deliver up indictments against Sonmans and two other Cornbury partisans. Thus did they go about "murdering the Reputation and good names" of gentlemen, though fortunately Cornbury's replacement, Governor John Lovelace, had put a stop to their proceedings. "New Jersey," Coxe continued, "is become A meer Pandora, out of which . . . issue such uncouth absurdityes and monstrous Villanys, both in Church and State, that I may defy any Collony in America to produce the like." The worst part of it was that "False and Villanous Storyes . . . hatcht and Contrived . . . by Scandalous men" were too often heard and believed at home. It all reminded him of the "old Saying, one tale is good till another is told." If the victims were given no opportunity to defend themselves, Coxe declared, they would lose their rights as Englishmen.[36]

Character assassination was certainly not the monopoly of any single faction in colonial America. In 1714 opponents of the liberal Governor Robert Hunter spread the rumor that he "had to doe with Lieutenant Riggs wife," which supposedly caused his own wife to miscarry. In another instance, Lewis Morris himself, the calumniator of Cornbury and Sonmans, was on the receiving end. An Anglican cleric politically opposed to Morris sent the Society for the Propagation of the Gospel a long list of complaints, including charges that Morris had publicly denied the authority of Scripture and had argued for "the Lawfulness of Polygamy." Morris meanwhile wrote the SPG to defend another clergyman with whom he was closely associated: "To tarnish his Caracter, an impudent whore has been prevailed upon to lay a Child to him," though "for my part I do believe he is most falsely accused." The Anglican minister at Jamaica, Queens County, was charged with similar misconduct, the stories having been floated by "a very wicked and Scandalous Wench" who purportedly was put up to it by the Dissenters of Long Island.[37]

All this was now standard fare in the colonies, especially those with royal charters or where politics was embittered between Anglicans and

Dissenters. In a time of flux and confusion, and during a popular reign when open criticism of those in power was particularly liable to be answered by severe measures, the opposition tended to remain underground. In the confined space its passions boiled and tumbled the stronger, finding occasional outlets in rumor and, increasingly, in anonymous printed satire.[38]

Thus far we mainly have noted spoken gossip. But, though the colonial press was still relatively undeveloped, Grub Street also had its denizens in early-eighteenth-century America. Many of their initial productions, like those in England, took the form of handwritten ditties and squibs that circulated among the gentry or were posted up in taverns and coffeehouses. In 1702 "A Satyr upon the Times" leveled a belated though now safe shot at the deceased former governor Bellomont and his minions:

> Twas Gold (that curst Tempter) that did bribe
> The grand Ringleader of this hellish Tribe
> Great by his Title[,] Vile in every action
> He's gon but has entail'd a Curse on's faction.[39]

Similar manuscript satires on Cornbury may have made the rounds, though none seems to have survived.

In the early eighteenth century such lampoons increasingly took aim at politicians. Lewis Morris in 1709 sought preferment with Lord Lovelace, briefly royal governor of New York and New Jersey, with a fulsome private address, "which made a Poeticall Spiritt, rise in some Gentlemen who on the next morning made the following Verses thereon which were all about the Town by noon":

> As Jack-puddings on Stages have different waies,
> From the rest of the Actors to meritt the Bayes [laurels],
> So Tall-Lewis-Morris o'retops all the rest,
> And by playing the fool Shows his Character best;
> He addresses alone, because tis his Part
> To differ from the Councill in Manner and Heart.

Urged to respond lest his silence "be a Reflection upon his Witt and Poetry," Morris, or possibly a member of his faction, retorted as follows:

> As Ravens and Night-owls their Voices betray,
> So asses are certainly known when they bray.
>
> . . . . . . . . . . . .
>
> The Pests of the Country, whose Practise has been
> To flatter the Governor, and Lie to the Queen,
> Have right to no favour in a well-govern'd State
> But to Swing in an Halter, or peep through a Grate.

This in turn elicited a response wherein a prideful Morris is made to lament "that Grubstreet writers should pervert my Muse":

> In fam'd Augusta's streets I am well known
> My Muse allow'd the Darling of the Town;
>
> . . . . . . . . .
>
> It paints the Miser, and the Spendthrift Beau,
> Tea-table-Scandal, and the Cuckolds row.[40]

Printed satire began to appear with some regularity around the end of the seventeenth century, despite the scarcity of printing presses and the government scrutiny of those that existed.[41] In the Middle Colonies, the first sustained pamphlet war took place in the 1690s between the Society of Friends and the Quaker reformer George Keith. The earliest pamphlets contained no sexual slurs, but their language was bitterly personal. A Presbyterian observer, detached from the fray, remarked that Keith's accusers presented him as a "Reviler of the Brethren, Brat of Babylon . . . Pope, Primate of Pennsylvania, [and] Father Confessor," whereas Keith in turn vilified his opponents as "Fools, Ignorant Heathens, Infidels, Silly Souls, Lyars, Hereticks, Rotten Ranters, [and] Muggletonians."[42] In the end, Keith's rationalist program led him and a number of followers into the Anglican fold, where they soon became allies of the new royal governor, Lord Cornbury. West Jersey Quakers, by contrast, joined the opposition to royal government, inciting a new pamphlet war between religious rivals now turned politicians.

Perhaps the best surviving example of early Middle Colony scandal-mongering is the work of Daniel Leeds, a former Quaker, now Anglican, whom Cornbury appointed to the New Jersey Council. A printer by trade, Leeds, with a convert's zeal, led the effort to discredit the Friends in New Jersey. His initial foray in the Grub Street style — perhaps prompted by the repeal of the Licensing Act — was a pamphlet titled *News of a Strumpet Co-habiting in the Wilderness; or, A Brief Abstract of the Spiritual and Carnal Whoredoms and Adulteries of the Quakers in America* (1701) (fig. 32). Offering twenty examples from his "Cage of Unclean Birds," Leeds raked Quaker history for subjects, whom he then listed along with their alleged unclean deeds. Samuel Jennings of New Jersey displayed intolerable pride and cheated the Indians of their land; Thomas Lord looted his children's estate; John Moon got his maidservant with child; Robert Ewer short-weighted his customers and was found on a bed with his neighbor's wife "with her Coats up"; Christopher Holder of Rhode Island was an "effeminate loving Preacher" who was taken "lying with another man'[s] wife in a field of Corn"; John Talbert was "charged with lying both with a white woman and a Negro woman"; Thomas Williams "had gotten his wifes Daughter with Child," and so on. The Quaker Caleb Pusey issued a hot denial: *Daniel Leeds: Justly Rebuked for Abusing William Penn, and His Foly and Falls-Hoods . . . Made Manifest* (1702). Leeds, undeterred, next published a pamphlet with a purported reprinting of two letters by George Fox, a founder of the Society of Friends, whose spelling and sentence structure he showered with ridicule. This "Minister of Anti-christ," Leeds jeered, could write "scarce Two lines good Sence." Leeds declared that Fox had hired others to do his public writing, giving "one Jew Thirty Pounds to do the greatest part" of his book, *A Battledore* (a child's primer).[43]

Pouncing on Fox's own concession that there were some "bad Spirits" among the Quakers, Leeds jubilantly supplied local examples, such as that of one lascivious brother who had "led a Sister into a Swamp after Meeting" and another who had "closed in with W. C.'s Wife in a Cornfield." Then there was *"Mary A——* of *Long-Island* [who] left her Husband to exercise her Talent [as a preacher] in Barbados, and became Pregnant in that fruitful Island, and returned to her Husband with Increase." Challenged by relatives and friends of the maligned woman,

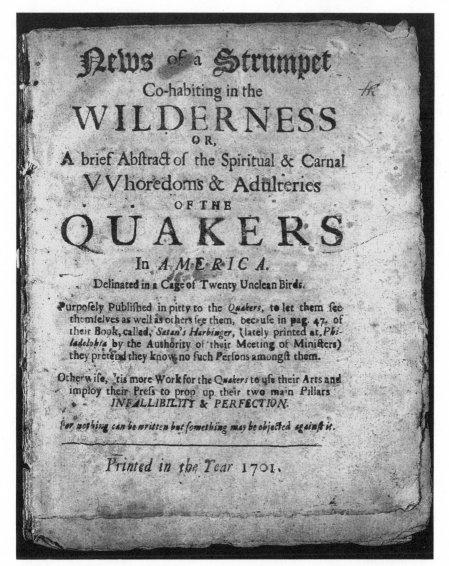

News of a Strumpet
Co-habiting in the

# WILDERNESS
### OR,
A brief Abſtract of the Spiritual & Carnal
VVhoredoms & Adulteries
### OF THE

# QUAKERS
In *AMERICA.*

Delinated in a Cage of Twenty Unclean Birds.

Purpoſely Publiſhed in pitty to the *Quakers*, to let them ſee themſelves as well as others ſee them, becauſe in pag. 47. of their Book, called, *Satan's Harbinger*, (lately printed at *Philadelphia* by the Authority of their Meeting of Miniſters) they pretend they know no ſuch Perſons amongſt them.

Otherwiſe, 'tis more Work for the *Quakers* to uſe their Arts and imploy their Preſs to prop up their two main Pillars *INFALLIBILITY* & *PERFECTION.*

*For nothing can be written but ſomething may be objected againſt it.*

Printed in the Year 1701.

Figure 32. *News of a Strumpet Co-habiting in the Wilderness.* . . . Title page of Daniel Leeds's pamphlet. 1701. *Permission, The Huntington Library, San Marino, California*

Leeds backed down somewhat, acknowledging that Mrs. A—— might have been impregnated by her own husband.[44]

If the Quakers were no match for the muckraking Leeds, such was not the case with other scribblers for the opposition. At the height of the New Jersey Assembly's assault on Governor Cornbury in 1706–1707, there appeared a tract bearing the title *Forget and Forgive, the Best Interest of New Jersey*. According to the imperial officer Robert Quary, "The heads of the faction in both Divisions [East and West Jersey] agreed on a most scandalous libell, of which they got a vast number printed, and took care to disperse them through the whole Province." He thought "perhaps there was never a more scandalous libell published." No copy of *Forget and Forgive* survives, so one can only wonder what was in it. At any rate, Cornbury was infuriated. After William Bradford, printer at New York, denied publishing the tract, Cornbury wrote to Governor Dudley of Massachusetts entreating him "to direct some inquiry to be made whether any such paper has been printed at Boston." For a time the Presbyterian preacher Francis Makemie came under suspicion as the author, though he wrote Cornbury denying any part in it.[45] Meanwhile, several members of the New Jersey opposition had been pointed out as the likely culprits. When the grand jury of locals — who reflected a broader spectrum of opinion than the Court party alone — refused to indict them, the attorney general brought suit via information (a common device in England) against the four men and two women "for publishing and dispersing a false and Scandalous Lible intitled forgett and forgive." One of the accused, when entering his plea, demanded that the charges against him be read; and so, as Lewis Morris gloatingly informed two political confederates, "forget and forgive was read in Open court from End to End to the Satisfaction of all."[46]

About this same time, informations were filed against another New Jerseyan for saying "the Church of England is a Carnall Church and none but Devils incarnate pretend to itt," and against still another for slandering Cornbury. When the accused slanderer pleaded guilty, he was ordered to apologize to the governor — a ritual similar to the French *réparation d'honneur* — and was then "committed prisoner for three months."[47]

Whether Cornbury was any more persistent than other colonial officers in using the courts to suppress libels and slanders is difficult to say, for such cases appear frequently in the legal records of all colonies. Lawsuits constituted the main defense such officials had against their provincial defamers, and Cornbury, perhaps more litigious than most, did not shrink from employing them. In a representative example, the governor of Pennsylvania in 1705 initiated a two-thousand-pound suit for slander against one William Biles, whose alleged attack was fairly tame: "He is but a boy and not fitt to be Our Governeur[,] we'll kick him out we'll kick 'm out." The jury awarded the governor three hundred pounds.[48]

Satirists sometimes avoided lawsuits by giving their targets fictive names. This technique was used in that notable example of early colonial Grub Street, the play *Androboros* (fig. 33), composed in 1714 by Cornbury's successor, Robert Hunter, from gossip fed to him by Lewis Morris, who had become the Whig governor's "perticular favorit." With Cornbury's supporters still dominating the New York Assembly during the early years of Hunter's administration (1710–1719), the new governor — disposed in any case to shift blame for present troubles to his predecessor — apparently decided to vent his frustrations in satiric wordplay.[49]

Grub Street is perhaps too low a term for *Androboros*. Its subject matter is sufficiently coarse — focusing as it does on a real incident, the defiling with excrement of Trinity Church's clerical robes. But its deft prose has an almost Swiftian flair.[50] Most of Hunter's New York opponents are held up to high ridicule in the thirty-one-page script. The action centers on stratagems employed by the outraged Anglicans to place blame on "The Keeper" (Governor Hunter) for the desecration of their vestments. They decide to dispatch an address to "Lord Oinobaros" — the sot (Cornbury) — since he, "being a Devotee to Long Robes of both Gendres, must highly Resent this Affront." A long argument ensues: what word best describes the soil on the robes? One side favors *ordure*, while the other prefers *turd*, "for a T—— is a T—— all the world over." They finally compromise on "Turdure."

A character named "Coxcomb" (Cornbury's New Jersey ally Daniel Coxe) suggests that they urge the return of Lord Oinobaros in place of the Keeper:

*Aesop* [of Hunter's faction]. If you should, my mind Forbodes you
   would repent the Change.

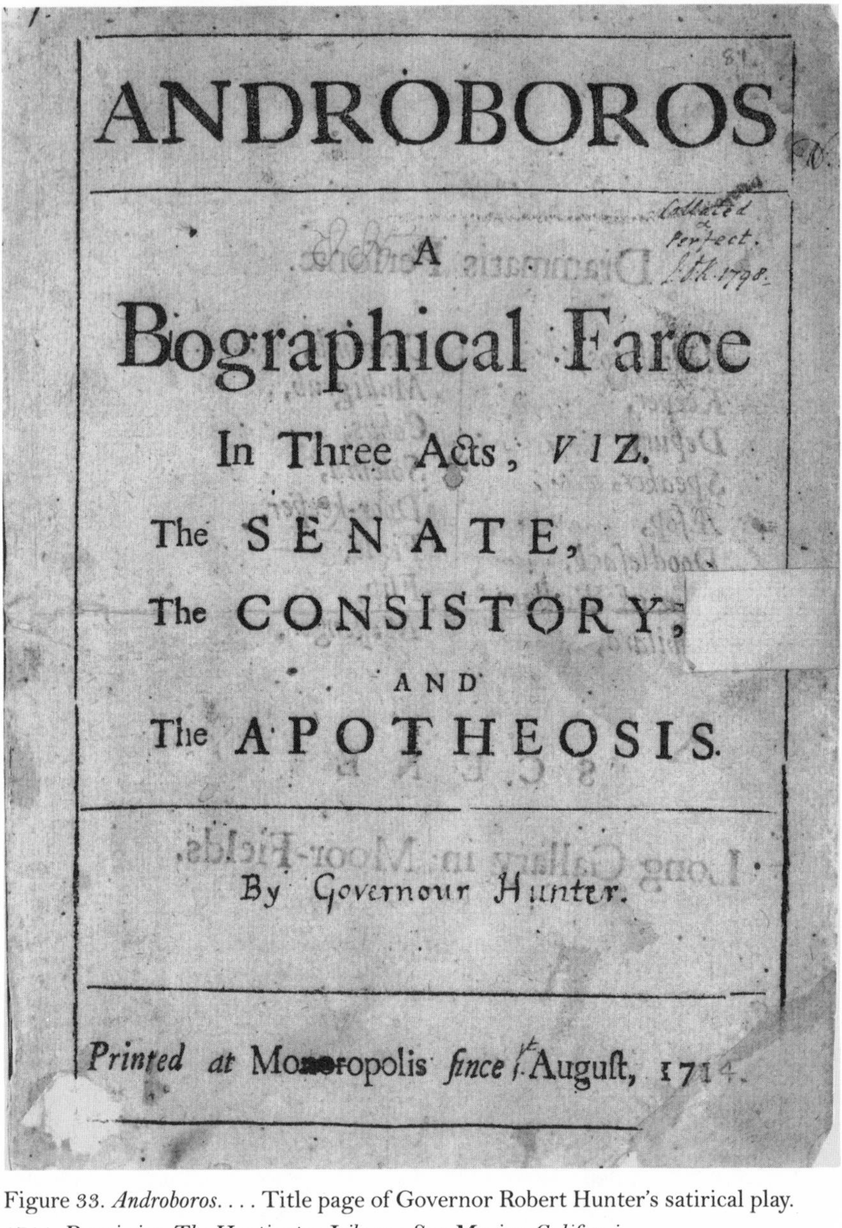

# ANDROBOROS

## A

# Biographical Farce

### In Three Acts, VIZ.

### The SENATE,

### The CONSISTORY,

### AND

### The APOTHEOSIS.

### By Governour Hunter.

Printed at Monoropolis since August, 1714.

Figure 33. *Androboros.* . . . Title page of Governor Robert Hunter's satirical play. 1714. *Permission, The Huntington Library, San Marino, California*

*Coxcomb.* Why?

*Aesop.* Why! why because a man who could never yet Govern himself, will make but a sorry Governour for others.

*Coxcomb.* Have a care what you say; That is *Scandalum Magnatum* [a libel].

[Offstage] *Doodlesack* [a Dutchman]. Pray, Mr. Tom. Wat is dat Lating [Latin]? Ick forestae't niet.

*Tom* [the English folk figure, Tom o'Bedlam]. He say, my Lord is in a very great Post, call'd, *The Scandalum Magnatum.*

*Doodlesack.* Is it given him lately[?]

*Tom.* No, he has it by inheritance.[51]

But wait. What was that about "Long Robes of both Gendres"?

# { 6 }  Sex and Gender in Early Modern English Culture

Rumors associating Lord Cornbury with transvestism, even if false, may still tell us something about the political culture of the late seventeenth and early eighteenth centuries. Courtiers and statesmen of that day, as we have seen, were subject to the lurid underside of an opposition rhetoric laced with charges of adultery, incest, sodomy, and assorted other sexual aberrances. Cross dressing, however, is somewhat more problematic, and we do not know as much about the subject as we would like. Though Governor Cornbury was hardly the only public official of his day to have had the finger pointed at him for dressing as a woman, the rumor is unusual enough to require some explanation.[1] How do we piece out the meaning of it? How much do we know about the subject of transvestism itself — and how much, especially, about the charge it carried in the early eighteenth century? Could the aristocracy have enjoyed a greater latitude in such behavior? Would Cornbury's English contemporaries have ignored the practice? condemned it? laughed at it?

## THE BOUNDARIES OF SEX AND GENDER

A good deal of evidence supports the current view of historians that sex roles were less clearly delineated in the sixteenth century than they would be by the eighteenth century. The blurring of gender boundaries in an agrarian society, particularly in the absence of a clear male-female division of labor, has been accounted a key factor. Moreover, sumptuary laws focused primarily on rank, not gender. Nonetheless, by the turn of the seventeenth century one of the most visible demarcators of gender among adults was clothing — women usually wore skirts, and men did not.[2]

Even so, cross dressing was practiced on a number of special occasions, such as seasonal festivals or religious spectacles. The inversion of sex roles that sometimes accompanied these public revels was seen by the community as a form of social expression, in many instances a derisive comment from below on a local aristocrat or some aspect of the culture higher up. In England, cross dressing might occur at rural morris dances and on other occasions that called for wearing costumes, not least on the stage, where men played women's roles. Among early modern English aristocrats, a favorite occasion for dressing up, sometimes in clothes of the opposite sex, was the masquerade ball (fig. 34).

Cross dressing was not limited to special occasions. Women were known to disguise themselves as men to gain employment in male occupations, most often as soldiers or sailors (fig. 35). Men sometimes dressed as women to hide their true identities during riots, to operate more effectively as spies, or to gain access to "women's quarters for purposes of seduction."[3]

Following the Restoration, a shift can be discerned in English attitudes toward public cross dressing. It was apparent first in the theater. Men and boys had traditionally played female roles, but now women began to take these parts. Other residual transvestite practices also fell out of favor; as one modern study notes, "By 1700 the power of female impersonation . . . [was] at the direct expense of normative masculinity." In the late seventeenth century, under the influence of the rather starchy monarchs William and Mary, the conviction grew that English society had been degenerating toward a self-indulgent effeminacy fostered by urban corruption, the baleful effects of French and Italian licentiousness, and a visible decline of the heroic virtues. As the author of *Mundus Foppensis* (1691) put it: "The World is chang'd I know not how, / For Men kiss Men, not Women now" (fig. 36). In *The Levellers: A Dialogue . . .* (1703), female characters complained that certain men were "grown full as effeminate as the Women. . . . They dress like Anticks and Stage-

Figure 34. *Royal Masquerade, Somerset House.* Engraving by Thomas Cook, 1805, from painting by William Hogarth, circa 1730s. *The woman playing cards at left sports a mustache; or was this a man disguised as a woman? Courtesy, Colonial Williamsburg Foundation*

Players, and are as ridiculous as Monkies." One fop was said to under-stand "Ribbons and Silk . . . Beauty Washes and Essences" as well as any mercer or chemist.[4]

Such public discussion was less a reflection of social reality than a measure of changing notions about appropriate masculine and feminine behavior and about the differentiation of the sexes. In the 1690s there had appeared the first reform societies, dedicated to suppressing what their sponsors saw as the promiscuous disorder of English life. As such groups proliferated, the raffish language and indulgent sexual attitudes we often associate with Restoration England came under increasing criticism and constraint.[5]

Figure 35. *Hannah Snell, the Female Soldier.* Engraving by John Faber, Jr., after a portrait by Richard Philips. 1750. *Hannah Snell, born at Worcester in 1723, disguised herself as a man and served for a number of years in the British army. Courtesy, Colonial Williamsburg Foundation*

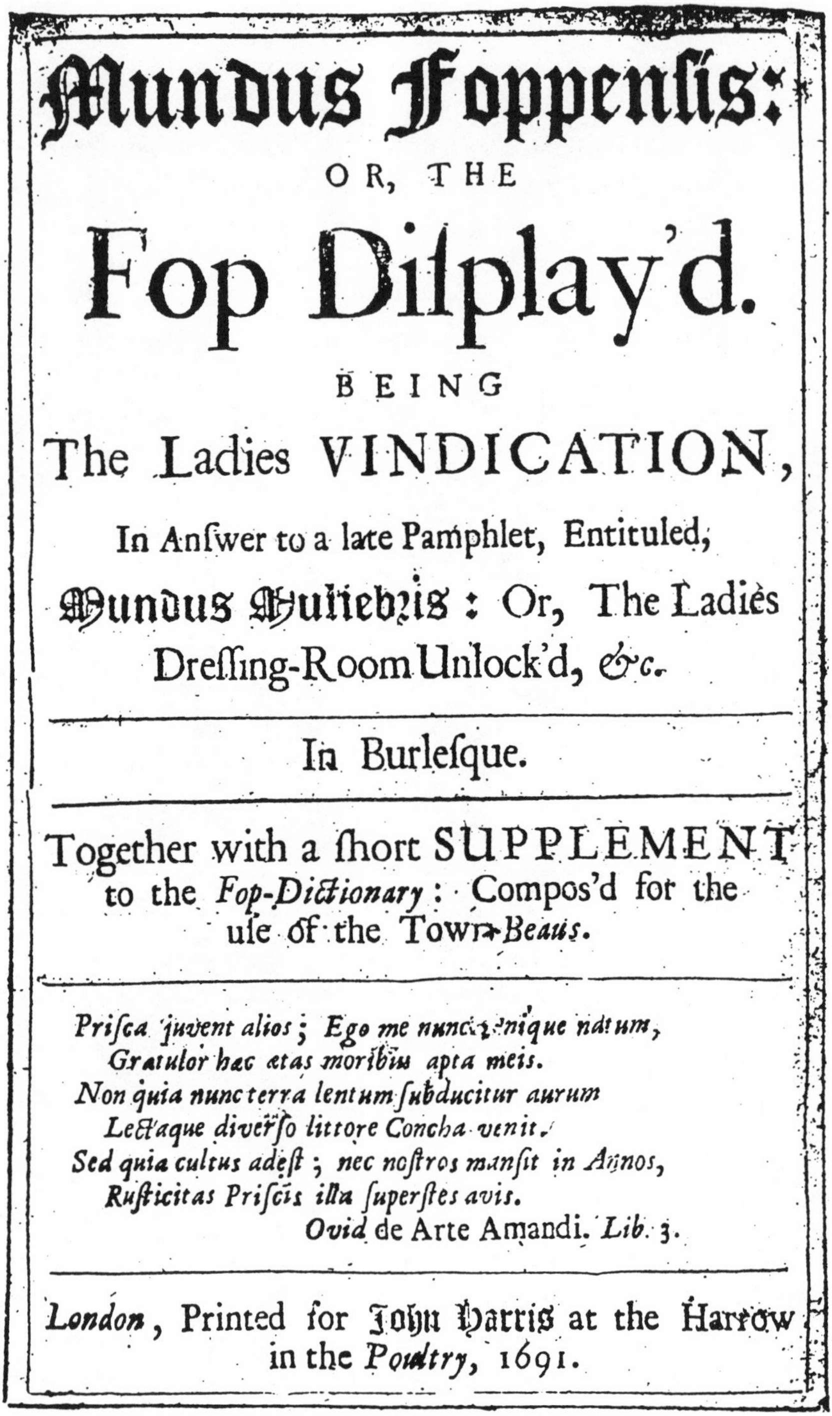

# Mundus Foppensis:

## OR, THE

# Fop Diſplay'd.

### BEING

## The Ladies VINDICATION,

In Anſwer to a late Pamphlet, Entituled,

## Mundus Muliebris : Or, The Ladies
## Dreſſing-Room Unlock'd, &c.

---

### In Burleſque.

---

### Together with a ſhort SUPPLEMENT
to the *Fop-Dictionary* : Compos'd for the
uſe of the Town-Beaus.

---

*Priſca juvent alios ; Ego me nunc ſ nique natum,*
*Gratulor hac atas moribus apta meis.*
*Non quia nunc terra lentum ſubducitur aurum*
*Lectaque diverſo littore Concha venit.*
*Sed quia cultus adeſt ; nec noſtros manſit in Annos,*
*Ruſticitas Priſcis illa ſuperſtes avis.*
        *Ovid* de Arte Amandi. *Lib.* 3.

---

*London*, Printed for John Harris at the Harrow
in the *Poultry*, 1691.

---

Figure 36. *Mundus Foppensis*, title page. 1691. *Courtesy, William Andrews Clark Memorial Library, University of California, Los Angeles*

The reformers enjoyed only partial success. Even as the reform societies took root, alternate structures emerged that facilitated the expression, though in encapsulated form, of by-then-proscribed erotic behavior, including cross dressing. The most visible of these was the masquerade ball, popular among the aristocracy since the sixteenth century and increasingly lavish in the second half of the seventeenth century. Samuel Pepys describes a masque at which almost everyone present cross dressed. By the early eighteenth century such balls were becoming more frequent and more inclusive, with masquerades at Lambeth Wells and Charing Cross being advertised in the newspapers and tickets sold for "Half a Guinea."[6]

Perhaps the most subversive element of the masquerade's appeal, in both its private and its increasingly public form, was the opportunity it gave participants to cross boundaries not only of class but of gender. Although most women dressed as shepherdesses and milkmaids, and men as Turks or hussars, some women seized the occasion to don boots and breeches while some men decked themselves out as bawds and serving-maids. Masks and disguises liberated the wearer from conventional inhibitions. Alarmed at such behavior, the reform societies warned that the anonymity of the masquerade was being taken as a license for sexual inversion. In 1711, Joseph Addison not only feared that unnatural "Mixtures of Dress" across the sexes threatened to turn "our publick Assemblies into a general Masquerade," but he specifically denounced the "Midnight Masque, which has of late been very frequently held in one of the most conspicuous Parts of the town," as a "libidinous Assembly" that often terminated in "Assignations and Intrigues" (fig. 37). The author of *The Danger of Masquerades and Raree-Shows* declared that "Avarice, and Lust, are the two Capital Inducements to meet upon such Occasions."[7]

The first full-scale, commercially organized public masquerade was held at the Haymarket Theatre in 1717, and others soon followed. These large public entertainments — "urban and non-exclusive in nature, cutting across historic lines of rank and privilege" — exemplified what one scholar has termed an eighteenth-century English "culture of travesty.... a persistent popular urge toward disguise and metamorphosis." Soon London's public masquerades, as urban representations of traditional country carnivals, were drawing up to eight hundred people a week.

Figure 37. *The Devil in Masquerade.* Engraving by F. Hoffmann. 1711. *Referring to a stabbing attack on Robert Harley on March 8, 1711, by the marquis of Guiscard, the print has a fold across the center, to be raised (right). The note at the upper left refers to Joseph Addison and Richard Steele's* Spectator. *Copyright © The British Museum*

There, as one newspaper reported, "the *Peer* and the *Apprentice,* the *Punk* and the *Duchess* are . . . upon an equal Foot," all for the price of a ticket. To the anonymous author of a pamphlet subtitled *Short Remarks upon the Original and Pernicious Consequences of Masquerades* (1721), the masquerade was simply a "Congress to an unclean end." This pamphlet has been

rightly characterized as "a barely-concealed assault on homosexual practices at the masquerade."[8]

Such confusions symbolized for many English moralists the sorry
plight of both society and state after more than a half-century of upheaval
that overturned one governmental regime after another. Gender inversion simply mirrored this topsy-turvy world of unstable authority. License and ambiguity clouded everything, magnifying anxieties about
who was in charge and where the boundaries of right conduct should be
drawn. These apprehensions may have heightened during Queen Anne's
reign, when the ladies of the queen's bedchamber, if rarely Anne herself,
were lampooned in opposition doggerel for supposedly exercising authority improper to their sex. All such tensions seem to have found voice
in the denunciations of cross dressing, which led to a further polarization
of gender distinctions and amplified criticism of those seen to violate the
newly drawn norms of male and female behavior. Hence in 1711 the *Spectator* deplored the coat and cravat worn by a female equestrian; to perceive how unnatural was such reversal, the lady need but "look upon a
Man who affects the Softness and Effeminacy of a Woman." "The Dress
and Air of a Man are not well to be divided."[9]

These same anxieties also manifested themselves in the sharpening
association of transvestism with male homosexuals. Transvestites, of
course, are not necessarily homosexual. Modern clinical studies assert,
in fact, that most male cross dressers lead heterosexual lives. Nonetheless, the close identification of transvestism with effeminate men (or
"mollies," as they were called) in late-seventeenth- and early-eighteenth-
century England suggests that further exploration of these themes may
provide the critical context in which to assess the allegations regarding
Cornbury.[10]

## THE EMERGENCE OF THE HOMOSEXUAL COMMUNITY
## IN ENGLAND

If masquerades offered a tantalizing occasion for London homosexuals to cross dress, the anonymity of urban life increasingly facilitated the coalescence of a clandestine all-male sexual community,
creating, in Randolph Trumbach's phrase, a "sodomitical subculture."[11]
Early-eighteenth-century court records and Grub Street both tell of

male transvestites disporting themselves in the mollyhouses of London. Drury Lane and Moorfields, with its "Sodomites' Walk," were well-known meeting grounds, and Holborn was a center of transvestism and male prostitution.[12]

Jonathan Wild, a professional police informer whose colorful reports on the early-eighteenth-century London underworld at times conform closely with testimony in the Old Bailey records, tells of a house of *"He-Whores"* near the courts. There, visitors were greeted as "Madam" and "Ladyship," "The Men calling one another 'My Dear,' hugging and kissing, tickling and feeling each other, as if they were a mixture of wanton Males and Females; and assuming effeminate Voices, Female Airs Etc., some telling others that they ought to be Whipp'd for not coming to School more frequently."[13]

As late as 1700, the almanac-like *Angliae Notitia* could innocently declare that "the Sin of Buggery, brought into England by the Lombards ... is now rarely practised amongst [the] English." Yet that same year Grub Street reported on a London bawdyhouse where customers had the choice of going up the stairs to female prostitutes or down to "the Sodomite cellar." In 1705 the *Wandering Spy*, a classic Grub Street rag, heatedly reprobated "that Inhabitant of Sodom ... that committed Fornication with his own Sex" and whose disciples "Rendezvous at that Sink and Sodom ... the famous *Blackmary's Hole."* In 1707, John Dunton, an irrepressible hack, published *The He-Strumpets: A Satyr on the Sodomite-Club*, in which he mocked a forty-three-member band of "He-Strumpets and He-Whores who indulge in He-Lechery and He-Lust." A street ballad also published in 1707, *The Women-Hater's Lamentation*, told of three men who killed themselves on being apprehended for sodomy, whereas "A Hundred more we hear, / Did to this Club belong" (fig. 38).[14]

Sensationalism may have been Grub Street's stock in trade, yet this did not lessen the public appetite for its vividly salacious offerings. Edward "Ned" Ward, a prolific Grub Streeter, in 1709 proclaimed a "Christian Abhorrance [of] a particular Gang of Sodomitical Wretches, in this Town, who call themselves the *Mollies."* Ward was ready with particulars. The mollies would "speak, walk, tattle, cur[t]sy, cry, scold, and mimic all Manner of Effeminacy," gossip about their "husbands," and on at least one occasion dress in women's clothes for the mock delivery of a baby. But their main reason for gathering was to "take those

Figure 38. The Suicides of Three Men. From *The Women-Hater's Lamentation*.
1707. *Broadside song about men who "Unnat'ral Lust pursu'd." Courtesy, the Guildhall
Library, London. Reproduction taken from the book* Homosexuality in Renaissance
England *by Alan Bray. Copyright © 1982, 1995 by Columbia University Press. Reprinted
with permission of the publisher*

infamous Liberties with one another, that no Man, who is not sunk into a
State of Devilism, can think on without Blushing." Though Ward claimed
that moral reform societies were putting an end to these "filthy scandalous Revels," court records tell a different story.[15]

In 1698 a naval captain named Edward Rigby was arrested and tried
at the Old Bailey for attempted sodomy; the incident had taken place in
Saint James's Park, a known haunt of the promiscuous. Though he was
acknowledged in the records as a gentleman, Rigby was not only fined
and imprisoned but sentenced to stand three times in the pillory at the
mercy of a hostile crowd. On his first exposure, Rigby, "dressed like a
*beau*," was so tightly surrounded by constables that none of the missiles
thrown at him could find their mark. A mollyhouse raid in 1699 netted a
clutch of men who were then tried and sent to Newgate Prison. More
raids took place in 1707 and were promptly brought to the public's attention in John Dunton's *He-Strumpets*.[16]

Perhaps best documented in a literature subject to hyperbole are the goings-on at Margaret Clap's in Holborn, where sodomites "Dress themselves in Women's Apparel for the Entertainment of others of the same Inclinations, in Dancing Etc. in imitation of the Fair Sex." Though "Mother Clap's" house had apparently been operating unmolested for some years, in 1714 a number of revelers were arrested, appearing the next morning before the lord mayor "in the same Dresses they were taken in. Some were compleatly Rigg'd in Gowns, Petticoats, Head cloths, fine lac'd Shoes, Furbelow Scarves, and Masks; some had Riding-hoods; some were dressed like Shepherdesses; others like Milk-Maids with fine Green Hatts, Wastcoats and Petticoats, and others had their Faces patched and painted, and wore very extensive Hoop-petticoats, which were then very lately introduced." The mayor committed the mollies to the workhouse, "and, as part of their Punishment, order'd them to be publickly convey'd thro' the Streets in their Female Habits." By the 1720s up to fifty men would gather of a Sunday evening at Mother Clap's "Academy," "kissing and hugging, and making Love (as they called it) in a very indecent Manner." A police raid in 1726 led to the arrest of a number of them along with the proprietress (fig. 39).[17]

Testimony resulting from this and other trials, following raids on some twenty such houses in the mid-1720s, makes clear that, despite efforts to shame the mollies, cross dressing continued to be practiced by a fair number in this subculture. Dancing and the mimicking of female talk — "O, Fie, Sir . . . Lord, how can you serve me so? . . . You're a wicked Devil" — were said to be commonplaces among those who wore female clothes. Mock marriages were also enacted, complete with veils and rings. According to one account, a man nicknamed "Miss Kitten" and his partner, a butcher, "stood as Bridesmaids" at the wedding of two male friends. Family scenes were also staged: "they sometimes have a Lying-inn" presided over by a "Midwife, and with a great Deal of Ceremony a jointed baby is brought from under the chair he [ 'she' ] sits on."[18]

Grub Street and the moral reform societies, both of which began their rise in the mid-1690s, were instrumental in bringing England's sodomitical underground first to public attention and then to public account in the arrests and trials of the early eighteenth century. The spate of molly-house raids was surely in significant part a consequence of the salacious reports broadcast by the new print culture, which in turn prompted a

Figure 39. Two Men Dancing /
Embracing / Kissing? From *The
Women-Hater's Lamentation.* 1707.
*Courtesy of the Guildhall Library, London.
Reproduction taken from the book*
Homosexuality in Renaissance England
*by Alan Bray. Copyright © 1982, 1995 by
Columbia University Press. Reprinted with
permission of the publisher*

surge of reform enthusiasm. As the *Observator* declared on March 13,
1703: "It is indeed a Labour worthy the Undertaking of a Pious Queen
to cleanse the Augean-Stable of Vice."

Spurred by royal proclamations, circular letters from Anglican bish-
ops, and accelerated prosecutions by local justices, the reform crusaders
soon enlisted an army of zealous citizens who joined Societies for the
Reformation of Manners dedicated to the extirpation of vice. And as reformers denounced the sodomitical demimonde, Grub Street continued
to expose it to the glare of publicity (fig. 40).[19]

The attention paid to foppery, the mollies, and the homosexual underground in the late seventeenth and early eighteenth centuries both reflected and accelerated the ongoing process of gender delineation, especially in such Protestant countries as England and the Netherlands. One
study of eighteenth-century Dutch sexual attitudes notes the emergence
of a bourgeois primness that led to "a genuine abhorrence of undressing,
variations of sexual positions, and especially of sodomy." One consequence was an intensified scrutiny by the magistrates of irregular sexual
behavior, including a homophobic frenzy in the years 1730–1732 that led
to the prosecution of 276 men for sodomy. British naval courts-martial

Figure 40. *This Is Not the Thing; or, Molly Exalted.* Broadside. Circa 1763. *A molly in the pillory. Courtesy, Print Collection, Lewis Walpole Library, Yale University*

for buggery rose sharply during the eighteenth-century wars from Queen Anne's time onward.[20] And if sodomy has sometimes been depicted as an aristocratic vice, early records provide ample testimony that it was not restricted to any one class.[21]

Just how changing attitudes toward deviant sexual behavior may have affected the peerage is difficult to gauge, elite precincts not being normally inclined to betray their secrets. Wealthy men could of course go abroad in pursuit of pleasure. Or they could remain at home and hope that their doings would be protected by the conventions of class solidarity. Many presumed sodomites seem to have been well known to those arbiters of court society the gossips. But if gossip about the mighty was confined to a relatively narrow orbit in the seventeenth century, in the early eighteenth century a number of reputed sodomites among the upper ranks were publicly exposed by members of their class. Such was the case with Cornbury's contemporaries James Stanhope, Lord John Hervey, and Viscount Bateman, and later with Lord George Germain. Thus, as Trumbach observes: "In 18th century England it is clear that the court no longer maintained the power to shield homosexual behavior that it had certainly possessed under James I and probably also as late as the time of Charles II."[22] Owing to Grub Street and the difficulty of proving that a charge was libelous, aristocrats were now vulnerable to exposure and the public scorn that often accompanied it. At the very least they might suffer ridicule; at the other extreme lay blackmail, voluntary exile, or prosecution.

Given the sharpening demarcation of male and female roles at the turn of the eighteenth century, the general climate of moral reform and public exposé, and the specific linkage of male transvestites to the feminine mollies, what is to be made of the stories about Lord Cornbury while he was governor of New York and New Jersey? That a royal governor could have publicly displayed himself in women's clothes, as Cornbury is alleged to have done, and escaped severe censure seems doubtful. The sight of a royal governor parading about the streets, or even the ramparts of the fort, in female dress would have scandalized friend and foe alike.

This would have been especially true in the colonies, where Calvinist influence was strong, biblical injunctions were familiar, and laws against cross dressing were enforced. At least twice in seventeenth-century New York men were arrested for appearing publicly in women's clothes, even though both incidents occurred during celebrations of Shrove Tuesday (known better today as Mardi Gras). In 1696, Massachusetts had enacted a statute against cross dressing by either sex. In 1703, shortly after Cornbury arrived in the colonies, one John Smith of Philadelphia was charged with being "Maskt, or Disgised in womens aparrell . . . it being against the Law of God, the Law of this province and the Law of nature, to the staining of holy profestion, and Incoridging of wickednes in this place."[23] And in 1709, Boston merchant Samuel Sewall branded transvestism an "abomination," taking both the word and the thought from the injunction to that effect in Deuteronomy 22:5.[24]

There is evidence from at least the late sixteenth century through the American Revolution that forcing a man to put on women's clothes was a common form of public shaming. Thus men involved in the English enclosure riots of 1598 were sentenced "to stand in the pillory in women's clothes"; and in 1776 a deserter from George Washington's army at New York was dressed in female apparel, given a wooden sword and musket, and "placed on the Back of an old Horse to be carried thro the Camp in this ridiculous Manner" as the troops pelted him with manure.[25] Proceedings like these make it doubtful that a public official or anyone else would have handed himself over to his political enemies by cross dressing in public.

Indeed, the most intriguing thing is, not the existence of letters from three of Governor Cornbury's most vocal enemies charging him with public cross dressing, but rather the absence of the much larger volume of noise such behavior would have aroused had it actually been observed. The extant record discloses no such evidence, even in private letters from Cornbury's critics within the imperial circle; it reveals instead repeated instances of support for his administration as well as expostulations over the way a few disgruntled colonials went about slandering their governor.

But even if essentially untrue, the rumor itself still calls for an explanation. Could it have been at least a half-truth? Does modern clinical thinking on transvestism offer any clues?

### TRANSVESTISM: A CLINICAL VIEW

The question now might be how Lord Cornbury's personality, on one hand, and reported style of cross dressing, on the other, accord with current views about the psychology of male transvestism and the variant forms it takes. Psychologists have proposed a spectrum of male transvestite behavior that ranges from the most casual and inconsequential wearing of a single item of female clothing to the extreme exhibitionism of the drag queen. In their search for a scientific understanding, clinicians have sorted cross dressers into five, seven, or nine categories.[26] These can be arranged into three general types: homosexual cross dressers, heterosexual transvestites, and those who fall somewhere in between.

Male homosexual cross dressers are perhaps the most familiar type. Such men identify erotically with members of their own sex; their aim in cross dressing seems to be gender role-playing rather than genital self-arousal. They often display effeminate traits such as a mincing walk and frequently have experimented with female clothing from an early age.

Among some members of this group, transvestite experiences are brief and intermittent; for others, notably female impersonators, cross dressing is central to their public persona and adorns a role in which they feel quite comfortable.[27]

With heterosexual transvestites, in contrast, cross dressing is a fetish employed specifically to stimulate self-arousal. It is manifested in a private, secretive manner rather than as a form of exhibitionism. Such heterosexual fetishists avowedly choose women as their sexual partners, both in practice and in their fantasies. Most are married and have fathered children. They are found in all the traditionally male professions, where their behavior, language, vocal expression, and clothing are "unremarkably masculine." Their own genitals are these men's main source of erotic pleasure, and during cross-dressing episodes their sexual excitement arises from the knowledge that a penis is hidden beneath their female garments. Transvestites of this category do not attempt to "pass" in public as women.[28]

The third type of male transvestite falls in a wide range between the other two and manifests in varying degrees an ill-formed or weakened gender orientation. Such men may be heterosexual, homosexual, or bisexual, and some tend to oscillate between male and female roles. This category, which here encompasses a number of ambivalent types identified by clinicians, ranges from the man who experiences a mild gender dysphoria, or sense of discomfort with his biologically assigned sex, to the transsexual who considers himself a female trapped in a man's body. Among those of special interest here — the more masculine, often married group — the wearing of female apparel is episodic and may be accompanied by psychological distress. Such heterosexual transvestites might, with age and greater experience as cross dressers, come to place a high value on deceiving the world by passing in public as women.[29]

The application of today's clinical understanding of transvestism back to Lord Cornbury's time requires a good deal of caution. Modern psychologists put considerable weight, for example, on their subjects' earliest, and often intense, experience with cross dressing, which frequently takes place around age five or six. In Cornbury's day, however, boys were regularly dressed in girls' clothing until about the age of six, when in a kind of rite of passage they were "breeched" (fig. 41).[30] Still, given that by the turn of the eighteenth century clothing was increasingly seen as

Figure 41. Henry Hyde, Future Second Earl of Clarendon. By Sir Peter Lely. Circa 1643. Oil. Present location unknown. *The father of Lord Cornbury, before he was breeched. Photograph Courtauld Institute of Art, London*

definitive of gender among adults, there might be some merit in weighing Cornbury's alleged transvestism in terms of the three categories sketched above.

There is no evidence to indicate that Cornbury was a homosexual transvestite. None of his contemporaries hinted that he displayed effeminate or even foppish traits, and except for the charge of transvestism, there was no suggestion of unusual appetites or scandalous behavior in his personal life. Such traits, had they existed, could hardly have escaped the notice of his political enemies. That modern clinicians, like early eighteenth-century commentators, tend to associate exhibitionistic cross dressing — that is, public female impersonation in which the subject openly displays himself in women's clothes — with homosexuality, calls into question the charge that Governor Cornbury publicly flaunted his transvestism, either on the streets of New York or on the ramparts of Fort Anne.[31]

Nor do contemporary descriptions of Cornbury's cross dressing conform with modern notions about the behavior of the second group, avowedly heterosexual transvestites. Such men are deeply secretive about wearing women's apparel and do not display themselves to the public. At most they might, after much preparation, disclose their fetish to a sympathetic wife or mistress.[32]

The broad middle category of transvestites seems worth exploring, especially at the more heterosexual end of the scale, since the sporadic nature of Lord Cornbury's supposed cross dressing marks at least one point of similarity. (The evidence regarding Cornbury's personal life is devoid of any of the traits of transgenderism or transsexualism that occupy the rest of this category.) Did Cornbury show any signs of the gender dysphoria sometimes displayed by those in this group? We could speculate, calling on another school of psychology, that his attachment to the military and to manly honor was a way of compensating for an incompletely developed masculine identity. Or that his alleged rages provided an outlet for the guilt and psychological distress he suffered as a fetishistic transvestite. As Cornbury aged, his fetish might have intensified, especially after the death of his wife in 1706, emboldening him to attempt to "pass" in public as a woman.

The difficulty with this construction is that Cornbury would have had to believe, not only according to modern experts but in terms of his own self-fashioning as a manly military leader, that he was "getting away with it," that he was truly deceiving the public when he strolled abroad in women's clothes. Yet in view of his accusers' statements that he attracted hordes of spectators and drew "many Censures" (see chapter 7), it is hard to imagine that Cornbury could either have been blind to the stir he was making or have believed that New Yorkers really thought he was a woman. Indeed, Elias Neau's letter reporting the rumor specifically claimed that the governor "knew all that was said of him."[33]

It appears that none of the transvestite types identified by today's clinicians fits closely or even shares significant features with the behavior described by Lord Cornbury's enemies. Though this is hardly conclusive when applied to a world so distant from our own, it does seem to reduce the likelihood that Cornbury so far forgot himself as to dress *publicly* in women's clothes and thus undo all he as royal governor had worked so hard to achieve. Yet as the material elements of the cross-dressing story blur, its metaphorical possibilities become more attractive. In a culture that relished masquerade and caricature, one that spawned a Grub Street press given to representational exorbitance, Governor Cornbury — whose office reflected the power of his cousin Queen Anne — may have been perceived by certain colonials as taking on her likeness, as enrobing himself in her persona and authority.

Before considering further the cross-dressing rumor and its possible sources, a closer examination of the letters that conveyed it to England, and of the transatlantic context in which imperial communication took place, might suggest additional ways of thinking about the uses to which news — and gossip — could be put in the early empire.

# { 7 }   "'Tis Said He Dresses as a Woman"

*Imperial Communication, Gossip, and the Search for Meaning*

Gossip seems to have certain universal properties that recur in different ages and cultures. Gossip fosters intimacy through rituals of confidence; it can also express a community's standards by marking the boundaries of approved behavior. Yet it also promotes social divisions, setting the gossipers against those being gossiped about. And its indirect, covert quality makes it a wonderful vehicle for the release of aggressions at low personal risk. Gossip, moreover, has an unhindered mobility: all profess to deplore it, few shut their ears to it.

In her discussion of gossip the literary theorist Patricia Meyer Spacks has touched on at least two forms that may apply to Cornbury's case. Gossip as "distilled malice," or slander, attacks reputations in order to increase the purveyor's power or to further a specific political or social objective. Such premeditated gossip, which as we have seen was a key weapon in the party battles of Cornbury's time, can inflict "incalculable harm." A second form of gossip might best be called "idle talk." It is less calculated and often frivolous: "Blunted awareness marks such gossip; involving little real consideration of the issues its discourse touches, it constitutes moral avoidance." But even such casual gossip can damage reputations.[1]

It is already clear that some colonial gossip took a highly poisonous form, though other instances may have been mere idle talk. No doubt the stories about Cornbury took different shapes according to the purposes of the gossiper. And purposes — conscious or otherwise — there surely were in that age of calumny. Gossip may have been particularly potent in bridging distance and intermittent communication in the early modern era, solidifying communities of listeners and creating insiders and outsiders through shared storytelling. The near-obsession of Anglo-Americans with gossip in Cornbury's time and well into the eighteenth century is perhaps most evident in plays ranging from William Wycherley's *Country Wife* (1675) to Richard Brinsley Sheridan's *School for Scandal* (1777) — pieces that revealed "a striking preoccupation with dark fantasies about what people say of one another," especially on the subject of sex.[2] That same preoccupation should serve as a clue, as we seek to understand transatlantic strategies of communication — the planting of rumors, the codes inherent in correspondence — in the politics of the early empire.

IMPERIAL COMMUNICATION IN THE AGE OF SAIL

Between 1707 and 1709, three colonists from New York and New Jersey — Robert Livingston, Lewis Morris, and Elias Neau — wrote a total of four letters to England containing allegations that Governor Cornbury dressed publicly in women's clothes. Historians have generally taken these letters at face value, but Cornbury's contemporaries were decidedly more cautious. They had to be. Much of the information pouring into government departments from the colonies was contradictory; officials knew, moreover, that gossip and calumny, together with party bias, were inherent in the very language of imperial communications. Which parts were trustworthy, which questionable? Experience and circumstances had taught English officials that they would do well to await the appearance of one more informant, another piece of evidence, before making up their minds about the truth or falsehood of anything. Thus, before looking at how accounts of Governor Cornbury's supposed derelictions were received in England, we might review something of the larger context in which all information was transmitted and received in early modern times.

The very conditions of communication — of space, time, and accident — made for a gross liability, full of complexities scarcely conceivable today. News carried across the ocean in the age of sail was invariably out of date when it reached the other side, a minimum of six months being required to send a letter and receive an answer. Because New York had no direct mail service to London until 1755, its governors' letter packets might lie in warehouses at Boston, Philadelphia, or Jamaica for weeks awaiting transfer to ships sailing for England. A substantial portion of official mail never reached its destination. Whitehall administrators pleaded repeatedly for records to be sent and queries answered, though the governors had long since dispatched the desired information. Colonial officials were equally frustrated, going months, even years, without receiving instructions from England on how to govern their provinces.[3] As a consequence, serious misunderstandings arose in every British colony, enlarging the breeding ground for suspicion, rumor, and intrigue.

Weather and war posed further hazards to imperial communication. Ice sometimes closed ports for weeks at a time. On the high seas storms delayed ships or sent them to the bottom with the loss of all hands and cargo. In wartime the risks multiplied. The Board of Trade instructed Governor Cornbury in 1703 to entrust mail packets only to "persons who will be prepared to sink them with weights" in the event of capture. Maintaining confidentiality was yet another obstacle. When Cornbury wished to write privately to his father, he sent a letter in the personal care of Colonel Quary lest it be "intercepted, as many of my letters have been both here and in England." He instructed his father to send his responses through certain trusted friends in New York and to make sure the letters bore neither superscription nor seal, as both Lord Clarendon's hand and the family seal were known in New York.[4]

Reputations and honor were frequently at the mercy of these hazardous and irreversible circumstances. Life itself sometimes hung on the frail thread of imperial communication. It certainly did so in late-seventeenth-century New York when Jacob Leisler, instead of dying a martyr's death on a New York scaffold as he did, might have been spared had exculpatory information about his part in the so-called Leisler's Rebellion of 1689 not been captured by a French privateer.[5]

Hostage though the colonials were to such perilous uncertainties, it is evident that as administration of the empire tightened in the 1690s and the volume of communication rose, those responsible for imperial intelligence found ways, perhaps without quite realizing it, to separate truth from fiction. Imperial officials, being familiar with the politics of England, were hardly naive about the part gossip and rumor played in correspondence from the colonies. And in that time of rampant party strife, their ability to discern partisan and personal misrepresentation seems to have sharpened. They knew, moreover, in their concern for a more efficient empire, that the appointment, regulation, and, if necessary, discipline of colonial functionaries had to be based on something more than conjecture.

### EVALUATING THE NEWS

As state and church officials in England sifted through the colonial reports for an accurate picture of events, they seem to have worked out an informal method for grading incoming news, dividing it roughly into three categories. Greatest weight was accorded to eye- or earwitness testimony, especially if it came from individuals personally known and trusted in England. Colonial correspondents were thus careful to state, if such was the case, that they had directly observed an action or participated in an incident. By specifying "eyewitness" or "earwitness" knowledge, the writer elevated his news above the common category of hearsay.

Descriptions of the actual arrangement of rooms and movements of the leading characters in a controversial episode lent further credibility to eyewitness reports while also conveying something of the tone and quality of the action. We have already glimpsed this kind of depiction in Cornbury's report on his diplomatic mission to Hanover (chapter 2) and in accounts of the dispute in 1706 between Cornbury and Thoroughgood Moore, the New Jersey clergyman who refused communion to the lieutenant governor (chapter 3). In the second episode, Cornbury's secretary, Peter Fauconnier, wrote the Society for the Propagation of the Gospel to relate what he himself had seen and heard during Cornbury and Moore's meeting at Perth Amboy. To validate his account, Fauconnier described the rooms in which the scene took place and the movements of each man. Governor Cornbury, he wrote, initially took Moore "privately into his own Room for very near half an hour, that at their comeing out, This Deponent heard his Lordship say (to the hearing of many others that were there)" that Moore was "Certainly in the wrong." When Moore later refused to enter the governor's barge for the trip to New York, Cornbury, after speaking to him "with a great deal of good humour and Calmness," finally "took him by the Arm . . . into his Barge."[6]

The respected imperial officer Robert Quary wrote a long letter to the bishop of London about the affair. Moore was well treated during his confinement at Fort Anne, being lodged with the chaplain and given "the command of my Lord's Cellar." "This I was an eye Witness of," declared Quary, having come from Boston just as Cornbury and Moore returned from Perth Amboy. And when Quary later visited Moore in his chambers, "I saw that he wanted nothing and had the priviledge of all the fort to walk in." Quary's detailed report, which blamed the defection of the Reverend Misters Moore and Brooke on a violent faction in New Jersey that aimed to "overset both Governor and Government," offered "the true History of these two Gentlemen," Quary informed the bishop. "What I have said is fact." The bishop of London appears to have been satisfied that this was so. He informed the SPG that accounts of the episode by Moore and Brooke were "ingeniously extended beyond the plain truth," and he consequently "lay[s] the blame on those Gentlemen."[7]

An especially striking example of the value placed on eyewitness testimony comes from Lewis Morris in 1712. As the leading supporter of then-governor Robert Hunter, Morris found himself in the position of defending an executive who had been accused by prominent Anglicans of failing to nurture England's established church. Morris firmly denied Hunter's culpability in a letter to the SPG. He closed with a flourish intended to seal the case: his knowledge of Hunter's concern for the church was solidly based on "what I have been Eye and Ear Witness to," as "can be prov'd on Oath if there is necessity."[8] Direct personal testimony, fortified by detailed descriptions of physical settings and the nuances of behavior, was most valued in an era when written words formed the primary medium of communication.

Another common means of substantiating eyewitness versions of events was to bolster them with sworn depositions. These were particularly effective when a number of statements agreed on the essential facts. In January 1712, depositions concerning Governor Cornbury's earlier dispute with the Reverend Mr. Moore were sworn in New York, possibly in preparation for a lawsuit. Seven have survived. Six support Cornbury's version of what happened at Perth Amboy and during Moore's confinement at Fort Anne. The seventh, that of John Grimes — the sentry who allowed Moore to walk out of the fort either through ignorance or in consequence of a bribe — simply states that Grimes had been issued no orders to stop Moore at the gate. Grimes's deposition was the only one signed with an "X," which suggests that he may have had some assistance in choosing the words that went into it.[9] We have already taken note of the statements sworn in New Jersey in 1707 to support the Morris party's assertions that Cornbury accepted bribes (chapter 4). But because in this instance the depositions provided widely variant versions of the facts, the Morrisites in multiplying them may have weakened rather than strengthened their case.

Cornbury himself knew the importance of proofs to support charges of wrongdoing, as he demonstrated in the complaints he lodged against that perennial pestilence — as he saw it — the colony of Connecticut. When one informant told him that Connecticut was sheltering pirates, he asked the man "if he could make oath of it. He said noe, but that he would inform himself better, and would give me a farther account." To prove that Connecticut persecuted "all Religions but their own," Cornbury forwarded notarized evidence to the Board of Trade; affidavits supported his charge that Connecticut offered haven to soldiers and sailors deserting at New York.[10] In short, it seems to have been understood, in the course of imperial communication, that if a thing were to be taken as true it had to be corroborated by all manner of proofs: eyewitness accounts, sworn depositions, detailed descriptions of physical settings, bodily gestures, and tone of voice — all in the interest of keeping fact separate from gossip and rumor.

Another level of information, a notch below eyewitness testimony though still significant, was the secondhand report. Here the reliability of the informant had to be established. Thus when Governor Bellomont in 1699 told about an incident that reflected on his predecessor, he affirmed: "This I had from the Lieutenant Governour at New Yorke, who is too much a man of honour to forge such a story."[11] That the lieutenant governor was known and respected at Whitehall gave the report added validity. When informants were not known in England, correspondents went to some lengths to establish their trustworthiness and objectivity by describing their good qualities or, as was said at the time, by "giving a character" of the individual.

Just as testimony from afar was more persuasive when supplied by someone possessing "a great character," so was it debased if the source were shown to have "an ill character." Cornbury's New York enemies urged London to doubt anything said about the colony's finances by the governor's secretary and collector of revenue, the "Frenchifyed" Peter

Fauconnier, whose origins alone presumably were sufficient to impeach his testimony. Cornbury countered with his own "character" of Fauconnier: "He is one of the best accomptants that ever I knew, he is a Man of very great application to and diligence in business; And I have by experience found him a very honest Man, he has been Naval Officer ever since I came into this province . . . he will give any security the Right Honorable Mylord High Treasurer shall please to require." [12]

Proofs, proofs: all parties were sensitive to their importance. Cornbury's opposition was represented in London by John Champante, the former agent of New York who aspired to hold that post again. In 1707, Champante energetically gathered evidence about Cornbury's alleged maladministration in an attempt to persuade the increasingly whiggish Board of Trade to recall him. Champante claimed to have laid before the board "very full accounts of his Lordships management which tho' I did not pretend to prove, yet I let their Lordships know that I had received them from some of the Principal Gentlemen of the Province and that I did not question but that upon a proper occasion full proofe could [be] made of every particular." A few days later he told a New York correspondent that "the Push we lately made here did not reach so far as we wished it might, yet it has given a considerable shock to his Lordships Interest and prepared the way for a general complaint if the Province has Spirit enough to make one." Champante, an experienced agent and lobbyist who well understood the art of plotting a governor's downfall, urged, however, that the colonials "must be sure that full proofe be made of every alleg[ation]." [13] In fact, the New Yorkers made no such complaint, and the opposition to Cornbury continued to be centered in New Jersey.

The lowest grade of imperial intelligence was the common rumor of the "'tis said" or "everybody knows" variety. Rumors of this kind pervaded imperial communications but were received with skepticism by officials on either side of the water. When in 1705 a report reached Cornbury that his local receiver of revenue countenanced illegal trade, "I told the person that informed me, that, that was a very general charge, and that unless he would come to a more particular one, I should take no notice of it." [14] On another occasion, a correspondent of Cornbury's chose not to repeat a scurrilous comment because it was only hearsay: "As to what Mr. Regnier was said to have spoke concerning your Lordships Peerage, I had it from

Mr. Bickley, but he having it by hearsay, could not find the certainty thereof and therefore can trouble your Lordship no further with it." Not everyone was this fastidious, of course, and a good deal of hearsay made its way to London. The response of departmental functionaries was usually to log such letters according to their substantive content and to ignore the gossip in their answering correspondence.[15]

Still, once gossip entered the stream of discourse — whether "distilled malice" or "idle talk" — its potential for damage was real, the more so if it came in written form. And if an item of gossip happened to benefit a particular faction, as much of the early-eighteenth-century gossip did, one would be tempted to give it credence. Nonetheless, many officials honestly tried to divide truth from falsehood. Their first response was normally skepticism, as when the Board of Trade got word in 1706 that Cornbury was appointing unqualified men to office. "What truth there is in this complaint," the secretary noted, "your Lordship can best judge." With so much contradictory information coming in from factious New York and New Jersey, administrators sometimes let the reports balance each other out; at other times they sought further character evaluations from leading men. When the Anglican minister of Westchester County was accused of neglecting his parish — probably by Lewis Morris, who disliked him — the SPG first withheld his salary pending further inquiry and then adjudged the charges as groundless after Cornbury furnished the clergyman with a good character. When bureaucrats were forced to act despite conflicting reports, they sometimes issued two sets of instructions, as they did to Cornbury in 1704 — one order to be followed if a story were true, another to be implemented if it were false.[16]

Sometimes these three levels of information — from eye- and earwitness to the more or less reliable secondary source to the general rumor — were hopelessly mixed in together and required lively construing. Such was the case with a letter from Governor Bellomont to the bishop of London, in which Bellomont flayed Godfriedus Dellius, the Anglicizing minister of Albany's Dutch Reformed Church and one of the governor's political opponents:

> I gave the Lords of the Council of Trade and the rest of the Ministers formerly an account of the wickednesse of that man, of being a most impudent lyar in my own hearing, and his being a drunkard and im-

moral man as can be prov'd by the testimony of undoubted credible persons. . . . There is yet a further Article against Mr. Dellius . . . [a letter from a French woman who] laments the disgrace of being with child by Dellius. . . . The letter is fallen into the hands of Mr. Nucella a Dutch Minister, at a Towne called Kings Towne in the Province of New Yorke, and I believe I shall have a copy of it. I have an account of this letter by three or four several hands from New Yorke, so that I cannot doubt of the truth of their being such a letter. If Mr. Nucella will part with it, I will send your Lordship a copy of it, that you may be convinc'd of the lewdness of that Man.[17]

In Bellomont's communication, only the charge that Dellius was an "impudent lyar" is offered on personal, in this case earwitness, testimony, though the governor promises the bishop evidence from reputable secondary sources (fig. 42). As for the accusations of drunkenness, immorality, and fornication, these were nothing more than hearsay unless proved, though Bellomont, long at loggerheads with Dellius, undoubtedly thought them true. The putative letter from the French woman apparently was never sent and probably did not exist. The result was that the bishop of London, inured to rumors of this sort, saw no good reason to withdraw his support from Dellius.[18]

The flurry of correspondence about Cornbury's dispute with the ministers Moore and Brooke included everything from eyewitness testimony to the most general hearsay. Here, owing to the serious nature of the case and the loss of the two clergymen at sea, the SPG secretary made a special effort to obtain an accurate picture. He thanked one New York missionary for writing of Lord Cornbury's many services to the provincial Church of England, especially in view of the "different accounts we have lately had concerning the Conduct of that Noble Lord with regard to Mssrs. Brooks and Moore." He pleaded with the rector of Trinity Church, whom he knew and respected, to send "a fair and full account of the business of Mr. Brooke and Moore, which that you may do the more freely, your name if you desire it shall be concealed." And he asked Colonel Quary, who he believed would give the least biased report, to write of the affair with great freedom and plainness, assuring Quary that he could "stand behind the Curtain." The secretary already knew Quary had written to the bishop of London about the two ministers and

Figure 42. Richard Coote, Earl of Bellomont, Governor of New York, 1698–1701.
*Courtesy, the Fine Arts Library, Harvard College Library*

that the bishop as a consequence "lays the blame on those Gentlemen," but he obviously wanted his own firsthand intelligence. The secretary was wont to urge ministers under his charge, as a matter of conscience, to write him nothing "but what you yourself know to be strictly and Literally true." [19]

Yet if London officials tended to cock a skeptical eye at rumors emanating from America, the colonials were beset by fears that gossip and innuendo would wreak havoc on their careers and reputations. Missionaries of the SPG regularly pleaded with the society to disregard "secret insinuations," at least until those accused could respond to charges leveled against them.[20] Knowing that time and distance put them at risk, the colonials sometimes attempted to preempt complaints. Thus the rector of Trinity Church begged the bishop of London's secretary to "doe me all the good offices in your power: for I shall have need of it, being at such a distance from my Lords Presence, and deprived of the opportunitys of giving a speedy answer to complaints, and setting all matters in a clear light." Similarly, Lord Cornbury asked the Board of Trade in 1704 not to "let any reports or stories make any impression upon your Lordships to my disadvantage, till I may have opportunity to Justify myself." Samuel Vetch, leader of the expedition of 1709 to Canada, petitioned the secretary of state: "Should any thing to my prejudice be Insinuated to your Lordship or any of the Ministry (as I hope there never will) I only begg your Lordship and they will please to Suspend your opinion, until your Lordship allow me an oppertunity to answer for myself." Even that master manipulator of news, Lewis Morris, acknowledged that "the vast distance from England, the Difficulty that attends applications in Controverted cases, [and] the possibility (after all) of their being thought in the wrong, and of being misrepresented" was a constant hazard for the provincials. It is ironic that Morris then went on in the same letter to accuse Cornbury of dressing in women's clothes.[21]

No one was more aware of the difficulty of defending reputations from afar than Governor Cornbury. As he wrote his father and uncle when preparing at last to depart from New York, "[once arrived in London] I can vindicate myself from all the clamours raised against me soe clearly that the worst of my Ennemys will be ashamed of believing what a parcell of Wretches here have writ, and which the whole Country here knows to be false." Still, it was hard to be turned out of his government "upon the complaints of a few people who when the matter is well examined will be found to be *wicked liars.*" It seemed as if "a Porter in the streets of London is a happier Man than a *Gouvernor in America*," for a porter could gain a hearing for the worst of crimes, whereas a governor "shall be condemned upon bare allegations." A few years later, Governor Robert Hunter reached the same conclusion. Though he confided to his friend Jonathan Swift that he had been "used like a dog" in New York, Hunter despaired at the thought of "the intolerable drudgery of answering false and malicious accusations or frivolous complaints."[22]

### ALLEGATIONS OF CROSS DRESSING

We may now turn to the specific correspondence alleging that Governor Cornbury was a transvestite. It consisted, as previously noted, of four letters: one each from Robert Livingston and Elias Neau and two from Lewis Morris. Robert Livingston, proprietor of Livingston Manor in Albany County, returned to New York in September 1706 from a three-year stay in London (fig. 43). As he wrote the Treasury office in June 1707, he had recently paid a visit to New York City (probably abuzz with chatter about the New Jersey Assembly's anti-Cornbury *Remonstrance* of May 1707). While there he heard such extraordinary stories about Governor Cornbury "that I durst not attempt to give your honor an account of them as not being possible to be believed." Having thus relieved himself of responsibility for the gossip, Livingston was now free to pass it on. "'Tis said he is wholly addicted to his pleasure . . . his dressing himself in womens Cloths Commonly [every?] morning is so unaccountable that if hundred[s] of spectators did not dayly see him it would be incredible."[23] At no point in the letter does Livingston claim that he personally witnessed any of this, and he provides next to no details. Nor does he offer an authoritative source; he names not one of his "hundreds of spectators." He is relaying a rumor and is giving it as broad a foundation as he can.

The next two letters are from Cornbury's longtime political nemesis, Lewis Morris. The first, though undated, appears from internal evidence to have been written in late 1707, shortly after — or possibly immediately after — the ministers Moore and Brooke departed from New York. Addressed to the SPG, it contains a long harangue about Cornbury's

Figure 43. Robert Livingston. Artist unknown. 1718. Oil. *Reproduced from the original portrait by courtesy of Henry H. Livingston*

arbitrary rule. After claiming that the governor owed money to every-one, Morris pushes on: But "the Scandal of his life is . . . he rarely fails of being dresst in Women's Cloaths every day, and almost half his time is spent that way, and seldome misses it on a Sacrament day, was in that Garb when his dead Lady was carried out of the Fort, and this not pri-vately but in face of the Sun and sight of the Town. But I'll not enter into his Privacies, his publick Vices are scandalous enough." Morris then concedes that his complaints against Cornbury, "of whom many good men have given large Encomiums, is not perhaps a procedure of the greatest prudence, and insted of diminishing his Caracter may very much lessen my own." But so it must be, for "I have a greater regard to God than Man."[24]

Notable in this letter is the rapid fire of Morris's charges, apparently recorded in a state of some agitation. His verbs are active and he enlivens his story with a few details. There is also an odd contradiction: "his Pri-vacies," a reference to behavior that has just been depicted as occurring in public. Then, acknowledging the potential damage to his own repu-tation for making such charges, Morris professes to throw off all caution in the interest of performing his moral duty.

The second letter, directed to an official in the offices of state, is dated February 9, 1708. Following mention of Cornbury, Morris writes: "of whom I must say something which perhaps no boddy will think worth their while to tell, and that is his dressing publiqly in womans Cloaths Every day and putting a Stop to all publique business while he is please-ing himselfe with that peculiar but detestable magot."[25] Once again ele-ments within the sentence work against each other. The assertiveness of Morris's "I must say something" contrasts with the blurred introduction of the information itself, "that is, his dressing." Morris does not say, I must tell you this because I *saw* him so, or even that it came from an unimpeachable source. The passive construction "his dressing" avoids attribution and implicates nobody, least of all himself.

Another issue this letter raises is why no one should "think worth their while to tell" of the governor's peculiar habit. There are at least two possibilities. It could be that Morris is seeking to give the story an en-hanced plausibility by pretending to downplay its importance. Actually, Morris was in something of a box. If the governor's alleged cross dress-ing was "detestable" and interfered with his official duties, as Morris asserted, the reports about it should have been backed by depositions or a public remonstrance — as had been the case with the multiple charges against Governor Dudley of Massachusetts, with Governor Nicholson of Virginia when accused of involvement in a lover's scandal, and even with Peter Sonmans of New Jersey when charged with adultery. But since no proofs were offered regarding Cornbury's cross dressing, Morris's language may have been an attempt to justify the absence of such documentation. Or it might simply be reflecting another eighteenth-century colloquial form: it would not be "worth" telling London about Cornbury's cross dressing because the teller's own reputation might thereby be damaged.[26] Nonetheless, in this letter as in the other, Morris makes no claim of having himself seen the governor in women's clothes, offering as witnesses only "the Sun and sight of the town." Without firsthand testimony, depositions, or other "proofs," these charges, for all their passion, could not have been viewed in London as other than overheated hearsay.

The fourth letter, dated February 27, 1709, and evidently written in response to the SPG secretary's request for more information about Cornbury's dispute with the Anglican ministers Moore and Brooke, is from the New York catechist Elias Neau. After praising the two clergymen, Neau continues: "My Lord Cornbury has and dos still make use of an unfortunate Custom of dressing himself in Womens Cloaths and of exposing himself in that Garb upon the Ramparts to the view of the public; in that dress he draws a World of Spectators about him and consequently as many Censures, especially for exposing himself in such a manner all the great Holy days and even in an hour or two after going to the Communion." He later adds, "I am assured that he continues to dress himself in Womens Cloths, but now 'tis after the Dutch manner."[27]

This rather curious letter is no more specific than the other three except that it situates Cornbury's perambulations on the ramparts of the fort, a location somewhat removed from the public thoroughfares. Actually Cornbury could not have been parading the ramparts in any kind of dress in February 1709, for two months earlier, at the arrival of Governor Lovelace, he had moved out of the fort into a small house. Perhaps Neau was referring to a previous period, as is insinuated by his saying that Cornbury "continues" to dress as a woman. In any case Neau, like the others, claims no eyewitness authority; and he was merely "assured" by someone that in 1709 Cornbury was dressing in the Dutch manner.[28]

These letters, all written at roughly the same time, have certain qualities in common (though there is no evidence of collusion among the three men). None of the writers claims to have been a firsthand witness; no informants are named by any of the three (no "Gentlemen of undoubted Honour"); and each writer — even Morris, with his "I must say something" — is careful to minimize his culpability for the story he is passing on. That politics was the prime motivation is evident. By this very time, the whiggish leanings of the ministry were well known and Cornbury's recall to England was increasingly likely. Robert Livingston, in his letter, comes close to giving the game away: "I thought it my duty to give your honor a hint off affairs, since it was your desire, and I know you will *make Such use of it* as will be for her majesties honor and Service and *our advantage.*" [29] The channels chosen for transmitting the rumor were both prominent and varied — the Treasury, the offices of state, and the SPG, all having access to broad networks — and it would seem that the colonials, despite the vagueness of their sources, hoped their gossip about Cornbury would ripple outward to an ever-wider reception.

That the rumor made so little headway among the English at home is therefore of interest, especially considering what a morsel the transvestism of the queen's near relation should have been in a gossip-loving society.[30] It could be that the incompatibility of the story with Cornbury and his family's general reputation for probity, as discussed earlier, was enough to sink the rumor in all but the most ardent Whig circles. It does not surface in any of the pertinent English correspondence, gossip-filled diaries, manuscript newsletters, or Grub Street satires of the time. Only a single noncolonial contemporary mention has ever been located, the previously noted letter of 1714 by the Hanoverian diplomat H. C. von Bothmer, which denigrated the Tory Cornbury as a fool who dressed as a woman to represent the queen when governor of the "Indies." Bothmer, who was cultivating connections with the Whigs, must have got wind of the story from party gossips. Yet only Bothmer, who lacked an English frame of reference within which to evaluate it, credited the rumor to the point of committing it to paper.[31]

More surprising is that the gossip about Cornbury's cross dressing had little contemporary staying power in the colonies. The Boston merchant Samuel Sewall had heard about it but wanted confirmation. Writing to a friend in New York about the laws during Plato's time, Sewall noted: *"Muliebri Veste uti,* is instanced in as against the Law of Nature. It has been reported that a certain Gentleman at N. York used to Practice that abomination. I should be glad to know the certainty of it." So far as we know, the letter was never answered. Even in New York the rumor showed no disposition to travel beyond the circle of Cornbury's most resolute enemies, despite the claim in all four letters that he paraded publicly in women's dress and drew a "World of Spectators" about him. Those spectators all remain silent. But for the letters, Sewall's remark, and the passing allusion in Governor Hunter's play, *Androboros,* no other contemporary reference to Cornbury's cross dressing has been found in colonial sources. (These references have been known to historians for many years.) No local scandalmonger passed the story on; no political rival other than Morris, Livingston, and Neau wrote to any friend, foe, or family member about the governor's fondness for women's clothes. Even the most determined critics inside Cornbury's administration, Thomas Byerly and George Clarke, say nothing about it in letters that otherwise censure their governor. Perhaps most remarkable, from those in the best position to observe Cornbury regularly — the soldiers and officers who lived with him in the fort, on whose ramparts he supposedly made his shameless rambles — there is not a mention. The resident military chaplain, John Sharpe, who saw Cornbury frequently, went hunting with him, and dined with him periodically, made a point of taking Cornbury's part against Lewis Morris.[32]

But if this particular cross-dressing story now seems somewhat more questionable than we once thought, that the accusation should have been leveled at all remains as intriguing as ever.

### POSSIBLE SOURCES OF THE RUMOR

What, then, could be the origin of the cross-dressing rumor? One possibility is that Governor Cornbury acquired in the colonists' eyes a kind of symbolic femininity by virtue of his near relationship to Queen Anne. There can be no doubt that Cornbury's power was in significant part owing to that connection, a point he was all too ready to press on those around him. Peevish colonials such as Lewis Morris and his New Jersey supporters — already somewhat alienated from a queen whose royal charter they had come to see as harmful to their interests — might have turned the connection around, associating Cornbury with traits of weakness and incapacity often applied to eighteenth-century women, especially political women.[33]

But is it conceivable that Cornbury could have identified himself with Queen Anne to the extent of actually dressing like her on some occasion? Because it is impossible to prove a negative, this cannot absolutely be ruled out. Perhaps Lord and Lady Cornbury introduced the masquerade ball to New York's elite, and the governor, no stranger to the extravagant flourish, dressed up like Queen Anne. Or perhaps on some other private occasion Cornbury chose literally to embody the queen. How well such scenarios fit with the more rounded view of Cornbury's character and personality laid out in this book the reader will have to judge. It does seem most unlikely, however, that Cornbury would have risked undermining his authority by a *public* act of cross dressing. That the governor's provincial contemporaries might casually have passed off such a performance as a personal quirk is belied by their words. Robert Livingston found the rumor of Cornbury's cross dressing "so unaccountable . . . [as to] be incredible," and Lewis Morris scorned Cornbury's supposed transvestism as "detestable" and "the Scandal of his life." Samuel Sewall condemned it as an "abomination," and Elias Neau considered it a possible cause for excommunication from the Church of England.[34]

Perhaps a more plausible explanation lies in the symbolic realm, in a scheme whereby Cornbury's political opponents would signify their grievances with a satirical attack on the physical body of their governor. Symbolism is the life and breath of political satire, and the tradition of assaults on a leader's body was long familiar in Western satire, dating back at least to the Greek tyrant plays. Later, Shakespeare and such Jacobean playwrights as Francis Beaumont and John Fletcher drew on this tradition, which may have reached a pinnacle in the Restoration theater. The tyrant was represented on stage in terms of sexuality and gender, his sensual appetites often overwhelming that most cherished of faculties, reason. Fragmenting into multiple forms, he sometimes was dressed in women's clothes. "The tyrant's love of pleasure, his impulse to shift shapes," led to the enfeeblement of his claim to power and to the assertion that he had been "feminized" — the mirror opposite of "an idealized, rational masculine self." New Yorkers of both English and Dutch descent would have been familiar with this form of political satire. And Cornbury's prowess as a military man might have made him a particularly inviting target for the invective of gender inversion. Hence to charge Cornbury with cross dressing was to capture in one lurid symbol the very traits his enemies wished to fasten on him — weakness, corruption, and illegitimacy.[35]

Or there may be a simpler explanation for the rumor. Perhaps some of Cornbury's critics within the ruling circle finally wearied of his frequent invocation of Queen Anne's name. Thomas Byerly, New York's receiver of customs, who kept up a running dispute with the governor, reported in 1705 that Cornbury had emphatically declared during one interview that "as he was Governor[,] his power here was the same as the Queen's in England." As he left the room Byerly might have been heard to growl, "He clothes himself in the authority of the Queen."[36] And the rest, one might say, is "history."

# { 8 }  The Politics of Reputation

The dark legend that has long clouded Governor Cornbury's name was shaped by an unusually harsh political climate, one that contributed centrally to the hostility he and a number of other imperial officials aroused in certain circles. We have noted that the early eighteenth century was a time of intense political cross-currents in both the colonies and England, a legacy from the Glorious Revolution. Local factions in New York and New Jersey were especially strident, beset as they were by religious and ethnic rivalries, clashing interest groups, and the very newness of royal government. Cornbury governed during a transition from the older, elitist imperialism of Charles II and James II to the newer, bureaucratically driven imperialism of the later Stuarts and their Whitehall collaborators. Another transition taking place in these colonies was from a century of settlement and disarray to one of consolidation and rapid growth, which in turn would pose a number of challenges to the imperial connection.

Cornbury was at heart an old imperialist. Yet his attachment to Queen Anne and loyalty to her policies — even in an era of administrative reform — called for a degree of flexibility, or at least a willingness to listen, when colonial needs and grievances were aired. A deeper look into the politics of Cornbury's administration may tell us something about both the imperial relationship at a critical point of development and what is perhaps the most obscure element of this story, the motives of Cornbury's detractors.

## WAR AND INDIAN AFFAIRS IN NEW YORK

Leisler's Rebellion, brought to a melancholy close with the execution of its two leaders in 1691, left a deposit of bitter division in New York politics. On arriving at New York in May 1702, Governor Cornbury, as we have seen, undertook to implement his instructions by reaching out to all New Yorkers — regardless of party — who displayed a readiness to support the royal government. In spite of these good intentions, unfinished business from the Leislerian era kept pushing itself onto the political stage of factious New York. Not only was the colony deeply in debt; Cornbury also found his predecessor, Lieutenant Governor Nanfan, and his Leislerian allies implicated in the hasty passage of a series of bills designed to "tie up the hands of the succeeding Governor and make him their slave." Cornbury's natural sympathies, whatever his efforts toward a detached neutrality, were bound to go with the more metropolitan, Anglicized anti-Leislerians, sometimes called the "English party." [1] According to one member of that faction, Robert Livingston, Cornbury had declared within days of his arrival that "he never could have beleevd they [the anti-Leislerians] had been so much abused if he had not come upon that spott to receive information." He promptly replaced five of the most vehemently partisan councillors with men of more balanced views, and following an investigation he suspended from office the sitting chief justice. Whitehall promptly approved each action. [2]

To be sure, Cornbury's efforts to readjust the political scales as well as to shore up New York's defenses in a time of financial exigency did not please everyone. Some of those he ousted from office marked time brooding over their grievances and looking for ways to strike back. Robert Livingston, "a restless meddling man," according to one contemporary, feared early on that the governor was falling "into the hands of those who are strangers to the wellmanagment of our affairs and who greedily pursue their own interest." [3] When Connecticut declined to provide its quota for frontier defense and allegedly gave sanctuary to soldiers who deserted their posts at Albany, Cornbury warned Governor Fitz-John Winthrop: "I shall be forced to acquaint the government at home with these proceedings." Royal governors often suspected the proprietary and charter colonies of disloyal tendencies, and Cornbury was no exception. But in spite of some colonists' efforts to drive a wedge between Cornbury and Winthrop — by, among other things, spreading rumors that Cornbury sought control of Connecticut and Rhode Island through certain latent claims of Lady Cornbury and their son — the two governors maintained an outwardly correct, if cool, association.[4] Given the time and place, Governor Cornbury had on the whole made a strong beginning, though probably neither he nor anyone else could have made it a totally smooth one.

Cornbury's imperial impulse found its fullest expression in the leadership he gave in the vital matter of Indian policy on the northern frontier, which after 1701 had entered a delicate phase. Some Iroquois, following devastating losses in King William's War and doubts about England's readiness to field troops should fighting resume, had adopted a more neutral posture toward the French in Canada. Because Cornbury as a military man fully appreciated the importance of the Five Nations to the defense of the frontier, one of his first acts on arriving in New York, as we have seen, was to confer with the Indians at Albany. His objectives are clearly revealed in the record of that conference. Cornbury sought at the very least to sow distrust of the French. "I doe not design to trust them," he told the Five Nations on July 15, 1702, "neither would I have the Brethren doe it but be upon their Guard." At the best, he might strengthen the faction within the Five Nations that favored the English, most prominent among the Mohawks and Oneida, by restoring their confidence in England's firmness of purpose.[5]

In his opening speech to the Five Nations, Cornbury declared that he would not ask the tribes to expose themselves as the "first aggressors" in a war. But if the French attacked, "we must joyn unanimously and make warr upon them with all Vigor, and not make a lingring war as the former was." He then announced that he would rebuild New York's frontier forts, where, he told the Indians, "you and your Wifes and Children may retire in time of danger where you shall be succor'd and protected from all assaults of the Enemy." To demonstrate that these all too familiar pledges would at last be redeemed, Cornbury on August 15 laid the cornerstone for the new stone fort he was determined to build at Albany. Four days later two-thirds of the foundation had been completed, and he expected the walls to reach five feet in height before the first frost. This was the very proof the Iroquois and Hudson River Indians wanted of England's concern for their well-being, and it led them to praise the governor's justice, circumspection, and "Paternall care." Robert Quary confirmed that the new fort at Albany gave "great satisfaction to our Indians, who lay the great stress of their security on the defence of those forts." Even Robert Livingston agreed that in this case Governor Cornbury "by his prudence and conduct, has much contributed to the steadying and securing of the Indians of the Five Nations."[6]

With the advent of Queen Anne's War in 1702, the French in Canada chose not to challenge New York, realizing that any provocation on their part would risk retaliation by the Indians. And when (false) rumors of a French attack did begin to circulate in 1704, Cornbury discovered that "the Indians of the Five Nations were so ready that they all left their Castles and were coming towards Albany before I could send them any orders."[7] Checked on the New York frontier, the French and their Indian allies turned on New England, attacking the town of Deerfield, Massachusetts, in the winter of 1704, and killing some forty-two inhabitants. Lord Cornbury had given timely warning to Governor Dudley of Massachusetts that the enemy was preparing an attack, which intelligence he had received from "some spys which I have kept in the Indian Country, ever since the warr has been declared." But, as he ruefully noted later, the New Englanders were negligent and "did not keep guard soe carefully as they should have done."[8]

Following the assault on Deerfield, Governors Dudley and Winthrop, with Cornbury's consent, moved to strengthen their ties with the Iroquois. Winthrop also requested that Cornbury lead a joint expedition against Canada, now supporting a policy that the New York governor and other local imperialists had advocated for years. How much faith Cornbury put in Winthrop or the New England militia he does not say, but by late 1704 he had no doubt that a much larger force, including English regulars, would be required to take Quebec. This was owing to new intelligence, obtained perhaps by his "spys," that the French had recently made Quebec "much stronger than it ever was, and have erected very good Batteries along the Water-side." According to one authority on Queen Anne's War, "New York certainly was not neutral in spirit, but was politically sophisticated enough to believe that only a military force from England directed against Quebec could defeat the Canadians."[9]

Governor Cornbury continued to advocate such an expedition throughout his years in New York, just as he persisted in urging closer ties with all the northern tribes. After his final meeting as governor with the Five Nations in 1708, Cornbury noted with pleasure that the Far Indians, or Great Lakes tribes, were at last beginning to trade at Albany, a link he and royal officials before him had encouraged as a means of wooing them from the French. When in 1709 an attack on Quebec was finally put into motion, the projected campaign adhered closely to the plan former Governor Cornbury and other New York imperialists had long championed. But the promised British expeditionary force was never dispatched. When troops finally were sent from England in 1711, the ships transporting them foundered in the Gulf of Saint Lawrence, and the attack had to be aborted.[10]

Cornbury and his merchant-imperialist allies believed every citizen should support policies that in their eyes benefited the greater empire. Not all New Yorkers agreed, especially the more provincial-minded ones. But because criticism was necessarily muted during wartime (particularly before diversification of the ministry in 1706–1707), those opposed to Cornbury's Indian and military policies were forced to bide their time at the margins of New York politics.

### GOVERNOR AND ASSEMBLY: THE BALANCE OF POWER IN NEW YORK

Another sphere to which Cornbury brought a definite measure of stability was the executive's relationship with the New York Assembly (though stability no doubt translated as control to colonials who favored a weak executive and greater local autonomy). In spite of the sharp drop in revenues consequent on Queen Anne's War, the assembly voted funds for Cornbury's salary and administrative needs with little resistance. Most legislators also supported Cornbury's defense policies, raising taxes to repair frontier forts and to strengthen military installations that protected New York City and its harbor. Thus Robert Quary could report some thirteen months into Cornbury's administration that the assembly "have a very great honour and veneration for His Excellency." Still, as England moved in these reforming years to shift a rising share of local defense costs to the provincials, some assemblymen began to chafe at the limited authority they exercised over the colony's money. At the least, they believed the legislature should have a share in the oversight of defense funds raised through local taxes, a notion Governor Cornbury initially resisted.[11] Because not only power over the purse but matters of imperial ideology were at stake in this debate, it reveals much about each side's conception of empire in the first decade of the eighteenth century.

The assembly, when considering defense appropriations in June 1703, claimed the right to appoint its own treasurer to oversee funds raised from local taxes, a move historians conventionally attribute to fears aroused by Cornbury's supposed "mismanagement and corrupt use of the public money." Yet the assembly journal plainly shows that the legislature's request for its own treasurer was a direct consequence of "the great Neglect, ill Management, and Misapplication of the Revenue, by those who *lately* exercised the Power of Government" — that is, Cornbury's predecessors. There is no evidence that the assembly's request was intended as a criticism of the sitting governor. For that matter, throughout Cornbury's administration the New York Assembly's complaints about the mishandling of money were directed almost entirely against former governors or the local Receivers General, who oversaw customs receipts as well as the sums raised by taxes. As the assembly noted in 1705, "not one of them [the Receivers] as yet has been able to avoid a Suspension," owing to bureaucratic conflicts with the various governors. This made it almost impossible for the assembly to obtain a detailed accounting of how its tax moneys were being spent.[12]

Cornbury at first objected to the assembly's proposal for a treasurer as being contrary to his royal instructions, which it was. He also saw it as one more effort by a "sawcy" assembly to gain for itself "all the same powers and priviledges, that a House of Commons in England enjoys." A dangerous notion, since "the holding of General Assembly in these parts of the world, has been settled neither by Act of Parliament in England, nor by Act of Assembly here, . . . [and] is purely by the grace and favour of the Crown." Here we see Cornbury at the top of his imperial form, though he hastens to add: "I am not pleading for the laying aside of Assembly's, it is far from my thoughts, but I think it my duty to acquaint you with what I take to be the Queen's right, especially when Assembly's begin to be refractory." He then asks the Board of Trade for a ruling on the issue.[13]

At its next session in 1705 the house restated its demand for a treasurer to monitor defense funds and actually named a man to that office. Cornbury characterized the action as "down right obstinacy, and a design to throw off the authority of the Queen," though he attributed the assembly's temper to but a few "factious people in the house" who had been troubling government since long before his time. These same few had persuaded the assembly that the council had no right to amend money bills "because the Commons of England will not suffer the Lords to make any amendments to a Money Bill there." Regarding that claim, Cornbury wrote to Whitehall: "I hope I may be pardoned, if I declare my opinion to be, that all these Colloneys, which are but twigs belonging to the main Tree (England), ought to be kept intirely dependent upon and subservient to England." He then urged the queen to signify her pleasure regarding such innovations, else the assembly would "be claiming New Rights every day."[14]

Whitehall believed with Cornbury that the New York Assembly was more presumptuous than any of its colonial counterparts about encroaching on the royal prerogative. Yet now that the cost of defending the northern frontier was being shifted to the Americans, New York's cooperation was essential. The ministry finally agreed in February 1706 to let the assembly name its own treasurer for the single purpose of overseeing "extraordinary supplyes for particular uses," that is, tax money for defense — a concession Her Majesty's government no doubt found expedient in time of war. Even so, such treasurer was to be accountable not only to the assembly but to the governor and council as well. Thus, once again, the strategic importance of New York gained it special privileges; and from this modest beginning the assembly's power over the purse would widen steadily in the years ahead. But once London had spoken, Governor Cornbury — obedient servant of the crown that he was — supported the plan, even to the point of heartily endorsing the man chosen by the assembly as treasurer.[15]

Whether Cornbury knew that Lewis Morris had a hand in the legislators' reach for power is unclear, because he identified his opposition only as three New York assemblymen and the colony's rural English Dissenters, "who are in no wise fond of monarchy." Yet the ambitious Morris, having rehearsed his political talents in the rural precincts of New Jersey, now sought a larger stage, and it was he who had drafted the New York Assembly's complaint asserting that it would be "left in the Dark" without its own treasurer. Cornbury was aware that Morris claimed powers for the provincial assemblies similar to those enjoyed by the House of Commons and had often told him "that he was mistaken . . . [the assemblies' power being] noe more than what every Corporation in England has, that is, to make by-laws for the well-governing of that Corporation." This correction, Cornbury observed, "offended Mr. Morris very much."[16] Nonetheless Governor Cornbury and the New York Assembly, once the issue of the treasurer was resolved, settled into a fairly pacific relationship, leaving Morris to concoct gossip out of doors as he strove to mobilize support for Cornbury's recall.

In the end, of course, Lewis Morris and the proponents of legislative power prevailed. When the Whig Robert Hunter (fig. 44) was appointed governor of New York in 1710, Morris became his friend and closest adviser. Given Hunter's political leanings and the tendency of all new governors to blame their predecessors for whatever troubles awaited them, Morris must have found it easy work to implant the notion that the imperious Cornbury had been a force for ill in New York. The satirical play *Androboros*, already mentioned, was but one product of their partnership. A far more significant legacy was Hunter's acquiescence, after holding out for five years and falling deeply into debt, to a bill greatly expanding the assembly treasurer's authority over provincial expenditures. This innovation opened the way for a decisive shift of fiscal control — the famous power of the purse — from England to the province.[17]

By the time the bill reached Whitehall, George I and his Whig supporters were in charge, and the course of empire in North America was no longer so clear. Thus, in spite of protests from Cornbury and a number of the old imperialists, the bill was approved.[18] By then the impulse

Figure 44. Robert Hunter, Governor of New York and New Jersey, 1710–1719. Attributed to Sir Godfrey Kneller. Oil. © *Collection of the New-York Historical Society*

to reform colonial administration, as imparted to the government by appointees of William and Mary and Queen Anne, was spent, and the transition to the age of Walpole and "salutary neglect" was under way. Rightly or wrongly, the opportunity to set the empire on a solid constitutional foundation — so dear to the old imperialists — was lost.

THE ROYAL COLONY OF NEW JERSEY

If Governor Cornbury's administration in New York ran a relatively smooth course, given the turbulent conditions that had awaited him in 1702, such was not the case in New Jersey. That colony, which in the seventeenth century had been parceled out to favored courtiers and investors in a series of proprietary grants, was wracked by perennial quarreling among rival land claimants. By the turn of the eighteenth century a number of gentlemen proprietors, led by Lewis Morris, had concluded that surrendering their proprietary charters for a royal frame of government might be the only way to save New Jersey from being partitioned between Pennsylvania and New York. In the spring of 1702, Queen Anne granted a charter combining the proprietary entities of East and West Jersey into the single royal colony of New Jersey.

Though Lewis Morris had hoped that his initiative in moving New Jersey into the royal fold might lead to his appointment as governor, the queen instead bestowed that office on her cousin Lord Cornbury. Cornbury was thereby confronted with a formidable challenge: to establish royal government in a region already full of fracture lines — not only the division between East and West Jersey but also the ceaseless frictions and cross-purposes among Scots, Dutch, and English as well as among Calvinists, Quakers, and Anglicans.[19]

In the face of all this, Cornbury made an auspicious beginning. When he published the queen's commission at Perth Amboy on August 11, 1703, he was "mett with neere 400 horse, each party striving to outvie each other in their respects to my Lord." On repeating the ceremony at Burlington two days later, he was again met with "universal satisfaction." He sat with the council for six days, appointing justices of the peace, sheriffs, and militia officers, "all of which," it was reported, "his Lordship hath done to the generall satisfaction of all partys, by mixing them so equally that he left no room for murmure." At its first meeting the assembly invited trouble by laying a tax that, in Robert Quary's opinion, favored the rich at the expense of the "poor industrious farmers . . . of 100 or 50 acres." But Cornbury — who knew the assemblymen "better than they know themselves, and managed them accordingly" — steadily asserted royal authority, offering hope that the people would soon be "freed by His Excellency's good Government." It was Cornbury's "generosity and prudence," according to another observer, that gained him "the love and affection of those people."[20]

Respect perhaps, but "love and affection" from a people long accustomed to having their own way was probably pushing things. The barest outline of New Jersey's factious politics, described as "a phenomenon of fantastic complexity," is clue enough to the difficulty that any governor would have faced in imposing royal authority there.[21] Roughly speaking, four major interests contended for control under the late-seventeenth-century proprietary government. English proprietors opposed Scottish proprietors in East Jersey; in West Jersey it was Quakers against Anglicans.

When the two Jerseys were united under royal government in 1702, new coalitions formed. Lewis Morris, having helped obtain a royal charter favorable to the interests of the Scottish proprietors, was rewarded with a lenient tax on his currently held Jersey lands and a large tract of new land. Then in July 1703, shortly before Governor Cornbury published his commission, Morris was appointed sole agent for the West Jersey Society of Proprietors. This brought him into closer touch with that section's Quakers, important members of the proprietary council, whose cooperation he needed to arrange for orderly land sales in the western part of the province.[22] Thus did Lewis Morris, whose Welsh, English, and Anglican background might under slightly different circumstances have placed him in the party that was forming around Cornbury, become instead the spokesman for a Scottish-Quaker alliance whose economic self-interest and religious outlook made a confrontation with the new royal governor all but inevitable.

True, all parties initially hoped that the seeming continuation of substantial proprietary authority over land grants in the royal charter would join with orderly royal government to produce a stable and prosperous colony. But in no time at all the combined circumstances of the new charter's ambiguous language, and reformers in England who frowned on any sort of proprietary privilege, made it ever less likely that the fragile fabric would hold. Local indignation was directed particularly on two issues: the New Jersey Assembly's decision in 1704 to tax the proprietors' unimproved lands, and the royal government's questioning of Quaker privileges together with the imposition of fines on Friends who sought exemption from militia service. When in addition the assembly broadened the franchise to include all freeholders in New Jersey, the political control long enjoyed by the proprietors had been struck a mortal blow. To Lewis Morris all this seemed like a betrayal of the arrangement he had helped negotiate with the crown. Eyeing the nearest symbol of crown authority, Lord Cornbury — the very model of the Tory imperialist apparently determined to bring New Jersey into line with other royal colonies — Morris had concluded by late 1705 that the best interests of both New Jersey and himself depended on getting rid of Cornbury.[23]

## POLITICAL "CONNEXIONS"

Considering Cornbury's close relationship to Queen Anne, his ties to prominent politicians in England, and the Board of Trade's approval of his leadership in New Jersey, the maneuver Morris contemplated might seem foolhardy. Yet the political weather in England was changing. In the spring of 1704, Cornbury's influential Tory patron, the earl of Nottingham, secretary of state for the Southern Department, was replaced by the moderate Robert Harley. In addition, as the star of John Churchill, duke of Marlborough, rose following his great victory at the Battle of Blenheim in August 1704, that of his rival, Lord Rochester, Cornbury's uncle and patron, fell. As early as May 1706, Marlborough and Lord Treasurer Godolphin were considering Cornbury's replacement. Rochester, earlier pushed from his post as lord lieutenant of Ireland and never a favorite of Queen Anne, clung to power until 1707, when he was dismissed from the Privy Council. But Marlborough continued to fear and hate him, telling his wife, Sarah, that they should give Rochester "all the mortefications which with justice may be done." When Godolphin acquired control over the Treasury, the position of Cornbury's friend William Blathwayt was rendered extremely precarious, and in 1707, with more and more Whigs being appointed to office, Blathwayt was driven from his long-held seat on the Board of Trade. By 1706–1707, Cornbury's patrons at home as well as the Tory party as a whole were in such acute eclipse that former New York agent John Champante, who had been nursing a grudge against Cornbury since 1702, energetically undertook to organize the campaign in London for his removal.[24]

Champante was convinced that if Cornbury's colonial opponents would "exert themselves and make a regular and publick complaint they might be morally certain of success," for politically "there never was a better Board [of Trade] than there is now." "In Short," Champante told his provincial correspondent, "I believe there is nobody here Great or Small who is not very much inclined to believe the worst of [Cornbury]." Champante also expected support for Cornbury's recall from certain English merchants trading to the colonies and from a number of the London directors of the East and West Jersey proprietary societies.[25]

All those individuals, many of them Whigs who had been excluded from office when Anne ascended the throne, now had the chance to reclaim what they saw as their rightful place in government. But to protect the political position of these men in England, it was required that the provincials themselves initiate the process of Cornbury's removal. And, as Champante prodded his New York correspondents, "the more gentlemen that complain the better." New Yorkers were not, in fact, moved to prepare a formal complaint against their governor.[26] Yet it was this same atmosphere of contracting Tory power and reviving Whig energy that gave Lewis Morris the confidence to launch his assault on Cornbury's financial and moral reputation.

Knowing that it would be impossible to attack Cornbury publicly from his place on the New Jersey Council, Morris resigned his seat. Then early in 1707 he gained election to the New Jersey Assembly along with his fellow conspirator, the Quaker firebrand Samuel Jennings, who also had vacated his council seat and was now chosen speaker of the assembly. Morris and Jennings used the more popular legislative forum, by then in the hands of Cornbury's opposition, to resurrect the memory of the so-called blind tax of 1703 and its supposed use to bribe the governor (see chapter 4).[27] In May 1707, Morris and Jennings also devised and pushed through the assembly the formal *Remonstrance* enumerating their grievances against Cornbury, including charges that he had interfered with land titles and intermeddled with or caused delays in the operation of the courts. They next drew up a petition to Queen Anne in the assembly's name reiterating their dissatisfaction with Cornbury and "Throw[ing] themselves at your MAJESTIES Royal feet Imploring Your *Majestie* to Relieve them from the oppressions they groan under by the arbitrary and Illegal Practices of his said Excellencie," the substance if not the tone of which was approved by a majority of assemblymen. When Governor Cornbury sent a copy of the *Remonstrance* with his answer to the earl of

Sunderland in November, he observed that it was not in his power to cure the tendency to "Faction and Private animosity" of a people who had "lived so long in licentiousnesse." [28]

We can infer that at about this same time the opposition's rumor mill also was set humming, because the letters from Robert Livingston, Lewis Morris, and Elias Neau accusing Cornbury of wearing women's clothes were written between mid-1707 and February 1709. And, as noted earlier, Livingston's letter of June 2, 1707, to the politically astute William Lowndes at the Treasury specifically suggested that Lowndes make use of the story for "our advantage." [29] Clearly, Cornbury's recall would serve political purposes on both sides of the Atlantic.

Through all the smoke and fury of these times, a number of leading partisans seemed to sense that fundamental political, and even constitutional, issues hung in the balance. Some interests were convinced that the empire would prosper most if English rights and local incentives were expanded. Other interests, especially after the unification with Scotland in 1707, rejoiced in the prospect of a centrally regulated and strongly defended kingdom of Great Britain. These competing perspectives did not align themselves neatly as colonials versus mother country but fragmented along the multiple stress lines of an Atlantic-wide polity. In New York and New Jersey, both the Cornbury royalists and the Morrisites — believing the future direction of the empire to be at stake — could perceive themselves to be true patriots defending the moral high ground.

It is often written that Governor Cornbury had by 1707 alienated almost everyone in New Jersey and New York. In fact, he had many warm supporters in both colonies: crown officials, most Anglican clergymen and leading lay members, provincial advocates of the British imperial enterprise, interests opposed to the Jersey proprietors, and even ordinary folk. It was with genuine feeling that the seasoned crown officer Robert Quary denounced Morris, Jennings, the New Jersey Assembly, and their *Remonstrance* as "false malitious unjust and most barbarously rude." They "shewed their resentments by scandalous . . . libells, and all that malice with *the help of Hell* could invent." Chief Justice Roger Mompesson, who esteemed himself "happy in being . . . under a Governour, who always dos encourage the due Administration of justice, and never interposes, with the proceedings of the courts," joined Lieutenant Governor Ingoldsby, Quary, and six other members of the New Jersey Council in responding to the assembly's attack on Cornbury with their own address to the queen. The entire conflict, they protested, was owing to the "unaccountable Humours, and pernicious Designs of some particular men. . . . Mr. Lewis Morris and Mr. Samuel Jennings, a Quaker, men notoriously known to be uneasy under all Governments." [30]

In New York, too, the council stood by Lord Cornbury to the end of his administration. Rejecting opposition rumors that the governor had browbeaten them or had misused public funds, the council declared in October 1708 that "Freedom and Liberty of Debate, has always been allowed upon every Instance and Occasion to Every [council] Member"; nor had Cornbury "received any money out of the publick Revenue other than by Warrants past in Council in the usual manner." Other trusted supporters included Roger Brett, an English gentleman living up the Hudson River at Fishkill, New York City Mayor Ebenezer Wilson, Captain Robert Lurting, and Attorney General May Bickley. To be sure, councilmen and other officials in New York as in New Jersey were expected to support the government, and many were beholden to Cornbury for their appointments to office. Yet it was just such investments of interest — self-interest and often something more — that undergirded political attachments, whether to Cornbury or Morris, Court or Country. [31]

Cornbury also received support from the Anglican clergy throughout his administration and long after he departed the colony in July 1710. Eight leading ministers of the provincial church looked back in 1711 on Cornbury's time in office as something of a golden age, praising his devotion to Anglicanism in the face of petitions and complaints from his foes. The two New Jersey ministers, Thoroughgood Moore and John Brooke, were obvious exceptions to this support, as was the New York catechist Elias Neau — each man no doubt believed he had valid reasons for joining Lewis Morris and the opposition faction. But otherwise the Anglican clergy and most lay members aligned themselves with the governor. The Reverend Mr. Halliday, who succeeded Moore at Saint Mary's Church in Burlington, expressed the royalist party position when he noted with stern disapproval that Lewis Morris, the New Jersey Anglican proprietor George Willocks, and "their Sett" had joined with the Quakers to subvert both the Church of England and Cornbury's government.[32]

Perhaps least to be expected is the support Lord Cornbury received from persons of lesser rank, for popular appreciation of a royalist governor might strike the modern sensibility as disjunctive. Yet as one of Cornbury's critics fumed, it was astonishing "how fond [a] great part of these wretches are of their departed Earle."[33] Among the governor's most loyal defenders were Benjamin Ashe and a Captain Sims, men sufficiently identified with the Court faction to have their credit attacked as soon as Cornbury departed New York. The two men asked Cornbury to assist them at home in obtaining appointment as masters of attendance so they could "live in Spite of your Lordships Enemies." It made Ashe's "blood boyle" to see the opposition triumph. When a rumor circulated that Cornbury would be restored as New York's governor, Ashe prayed that it might be true; such a day would be "a very Joyfull one" to all his friends. Then there is a letter in 1714 from the minor placeman William Carter asking Cornbury — "my very good Friend here" — to support his reappointment as a customs collector at New York. Recalling that as governor Cornbury had built a fireplace in the Customs House to keep the men warm, Carter reported that Receiver of Customs Thomas Byerly had since usurped it for himself and the officers, leaving only two lower rooms for the customs men "to blow our fingers in." It is likely that Cornbury responded to these appeals, as he did to the plight of New York County Sheriff William Anderson when the opposition threatened to sue him for allowing Cornbury, on acceding to the earldom of Clarendon, to depart for England before discharging his debts.[34]

An incident that occurred in New Jersey on November 1, 1710, several months after Cornbury had left the colonies, captures something of the strength and breadth not only of Cornbury's supporters but of those who opposed him. On that day one Beyer Schermerhorn was drinking a glass of wine at a tavern in Perth Amboy. Among the assorted company in the room were Dr. John Johnston, Thomas Gordon, and other men identified with the Morrisite party. Schermerhorn — perhaps emboldened by drink — proposed that "my Lord Cornbury's good health be drank," to which Dr. Johnston replied, "I will drink no such health." When Schermerhorn insisted, Johnston declared that Cornbury was "a villain and a Rascall[,] whereupon the said Schermerhorn said[,] then we are both Rascalls." At this point, Johnston "gott up out of his Chair and gave the said Schermerhorn divers blows upon the face and Eyes that his Nose bled and his left Eye . . . was very black and swelled mightily." Johnston continued the beating "until some of his company took him the said Johnstone away." All this while the local constable, apparently sympathetic to Johnston's faction, sat idly at a table. When the constable later took Schermerhorn into custody, Schermerhorn protested that "he did not know that he had done any wrong." [35] Clearly, Johnston and Schermerhorn each passionately believed himself in the right about Cornbury. But the lack of parties or other systematic means for mediating such political conflicts meant that they often found expression in barroom brawls, slander, and character assassination.

The final scenes of vengeful warfare between Cornbury's opponents and supporters occurred after he had been replaced as governor, especially in New Jersey, where a political vacuum was created by the sudden death in May 1709 of his successor, Governor Lovelace. The Morrisites, as Councilman Peter Sonmans wrote Cornbury, made "a plain Declaration of Warr against the Council and all those who have had the honour of being esteemed or called your Lordships friends," loading Cornbury and his followers with "personall and shameful Crimes." The Morrisites also sought to prevent Lieutenant Governor Ingoldsby from assuming the acting governorship of New Jersey, claiming that right for Morris as senior councillor, he having rejoined the council after Cornbury's departure. And in 1710 they greeted Governor Robert Hunter with an address that denounced the Court party and specifically catalogued Cornbury's vices, among them avarice, arbitrary rule, and "the Depravity of his Nature." [36] Not to be outdone, the pro-Cornbury majority on the New Jersey Council leveled its guns at Lewis Morris, urging the attorney general to prosecute him for "high Crimes and misdemeanours" for "unlawfully assuming to himself the title of Governor of this Province [following Lovelace's death] and for breaking open a packet from the Queen," pending which Ingoldsby suspended Morris from the council. [37]

In June 1710, newly arrived Governor Robert Hunter noted that forces favorable to Lord Cornbury still controlled not only the New Jersey Council but the New York General Assembly. [38] And the Morrisites warned that no "Liberties or Properties [would be] safe" until such men were removed. Councilman Daniel Coxe of New Jersey had seen as early as 1709, however, that the real battle for political supremacy should be waged in England. Since "Morris and his Tools" were now ascendant with the Board of Trade, Coxe did his best to denigrate that party among his English acquaintances, writing to one sympathetic proprietor that Morris's second-in-command in the New Jersey Council was "poor Ignorant George Deacon the miller . . . [who] can scarce say bo to a Goose." Moreover, the latest "masterpiece of Mr. Morris and that Confederate Gang" was to pack a grand jury at Perth Amboy and deliver up indictments against such Cornbury friends as Peter Sonmans, Jeremiah Basse, and "honest Bickley," the attorney general. Thus did the Morrisites (and the Cornburyites as well) go about "murdering the Reputation and good names" of their enemies.[39]

## A NEUTRAL OBSERVER TAKES CORNBURY'S MEASURE

With factional fighting so vicious during these years and charges on both sides so unbridled, it would be of value to find some contemporary of Cornbury who could assess his character from a relatively impartial point of view. James Logan, William Penn's secretary and resident representative in Pennsylvania since 1699, who was also a close observer of politics in New York and New Jersey, may have been just such a person. A number of qualities allowed Logan to maintain a fairly balanced view of Governor Cornbury and his administration. He was a moderate in politics, a substantial landholder, an ally of the large Quaker merchants, and an admirer of an imperial order that protected property while guarding traditional English liberties. At the same time he was a member of the Society of Friends, sympathetic to the Quakers' special concern for religious freedom, and dedicated to William Penn's proprietary charter as the best instrument for governing Pennsylvania.[40]

We have already seen that Logan was deferential toward the English aristocracy, specifically the queen's first cousin; balancing this was an equal deference toward the wishes of William Penn, who feared that Cornbury's strong attachment to royalist principles might pose a threat to proprietary Pennsylvania. Perhaps most important was Logan's mild temperament and rational mien, as well as a sufficient political experience to make him wary of partisan rumors and gossip.

All of this prepared Logan to greet Governor Cornbury's arrival in the colonies with a certain equanimity. In June 1702, Logan noted that Cornbury offered "Great Civilities" to New Jersey's leaders, that he was critical of excessive Anglican "Warmth" in Pennsylvania, and that the Quakers appreciated Cornbury's "Excellent Temper" while New Yorkers "Look on him as their Savior." In January 1703, the first doubts crept into Logan's letters to Penn after he heard that Lewis Morris's commission to be governor of the now royal colony of New Jersey was "stopt by Lord[s] Rochester and Clarendon in behalf of Lord Cornbury," whose appointment Logan seems not to have anticipated. "Lord Cornbury I perceive is a Courtier from whom fair words are Common[;] few of them I know are Sincere but he has a good Stock." Six months later he writes: "P[aroclus] Parm[yter] [a naval officer] . . . affirms Lord Cornbury is in the wrong Interest for this place [Pennsylvania] notwithstanding professions. He desires this government to be annexed." But, Logan adds, Parmyter "is not in favour with Lord Cornbury which makes his Information the less certain but it may be too true."[41]

Logan was apparently among those in attendance when Cornbury published his commission for New Jersey, for in describing the governor's response to addresses in his honor Logan noted that Cornbury was "very good at Extemporary Speeches." Afterward Cornbury traveled to Philadelphia, where Logan sought and followed his advice regarding a legal matter. He also, however, wrote to Penn in September 1703: "Tis now but too Manifest I think that he Designs to have this Government (if it be Effected) annexed to his." He further noted that Lewis Morris now "hates him and all his Party." Many men in East Jersey and New York "would be glad the Queen his Cousin would be graciously Pleased to give him a better Post Nearer home," added Logan, continuing, "for though really a Man of good Parts himself he has not one such about him[.] [B]esides that a great Man has great Necessities." This last simply acknowledged that a peer cost more than a commoner to support in a governorship. A year later Logan scotched a report that Cornbury would claim Pennsylvania's lower counties for royal government; when he traveled to New Castle to investigate the rumor, he "found nothing like what had been so freely talked of."[42]

When the New Jersey Assembly presented its *Remonstrance* to Governor Cornbury in May 1707, Logan was clearly distressed. "It was drawn by Lewis Morris, 'tis said," but styled in "Friends Language, which I think was very Indiscreet," he informed Penn. And if "there are some things that Nobleman has doubtless overstrained," Logan feared that in England the opposition's complaints would cast odium on the Quakers in both New Jersey and Pennsylvania. "I discoursed Samuel Jennings closely as to this purpose the day before their Assembly mett, but his head strong temper will never admitt a Rein." Penn himself was always more skeptical of the Middle Colony royalists than was Logan, who dealt regularly with "honest Col. Ingoldsby" and Colonel Quary, whom he "ever found . . . true here to what he professed."[43]

In 1709, James Logan looked back on "the time the Lord Cornbury so widely differed with the Assembly of Jersey, whose treatment of him as their Governour (whether in the Right or Wrong in other points) was certainly Scurrilous and provoking." Colonel Quary's report to London on the episode was undoubtedly severe, Logan conceded, but "the Provocations on our side were so great that it was exceeding difficult for any man of sense . . . not to lay them out in their proper Colors."[44] That Logan found the treatment of Cornbury "Scurrilous" — that is, indecent and vulgar — while also remaining critical of Cornbury's royalist policies, shows a balance of judgment and restraint of partisanship rare for his time.

# { 9 }   An Age of Scurrility

On September 5, 1709, Daniel Parke, royal governor of the British West Indian Leeward Islands, was shot in the arm during a failed assassination attempt. The assassin had been hired by a wrathful local opposition of gentry and merchants who detested Governor Parke and his royalist policies as destructive of their private interests. A year later, Parke's enemies, armed and backed by a mob, confronted him openly at government headquarters, demanding he resign on the spot. The governor resisted, shots were fired, and Parke took a musket ball in the thigh. As the wounded governor lay bleeding, begging for water and mercy, the mob, according to one account, "tore off his cloaths, draged him by the members about his house, bruised his head, and broke his back with the butt end of theire pieces." Two hours later, Parke was dead.[1] Considering what happened to Parke, his contemporary Governor Cornbury may not have fared so badly after all, Cornbury's political enemies being content merely to assassinate his character.

The abuses suffered by Cornbury, Parke, and other royal governors at the hands of provincials in the late seventeenth and early eighteenth centuries reflected the seething volatility of imperial relations in a time of political innovation, administrative transformation, and pervasive anxiety. Only in the past quarter-century have scholars come to appreciate fully the dizzying series of changes that overtook England in late Stuart times. Political nerves were chronically exposed in an Anglophone society still rocking from a half-century of upheaval that began and ended with revolution. These unsteady conditions — in the absence of a systematic ideology of party to channel and legitimate opposition to government — led, as argued here, to a politics of slander and sexual innuendo and to the emergence of a rough-hewn Country attitude.

The shrill debates among Whigs, Tories, Jacobites, and a welter of subfactions following the Revolution of 1688–1689 might in any case have prompted an explosion of scurrilous political rhetoric. The simultaneous emergence of the Grub Street press guaranteed it. Grub Street recast political communication by enlarging the audience for gossip and scandal about the great and by packaging its revelations in pungent prose that entertained as well as informed. These combined to spark new fears about the evils of concentrated power and the manipulation of hidden interests, central components of opposition thought. The Country vocabulary of virtue — and of malice and conspiracy — hung heavily in the very air.[2]

But how does this emergent opposition mentality fit with, or illuminate, the politics of early-eighteenth-century colonial America? Though the colonists may have lagged behind in sophistication, they were by this time increasingly aware of the political currents of the English-speaking world and of the Atlantic world at large. Travel back and forth across the ocean became more regular following the Glorious Revolution. Commerce, immigration, and the rise of transatlantic interest groups made for significant channels of communication, as did the trade in English-language books, pamphlets, and newspapers.[3] Lewis Morris borrowed words and phrases from the English satirists of the late seventeenth and early eighteenth centuries to liven his attacks on Governor Cornbury. The clique bent on calumniating Cornbury was sure to have had some familiarity with Grub Street as well, given their transatlantic travels and high literacy. Nor could they have been ignorant of the Western tradition of subverting a leader's authority by ridiculing his sexual person. With the arrival in 1710 of Governor Robert Hunter — friend of Swift, Addison, and Steele — came the "freshest advices" regarding the gyrations of political life at home, and it was in these very years that the Cornbury legend took permanent shape.

In one sense all the colonists were, by their very location, of the Country persuasion, predisposed as they were to see any executive person sent from England as a potential threat to local interests. And if the royal governors in fact exercised only a pale semblance of executive power, the forces that tended to weaken their authority did not bear on all colonies equally.[4] New York, in particular, was a special case, one with at least some approximation of a Court-Country equilibrium. It was the only mainland colony with a "standing army" (and a heavy land tax to support it), a fact of life that New Yorkers endured with no more than moderate grumbling in view of the frequency with which their physical safety was threatened from French Canada. New York was also the center of imperial diplomacy, the prime focus of the Church of England's missionary efforts in the North, and a commercial colony of rising importance. In each of these roles New York attracted British officials and a certain influence, and the colony's governors, in turn, became something of a rallying point for local men of ambition. But the governors and their company of "courtiers," as they were sometimes called, also became targets for other ambitious men who stood outside the circle of power. As those opposing the governors came increasingly to be centered in the assembly, fierce struggles arose from time to time between executive and legislature.

Cornbury, an old imperialist and staunch believer in prerogative power, held off the local opposition forces with some success. But in later years, executive authority was compelled periodically to make strategic retreats. Where the preponderance of power might lie during any given administration depended on a number of ingredients: the political skills and "interest" of the governor, the determination and political talents of his opponents, the presence or absence of war, the expedients of metropolitan politics. Setting aside our inherited whiggish historical formulas, we might discern — in place of the truisms of "salutary neglect" and thereafter a linear shift of loyalty from governors to colonial assemblies — a more complex, more interesting, and conceivably more lifelike pattern in Americans' attachment to royal government. As Gordon Wood has reminded us, there were many diverse reasons for provincials to value their bond to crown and empire.[5] What role, it might be asked, did the circles of colonial courtiers play in rallying support for imperial ambitions? Did they, as true Anglo-Americans, act as mediators during times of tension between colonies and mother country?[6] A detached examination of those who supported the colonial governors as well as of the opposition forces that intermittently rose against them might reveal new contours, new patterns of ebb and flow, to the colonists' loyalty to Britain — a loyalty that, on the part of considerable numbers, persisted to the very outbreak of the Revolution, and in many a case well beyond.

Cornbury's governorship, of course, took place at an earlier, less mature period of imperial politics when matters of the gravest significance — touching on the very survival of civil and religious institutions — appeared to be at stake. And it was in the recently royalized colonies over which Cornbury presided that the boldest experiments in imperial reform and Anglicization were undertaken. Accordingly, the uses to which the Country persuasion could be put in British America were perhaps most fully played out in the factious politics of New York and New Jersey. Lewis Morris and his set — caught up in the conspiratorial imaginings and partisan passions of late Stuart politics, acquainted with the techniques of Grub Street, and fully at home in an age of gossip and sexual defamation — aspersed Governor Cornbury with an abandoned ferocity. These contentions occurred at a time when a generally accepted logic of organized opposition lay far in the future, a time when party and faction were still universally condemned as reprehensible and wicked.

Yet in fact far more wicked was this poisonous setting wherein individuals were largely limited to going after individuals, wherein politics was personalized and reduced to slander, libel, and the destruction of reputations — to "Smut and Satyr," as one contemporary put it.[7] It was the bad historical destiny of Lord Cornbury to have been a prime victim of the Country impulse in its earliest, crudest, most ruthless stage.

# Abbreviations

| | |
|---|---|
| BL | British Library, London |
| Bodl. Lib. | Bodleian Library, Oxford |
| CO | Colonial Office |
| *CSPC* | Great Britain, Public Record Office, *Calendar of State Papers, Colonial Series, America and West Indies*, 35 vols., ed. W. Noel Sainsbury et al. (London, 1860–1939) |
| *CSPD* | Great Britain, Public Record Office, *Calendar of State Papers, Domestic Series* |
| | *Charles II*, 28 vols. (London, 1860–1938) |
| | *James II*, 2 vols. (London, 1960–1964) |
| | *William and Mary*, 5 vols. (London, 1895–1906) |
| | *William III*, 6 vols. (1908–1937) |
| *DHNY* | *The Documentary History of the State of New-York*, ed. E. B. O'Callaghan, 4 vols. (Albany, 1849–1851) |
| *DNB* | *Dictionary of National Biography* |
| *Eccl. Recs.* | *Ecclesiastical Records of the State of New York*, 8 vols. (Albany, 1901–1916) |
| HHV | Historic Hudson Valley, Tarrytown, N.Y. |
| HL | Huntington Library, San Marino, Calif. |
| HMC | Historical Manuscripts Commission |
| HSP | Historical Society of Pennsylvania, Philadelphia |
| JCBL | John Carter Brown Library, Providence, R.I. |
| LOC | Library of Congress, Washington, D.C. |
| MHS, *Colls.* | Massachusetts Historical Society, *Collections* |
| MHS, *Procs.* | Massachusetts Historical Society, *Proceedings* |
| *NJA* | *New Jersey Archives: Documents Relating to the Colonial History of the State of New Jersey*, 1st Ser., ed. William A. Whitehead et al., 37 vols. (Newark et al., 1880–1942) |
| *NYCD* | *Documents Relative to the Colonial History of the State of New-York*, ed. E. B. O'Callaghan and Berthold Fernow, 15 vols. (Albany, 1856–1887) |
| NY Col. Mss. | New York Colonial Manuscripts, New York State Library, Albany |
| NYHS | New-York Historical Society, New York City |
| NYPL | New York Public Library, New York City |
| NYSL | New York State Library, Albany |
| PC | Privy Council |

| | |
|---|---|
| PRO | Public Record Office, London |
| SP | State Papers |
| SPG | Society for the Propagation of the Gospel in Foreign Parts |
| T | Treasury |
| *WMQ* | *William and Mary Quarterly* |

# Notes

INTRODUCTION

1. Tim Harris, *Politics under the Later Stuarts: Party Conflict in a Divided Society, 1660–1715* (New York, 1993); Gary Stuart De Krey, *A Fractured Society: The Politics of London in the First Age of Party, 1688–1715* (Oxford, 1985); J. R. Jones, *Country and Court: England, 1658–1714* (Cambridge, Mass., 1978). And see Gordon S. Wood, "Conspiracy and the Paranoid Style: Causality and Deceit in the Eighteenth Century," *WMQ,* 3d Ser., XXXIX (1982), 401–441.

2. Exemplary studies in these areas include Harris, *Politics under the Later Stuarts;* W. A. Speck, *The Birth of Britain: A New Nation, 1700–1710* (Oxford, 1994); John Brewer, *The Sinews of Power: War, Money, and the English State, 1688–1783* (New York, 1989); and Lawrence E. Klein, *Shaftesbury and the Culture of Politeness: Moral Discourse and Cultural Politics in Early Eighteenth-Century England* (Cambridge, 1994).

3. William Smith, Jr., *The History of the Province of New-York: From the First Discovery to the Year 1732* (1757), ed. Michael Kammen, 2 vols. (Cambridge, Mass., 1972), I, 117–130; James Grahame, *The History of the United States of North America,* 4 vols. (Boston, 1845), II, quotation on 250; James Grant Wilson, *The Memorial History of the City of New York,* 4 vols. (New York, 1892–1893), II, 88 (the chapter on Lord Cornbury, 55–92, was written by William L. Stone).

4. George Bancroft, *History of the United States from the Discovery of the American Continent,* 19th ed., III (Boston, 1866), 60; William Wilson Manross, *A History of the American Episcopal Church* (New York, 1935), 117; Hugh Edward Egerton, *A Short History of British Colonial Policy* (London, 1897), 112. For other 19th-century accounts, see Agnes Strickland, *Lives of the Queens of England,* 12 vols. (London, 1820–1847), XII, 132; and Lord Mahon [Philip H. Stanhope], *History of England from the Peace of Utrecht to the Peace of Versailles, 1713–1783,* 3d ed., I (London, 1853), 79.

5. Ormonde de Kay, Jr., "His Most Detestable High Mightiness," *American Heritage,* XXVII, no. 3 (April 1976), 60–61, 89; The *Daily News* story, June 19, 1988, is an excerpt from a book by Shelley Ross, *Fall from Grace: Sex, Scandal, and Corruption in American Politics, from 1702 to the Present* (New York, 1988), whose tales of sexual misconduct in American public life begin with Cornbury. Cornbury has recently been depicted in another popular genre, the comic strip; see Patrick M. Reynolds, *Big Apple Almanac* (Willow Street, Pa., 1989–), I, 33–34.

6. Leonard Woods Labaree, *Royal Government in America: A Study of the Brit-

*ish Colonial System before 1783* (New York, 1958), 42; the second quotation is from Stephen Saunders Webb, "William Blathwayt, Imperial Fixer: Muddling through to Empire, 1689–1717," *WMQ*, 3d Ser., XXVI (1969), 412. An early skeptic, Charles Worthen Spencer, noted that the vehemence with which historians write about Cornbury "might easily prompt the stirrings of doubt." Yet after completing his own investigation of the then-available evidence, Spencer concluded that "enough remains of the legend to entitle it substantially to acceptance." "The Cornbury Legend," New York State Historical Association, *Proceedings*, XIII (1914), 309–320.

7. The letters forwarding the cross-dressing rumor are Robert Livingston to [William] Lowndes, New London, June 2, 1707, T 1/102, fols. 130–131, PRO (microfilm), HHV; Col. [Lewis] Morris to the Secretary concerning the State of the Church in New York and the Jerseys, [late 1707–early 1708], SPG, Letterbook C, I, no. 2 (microfilm); Lewis Morris to Secretary of State, New York, Feb. 9, 1708, in Eugene R. Sheridan, ed., *The Papers of Lewis Morris*, 3 vols. (Newark, N.J., 1991–1993), I, 78; Elias Neau to the Secretary, New York, Feb. 27, 1709, SPG, Letterbook A, IV, 402–413. The published memoir, in Julia Delafield, *Biographies of Francis Lewis and Morgan Lewis*, 2 vols. (New York, 1877), I, 205, 206, is based on the manuscript memoir recently deposited at Princeton University (see Edward Livingston Papers, Series VI, box 113, fols. H and I, Rare Book Room, Princeton University Library).

8. Gertrude Van Cortlandt Beekman (1688–1777) might have "inherited" a grudge against Cornbury from her mother, also named Gertrude (1654–1719). Shortly after Cornbury arrived in New York in 1702, the senior Gertrude applied to him for £1,386 she claimed was owed to the estate of her deceased husband, Stephanus Van Cortlandt, victualer to the New York regiment during Governor Bellomont's administration. Such reimbursement — always subject to long delays, especially when the debt was contracted by a prior administration — was further complicated in this case by the widow's acknowledgment that she possessed no warrants proving the expenditures; NY Col. Mss., XLVI, fols. 79a, 79b (2), 81 (1), NYSL. She later wrote William Blathwayt at the Board of Trade that she had begged Cornbury to pay the money "Due to a wedew and So much fatherles Children." Gertrude Van Cortlandt to Blathwayt, New York, Apr. 24, 1704, BL 153, HL.

9. Richard Hofstadter, noting that "political discussion in eighteenth-century England and America was pervaded by a kind of anti-party cant," quotes Jonathan Swift as writing, "Party is the madness of many, for the gain of the few," in *The Idea of a Party System: The Rise of Legitimate Opposition in the United States, 1780–1840* (Berkeley, Calif., 1969), 2.

10. H. T. Dickinson, "The Precursors of Political Radicalism in Augustan

Britain," in Clyve Jones, ed., *Britain in the First Age of Party, 1680–1750* (London, 1987), 72; and Dickinson, *Liberty and Property: Political Ideology in Eighteenth-Century Britain* (London, 1977) (for William's army, see 105; the quotation is on 106–107). See also P. G. M. Dickson, *The Financial Revolution in England: A Study in the Development of Public Credit, 1688–1756*, 2d ed. (Aldershot, Hampshire, 1993), 24–29; and Brewer, *Sinews of Power*.

11. For the connections between moral reform, religion, and the Country persuasion, see David Hayton, "Moral Reform and Country Politics in the Late Seventeenth-Century House of Commons," *Past and Present*, no. 128 (August 1990), 48–91. Especially pertinent to this study is Hayton's assertion that among post-Revolution politicians "the imagery through which corruption was denounced was often sexual" (84). For both Whigs and Tories' being represented in the Country opposition, see 77–79. Another useful discussion of the Country mentality is Colin Brooks, "The Country Persuasion and Political Responsibility in England in the 1690s," *Parliaments, Estates and Representation*, IV, no. 2 (December 1984), 135–146. My emphasis falls on the pessimistic and mistrustful strands of early Country thought, and particularly on the fear that the state was being subverted by corrupt and immoral placemen.

12. Daniel Coxe to [William Dockwra], Burlington, N.J., Jan. 17, 1709, HM 22302, HL.

13. Dickinson, *Liberty and Property*, 93; Brewer, *Sinews of Power*, 155–161. Earlier scholars writing about the Country mentality focused primarily on its intellectual genealogy and deployment after 1715 at the higher levels of government. Especially pertinent to imperial political history are J. G. A. Pocock, *The Machiavellian Moment: Florentine Political Thought and the Atlantic Republican Tradition* (Princeton, N.J., 1975); Bernard Bailyn, *The Ideological Origins of the American Revolution* (Cambridge, Mass., 1967); and Gordon S. Wood, *The Creation of the American Republic, 1776–1787* (Chapel Hill, N.C., 1969). For a concise synthesis of the Court-Country polarity and a comparison of its functioning in Hanoverian England and in colonial and early republican America, see Stanley Elkins and Eric McKitrick, *The Age of Federalism* (New York, 1993), 4–18.

14. It was the very incivility of such political rhetoric, prompted in part by the post-Revolution emergence of the Whig Junto and then by the Tory resurgence under Queen Anne, that led to the concerns about civic discourse explored by Klein in *Shaftesbury and the Culture of Politeness*.

15. James Logan to William Penn, July 9, 1703, James Logan Letterbook, I, 104, HSP.

16. For attitudes toward the empire in the early 18th century, see Eric Hinderaker, "The 'Four Indian Kings' and the Imaginative Construction of the First British Empire," *WMQ*, 3d Ser., LIII (1996), 487–526. Gordon S. Wood sees

Franklin as a complete imperialist and Anglophile in the 1750s and early 1760s; in *New York Review of Books*, June 6, 1996, 48–49.

## CHAPTER ONE

1. Francis Bickley, ed., *The Diaries of Sylvester Douglas (Lord Glenbervie)*, 2 vols. (London, 1928), I, 76–77 (Oct. 9, 1796).

2. For Walpole quotation, see Peter Sabor, "Horace Walpole as a Historian," *Eighteenth-Century Life*, XI (1987), 5. Sabor concludes that Walpole's primary interpretive aim as a historian "was to be original, tendentious, and, above all, interesting" (8). Bickley, ed., *Diaries of Douglas*, I, vii; *Dictionary of National Biography* (hereafter *DNB*), LXI, 400–401; John Heneage Jesse, *Memoirs of the Court of England: George Selwyn and His Contemporaries*, I (Boston, 1843), esp. 121–159.

3. Williams's father, William Peere Williams, died in 1736, when his son was either 16 or 17 years of age (*DNB*, LXI, 469–470). Gerald Howson, *Thief-Taker General: The Rise and Fall of Jonathan Wild* (London, 1970), 62–63; Randolph Trumbach, "London's Sodomites: Homosexual Behavior and Western Culture in the Eighteenth Century," *Journal of Social History*, XI (1977–1978), 1–33.

Cornbury's London residence at the time was Somerset House, a former royal palace, whose windows were at a safe remove from the public gaze. Raymond Needham and Alexander Webster, *Somerset House, Past and Present* (London, 1905).

4. Whether Sandys's letter was written before or after Williams's visit to Worcestershire is unknown. The letter is included in Musgrave's manuscript catalogue, "Painted Portraits in Many of the Publick Buildings and Capital Mansions of England," Add. Mss. 6391, fol. 239, BL.

An inventory of furnishings, including paintings, at the Pakington estate in 1786 makes no reference to a Clarendon painting; see Hampton Collection, accession no. 4739, parcel I (viii), fol. 1 (microfilm), Worcestershire Records Office, Worcester, England.

5. The most thoroughly researched biography is Gary Kates, *Monsieur d'Eon Is a Woman: A Tale of Political Intrigue and Sexual Masquerade* (New York, 1995); see also Kates, "D'Eon Returns to France: Gender and Power in 1777," in Julia Epstein and Kristina Straub, eds., *Body Guards: The Cultural Politics of Gender Ambiguity* (New York, 1991), 189. Consult with some caution Cynthia Cox, *The Enigma of the Age: The Strange Story of the Chevalier d'Eon* (London, 1966); and Marjorie Garber, *Vested Interests: Cross-Dressing and Cultural Anxiety* (New York, 1992), 259–266. The chevalier's published memoirs are in significant part spurious; see Antonia White, trans., and Robert Baldick, intro., *Memoirs of Chevalier d'Eon* (London, 1970), xiv; and J. Buchan Telfer, *The Strange Career of the Chevalier D'Eon de Beaumont* . . . (London, 1885).

6. Lynne Friedli, "'Passing Women' — A Study of Gender Boundaries in the Eighteenth Century," in G. S. Rousseau and Roy Porter, eds., *Sexual Underworlds of the Enlightenment* (Chapel Hill, N.C., 1988), 245; Cox, *Enigma of the Age*, 84, 126– 127, 132–133. For these duels the chevalier is said to have been garbed either as a woman or in the uniform of a dragoon (ibid., 126–127). The British Library possesses putative journals and letterbooks of d'Eon in which he is alternately addressed as "Chevalier" or "Mademoiselle"; see Add. Mss. 29993, 29994.

7. The description, though slightly altered for the label, is attributed to Agnes Strickland (*Lives of the Queens of England*, 12 vols. [London, 1847], XII, 132). The New-York Historical Society added its own descriptive label in 1995 indicating that the identity of the sitter has been challenged; it reads: "Unidentified artist, early 18th century. *Edward Hyde (Viscount Cornbury) (1661–1723)*. Oil on canvas. Purchase 1952.80. The name of Edward Hyde, Viscount Cornbury, royal governor of New York Colony (1702–1708), was first associated with this portrait at the end of the 18th century. Recent research done on the painting has called the identity of the sitter into question."

8. Baron von Bothmer to Jean de Robethon, The Hague, June 16, 1714, Stowe Mss. 227, fols. 117–119, BL. The rumor, spread to Whig circles in England (with which Bothmer was allied) in correspondence from three colonials (see chap. 4), may have taken on new life after 1775 when Bothmer's letter was translated from French to English. See James Macpherson, comp., *Original Papers; Containing the Secret History of Great Britain, from the Restoration to the Accession of the House of Hannover*, 2 vols. (London, 1775), II, 626.

The catalogue description reads in full: "Edward Hyde, Lord Cornbury, afterward 3d Earl of Clarendon (–1723). Painter [ ]. Sir J. S. Pakington, Bt. M.P. Only s. of Henry, 2d E.; Master of the Horse to P. George of Denmark; Gov. of New York in the reign of Anne; marr. Catherine, dau. of Henry, Lord O'Brien, eld. son of Henry E. of Thomond; is said to have dressed himself in woman's clothes in order to represent her Majesty Q. Anne at New York; d. 31 March, 1723. Half-length, standing; in female dress, with low body and jewels. Canvas, 49 × 39 in." *Catalogue of the Second Special Exhibition of National Portraits, Commencing with the Reign of William and Mary and Ending with the Year MDCCC, on Loan to the South Kensington Museum, May 1, 1867* (London, 1867), 40. Though the figure is more or less seated, the painting described is unquestionably the one that hangs today in the New-York Historical Society.

9. See, e.g., "A Governor in Petticoats," *Historical Magazine* (Morrisania, N.Y.), 2d Ser., II (1867), 169, J. Romeyn Brodhead, "Lord Cornbury," III (January 1868), 71–72; James W. Gerard, "The Dongan Charter of the City of New York," *Magazine of American History*, XVI (July 1886), 41; and James Grant Wilson, *The Memorial History of the City of New York: From Its First Settlement to the Year 1892*, 4 vols. (New York, 1892–1893), II, 88.

10. The late Mary Black, former curator of painting at the New-York Historical Society, wrote: "I do not think the painting is of the period of Cornbury's presence in the province. . . . I doubt that it was painted in America." Moreover, in her survey of artists' account books and diaries in the society archives, she encountered no mention of the painting (Black to author, May 17, 1989). Ruth Piwonka, New York museum and history consultant, notes, "The portrait does not resemble the style of any painters known to be working in America circa 1705" (Piwonka to author, May 18, 1986).

Ellen G. Miles of the National Portrait Gallery, Washington, D.C., does not rule out a colonial artist, pointing to New York's Gerardus Duyckinck (1695– 1746) as a painter worthy of consideration, though Gerardus, only 15 when Cornbury returned to England in 1710, would have had to paint him at a later date. Miles further notes that the New-York Historical Society painting is in the style of early-18th-century portraiture; she believes it is, not a caricature, but a serious painting (Miles to author, Feb. 15, 1989, August 1993). For more on Gerardus Duyckinck, see Richard H. Saunders and Ellen G. Miles, *American Colonial Portraits, 1700–1776* (Washington, D.C., 1987), 144–147.

11. For these and other 18th-century painters, see Waldron Phoenix Belknap, Jr., *American Colonial Painting: Materials for a History* (Cambridge, Mass., 1959); Ian M. G. Quimby, ed., *American Painting to 1776: A Reappraisal* (Charlottesville, Va., 1971); Mary Black, "Contributions toward a History of Early Eighteenth-Century New York Portraiture: Identification of the Aetatis Suae and Wendell Limners," *American Art Journal*, XII, no. 4 (Autumn 1980), 4–31; John Hill Morgan, *John Watson, Painter, Merchant, and Capitalist of New Jersey, 1685–1768* (Worcester, Mass., 1941 [orig. publ. as American Antiquarian Society, *Proceedings*, L, pt. 1 (1940), 225–317]); and Saunders and Miles, *American Colonial Portraits*. For more on the use of mezzotints, see Belknap, *American Colonial Painting* Charles Coleman Sellers, "Mezzotint Prototypes of Colonial Portraiture . . . ," *Art Quarterly*, XX (1957), 407–468, and Frederick A. Sweet, "Mezzotint Sources of American Colonial Portraits," XIV (1951), 148–157.

12. Robin Gibson to author, July 30, 1990. See Gibson's *Catalogue of Portraits in the Collection of the Earl of Clarendon* (Wallop, Hampshire, 1977).

13. Nor is there any mention in Vertue's voluminous writings on early-18th-century English painting of an unusual portrait of Lord Cornbury. The original Vertue notebooks are in the British Library; for Cornbury Hall entries, see Add. Mss. 23070, fol. 66, BL. A detailed inventory of the Clarendon Collection, made in 1751 when Cornbury Hall was sold by the Hyde family, appears in Vernon J. Watney, *Cornbury and the Forest of Wychwood* (London, 1910), app. XVIII; and in Lady Theresa Lewis, *Lives of the Friends and Contemporaries of Lord Chancellor Clarendon: Illustrative of Portraits in His Gallery*, 3 vols. (London, 1852), III, 239–435.

Among viewers of the collection was Horace Walpole. In 1751 the paintings were divided between two lines of Hyde descendants. Walpole saw one half of the collection in 1761 and the other half in 1786 while visiting the owners' estates. He gives a fairly detailed description of the paintings but remarks no oddities; see Paget Toynbee, ed., "Horace Walpole's Journals of Visits to Country Seats etc.," *Walpole Society*, XVI (1927–1928), 38; W. S. Lewis et al., eds., *Horace Walpole's Correspondence*, XXXIII (New Haven, Conn., 1965), 541.

14. The drawing was one of many included in an illustrated edition of the first earl of Clarendon's *History of the Rebellion and Civil Wars in England* (1702–1704), 31 vols. (Oxford, 1837), IV, 102, a celebrated eyewitness account. David Piper, comp., *Catalogue of Seventeenth-Century Portraits in the National Portrait Gallery, 1625–1714* (Cambridge, 1963), 89 and plates; M. H. Spielmann, *British Portrait Painting to the Opening of the Nineteenth Century*, 2 vols. (London, 1910), I.

15. For Hyde family members, see Gibson, *Catalogue of Portraits*, plates 27–30. But see also Timothy H. Breen, "The Meaning of 'Likeness': American Portrait Painting in an Eighteenth-Century Consumer Society," *Word and Image*, VI (1990), 325–350.

To continue the "likeness" game — a particularly conjectural sport when dealing with formal 18th-century portraiture — a glance at extant paintings of Cornbury's immediate family members suggests a certain refinement of feature and bearing as well as a fairness of complexion and hair, characteristics significantly absent in the New-York Historical Society portrait (see figs. 6–8). On such grounds as these one might be more inclined to connect the painting to the Pakington family, judging from the rather coarse features of Sir John Pakington (1672–1727) as depicted in a portrait that hangs today in the Worcester Guildhall.

16. Compare the initial illustration in Francis Bazley Lee, *New Jersey as a Colony and as a State*, 4 vols. (New York, 1902), I, facing 390, with that in Duane Lockard, *The New Jersey Governor: A Study in Political Power* (Princeton, N.J., 1964), 25. The retouched print was then used to illustrate a story about Lord Cornbury in the *New York Times*, June 3, 1990. For the original illustrations, see Wilson, *Memorial History of New York*, II, 59, 71, 55. Lee's account of Cornbury's governorship is in *New Jersey as Colony and State*, I, chaps. 11–12. This representational sequence illustrates two of this book's themes: the untrustworthiness of pictorial evidence and the subjectivity of history.

17. Inventory item no. G 60, Miniatures Series, Musée d'Art et d'Histoire, Geneva; Fabienne X. Sturm, conservator, Musée de l'Horlogerie et de l'Emaillerie, Section du Musée d'Art et d'Histoire, to author, July 7, 1992. I am much indebted to Sturm, to archivists at the State Archives of Geneva, and to Livio Fornara at the Bibliothèque d'Art et d'Archéologie for assistance in researching Cornbury's sojourn in that city.

The handwritten inscription on the back of the miniature, it might be noted, is in the style of the later 17th and early 18th centuries.

18. Charles Borgeaud, *Histoire de l'Université de Genève*, I, *L'académie de Calvin, 1559–1796* (Geneva, 1900), 441. According to a local history, in 1680, "Le comte de Cornbury tenta sa chance, il fit deux coups meilleurs que son prédécesseur, 'et le dernier proche la broche'"; Eugène-Louis Dumont, *Exercices de l'arquebuze et de la navagation* (Geneva, 1979), 114, n. 3. For the history of the festival and Cornbury's investiture as king in 1680, see Ernest Naef, "Les exercices militaire à Genève," *Genava: Bulletin du Musée d'Art et d'Histoire de Genève*, XI (1933), 110–120; for 1681, see N.S., XIV (1966), 59 and n. 10.

Durant, a native of Geneva, was known primarily as an ornamental engraver and painter in enamel; see Leo R. Schidlof, *La miniature en Europe . . .*, I (Graz, 1964), 236.

19. For the description of Cornbury's mother, see Anthony Hamilton, *Memoirs of the Comte de Gramont* (London, 1930), 112.

20. Hampton Collection, accession no. 4739, parcel I (viii), fol. 1 (microfilm). The closest link between the two families is that Sir John Pakington's first wife's mother was Margaret Hyde, daughter of the Right Reverend Alexander Hyde, bishop of Salisbury (1665–1667), who was a first cousin of Cornbury's grandfather, the first earl of Clarendon. See John Pakington to Mr. Wotton, Oct. 22, 1726, Add. Ms. 24121, II, fol. 142, BL; E. A. B. Barnard, "The Pakingtons of Westwood," *Worcestershire Archeological Society, Transactions*, N.S., XIII (1937), 28–47; and *DNB*, XV, 91–95. It is possible that Cornbury and Sir John (1671–1727) knew each other, because both were Tories and served together in the House of Commons in the late 17th century. Yet there is no evidence of correspondence between them or any other indication in family or official papers that they were in any way close.

21. Richard Davenport-Hines to *Times Literary Supplement*, May 18–24, 1990; Lewis, *Lives of Friends and Contemporaries of Clarendon*, I, 33–34. Lady Theresa could find no link between the Pakington and Hyde families and no account of how the portrait became part of the Pakington collection.

22. The chiaroscuro, or shadowing, of the sitter's face (which the casual observer might mistake as evidence of a latent beard and mustache) was characteristic, however, of painting at the turn of the 18th century.

23. This information is based on a number of consultations with Holly Hotchner and Richard Kowall of the New-York Historical Society Conservation Laboratory and Kowall to author, Jan. 4, 1990. I gratefully acknowledge their assistance.

24. Though the London editor called the story "improbable," he ran it on the front page beside other foreign news. Washington's secret was supposedly revealed in a deathbed confession by his wife; that Martha Washington did not die

until 1802 seems not to have deterred the scandalmongers. See the *Daily Advertiser* (London), Jan. 25, 1783. The *Advertiser* gave as its original source the *Pennsylvania Gazette* of November 1782; a scan of the newspaper for those and other likely dates turns up no such story.

25. Peter Wagner, *Eros Revived: Erotica of the Enlightenment in England and America* (London, 1988); George deF. Lord et al., eds., *Poems on Affairs of State: Augustan Satirical Verse, 1660–1714*, 7 vols. (New Haven, Conn., 1963–1975); David Foxon, *Libertine Literature in England, 1660–1745* (New Hyde Park, N.Y., 1965); W. A. Speck, "Political Propaganda in Augustan England," Royal Historical Society, *Transactions*, 5th Ser., XXII (1972), 17–32.

CHAPTER TWO

1. Edward Gregg, *Queen Anne* (London, 1980), 3.

2. Ibid., 3–4; Richard Ollard, *Clarendon and His Friends* (New York, 1988), quotation on 230; Vicary Gibbs, ed., *The Complete Peerage . . .*, new ed., VIII (London, 1913), 267–268; Milton Rubincam, "The Formative Years of Lord Cornbury, the First Royal Governor of New York and New Jersey," *New York Genealogical and Biographical Record*, LXXI (1940), 106–116. Eight children were born of this marriage, though only Mary and Anne survived. Anne Hyde died in 1671; ibid.

3. J. V. Beckett, *The Aristocracy in England, 1660–1914* (Oxford, 1986); Lawrence Stone and Jeanne C. Fawtier Stone, *An Open Elite? England, 1540–1880* (Oxford, 1984). The quotation is from David Harris Sacks, "Searching for 'Culture' in the English Renaissance," *Shakespeare Quarterly*, XXXIX (1988), 476–477, who acknowledges that only first sons were fully admitted to the nobility.

4. Ollard, *Clarendon and His Friends*, 223–230, 287–297, chap. 19; Paul Seaward, *The Cavalier Parliament and the Reconstruction of the Old Regime, 1661–1667* (Cambridge, 1989), 320–322.

5. Samuel Weller Singer, ed., *The Correspondence of Henry Hyde, Earl of Clarendon, and of His Brother Laurence Hyde, Earl of Rochester; with the Diary of Lord Clarendon from 1687 to 1690 . . .*, 2 vols. (London, 1828), I, viii–ix, xvi (hereafter cited as *Hyde Correspondence*); Vernon J. Watney, *Cornbury and the Forest of Wychwood* (London, 1910), 149; Lady Theresa Lewis, *Lives of Friends and Contemporaries of Lord Chancellor Clarendon: Illustrative of Portraits in His Gallery*, 3 vols. (London, 1852), II, chap. 11.

6. So wrote Daniel Defoe, as noted in Beckett, *Aristocracy in England*, 93.

7. For gentlemen to matriculate at 15 was not unusual, but to do so at 13 was rare. Christ Church was known for its Puritan and Presbyterian sympathies. E. G. W. Bill, *Education at Christ Church, Oxford, 1660–1800* (Oxford, 1988), 18, 172; Joseph Foster, comp., *Alumni Oxonienses . . . 1500–1714* (1888; rpt. Nendeln, Liechtenstein, 1968), 781.

8. Charles Borgeaud, *Histoire de l'Université de Genève*, I, *L'académie de Calvin, 1559–1798* (Geneva, 1900), 441. Eugène-Louis Dumont, *Exercices de l'arquebuze et de la navagation* (Geneva, 1979), 114; Ernest Naef, "Les exercices militaire à Genève," *Genava: Bulletin du Musée d'Art et d'Histoire de Genève*, XI (1933), 110–120; Lord Cornbury to Secretary Bromley, Hanover, Aug. 3, 1714, Stowe Mss. 242, fol. 158, BL; Lord Preston to the earl of Clarendon, Paris, 1682, HMC, *Seventh Report* (1879; rpt. London, 1979), 266.

9. *CSPD, James II*, III, 13. C. T. Atkinson, *History of the Royal Dragoons, 1661–1934* (Glasgow, 1934), 34, 40, 46–47, 51; Stephen Saunders Webb, *Lord Churchill's Coup: The Anglo-American Empire and the Glorious Revolution Reconsidered* (New York, 1995), 71, quotation on 95; Clarendon to the earl of Rochester, May 8, 1686, *Hyde Correspondence*, I, 325.

10. [Sir Edward Hungerford?] to Robert Harley, Feb. 12, Mar. 10, [1690], HMC, *Fourteenth Report*, Appendix, Part II, *The Manuscripts of His Grace the Duke of Portland, K.G., Preserved at Welbeck Abbey*, III (London, 1894), 28; Gibbs, ed., *Complete Peerage*, 267–268; E. S. de Beer, ed., *The Diary of John Evelyn*, 6 vols. (Oxford, 1955), IV, 559.

11. The description of Flower Backhouse is from Austin Dobson, ed., *The Diary of Sir John Evelyn*, 3 vols. (London, 1906–1908), I, 238n; *Hyde Correspondence*, July 10, 1688, II, 181. For a sampling of Lady Clarendon's articulate and witty letters, see ibid., I, 237–238. For Henry's appointments, see Feb. 27, 1685, *CSPD, James II*, I, 49, 403, 409. See entries in *CSPD, Charles II*, XXVII, and *James II*, I, from mid-1684 to mid-1685 for Henry's entertainment of the duke and duchess of York as well as other dignitaries at Cornbury Park.

12. The quotation is from Stone and Stone, *Open Elite?* 393.

13. Watney, *Cornbury*, 1–6, 134n; de Beer, ed., *Diary of Evelyn*, III, 381–382, 481–482 and n. 1; Notes on Collections, Swallowfield, National Portrait Gallery Archives, London; Lady Charlotte C. Russell, *Swallowfield and Its Owners* (London, 1901), chap. 18; Clarendon to Rochester, Dec. 30, 1685, *Hyde Correspondence*, I, 198–201.

14. Clarendon to Rochester, Dec. 26, 30, 1685, Mar. 14, 1686, *Hyde Correspondence*, I, 193–195, 198–201, 303–304. The editor speculates that this courtship involved Cornbury's eventual wife, Katherine; but because she was only 12 or 13 at this time, it seems unlikely she would have been of marriageable age, much less a widow.

15. Ibid., Mar. 14, Apr. 3, 1686, 303–304, 327–328.

16. Ibid., Mar. 14, Apr. 3, 20, 1686, 303–304, 327–328, 356. Meanwhile, the sister of Henry's first wife was also suggesting matches with either Lord Chesterfield's daughter or the widow Howland: duchess of Beaufort to Clarendon, Sept. 4, 1685, Nov. 17, 1686, ibid., 158–159, II, 67–68. Compare Henry's negotiations to those of the earl of Sunderland in 1694 regarding his son's marriage,

in which Sunderland settled a £25,000 dowry and from £4,800 to £5,700 a year income on the couple; see J. P. Kenyon, *Robert Spencer, Earl of Sunderland, 1641–1702* (London, 1958), 267–268.

17. Diary entries of May 31, 1688, *Hyde Correspondence*, II, 174; May 8, 1686, Aug. 6, 1688, I, 380, II, 184; Clarendon to Rochester, Apr. 3, Nov. 13, 1686, I, 328, II, 60.

18. July 10, 1688, ibid., II, 181. In addition to the financial inconvenience, Henry thought it "a base thing, and unbecoming a man of honour to steal a child from a parent."

Katherine's name is spelled with a *K* in this study; she signed it so in a power of attorney executed in 1701 before leaving for New York; Lord and Lady Cornbury's Power of Attorney, Add. Mss. 15895, fol. 337, BL.

19. July 11, 1688, *Hyde Correspondence*, II, 181. As it happened, Lady Cornbury did eventually inherit her mother's estate as heiress of the duke of Richmond and Lenox, though what she got is unclear; Gibbs, ed., *Complete Peerage*, 267–268. It took the bride's parents somewhat longer to reconcile themselves to the marriage. As Clarendon noted when he paid a call on the family, Katherine's stepfather, the diplomat Sir Joseph Williamson, displayed "a wonderful stiffness" (July 12, 1688, *Hyde Correspondence*, II, 181).

20. *Hyde Correspondence*, II, 246. W. A. Speck, *Reluctant Revolutionaries: Englishmen and the Revolution of 1688* (Oxford, 1988), 14, 64; J. R. Jones, *Country and Court: England, 1658–1714* (Cambridge, Mass., 1978), 23.

21. Gregg, *Queen Anne*, 59–63; John Childs, *The Army, James II, and the Glorious Revolution* (New York, 1980), 148–149.

Earlier, Rochester's faction was seen to favor the Dutch states over France; see Speck, *Reluctant Revolutionaries*, 62. There is no specific evidence that Laurence and Cornbury were in communication before Cornbury's defection. But, unlike Clarendon, Rochester later took the oath of loyalty to William and Mary.

22. Gregg, *Queen Anne*, 63. A typical Whig interpretation is Thomas Babington Macaulay's in *The History of England from the Accession of James II*, first published in 1849–1861; Charles Harding Firth's edition is used here, 6 vols. (1914; rpt. New York, 1968), III, 1147.

23. [Ambrose Norton?], "An Account of the Revolution of the Army in 1688. In a Letter to a Friend, written in London Oct. 16, 1713," 4–7, Rawlinson Mss., D 148, Bodl. Lib.; Atkinson, *History of the Royal Dragoons*, 55. Historians date Cornbury's defection anywhere from November 10 to 16. The eyewitness states that after a two-day march the troops entered William's camp on a Sunday, which would have been November 11 or possibly very early on the November 12. A London newsletter carried word of the defection on November 15: Newdigate Newsletters, L.C. 1935, Folger Library, Washington, D.C.

Childs writes that Cornbury "panicked" (*The Army, James II, and the Glorious*

*Revolution,* 186) when confronted by his (Catholic) major, though he seems to have confused Cornbury with Compton. The eyewitness account states that Cornbury "stole away [to the Prince of Orange] with his Lt. Coll. Heyfed [Anthony Heyford], who was more resolute, and had most of his own Troops and some few others not exceeding 50." Yet Heyford's resolution was being contrasted, not with Cornbury's, but with that of some other regimental officers. The author makes clear throughout his account that Cornbury and Langston were the leaders of the defection; see [Norton], "Account of the Revolution," 7.

In Bishop Gilbert Burnet's *Burnet's History of His Own Time . . .* (1724–1734; London, 1883), Cornbury and Compton also were mixed up, Burnet writing that "Lord Cornbury had not the presence of mind that so critical a thing required" (501). But in a firsthand report of November 1688 from the scene of the action itself, Burnet blamed, not Cornbury, but the confusion of the night and "Sir Francis Compton's want of head and heart[,] together with the vigour of some Popish officers among them" for the disappointingly low number of soldiers defecting to William: Burnet to Admiral Herbert, Nov. 16, 1688, in H. C. Foxcroft, ed., *A Supplement to Burnet's History of My Own Time* (Oxford, 1902), 530.

24. [? to ?], Nov. 13, 1688, Add. Mss. 41805, fol. 200, BL; Childs, *The Army, James II, and the Glorious Revolution,* 187–188; Atkinson, *Royal Dragoons,* 54–56; [Norton], "Account of the Revolution," 9–10. One of the earliest narratives credits Cornbury with being the first "person of Quality" to defect to William, which "News caused a great Consternation at Whitehall"; see [Edmund Bohun], *The History of the Desertion . . .* (1688), in *A Collection of State Tracts, Publish'd on Occasion of the Late Revolution in 1688, and during the Reign of King William III,* I (London, 1705), 62. The duke of Berwick, nominal head of the troops at Salisbury though absent, confirms that Cornbury's defection preceded that of Churchill, in *Memoirs of the Marshal Duke of Berwick,* 2 vols. (London, 1779), I, 28–30. Men around the king also pointed to Cornbury, at least one describing him as "the leader" of the defection; Sir Henry Shere to Lord Dartmouth, Hartley Row, Nov. 25, 1688, HMC, *Fifteenth Report,* Appendix, Part IV, *The Manuscripts of His Grace the Duke of Portland, Preserved at Welbeck Abbey,* IV, *Harley Letters and Papers,* II (London, 1897), 133; see also ibid., 204, 210; and HMC, *Eleventh Report,* Appendix, Part VII, *The Manuscripts of the Duke of Leeds . . .* (London, 1888), 23.

25. Or, at least, to most of them. One Jacobite, possibly Ambrose Norton, reported that the duke of Schomberg was disappointed that Cornbury had not delivered more troops to the Orangist cause: "Lord Cornbury was not welcom to Schomberg having failed of his promis of what he promised to bring in, and told him that he had done the king greater service, in what he had done, then if he had stayed"; see Richard Hast to Sir Walter Vavasour at York, Nov. 20, 1688, Egerton Mss. 3335, fol. 40, BL. Yet the circle of intrigue was necessarily limited, and as Childs observes, "The conspiracy, based as it was upon the self-interest of

a small number of officers, was not strong enough to overcome the attachment of the majority of officers and soldiers to their sovereign" (*The Army, James II, and the Glorious Revolution*, 187).

26. *Hyde Correspondence*, II, 216; Nov. 15, 20, 1688, 204, 206, 213–215. Henry later recorded that when he "went in to the Prince of Orange [at Salisbury] . . . it was not to be against the King," because he expected William and James "to treat" with each other (Jan. 14, 1689, ibid., 246). Given Clarendon's subsequent refusal to recognize William III as king, this is entirely plausible.

27. Henry Horwitz, *Parliament, Policy, and Politics in the Reign of William III* (Manchester, 1977), 338; Gregg, *Queen Anne*, 69–71. Cornbury apparently had been elected to the Convention Parliament, probably from Wiltshire. For more on the convention, see Speck, *Reluctant Revolutionaries*, chap. 5.

28. Stephen B. Baxter, *William III and the Defense of European Liberty, 1650–1702* (London, 1966), 255–256; Gregg, *Queen Anne*, 78–80.

29. Gregg, *Queen Anne*, 79–80; *Hyde Correspondence*, II, 263–264, 268, 314. The convention agreed that Anne's heirs would take precedence over any children of a second marriage by William. See Henry Horwitz, *Revolution Politicks: The Career of Daniel Finch, Second Earl of Nottingham, 1647–1730* (Cambridge, 1968), 79–80; see also Webb, *Lord Churchill's Coup*, 174–175.

30. Narcissus Luttrell, *A Brief Historical Relation of State Affairs from September 1678 to April 1714*, 6 vols. (Oxford, 1857), I, 560. Stephen Saunders Webb says that William's decision to take away Cornbury's regiment was directly owing to Cornbury's connection to Anne's court and to Churchill, in *Lord Churchill's Coup*, 230–231. Clarendon's reaction to the news was remarkably stern: "God grant it may make my son reflect . . . on the abominable action he committed in deserting the King; which will be a stain in his life, and will stick heavy at my heart as long as I live" (July 19, 1689, *Hyde Correspondence*, II, 283).

31. May 30, 1690, *Hyde Correspondence*, II, 314–315.

32. Mar. 27, June 26, 1690, Feb. 2, 1691, *CSPD, William and Mary*, I, 528, II, 41, 219; *Hyde Correspondence*, II, 319–330. Henry was discharged to the care of a warder; of the £20,000 bond, Clarendon apparently put up half, Laurence £5,000, and John Lord Lovelace £5,000; (*CSPD, William and Mary*, II, 433). Cornbury visited his father frequently during his incarceration.

33. Burnet, *Burnet's History of His Own Time*, 446; Watney, *Cornbury and the Forest of Wychwood*, 150–153.

34. Shortly after Cornbury's defection to William, some 30 Wiltshire gentlemen who gathered at the Vine, a tavern in Salisbury, told his father that they "all agreed upon my son to be one of the Knights for this County." But when Cornbury put his name forth in 1690, with his father still refusing the oath, he discovered "he was like to find a great opposition in his election." In the face of a "very hard struggle," he was chosen. See *Hyde Correspondence*, II, 216,

304–308; [Hungerford?] to Harley, Feb. 12, Mar. 10, [1690], HMC, *Fourteenth Report*, 28. Earlier Cornbury had sought to represent the Corporation of Reading, Berks., but two other gentlemen were chosen to stand, "in pursuance of a circular letter from the Prince of Orange" (Jan. 9/10, 1688/1689, Manuscripts of the Reading Corporation, HMC, *Eleventh Report*, 202).

As for Cornbury's other activities in this period, he had been included in the party that greeted Mary at Spithead in early 1690; in 1693 it was rumored that he would be appointed governor of the Isle of Wight, though nothing ever came of it; see Feb. 1, 1690, *CSPD, William and Mary*, I, 442; and Feb. 21, 1693, Luttrell, *Brief Relation*, III, 39.

35. Jan. 11, 1690, *Hyde Correspondence*, II, 301; Nov. 26, 1697, *CSPD, William III*, III, 486, Apr. 2, 1696, II, 115; Cornbury to Sir William Trumbull, Aug. 19, 1697, HMC, *[Eighteenth Report]*, *Report of the Manuscripts of the Marquess of Downshire*, I, *Papers of Sir William Trumbull*, Part II (London, 1924), I, 762.

36. Cornbury to Clarendon, London, Oct. 30, 1697, Cornbury Mss., NYHS.

Of seven children born to Edward and Katherine, three survived, two daughters and one son. John Sharpe, *A Sermon Preached at the Funeral of the Right Honorable Katherine Lady Cornbury, the Thirteenth of August, 1706* (New York, 1706); Gibbs, ed., *Complete Peerage*, 267–268.

37. Mr. Champneys to Lord Ambassador [Joseph] Williamson, Jan. 18, 1698, State Papers 32/9, fol. 70, PRO. In a similar usage, for example, it was reported that the duke of Ormonde "hath been shut up" since his daughter's death; Jan. 9, 1713, Add. Mss. 22220, fol. 46, BL. The anachronistic interpretation is that of Rubincam in "Formative Years," *N.Y. Geneal. Biog. Rec.*, LXXI (1940), 115.

38. Lewis, *Lives of Friends and Contemporaries of Clarendon*, I, 42–44, 46; Watney, *Cornbury and the Forest of Wychwood*, 143; Champneys to Sir Joseph Williamson, Nov. 26, 1697, *CSPD, William III*, III, 486. Swallowfield was eventually inherited by Cornbury, who sold it to Thomas Pitt in 1719; see Russell, *Swallowfield*, 192.

Clarendon would only partially recover at the accession of Queen Anne in 1702, when he finally took the oath of loyalty, regained his seat in the House of Lords, and was granted a pension of £1,500 per annum; see J. Wotton to the earl of Rutland, London, Mar. 19, 1702, HMC, *Twelfth Report*, Appendix, Part V, *The Manuscripts of the Duke of Rutland . . .* , II (London, 1889), 170; Watney, *Cornbury and the Forest of Wychwood*, 168. Wotton had heard that Clarendon took the oath at Queen Anne's accession, but as late as August 1702, Clarendon himself suggests otherwise (Clarendon to Queen Anne, Aug. 14, 1702, Add. Mss. 61416, fol. 9, BL).

39. Gregg, *Queen Anne*, 101–104. Rochester, who kept a tighter rein on his high Toryism, served briefly in William and Mary's Privy Council and in 1700 gained appointment as lord lieutenant of Ireland (*Hyde Correspondence*, II, 348n).

For more on the politics of these years, see Tim Harris, *Politics under the Late Stuarts: Party Conflict in a Divided Society, 1660—1715* (New York, 1993), 131—153.

40. Horwitz, *Parliament, Policy, and Politics*, 319, 326, n. 40, 338—339, 349. (For Sir John Fenwick, see Jones, *Country and Court*, 277.) August 6, 1698, Luttrell, *Brief Relation*, IV, 411.

41. See, e.g., Rubincam, "Formative Years," *N.Y. Geneal. Biog. Rec.*, LXXI (1940), 115. The appointment is noted in May 1, June 13, 1701, *CSPD, William III*, VI, 310, 363. Histories of the period often state that the appointment was made by Queen Anne, which is clearly wrong. For the Tory resurgence, see Harris, *Politics under the Later Stuarts*, 151—153.

42. Ian K. Steele, *The English Atlantic, 1675—1740: An Exploration of Communication and Community* (New York, 1986), chap. 12; W. A. Speck, "The International and Imperial Context," in Jack P. Greene and J. R. Pole, eds., *Colonial British America: Essays in the New History of the Early Modern Era* (Baltimore, 1984), 384—407; John Brewer, *The Sinews of Power: War, Money, and the English State, 1688—1783* (New York, 1989), quotation on 74. For the absurdity of historians' assuming that 18th-century patronage was "little more than private charity," see J. H. Plumb, *The Growth of Political Stability in England, 1675—1725* (London, 1967), 188.

43. Board of Trade to the earl of Manchester, Enclosing a Representation to the King, Jan. 24, 1702, *CSPC*, XX, no. 55.

44. Such delays were not unusual for colonial appointees. Cornbury's lobbying efforts can be followed in Cornbury to William Blathwayt, Hammersmith, Sept. 9, 16, Nov. 8, 1701, BL, HL; and *CSPC*, XIX.

45. Secretary of State James Vernon to the king, Aug. 22, 26, 1701, Add. Mss. 40775, fols. 85, 93, BL.

The timing of these events makes plausible the reconstruction offered here. The lawsuit was instituted in August 1701. In September, William ordered the Treasury to pay Cornbury £1,000, the money being taken from the secret service fund "to avoid making precedents": *Calendar of Treasury Papers, 1697—1702*, II (London, 1871), 526, and see also 540. On Oct. 21, 1701, the Treasury noted that Cornbury's "130 tons of goods and equipage to New York" cost £390, the equipage fee being unusually large because Cornbury carried the new uniforms with him. This leaves a balance of £610, the very amount needed to repay Cornbury's debt. That Cornbury received no respites while in New York suggests that these were turned back to the Treasury, in part to repay the king's loan; see William A. Shaw, ed., *Calendar of Treasury Books*, XVI, *1 October 1700 to 31 December 1701* (London, 1938), 376. For the respites, see Apr. 3, 1703, PC 2/79, fols. 344—345, PRO (microfilm), HHV; Cornbury to Clarendon, Mar. 9, 1709, Add. Mss. 15895, BL.

46. Cornbury to William Popple, Nov. 28, 1701, *CSPC*, XIX, no. 1037; CO 5/

1084, LOC (microfilm); May 1, 1702, M. Halsey Thomas, ed., *The Diary of Samuel Sewall, 1674–1729*, 2 vols. (New York, 1973), I, 466. On October 29, Lord and Lady Cornbury had assigned power of attorney to Lords Clarendon and Rochester (Add. Mss. 15895, fol. 337, BL).

47. Cornbury to Rochester, Feb. 21, 1709, New York, A Collection of Original Letters, JCBL; Cornbury to Clarendon, Mar. 9, 1709, [New York], Add. Mss. 15895, fol. 339, BL; Extracts from Some Letters and Memorials relating to the Rt. Hon. the Lord Clarendon Whilst Governor of New York etc., n.d., Clarendon Papers, CII, fols. 150–155, Bodl. Lib.; depositions of Peter Fauconnier, William Anderson, and Ebenezer Wilson, Jan. 19, 1712, and Clarendon to SPG, Somerset House, May 12, 1712, SPG, Letterbooks C, I (microfilm); The Voluntary Deposition of Roger Brett, Apr. 19, 1709, Add. Mss. 15895, fol. 363, BL. Cornbury regained the queen's confidence, if he had ever lost it, long before this evidence was collected.

Regarding Cornbury's accounts see, e.g., An Account of what I am accused of and my answers, and Account of Debts, Mar. 9, 1709, Add. Mss. 15895, fols. 347–354, BL; Clarendon Mss., CII, esp. fols. 54–55, 88–89, 90–94, 106–107, Bodl. Lib. Regarding money owed to the four companies, which Cornbury asserted was actually a debt contracted by previous governors, see Cornbury to Treasury, Somerset House, Mar. 26, 1711, and n.d. [March 1711?], T 1/146, fols. 83–85, PRO.

48. For example, Governor Benjamin Fletcher (1692–1698) of New York, whose recall was "not done out of any dissatisfaction the King had in him, but in favour of the Earl of Bellomont," nonetheless had to defend his financial actions on returning to England. *Calendar of Treasury Papers*, II, 541–542.

49. Chesterfield is quoted in Lord Mahon [Philip H. Stanhope], *History of England, Comprising the Reign of Queen Anne until the Peace of Utrecht*, 2d ed. (London, 1870), 566. For Cornbury's appointments, see Gibbs, ed., *Complete Peerage*, 267–268; Luttrell, *Brief Relation*, VI, 720. It is unclear whether he ever served as commissioner of the Admiralty, so the report may have been erroneous.

On Somerset House, see Dec. 21, 1710, Luttrell, *Brief Relation*, VI, 668. The palace, formerly the home of queen mothers, had in 1694 been divided into apartments, where a number of earls, countesses, and the like lived. Though it later fell on hard times and was converted to a barracks, Somerset House was an elegant address when Cornbury resided there. In 1712 the duke D'Aumont, one of the residents, gave a masked ball for 600. Its piazza, designed by Inigo Jones, ran down to the Thames; the property included gardens and a bowling green. At the crown's expense the palace was maintained by "two sentinels at the gate, a porter, a housekeeper, a chaplain, and a lay reader" — an ideal arrangement for a widower like Cornbury. Raymond Needham and Alexander Webster, *Somerset House, Past and Present* (London, 1905), chap. 4.

50. Geoffrey Holmes, *British Politics in the Age of Anne* (London, 1967), app. B.

Robert Harley, Anne's chief minister, had inserted a clause forbidding the alien-ation of any part of the pension, making it impossible for Cornbury to use it to pay off his debts (State Papers, Domestic, George II [sic], n.d., bundle 155, fol. 196, LOC Transcripts). Queen Anne's order lifting the restriction is dated June 10, 1714, Clarendon Mss., LXXXX, fol. 203. Anne, not only widowed in 1708 but at about that same time becoming estranged from her closest friend, Sarah Marlborough (and soon from the duke), may have turned more frequently to her few remaining family members in these years.

51. Holmes, *British Politics in the Age of Anne*, app. A; Gregg, *Queen Anne*, 385; Jones, *Country and Court*, 326–327, 350–356; Peter Wentworth to his brother Thomas, London, June 4, 1714, James J. Cartwright, ed., *The Wentworth Papers, 1705–1739 . . . Correspondence of Thomas Wentworth . . . Earl of Strafford* (London, 1883), 387. For more on Bolingbroke's position, see Isaac Kramnick, *Bolingbroke and His Circle: The Politics of Nostalgia in the Age of Walpole* (Cambridge, Mass., 1968), 14, 271, n. 17.

52. May Bickley to Clarendon, New York, Nov. 10, 1714, Collection of Origi-nal Letters, fols. 235–238; Anne to the elector of Brunswick, Kensington, June 19, 1714, and Secretary Bromley to Clarendon, Whitehall, July 27, 31, 1714, Stowe Mss. 242, fols. 143, 154–156.

53. Cornbury to Bromley, Hanover, Aug. 3, 7, 1714, Stowe Mss. 242, fols. 158, 161.

54. Ibid., Aug. 10–17, 1714, fols. 162–165; Lewis Melville [pseud. of Lewis Saul Benjamin], *Life and Letters of John Gay . . .* (London, 1921), 33.

55. Bothmer to Robethon [at Hanover], The Hague, June 16, 1714, Stowe Mss. 227, fols. 117–119. The original letter is in French; a translation of extracts, apparently the first, is in James Macpherson, comp., *Original Papers: Containing the Secret History of Great Britain, from the Restoration to the Accession of the House of Hannover*, 2 vols. (London, 1775), II, 626. The translation is accurate, though it does not include Bothmer's assertion in the original letter that Cornbury not only dressed as a woman but did his hair in a female style. That charge appears to have been but the first of many embellishments on the Cornbury legend, since none of the colonists who transmitted the cross-dressing gossip mentioned Cornbury's hairstyle. For more on Bothmer, see Gregg, *Queen Anne*, 317, 327, 328, 345–346; and Jones, *Country and Court*, 298, 351–354. Bothmer, who was Hanover's envoy alternately to London and The Hague during these years, also denigrated the Tory envoy to Utrecht (Bothmer to Bernsdorff, Aug. 13, 1714, Macpherson, *Original Papers*, II, 642). Bothmer's is the only reference to the cross-dressing gossip I have found in noncolonial documents before 1796.

56. Clarendon to the earl of Strafford, Hanover, Aug. 17, 1714, Add. Mss. 22211, fol. 55, and Clarendon to Bromley, Hanover, Aug. 17, 1714, Stowe Mss. 242, fol. 165.

57. Strafford to Clarendon, The Hague, Aug. 20, 1714, Add. Mss. 22211, fol. 57, BL. That George was inclined to show some favor to the Tories is the view of Whig John Perceval, first Lord Egmont. Egmont states that the king offered good posts to certain prominent Tories, but when they asked for more, the king turned to the Whigs; a number of leading Tories then attempted to form an opposition. Cornbury's name does not appear in Egmont's list of the hottest Tories; see Letterbook of John Perceval, First Lord Egmont, Add. Mss. 47027, esp. fols. 170–181, BL.

58. For Cornbury's service in the Lords, consult Clyve Jones, "The House of Lords and the Growth of Parliamentary Stability, 1704–1742," in Jones, ed., *Britain in the First Age of Party, 1680–1750: Essays Presented to Geoffrey Holmes* (London, 1987), 96–97; Clyve Jones and Geoffrey Holmes, eds., *The London Diaries of William Nicolson, Bishop of Carlisle, 1702–1718* (Oxford, 1985), 37; Holmes, *Politics in the Age of Anne*, app. A. Bishop Gilbert Burnet, for example, chaired the Committee of the Whole House 21 times in that period (Jones and Holmes, eds., *London Diaries of William Nicholson*, 37).

Regarding Cornbury's support for the king, when urged to attend an important session of the House of Lords in 1719, he responded that just as he had "always been ready to doe his Majesty the best service in my poor Power, soe I shall readily doe the same now"; Clarendon to Mr. DeLaFaye, Edminton, Aug. 17, 1719, State Papers 35/17/182 [old no. 101], PRO. Linda Colley's assertion that Cornbury was a Tory apostate by 1719 is questionable; see *In Defiance of Oligarchy: The Tory Party, 1714–60* (Cambridge, 1982), 62.

For Cornbury's declining role in the Lords, see Luttrell, *Brief Relation*, VI, 661; [Ebenezer Timberland], *The History and Proceedings of the House of Lords . . .* , II (London, 1742), 351, 359; William Cobbett, ed., *Parliamentary History of England, from the Norman Conquest in 1066 to the Year 1803*, VI (London, 1810), 1344; and Leo Francis Stock, ed., *Proceedings and Debates of the British Parliaments respecting North America*, 5 vols. (Washington, D.C., 1924–1941), III, 381, 404, 417, 426, 438.

59. Sharpe, *Sermon Preached at the Funeral of Lady Cornbury*; Rubincam, "Formative Years," *N.Y. Geneal. Biog. Rec.*, LXXI (1940), 112.

Katherine's age is often given as 34, in accordance with old style "in the 34th year of her age," but she was by modern count 33.

60. According to Thomas Hearne, the young Viscount Cornbury had "inflamed his spirits by hard drinking." He adds: "I was particularly acquainted with him. He was a very fine, pretty gentleman, of a tall, but thin stature, very good natured, loyal, and well principled in other respects." Philip Bliss, comp., *Reliquiae Hearnianae: The Remains of Thomas Hearne . . . Being Extracts from His MS. Diaries*, I (Oxford, 1857), 282–283.

Lord Berkeley of Stratton reported that Edward and his companions "drank as many quarts of Uskquebath [Usquaebach] as is usual of wine." Lady Strafford noted that the young viscount was just going "to have Lord Windsor's Regiment," and that the queen had twice sent for word of his condition. When he died, Queen Anne paid for his burial at Westminster Abbey. Lord Berkeley of Stratton to ?, [Feb.] 13, 1713, Lady Strafford to ?, Feb. 17, 20, 1713, Cartwright, ed., *Wentworth Papers*, 314, 320–321.

61. Berkeley of Stratton to ?, [Feb.] 13, 27, 1713, Cartwright, ed., *Wentworth Papers*, 314, 322; C. E. Doble et al., eds., *Remarks and Collections of Thomas Hearne*, VIII (Oxford, 1907), 64.

62. Cited in Gibbs, ed., *Complete Peerage*, 267n. I have been unable to locate any trace of the original Bible.

63. The sexual connotations of the word *folly* declined after the early 17th century according to *The Oxford English Dictionary*, with *foolish* becoming the primary synonym. For example, Cornbury's well-principled father, Henry, second earl of Clarendon, on reaching 50 took a kind of moral accounting of his life to that date: he enjoyed many blessings, but, alas, he was too fond of "the follies and ambition of this deceitful world," for which he begged God's forgiveness (June 2, 1688, *Hyde Correspondence*, II, 174). William Penn in 1703 contrasted Governor Cornbury's "prudence" with the Philadelphia Anglicans' "Folly" when the Anglicans requested a royal charter for Pennsylvania; see Penn to Provincial Council, London, Dec. 31, 1703, Mary Maples Dunn, Richard S. Dunn, et al., eds., *The Papers of William Penn*, 5 vols. (Philadelphia, 1981–1987), IV, 253–254.

CHAPTER THREE

1. For Leisler's Rebellion, see Michael G. Hall et al., eds., *The Glorious Revolution in America: Documents on the Colonial Crisis of 1689* (Chapel Hill, N.C., 1964), pt. 2; for a later interpretation that emphasizes religion rather than democratic strivings as the central issue of Leisler's Rebellion, see David William Voorhees, "'In Behalf of the True Protestants Religion': The Glorious Revolution in New York" (Ph.D. diss., New York University, 1988). For the Bayard episode, consult Adrian Howe, "The Bayard Treason Trial: Dramatizing Anglo-Dutch Politics in Early Eighteenth-Century New York City," *WMQ*, 3d Ser., XLVII (1990), 57–89.

2. Robert Livingston to Fitz-John Winthrop, New York, May 11, 1702, MHS, *Colls.*, 6th Ser., III (1889), 93–94; Samuel Broughton to William Popple, May 4, 1702, *CSPC*, XX, 410; To the Queen's Most Excellent Majesty, New York, 1702, CO 5/1048 (microfilm), HHV. The formal addresses are dated Oct. 2, 1702, though signatures were no doubt collected over many weeks (*NYCD*, IV, 1005–1010). The Ulster Co. signers regretted that their address was not offered "in

the name of the whole for these wedges that have been formerly forged, these last four years [during Bellomont's and Nanfan's administrations] . . . have split the County, almost into two halves."

3. Cornbury to Board of Trade, May 18, 1702, *CSPC*, XX, 496.

4. John Campbell Newsletter, May 17, 1703, MHS, *Procs.*, 1st Ser., IX (1867), 492.

5. The first earl of Clarendon's famous *History of the Rebellion*, the preeminent contemporary account of the English Civil War, was in part a defense of his conduct as Charles II's chancellor; Laurence and Henry's introduction to a later edition of the *History* was a further effort to correct what they saw as slurs on the family name. In the 1690s, Henry successfully sued and drove from office the Oxford antiquarian Anthony Wood for libeling his father as a bribe-taker (Andrew Clark, ed., *The Life and Times of Anthony Wood, Antiquary, of Oxford, 1632–1695, Described by Himself* [Oxford, 1895], B). And as we have seen, Henry and Laurence both gave up lucrative offices in the late 1680s rather than submit to James II's pressure on the Catholic issue (chap. 2).

6. Governor Cornbury's Answer to the River Indians, Aug. 15, 1702; Cornbury to Board of Trade, Oct. 1, 1702, *NYCD*, IV, 997–998, 1001; see also 994.

7. William Anderson to Cornbury, May 3, 1708, Clarendon Papers, CII, fol. 164, Bodl. Lib.; New Jersey Council to Governor Lovelace, April 1709, *NJA*, III, 409–410.

8. Anderson to Cornbury, May 3, 1708, Clarendon Papers, CII, fol. 164; New Jersey Council to Lovelace, April 1709, *NJA*, III, 409–410. On impressment, see Cornbury to Board of Trade, New York, Dec. 14, 1706, Admiralty 1/3815; Extract of a letter from Cornbury regarding the behavior of Captain Miles, Dec. 6, 1706, Admiralty 1/3814, PRO (microfilm), HHV.

9. The quotation is from William Byrd II in Louis B. Wright and Marion Tinling, eds., *The Secret Diary of William Byrd of Westover, 1709–1712* (Richmond, Va., 1941), 159. The basic structures of the First British Empire were, according to Stephen Saunders Webb, shaped by military men "intent on establishing security and imposing social order within their jurisdictions and determined to spread crusading Christianity and English authority over conquered territories"; see *The Governors-General: The English Army and the Definition of the Empire, 1569–1681* (Chapel Hill, N.C., 1979), 438.

10. In addition, Connecticut was to provide £450, Pennsylvania £350, Maryland £650, and East and West Jersey £250 each (Privy Council 5/2, n.d., fols. 146–173, PRO [microfilm], HHV). The Carolinas were not mentioned, possibly because they were considered within the purview of forces at Jamaica; Massachusetts's funds were apparently under the authority of its governor, Joseph Dudley. The militia quotas were Massachusetts 350 men, New Hampshire 40, Rhode Island 48, Connecticut 120, New York 200, East Jersey 60, West Jersey 60, Penn-

sylvania 80, Maryland 160, and Virginia 240. Ibid.; Draught of Commission, July 8, 1702, *CSPC*, XX, no. 715.

11. Cornbury to William Blathwayt, Hammersmith, Aug. 5, 1701, Blathwayt Papers, HL; John Nanfan to Board of Trade, Feb. 4, 1703, *CSPC*, XXI, no. 295. When Cornbury arrived, the four companies were owed "from 1691 nearly £20,000"; see Stanley McCrory Pargellis, "The Four Independent Companies of New York," in *Essays in Colonial History Presented to Charles McLean Andrews by His Students* (1931; rpt. Freeport, N.Y., 1966), 107.

For Cornbury's lobbying efforts, see his letters to Blathwayt, Hammersmith, Aug. 5, Sept. 9, 16, Nov. 8, 1701, Blathwayt Papers; and June 28, 1701, PC 2/78, fols. 221–224, Apr. 3, 1703, PC 2/79, fol. 347, PRO (microfilm), HHV; and Leo Francis Stock, ed., *Proceedings and Debates of the British Parliaments respecting North America*, 5 vols. (1924–1941), III, 21–22. How much of the requested ordnance was ever delivered is hard to say, though Cornbury may have brought some of it with him to New York in 1702.

12. Cornbury to Secretary Popple, Dec. 20, 1701, *CSPC*, XIX, no. 1096; Cornbury to Board of Trade, Dec. 12, 1702, XXI, no. 41; John Champante to Board of Trade, Mar. 22, 1703, no. 489; Journal of the Board of Trade, May 25, June 4, 1703, nos. 732, 794. And see Champante's letters in the Rawlinson Mss., A272, Bodl. Lib. For Champante's efforts to get Cornbury dismissed, see chap. 7.

13. Nanfan to Champante, New York, Oct. 5, 1702, Rawlinson Mss., fol. 167. Given that Nanfan, no friend of Cornbury's, was the auditor, the description carried an ironic edge.

14. June 2, 1703, PC 2/79, fol. 347 (microfilm), HHV; Cornbury to Lords of Trade, Orange Co., N.Y., Sept. 24, 1702, *NYCD*, IV, 967; Sir Thomas Laurence to Board of Trade, Oct. 25, 1703, *CSPC*, XXI, no. 1190. On the Albany fort, see Cornbury to Board of Trade, Orange Co., N.Y., Sept. 24, 1702, *NYCD*, IV, 969–971.

15. Humble Address of the Mayor, Recorder, Aldermen, and Assistants of the City of Albany convened in common Councill, Albany, Aug. 19, 1702, CO 5/1047 (microfilm), HHV. (A similar address from Ulster Co. is in *NYCD*, IV, 1009.) Pargellis, "Four Companies," in *Essays in Colonial History*, 104.

16. Cornbury to Board of Trade, Orange Co., N.Y., Sept. 24, 1702, *NYCD*, IV, 968. For an earlier proposal to build fortifications at the Narrows, see "Report of Colonel Romer on the Harbor of New-York," Jan. 13, 1701, ibid., 836. Cornbury's actions were praised in a Memorial from Mr. [Robert] Livingston about New-York to the Lords of Trade, n.d. [1703?], ibid., 1067–1069; Colonel Robert Quary to Board of Trade, New York, June 16, 1703, ibid., 1052–1055; Laurence to Board of Trade, Oct. 25, 1703, *CSPC*, XXI, no. 1190. Governor Fitz-John Winthrop of Connecticut had earlier told Cornbury he had "made glad the hearts of all good men. . . . Your Excellencye's conduct thus far fills every habitation

with joy." Winthrop to Cornbury, New London, June 24, 1702, MHS, *Colls.*, 6th Ser., III (1889), 100.

17. Cornbury to Board of Trade, December 1702, *NYCD*, IV, 1004, October 1706, 1183. Governor Francis Nicholson contributed Virginia's quota of £900 from his own pocket when the Assembly refused to pay its share (Nicholson to Board of Trade, July 23, 1703, *CSPC*, XXI, no. 944). Maryland's royal governor persuaded his assembly to provide £300 of its £650 share (Minute of the Council of Maryland, June 15, 1703, ibid., no. 828). Pennsylvania and Connecticut gave nothing; the governor of Rhode Island was "full of Protestations of Loyalty and fidelity to the Crown but no money" (Cornbury to Board of Trade, New York, June 30, 1703, ibid., no. 861).

On defense costs, see Address of the New York Assembly and Governor Cornbury's response, May 27, 1703, *CSPC*, XXI, no. 748; Cornbury to Board of Trade, June 30, 1703, no. 861. The New York Assembly's address contained an eloquent plea for Cornbury to intercede with Queen Anne regarding the colony's high taxes. The assembly claimed to have paid £22,000 for defense, much of which had been misapplied by past administrations; thus, wrote Cornbury, it was little wonder that the people were now "averse to giveing." The final quotation is in Cornbury to Board of Trade, June 30, 1703.

18. Cornbury to Board of Trade, Orange Co., N.Y., Sept. 29, 1702, *NYCD*, IV, 977–978; Stock, ed., *Proceedings of Parliament*, III, 73. The Board of Trade thanked Cornbury in 1707 for putting New York City into a sound defensive posture (*NYCD*, V, 2).

19. *NYCD*, IV, 1172. *Lowestoffe* was a fifth-rate frigate of 32 guns and 145 men, *Triton's Prize* a sixth-rate frigate of 30 guns and 115 men.

20. Cornbury to Board of Trade, New York, Dec. 14, 1706, Admiralty 1/3815, PRO (microfilm), HHV.

21. See, e.g., Cornbury to Board of Trade, December 1702, *CSPC*, XXI, no. 29; and Cornbury to Board of Trade, Oct. 3, 1706, *NYCD*, IV, 1184–1185. John Brewer, *The Sinews of Power: War, Money, and the English State, 1688–1783* (New York, 1989), 11–12, 29–31.

22. These very years saw the emergence of a naval officer class "with excellent *esprit de corps*. . . . Officers flaunted their bellicosity . . . [and] held themselves in high esteem." Brewer, *Sinews of Power*, 58, 59.

23. On Captain Fane, see Cornbury to Board of Trade, New York, Dec. 14, 1706, Admiralty 1/3815, PRO (microfilm), HHV. On Richard Davis, see Cornbury to Davis, Dec. 9, 1706, 1/1693, no. 18; Davis to Cornbury, Dec. 10, 1706; and Order in Council to Lieutenant Richard Davis, Dec. 11, 1706. In declining to attend Cornbury, Davis added: "But Shall Allways put in Execution your Lordships Commands for the Service of her Majesty" (Davis to Cornbury, Dec. 12, 1706). See also Cornbury to Board of Trade, New York, Dec. 14, 1706.

24. According to Cornbury, Davis had declared that if soldiers were sent to get him, "he would give them as warm a reception as ever they had in their lives" (Cornbury to Board of Trade, New York, Dec. 14, 1706, ibid.). Cornbury sent the Admiralty copies of all his orders, the responses they elicited, and affidavits from New Yorkers who served as messengers during the episode. See ibid.; Order of His Excellency Edward Viscount Cornbury to Captain John Riggs, Ft. Anne, Dec. 17, 1706, ibid.

25. Davis to Admiralty, Ft. Anne, Dec. 22, 1706, ibid.

26. Cornbury to James Hull, chief mate, Jan. 1, 1707, ibid.; Davis to the Admiralty, Jan. 7, 1707. The engagement is vividly described in separate accounts by Davis and Cornbury; Davis to Admiralty, June 3, 1707, ibid.; Cornbury to Board of Trade, New York, July 20, 1707, *NYCD*, V, 20–21. Cornbury and Davis continued to enjoy cordial relations in later years; see their correspondence, including a letter dated Nov. 19, 1711, in Admiralty 1/1693, no. 18, PRO (microfilm), HHV. It was on a ship under Davis's command that Cornbury returned to England in 1710 (Davis to Admiralty, Oct. 9, 1710).

27. Cornbury to Board of Trade, Oct. 3, 1706, *NYCD*, IV, 1181–1185. Mr. Burchett, secretary of the Admiralty, to Popple, Dec. 10, 1706, 1188. But see also Burchett to Captain Miles, Dec. 10, 1706, 1189.

28. Burchett to Popple, Admiralty Office, Apr. 30, 1707, ibid., V, 4. Having lost this particular struggle, the Board of Trade transmitted the Admiralty's ruling to Cornbury without comment.

29. Two Anglican missionaries stationed in New York characterized him as "a true nursing father" to the church: William Urquhart and John Thomas to the secretary, Long Island, July 4, 1705, SPG, Letterbook A, II, 105 (microfilm).

30. The Queen's Farm stretched from Broadway to the Hudson River (then along present-day Trinity Place) and from modern-day Fulton Street to approximately Christopher Street in Greenwich Village. Cornbury to the secretary, New York, Sept. 22, 1705, ibid., 105 (microfilm); Queen Anne to Governor Hunter, Apr. 14, 1714, IX, 177; Trinity Churchwardens and Vestry to the queen, May 11, 1714, 181.

31. State of the Church, Oct. 11, 1704, William Vesey to SPG, SPG Journals, App. A, no. 58 (London: Micro Methods, 1964); A Summary Account of the State of the Church in the Province of New York, Oct. 5, 1704, *DHNY*, III, 74–76; Elias Neau to John Chamberlayne, New York, Aug. 29, 1704, SPG, Letterbook A, II, 19 (microfilm).

Anglicans praised Cornbury throughout his administration, and indeed long afterward, for his devotion to the well-being of the colonial church. And in a colony riddled with religious conflict, Dissenters as frequently objected to Cornbury's treatment of them. See Thomas to SPG, New York, Mar. 1, 1705, SPG, Letterbook A, II, 71; Memorial of the Clergy, Nov. 13, 1711, VII, 295–304;

churchwardens of St. Mary's, Burlington, N.J., to the bishop of London, Mar. 25, 1714, IX, 98–101 (microfilm); secretary to Cornbury, Westminster, Apr. 18, 1706; American Papers of the SPG, Lambeth Palace, XIII, 198 (London: World Microfilm). For the Dissenters, consult [Francis Makemie], *A Narrative of a New and Unusual American Imprisonment of Two Presbyterian Ministers: And Prosecution of Mr. Francis Makemie, One of Them, for Preaching One Sermon at the City of New-York* (London, 1707), in Peter Force, comp., *Tracts and Other Papers, Relating Principally to the Origins, Settlement, and Progress of the Colonies of North America*, IV (1847; rpt. New York, 1947), no. 4; and Randall Balmer, *A Perfect Babel of Confusion: Dutch Religion and English Culture in the Middle Colonies* (New York, 1989).

32. Thomas Hutchinson, *History of the Colony and Province of Massachusetts-Bay* (1760–1768), ed. Lawrence Shaw Mayo, 3 vols. (1936; rpt. New York, 1970), II, 92n. Cornbury to the secretary, Nov. 9, 1705, SPG, Letterbook A, II, 131 (microfilm).

It is not clear that Cornbury had the legal right to license any except school-teachers, though the difference between teachers and ministers was often blurred in these years. Still, a number of clergymen accepted licenses from Cornbury, perhaps simply to keep the peace, as they did from governors before and after him. See License to Stephen Gasheris from Lord Cornbury (to read the service at the Dutch church in Kingston and to keep a "Writing and Reading School"), Aug. 10, 1704, NY Col. Mss., XLIX, fol. 165b, NYSL; Journal of Domine Beys, January–March 1706, E. T. Corwin, ed., *Ecclesiastical Records of the State of New York*, 7 vols. (Albany, N.Y., 1901–1916), III, 1615–1616; license to Mr. Goodhue (Presbyterian), January 1706, ibid., 1620; Petition to Lieutenant Governor Ingoldsby from D. Provoost, A. DePeyster, and J. DePeyster, n.d. [1709?], fols. 203–204 (and see fols. 205, 206, 225), A Collection of Original Letters, JCBL.

In 1863, the historian John Romeyn Brodhead accused Cornbury of forging an instruction from Queen Anne during the Makemie trial (discussed later) to support his claim of a licensing power ("Mr. Brodhead's Impeachment of Lord Cornbury as a Forger," *Historical Magazine* [Morrisania, N.Y.], 1st Ser., VII [November 1863], 329–331), though the defendant and his supporters themselves acknowledged the authenticity of the document. The language of Cornbury's instructions from both William III and Queen Anne was somewhat ambiguous at a time when the application of English law to the colonies was still being worked out.

33. Witnesses described the Hubbard incident as a riot, with a great "Hawling and Tugging of Seats; shoving one the other off," violently disrupting the Anglican service; see John Bartow to the secretary, Westchester, N.Y., Dec. 1, 1708, SPG, Letterbook A, III, 524–534 (microfilm). For Cornbury's actions against Hubbard, see ibid., 527–530; Corwin, ed., *Ecclesiastical Records*, III, 1531, 1570; Memorial of the Clergy, Nov. 13, 1711, *DHNY*, III, 230. For subsequent treat-

ment of the episode, see William Smith, Jr., *The History of the Province of New York: From the First Discovery to the Year 1732* (1757), ed. Michael Kammen, 2 vols. (Cambridge, Mass., 1972), I, 118–119; [William Livingston et al.], "Watch Tower," *New-York Mercury*, June 2, 1755. Anglican objections are expressed in James Honeyman to Lewis Morris, Jamaica, June 12, 1704, and John Talbot to George Keith, New York, Oct. 20, 1704, SPG, Letterbook A, I, 172, II, 23 (microfilm).

34. Cornbury to Board of Trade, New York, Oct. 14, 1706, *NYCD*, IV, 1186–1187. Cornbury's letter, dated 1706, places Makemie's arrest and trial in that year, but this is apparently an error of transcription.

Makemie incorporated in his account part of a dialogue between himself and Cornbury that at every turn shows the clergyman outwitting the governor on legal points; see *Narrative of a New and Unusual American Imprisonment*, in Force, *Tracts and Other Papers*, IV, no. 4. William Livingston reprinted the *Narrative* in 1755 (a time of tension between Presbyterians and Anglicans over the founding of King's College), describing the Makemie episode as "an eternal monument of the danger of bigotry, supported by power" ("Watch Tower," *New-York Mercury*, June 2, 1755). Dissenters were particularly angered when, following Makemie's acquittal by a New York jury, Cornbury's government compelled the clergyman to pay court charges of some £81. This was an instrument commonly used in England to enforce the government's will; see Leonard W. Levy, *Legacy of Suppression: Freedom of Speech and Press in Early American History* (New York, 1963), 11n. For a typical treatment of the case by a historian, see Carl Bridenbaugh, *Mitre and Sceptre: Transatlantic Faiths, Ideas, Personalities, and Politics, 1689–1775* (New York, 1962), 122–124.

35. The Reverend Thoroughgood Moore to the secretary, New York, Oct. 24, 1704, American Papers of the SPG, Lambeth Palace, I, 88 (microfilm); Cornbury to the secretary, New York, Nov. 9, 1705, SPG, Letterbook A, II, 131 (microfilm); Mr. [Peter] Fauconnier's Deposition in Justification of the Earle of Clarendon, Jan. 19, 1712, ibid., VII, 342–347 (microfilm). For the provision of an interpreter, see NY Col. Mss., L, fol. 34a. Moore's move to New Jersey is discussed in Fauconnier's Deposition, Jan. 19, 1712, SPG, Letterbook A, II, 342–347; Cornbury to the secretary, New York, Oct. 20, 1705, American Papers of the SPG, Lambeth Palace, XIII, 175 (microfilm). The final quotation is from the secretary to Cornbury, Westminster, Apr. 18, 1706, ibid., XIII, 198 (microfilm). For Moore's background, see Frederick Lewis Weis, *The Colonial Clergy of the Middle Colonies* (1957; rpt. Baltimore, 1978), 109.

36. His Majesty's Instructions for Edward Hyde Esq., n.d. [1702], PC 5/2, fols. 146–173, PRO (microfilm); Commission to Be Governor of New York, July 9, 1702, fols. 372–380 (microfilm), HHV.

37. For the Albany incident, see Fauconnier's Deposition, Jan. 19, 1712, SPG,

Letterbook A, II, 342–347 (microfilm). There are four major sources for the Ingoldsby episode: Quary to the bishop of London, Philadelphia, Jan. 20, 1708, IV, 90–110; Fauconnier's Deposition, Jan 19, 1712, VII, 342–347; Deposition of William Anderson, Jan. 19, 1712, Letterbook C, I, n.p.; Lewis Morris, State of the Church in New York and the Jerseys, n.d. [1708?], ibid. (microfilm). Elias Neau states that Moore had refused Ingoldsby Communion "upon the account of some Debauch and abominable Swearing, to which that Gentleman is unfortunately Addicted"; Neau to the secretary, New York, Feb. 27, 1709, Letterbook A, IV, 402–413. It was in this same scandal-bearing letter that Neau accused Cornbury of cross dressing.

For Anglican opposition to dueling in the early 18th century, see Donna T. Andrew, "The Code of Honour and Its Critics: The Opposition to Duelling in England, 1700–1850," *Social History*, V (1980), esp. 416–420.

38. The quoted passages are in Quary to the bishop of London, Philadelphia, Jan. 20, 1708, SPG, Letterbook A, IV, 90–110; even Robert Quary, the royalist New Jersey councillor, thought that the lieutenant governor "carried his resentments too high," and he advised Moore to make only a private apology. And see Fauconnier's Deposition, Jan 19, 1712, ibid., VII, 342–347 (microfilm).

39. Quary to the bishop of London, Jan. 20, 1708, ibid., IV, 90–110; Fauconnier's Deposition, Jan. 19, 1712, VII, 342–347 (microfilm).

Cornbury had also reprimanded Moore for offering Communion too frequently, often every two weeks. Moore meanwhile asserted that Cornbury could not give orders affecting New Jersey from New York, a view Whitehall firmly rejected. Moore to the secretary, Ft. Anne, August 1707, ibid., IV, 182–187; Moore to the secretary, Ft. Anne, Aug. 27, 1707, III, 348–359 (microfilm); Board of Trade to Lord Lovelace, Whitehall, June 28, 1708, *NYCD*, V, 47.

40. Moore to the secretary, Ft. Anne, Aug. 27, 1707, SPG, Letterbook A, III, 348–359; Fauconnier's Deposition, VII, 342–347 (microfilm). Regarding his suspension, Moore said he had been placed at Burlington by the bishop of London (the bishop having confirmed Cornbury's decision to move Moore from Albany). Cornbury replied that the queen had invested him with the "sole power" to place ministers in his government (which also was true pending confirmation by the bishop). Moore to the secretary, Ft. Anne, Aug. 27, 1707, ibid., III, 348–359 (microfilm).

41. Moore to the secretary, Ft. Anne, Aug. 27, August 1707, ibid., III, 348–359, IV, 182–187 (microfilm).

Elias Neau and Lewis Morris later claimed that Moore was aware of rumors about Cornbury's dressing as a woman and censured the New York clergy for failing to excommunicate him. Neau to the secretary, New York, Feb. 27, 1709, ibid., 402–413; Morris, State of the Church in New York and the Jerseys, n.d.

[1707?], SPG, Letterbook C, I, no. 1 (microfilm). But Moore specifically states in his letter that "the chief nay only cause" of his removal was that he opposed Cornbury's political program in New Jersey. And just before his dispute with Cornbury erupted, Moore had informed the SPG that he was "very well contented" at Burlington and "wouldn't change my 60 pound per annum here, for 600 . . . in any part of Europe" (July 17, 1707, American Papers of the SPG, Lambeth Palace, XII, 223, Lambeth Palace Library, London).

42. The readiness of these men to boldly confront their governor was very likely prompted by their knowledge that Cornbury's Tory patrons had fallen from power in England and that Cornbury himself was now subject to recall. For more on the relevant politics, see chaps. 7 and 8.

43. Cornbury to the secretary, Nov. 29, 1707, SPG, Letterbook A, III, 404–414 (microfilm). Whether the guard, who alone among the soldiers later questioned claimed he had no orders to detain Moore, was bribed or was simply a bit slow is impossible to determine. See affidavits of Lt. John Riggs, James Walters, Sgt. Francis Sheirman, and John Grimes, Jan. 2, 3, 1712, American Papers of the SPG, Lambeth Palace, VII, 248–251 (microfilm). Grimes, the sentinel who allowed Moore to escape, signed his affidavit with an *X;* he also noted that as punishment for allowing Moore to escape he was placed in irons for "five weeks and one day in very great Misery."

Brooke, a graduate of Emmanuel College, Cambridge, was posted to New Jersey by the SPG in 1705. He served as minister at Saint John's Church in Elizabethtown and itinerated among nine other congregations in the colony. Weis, *Colonial Clergy,* 21; Edwin F. Hatfield, *History of Elizabeth, New Jersey* (New York, 1868), chap. 1.

Neau to the secretary, New York, Feb. 27, 1709, SPG, Letterbook A, IV, 402–413 (Neau also denied he had assisted Moore's escape from the fort); Deposition of [Mayor] Ebenezer Wilson, Jan. 19, 1712, SPG, Letterbook C, I, n.p. (microfilm). Peter Fauconnier states that Moore and Brooke took shelter seven miles from New York in a country house belonging to "a Gentleman publickly known to be engaged in the Malcontent Party" (Morris had an estate in Westchester Co.). Fauconnier's Deposition, Jan. 19, 1712, SPG, Letterbook A, VII, 342–347 (microfilm).

44. The Reverend John Talbot to the secretary, Aug. 24, 1708, SPG, Letterbook A, IV, 176–181 (microfilm); George Morgan Hills, *History of the Church in Burlington* (Trenton, N.J., 1876), 66–83. For the fate of Moore and Brooke, see David Humphreys, *An Historical Account of the Incorporated Society for the Propagation of the Gospel in Foreign Parts . . .* (London, 1730), 291.

45. Thus were Cornbury's opponents derided in a Memorial of the Clergy, Nov. 13, 1711, SPG, Letterbook A, VII, 295–304 (microfilm). The imperial con-

stitutional context in these years is examined in Jack P. Greene, *Peripheries and Center: Constitutional Development in the Extended Polities of the British Empire and the United States, 1607–1788* (Athens, Ga., 1986), esp. chap. 3.

CHAPTER FOUR

1. The depiction of Cornbury in Leonard Woods Labaree, *Royal Government in America: A Study of the British Colonial System before 1783* (New York, 1958), 283, is typical; no evidence is offered for Cornbury's alleged corruption. Oliver Morton Dickerson, in *American Colonial Government, 1696–1765 . . .* (Cleveland, Ohio, 1912), 160, cites a letter from Cornbury himself as evidence of his misdeeds, though it contains nothing to implicate him.

2. P. G. M. Dickson, *The Financial Revolution in England: A Study in the Development of Public Credit, 1688–1756,* 2d ed. (Aldershot, Hampshire, 1993); Dora Mae Clark, *The Rise of the British Treasury: Colonial Administration in the Eighteenth Century* (New Haven, Conn., 1960); Robert C. Ritchie, *Captain Kidd and the War against the Pirates* (Cambridge, Mass., 1986), 148–151; Ian K. Steele, *Politics of Colonial Policy: The Board of Trade in Colonial Administration, 1696–1720* (Oxford, 1968).

3. Tim Harris, *Politics under the Later Stuarts: Party Conflict in a Divided Society, 1660–1715* (New York, 1993); John Brewer, *The Sinews of Power: War, Money, and the English State, 1688–1783* (New York, 1989).

4. Labaree, *Royal Government in America,* 112, chap. 8; Mary Lou Lustig, *Robert Hunter, 1666–1734: New York's Augustan Statesman* (Syracuse, N.Y., 1983), esp. 100–101; J. G. A. Pocock, *The Machiavellian Moment: Florentine Political Thought and the Atlantic Republican Tradition* (Princeton, N.J., 1975), esp. 423–427; J. M. Sosin, *English America and Imperial Inconstancy: The Rise of Provincial Autonomy, 1696–1715* (Lincoln, Nebr., 1985), 18–32, 35.

5. Past assessments have also been limited by incomplete sources, most writers drawing their information from provincial gossip and selected English documents relating to New York and New Jersey published during the 19th century. A much larger body of original documents in England as well as important collections in American archives is used here.

6. "Remonstrance of the Assembly of New Jersey, against certain evils, to which the Province was subjected, and Lord Cornbury's Answer," May 5, 12, 1707, William A. Whitehead et al., eds., *NJA,* 1st Ser., 43 vols. (Newark, N.J., 1880–1949), III, 179, 196, 194. It might be noted that the depositions taken by Morris's committee (198–219) were more likely to name Cornbury as the recipient of bribes than were those sworn before other authorities.

Lewis Morris (1671–1746), precocious politician and frequent troubler of colonial governments in New Jersey and New York, held landed estates in both colonies. For his peripatetic, interest-driven travels between Court and Country positions in provincial politics, see Eugene R. Sheridan, *Lewis Morris, 1671–1746: A Study in Early American Politics* (Syracuse, N.Y., 1981); Stanley Nider Katz, *Newcastle's New York: Anglo-American Politics, 1732–1753* (Cambridge, Mass., 1968), chaps. 4–5; and Patricia U. Bonomi, *A Factious People: Politics and Society in Colonial New York* (New York, 1971), chaps. 3–4.

7. Deposition of John Johnstone, *NJA*, III, 208. Regarding such presents, see Minutes of the Privy Council, Whitehall, Sept. 5, 1700, PC 2/78, fol. 79, PRO. For a discussion of presents given to southern governors, see Jack P. Greene, *The Quest for Power: The Lower Houses of Assembly in the Southern Royal Colonies, 1689–1776* (1963; rpt. New York, 1972), 131–132.

8. A "present" was no bribe before 1703, but simply money that was within the gift of the assemblies. The crown much preferred that governors' salaries be paid at a set rate from customs and excise revenues, over which it had more control. The present in this case was offered by an individual because the new assembly was still in formation. For imperial policy (which placed presents in a more ambiguous category after 1703), see Minutes of the Privy Council, Whitehall, Apr. 10, 1703, PC 2/79, fols. 354–356, PRO.

9. Deposition of John Johnstone, *NJA*, III, 208–209 (abbreviations expanded). For Cornbury's order regarding presents, see ibid., 10.

10. Ibid., 179, 198–219, 277; "Minutes and Rules of the [New Jersey] Supreme Court, 1704–1715," 7–9, 12–13, New Jersey State Archives, Trenton.

11. *NJA*, III, 201–202, 210, 212, 213, 214, 216, 217. The original depositions, dated April and May 1707, are in CO 5/1091, fol. 13 (vii), PRO.

12. *NJA*, III, 203–204, 207, 277–278. Morris asserted that he could prove the money got at least as far as Cornbury's New York chief justice, though he does not say how (277). And see the letter from Samuel Jennings (though apparently written in Lewis Morris's hand) to Lord Sunderland, May 5, 1707, HM 22301, Sunderland Collection, HL. For the assembly's retreat, see *NJA*, III, 262.

13. *NJA*, III, 228 (first quotation), 288–289 (second and third quotations), 288–289 (fourth quotation).

14. Cornbury estimated the actual cost of two batteries at about £2,025; see Cornbury to Board of Trade, N.Y., June 30, 1703, *NYCD*, IV, 1058. For the stonework, see Mr. Congreve to Board of Trade, July 1704, 1129.

That Cornbury's governorship coincided with Queen Anne's War (1702–1713) greatly complicated his efforts to rule, especially since one of the Treasury Department's reforms involved shifting the cost of local defense to the colonials themselves; see Clark, *Rise of the British Treasury*, 13. Such costs, defrayed by a tax on property, were unusually heavy in New York because it was the gateway to French Canada. Robert Quary, like Cornbury, had observed in 1704 that New Yorkers' "circumstances are very low" owing to the war; see Quary to Board of

Trade, Virginia, May 30, 1704, *NYCD*, IV, 1084. For a discussion of property taxes during wartime, see Bonomi, *A Factious People*, 80.

15. The "pleasure house" comment is in the Colden Letters on Smith's History, NYHS, *Collections*, I (1868), 204. Cadwallader Colden was not an eyewitness to these events because he did not arrive in the colony until 1718. See also William Smith, Jr., *The History of the Province of New-York: From the First Discovery to the Year 1732* (1757), ed. Michael Kammen, 2 vols. (Cambridge, Mass., 1972), I, 122.

The bills are in Mr. Denn's Account, 1702–1704, Clarendon Papers, CII, fol. 88, Bodl. Lib. The sum of £100 is plausible; timber for the ground floor cost £15 and labor £48 (the bill listing 160 man-days of work at 6s. per day).

16. *Journal of the Votes and Proceedings of the General Assembly of the Colony of New York, 1691–1765*, 2 vols. (New York, 1764–1766), I, 208, 212. In spite of this long-available evidence, historians repeatedly state that Cornbury misapplied the £1,500.

17. Ibid., 213. For evidence of Morris's part in Cornbury's New York Assembly opposition, see his political writings in the Robert Morris Papers, box I, 1698–1709, Special Collections, Alexander Library, Rutgers University.

18. [William Blathwayt], Observations on the New York Accounts which are to be Rectifyed Accordingly, Under the Management of the Council from the 30th June 1702 to the 25th of March 1703, NY Col. Mss., n.d. [1704?], XLIX, fol. 16, NYSL.

19. Clark, *Rise of the British Treasury*, 25, 36. As Thomas C. Barrow notes, between 1696 and 1710 imperial authorities fleshed out the system outlined in the Act of 1696; see *Trade and Empire: The British Customs Service in Colonial America, 1660–1775* (Cambridge, Mass., 1967), 60.

20. Given that Cornbury's administration coincided with the War of the Spanish Succession (Queen Anne's War), the War Office and Admiralty also got involved in defense expenditures and planning. Under these circumstances, overlapping jurisdictions and contests for power were inevitable. For more on the administrative complexities of this period, see W. A. Speck, "The International and Imperial Context," in Jack P. Greene and J. R. Pole, eds., *Colonial British America: Essays in the New History of the Early Modern Era* (Baltimore, 1984), 384–407. For the growth of government departments in these years, see Brewer, *Sinews of Power*, esp. 64–69.

21. Blathwayt to [George Clarke], May 23, Aug. 27, 1704, NY Col. Mss., V, box 49, fols. 79, 170. Clarke was also distantly related to Lord Cornbury, having married a Hyde.

Blathwayt had been one of Cornbury's supporters in obtaining the New York governorship; when the Jersey proprietorships were to be combined into a single royal colony, he wrote Cornbury, "In my poor opinion these Governments would be more properly in your Lordships hands." Blathwayt to Cornbury, May 8, 1702, Blathwayt Papers, VIII, Colonial Williamsburg Foundation, Williamsburg, Va. (microfilm).

22. Under both the old and the new regime, the governor and council also had to certify local expenditures. See, e.g., Blathwayt to Clarke, Apr. 10, 1705, Treasury 64/90, PRO (microfilm), HHV. For Clarke's view of how the system was supposed to work in New York, see his State of Revenue in New York . . . offered to William Blathwayt, n.d. [1706?], NY Col. Mss., LII, fol. 87a. On Blathwayt's career, see Stephen Saunders Webb, "William Blathwayt, Imperial Fixer: Muddling through to Empire, 1689–1717," *WMQ*, 3d Ser., XXVI (1969), esp. 412–414.

23. Clarke to Blathwayt, New York, Feb. 23, 1705, BL 155; Clarke to Blathwayt, Virginia, July 23, 1705, BL 207, HL; Thomas Byerly, Journall or Particular . . . transactions, June 10, 1704–1707/8, CO 5/1084, fol. 62, PRO (microfilm), HHV. Cornbury also charged Byerly with allowing trade in "enumerated Comodities," which he considered "a manifest breach of the Laws of Trade"; Cornbury to [the treasurer?], New York, June 13, 1705, T 1/94, 389 (microfilm), HHV. The rules regarding what was or was not illegal trade were "far from precise" in these years, leading to many such disputes; see Clark, *Rise of the Treasury*, 20, 24.

The last quotation is in Clarke to Blathwayt, Virginia, July 23, 1705, BL 207, HL. Clarke and Byerly had come to New York by the same ship in 1703 (E. B. O'Callaghan, ed., *Voyage of George Clarke, Esq., to America* [Albany, N.Y., 1867]). New York was the only colony in which the collector of the customs was also the receiver (and distributor) of provincial revenue, which meant that New York's receiver was frequently entangled in politics (Barrow, *Trade and Empire*, 66).

24. Clarke to Byerly, New York, Sept. 5, 1705, and Clarke to Blathwayt, Sept. 6, 1705, BL 210–211, HL.

25. Clarke to Blathwayt, Sept. 6, 1705, BL 210–211, HL.

26. On Cornbury's secretary (Peter Fauconnier), see ibid., 211. Peter Schuyler discovered that "Mr. Clarke, auditor, would not allow the bills for firewood at Albany, neither can Mr. DeLancey to whom I paid one hundred and fifty Pounds in such bills get the same allowed on his Customs which makes him very uneasy" (Clarendon Papers, CII, fols. 101–102, Bodl. Lib.). See also Cornbury to Blathwayt, Nov. 28, 1708, Blathwayt Papers, VIII, no. 7, Colonial Williamsburg (microfilm); and NY Col. Mss., L, fols. 117, 145a; Observations on Mr. Fauconnier's Account [burned] of Candles for the Fort, etc., n.d., LII, fol. 25. For the petty expenses, see Observations on Mr. Fauconnier's Account of Contingent Charges, 1705–1707, LII, fol. 30.

Even deciding which agency to apply to for reimbursement was complex. In one audit the Treasury ordered that freight costs for new uniforms for the New York companies of foot should not be charged to the "Civil Revenue," but presumably to the ordnance office; see [Blathwayt], Observations on the New York Accounts . . . , ibid., n.d. [1704?], XLIX, fol. 16.

27. NY Col. Mss., LIII, fol. 47; An Account of Warrants . . . , Mar. 4, 1709, Cornbury Mss., NYHS.

28. Clarke to Blathwayt, New York, Nov. 23, 1705, Copy, BL, 161, HL.

29. Ibid., Sept. 6, Nov. 28, 1705, 211–212; Clarke to [Blathwayt], [January 1706?], Clarke Mss., NYHS. The letter of November 28 is especially interesting. In one passage Clarke asserts that Cornbury "gave me such like base language that a gentleman would Scorn to use to a Negro." But he followed this with: "My Lords a Gentleman of very good sence, which cannot be so greatly misguided without some alloy of interest."

Clarke's description of Cornbury's temperament probably did not much impress Blathwayt, it being a convention of this time to accuse a political rival of excessive passion, thereby implying that the most prized of mental faculties — reason — was being subverted by baser instincts. (Note that Clarke used identical language in denouncing Cornbury's secretary; see above.) Clarke himself was apparently a man of some passion, having been arrested and fined in 1701 for assault and battery against a merchant in Dublin (O'Callaghan, ed., *Voyage of George Clarke*).

30. Cornbury to Lord Clarendon, Sept. 1, 1705, Mss. Doc. 619, Albany Institute of History and Art, Albany, N.Y.

31. On Fletcher's administration, see Governor Bellomont to Board of Trade, New York, May 8, 18, 1698, *NYCD*, IV, 302–310; Colonel Fletcher's Answers to the Complaints against him, London, Dec. 24, 1698, 443–451; Cornbury to Board of Trade, Sept. 27, 1702, 973. James S. Leamon concludes that Bellomont attempted to blacken Fletcher's reputation for political reasons ("Governor Fletcher's Recall," *WMQ*, 3d Ser., XX [1963], 527–542); see also John D. Runcie, "The Problem of Anglo-American Politics in Bellomont's New York," *WMQ*, 3d Ser., XXVI (1969), 191–217.

For Governor Bellomont, see Quary to Board of Trade, June 16, 1703, *NYCD*, IV, 1052; Colonel Ingoldsby to Blathwayt, May 26, 1704, BV, New Netherland, fol. 43, NYHS; Cornbury to Board of Trade, June 17, 1704, *NYCD*, IV, 1095; Caleb Heathcote to Gilbert Heathcote, [1701], BL 206, HL; Herbert L. Osgood, *The American Colonies in the Eighteenth Century*, 4 vols. (New York, 1924–1925), II, 66.

Alison Gilbert Olson discusses transatlantic influences in *Anglo-American Politics, 1660–1775: The Relationship between Parties in England and Colonial America* (New York, 1973).

32. For John Nanfan, see *Journal of the Assembly of New York*, I, 171; Memorial of Mr. Champante to the Board of Trade, Feb. 4, 1703, *NYCD*, IV, 1027–1028;

Affidavit of Mr. Ebenezer Wilson, June 1704, Rawlinson Papers, D 916, fol. 180, Bodl. Lib. (microfilm), HHV.

For Lady Bellomont, *CSPC*, XXI, 30; Petition of Peter Schuyler, Killian Van Rensselaer, and Dirck Wessels to Cornbury, 1703, NY Col. Mss., XLVII, fols. 79a–b.

33. The Petition and Case of Robert Livingston, June 1704, T 1/90, fols. 356–359, PRO (microfilm), HHV; Robert Hunter to Board of Trade, May 21, 1715, *NYCD*, V, 402–403. For an explanation of Hunter's delay in lodging charges against Cornbury, see Eugene R. Sheridan, ed., *The Papers of Lewis Morris*, 3 vols. (Newark, N.J., 1991–1993), I, 130, n. 1; and Lustig, *Robert Hunter*, 127. For accusations against Hunter's administration, see ibid., 119–120, 123.

34. Stanley McCrory Pargellis, "The Four Independent Companies of New York," in *Essays in Colonial History Presented to Charles McLean Andrews by His Students* (1931; rpt. New York, 1966), quotation on 105; Cornbury to Board of Trade, June 17, 1704, *NYCD*, IV, 1095.

35. Petitions of Captain Weemes and Lieutenant Matthew Shank to Cornbury, Nov. 11, 1702, NY Col. Mss., XLVI, 108, 113; Cornbury to Treasury, Oct. 18, 1708, Mar. 26, 1711, T 1/146, fols. 83, 85, PRO (microfilm), HHV; Affidavit of Mr. Ebenezer Wilson, June 1704, Rawlinson Papers, D 916, fol. 180 (microfilm), HHV; Account of [Cornbury] Debts, Mar. 9, 1709, Add. Mss. 15895, fol. 349, BL. The quotation is from Pargellis, "Four Independent Companies," in *Essays in Colonial History*, 106.

Cornbury's administration was apparently quite punctual in paying the troops, at least in the early years; see July 1704, *CSPC*, XXII, nos. 643i–xi. This is the more remarkable considering that Cornbury did not retain the "respites" (the portion of soldiers' pay usually reserved for the commanding officer), these being used instead to recruit the four companies' full complement of men and, as noted earlier, to buy new uniforms; see Apr. 3, 1703, PC 2/79, fols. 344–345, PRO (microfilm), HHV; Cornbury to Clarendon, Mar. 9, 1709, Add. Mss. 15895, BL.

36. October 21, 1701, William A. Shaw, ed., *Calendar of Treasury Books*, XVI (London, 1938), 376. George Keith, *A Journal of Travels from New-Hampshire to Caratuck* (London, 1706), 55; Sir Thomas Laurence to Board of Trade, Virginia, Oct. 25, 1703, *CSPC*, XXI, no. 1190; Sales of Sundry Merchandize at Public Vendue, Nov. 18, 1708, Clarendon Papers, LII, fols. 180–182, Bodl. Lib.; Sold to Mr. Swift, Jan. 18, 1709, ibid., n.p.; Mr. Denn's Account, 1702–1704, ibid., fol. 89. For a discussion of the colonials' growing interest in gentility after 1700, see Richard L. Bushman, *The Refinement of America: Persons, Houses, Cities* (New York, 1992).

37. Sales of Sundry Merchandize at Public Vendue, Nov. 18, 1708, Clarendon Papers, LII, fols. 180–182, Bodl. Lib. It is unlikely that any of the pictures was

from the celebrated Clarendon Collection begun by Cornbury's grandfather; all sold for around £1 or £2 with the exception of Saint Jerome, which went for £10. This compares with the £5–£15 paid for a suite of calico curtains.

38. "Journal of Rev. John Sharpe," *Pennsylvania Magazine of History and Biography*, XL (1916), 270; Lord Cornbury's Account, 1702–1704, Clarendon Papers, CII, fol. 54, Bodl. Lib.

39. NY Col. Mss., LIII, fol. 47, XLVI, pt. 2, fol. 8; Lord Cornbury's General Accounts, May 6, 1707, Clarendon Papers, CII, fol. 192c, Bodl. Lib.; T 1/91, fol. 138, PRO (microfilm), HHV. Morris's comment appears in the *New-York Weekly Journal*, Dec. 24, 1733; the draft of this essay, in Morris's hand, is in the Rutherfurd Collection, NYHS.

Some writers have assumed that bills amounting to £500 for 20 pipes of madeira supplied to Cornbury by New York merchant Abraham DePeyster were evidence Cornbury was a drunkard (see, e.g., Charles W. Spencer, "The Cornbury Legend," New York State Historical Association, *Proceedings*, XIII [1914], 310–311). Yet this ignores not only Cornbury's active table but the custom of treating, which must have accounted for much of the expenditure for wine. DePeyster was apparently a major supplier; see his £30 bill to Governor Bellomont for one pipe of madeira "for the city regiment, the soldiers in the fort, and the men of war, on the king's birthday" (Nov. 4, 1700, no. 10586, Emmet Collection, NYPL).

40. James Logan to William Penn, June 23, 25, 1702, James Logan Letterbook I, 31, HSP. Cornbury also took the occasion to tell Logan that he was "much averse to the Warmth" of the Philadelphia Anglicans, a strident High Church clique then troubling Logan (June 25, 1702, ibid). Of course, Logan was not blind to the potential value of Cornbury's friendship, noting that his close relation to the crown could be of service to Pennsylvania in future.

41. Logan to Penn, Aug. 13, 1702, Logan Letterbook I, 44, HSP; NY Col. Mss., XLVI, pt. 3, fol. 46.

42. NY Col. Mss., XLVI, pt. 2, fols. 3, 9, 11, pt. 3, fols. 6, 7, 9.

43. Ibid., pt. 3, fol. 13; Conference of Lord Cornbury with the Indians, 1702, *NYCD*, IV, 986, 980, 979, 992, 984. Cornbury in addition offered medical assistance to an Indian woman afflicted with smallpox, and among his accounts is an entry for paying "Dr. Rookeby for Medicines and Attendance in Looking after some of the Indian Sachims." NY Col. Mss., XLVI, pt. 2, fol. 2.

44. Neals Account for Washing, Sept. 22, 1702, NY Col. Mss., XLVI, pt. 3, fols. 23–25, 53. The Albany accounts include a bill of £3, 12s. "for a Cow [for] the wife of the Governor," which suggests that one of Governor and Lady Cornbury's four nonsurviving infants was with them at Albany. Regarding the baptisms, Lady Cornbury is recorded as sponsor of Maria, daughter of Maria Van Cortlandt and Killian Van Rensselaer; the governor stood with Maria Van Rens-

selaer as sponsor of Edward, son of Henry Holland; in 1704, Cornbury sponsored another Edward, son of John Collins and Margarita Schuyler. Edward was an unusual name for a Dutch-American child. Joel Munsell, *The Annals of Albany* (Albany, N.Y., 1852), III, 93, 94, 102.

The quotation is in *NYCD*, IV, 987–988. For more on Cornbury's negotiations of 1702, see chap. 8.

45. Livingston to William Lowndes, New London, June 2, 1707, T 1/102, pp. 130–131, PRO (microfilm), HHV (this letter also relayed the cross-dressing rumor). Livingston had recently returned after nearly three years in London seeking reimbursement for official expenses contracted before Cornbury's arrival. His falling-out with Cornbury may be owing to the "great opposition" he found in London to the settlement of his accounts, which he blamed on Cornbury and his father, the earl of Clarendon. He was "informed it was from that corner it came. . . . All cunning was devised to clogg my warrant." Livingston to Fitz-John Winthrop, London, May 7, 1705, MHS, *Colls.*, 6th Ser., III (1899), 292. His probable suspicion that the governor would soon be replaced, given the political turn in the ministry, may also have made him especially susceptible to the opposition's rumors about Cornbury. For Livingston's experience in London and return to New York, see Lawrence H. Leder, *Robert Livingston, 1654–1728, and the Politics of Colonial New York* (Chapel Hill, N.C., 1961), 180–204.

46. When awarding patents to political supporters, Cornbury tended to observe the 2,000-acre limit imposed by the crown. And, contrary to the history books, he spoke against "exorbitant Grants" as discouraging to settlement in New York, especially the 300,000-acre Evans Patent in Orange Co.; he recommended that it and a number of Governor Fletcher's large grants be vacated; see June 30, 1704, *CSPC*, XXII, no. 428. Some of the larger patents he did approve were for townships (e.g., 23,000 acres to the Town of Bedford), while others, such as the Westenhook Patent on the Housatonic River, were likely made in support of the crown's effort to preempt claims by Connecticut to New York's eastern borderlands. See the list of grants patented by Cornbury and other governors in Abstract of the Record of all Grants of Land in New York Colony to 1760, CO 5/1134 (microfilm), HHV.

The confusion about Cornbury's and other New York governors' land policies arises from shifting imperial instructions and the vagueness of markers in the early deeds. Some patentees later "Streched the bounds" of their grants, as one New Yorker put it, by intentionally misreading them; James Alexander to Hunter, n.d. (post 1721), draft, Rutherfurd Collection, NYHS. Such was the case, for example, with the huge Hardenbergh Patent in Ulster Co., patented initially by Cornbury as a "small" grant, according to a lawyer pursuing claims in 1770 against the then patentees. (See the legal papers in American Antiquarian Society, *Proceedings*, N.S., XIX [Worcester, Mass., 1908–1909], 151–181).

47. Cornbury writes: "Because the Assembly of New Jersey would not settle any Revenue,... I have been forced to carry money with me from New York to bear my charges in New Jersey [which] has run me into debt in New York" (An Account of money due to me in the Provinces of New York and New Jersey for which I have not yet any Warrants, Feb. 24, 1709, Cornbury Papers, NYHS). The governor's secretary, Peter Fauconnier, confirmed that Cornbury received no money from New Jersey after Dec. 13, 1706; Fauconnier to [Governor Lovelace], Feb. 8, 1709, *CSPC*, XXIV, no. 847. On Byerly, see Cornbury to Treasury(?), New York, Sept. 24, 1707, CO 5/103, fol. 72, PRO; Petition of Cornbury to Lovelace [1709], NY Col. Mss., LIII, fol. 19; Cornbury to the queen [ca. March 1711], SP 44/245, fols. 268–271, PRO.

Charles Worthen Spencer estimated that between 1687 and 1717, New York's public debt amounted to about £44,000, "more than one-sixth" of which, he figured, could be charged to Cornbury ("Cornbury Legend," N.Y. State Hist. Ass., *Procs.*, XIII [1914], 314, n. 2). Yet Cornbury was governor for *more than a fifth* of those years, which means that his administration's share of the debt was proportionately less than that accumulated on average by other governors of the time.

CHAPTER FIVE

1. Lawrence E. Klein, *Shaftesbury and the Culture of Politeness: Moral Discourse and Cultural Politics in Early Eighteenth-Century England* (Cambridge, 1994).

2. *The Dangers of Europe from the Growing Power of France*, quoted in J. P. Kenyon, *Revolution Principles: The Politics of Party, 1689–1720* (Cambridge, 1977), 55.

3. As J. H. Plumb has observed, between 1689 and 1720 politics in England were "as violent as at any time in our history"; *The Growth of Political Stability in England, 1675–1725* (London, 1967), 133. For scholarship supporting this interpretation, see Tim Harris, *Politics under the Later Stuarts: Party Conflict in a Divided Society, 1660–1715* (New York, 1993); W. A. Speck, *Reluctant Revolutionaries: Englishmen and the Revolution of 1688* (Oxford, 1988); J. C. D. Clark, *English Society, 1688–1832: Ideology, Social Structure, and Political Practice during the Ancien Regime* (New York, 1985). Richard R. Johnson compares the period after 1689 in England with that following 1787 in the United States: both were times of "slow and often painful resolution of business left unfinished" ("Politics Redefined: An Assessment of Recent Writings on the Late Stuart Period of English History, 1660–1714," *WMQ*, 3d Ser., XXXV [1978], 691–732, quotation on 702). See also Gary Stuart De Krey, *A Fractured Society: The Politics of London in the First Age of Party, 1688–1715* (Oxford, 1985).

4. Geoffrey Holmes, *British Politics in the Age of Anne*, rev. ed. (London, 1987), 20–21. Tim Harris observes that "party strife undoubtedly reached a peak of intensity under Anne" (*Politics under the Late Stuarts*, 160). Linda Colley, however,

sees late Stuart party rhetoric as "stylized" if often "ruthless" (*In Defiance of Oligarchy: The Tory Party, 1714–60* [New York, 1982], 12).

5. William Shippen, *Moderation Display'd* (1704), in George deF. Lord et al., eds., *Poems on Affairs of State: Augustan Satirical Verse, 1660–1714,* 7 vols. (New Haven, Conn., 1963–1975), VII, 30. Robert Harley, the leading moderate after 1704, seemed to have a precocious understanding of the possibilities of coalition government (ibid., 19–20). Still, when he was challenged by Bolingbroke in the later years of Queen Anne's reign, the struggle between the two men became, according to J. H. Plumb, "almost paranoic" (*Growth of Political Stability in England,* 155).

6. As Richard Hofstadter has written, the notion of a "legitimate opposition — recognized opposition, organized and free enough in its activities to be able to displace an existing government by peaceful means — is an immensely sophisticated idea"; see *The Idea of a Party System* (Berkeley, Calif., 1969), 8. For the Shaftesbury quotation, see Klein, *Shaftesbury and the Culture of Politeness,* 152.

7. Gordon S. Wood, "Conspiracy and the Paranoid Style: Causality and Deceit in the Eighteenth Century," *WMQ,* 3d Ser., XXXIX (1982), 411.

8. Dustin Griffin, *Satire: A Critical Reintroduction* (Lexington, Ky., 1994), 10–11; Steven N. Zwicker, *Politics and Language in Dryden's Poetry* (Princeton, N.J., 1984), chap. 1; John H. O'Neill, "Sexuality, Deviance, and Moral Character in the Personal Satire of the Restoration," *Eighteenth-Century Life,* II (1975–1976), quotation on 16. See also Harold Love, "Rochester and the Traditions of Satire," in Love, ed., *Restoration Literature: Critical Approaches* (London, 1972), 145–175. For earlier Jacobean ballads and satirical broadsheets, consult Adam Fox, "Ballads, Libels, and Popular Ridicule in Jacobean England," *Past and Present,* no. 145 (November 1994), 47–83.

9. For an elaboration of this reading, see Rachel Weil, "Sometimes a Scepter Is Only a Scepter: Pornography and Politics in Restoration England," in Lynn Hunt, ed., *The Invention of Pornography: Obscenity and the Origins of Modernity, 1500–1800* (New York, 1993), 125–153. "The tendency to associate political positions with sexual styles, and the tendency to use images of and stories about the king's body for a variety of political purposes, make it hard to separate pornographic political poems from other kinds of political theory and commentary" (140). And see Richard Braverman, *Plots and Counterplots: Sexual Politics and the Body Politic in English Literature, 1660–1730* (Cambridge, 1993), 115–116.

10. Lacy, *Satire* (1677), in Lord et al., eds., *Poems on Affairs of State,* I, 427, 426. This offering was in manuscript, as were most satires in the 1670s (xxxii). Nymphomania was commonly attributed to the king's' mistresses; see "Quoth the Duchess of Cleveland to Counselor Knight," in O'Neill, "Sexuality, Deviance, and Moral Character," *Eighteenth-Century Life,* II (1975–1976), 16; Weil, "Sometimes a Scepter," in Hunt, ed., *Invention of Pornography,* 147–148.

11. Charles Sackville, *Colin* (1679), in Lord et al., eds., *Poems on Affairs of State*, II, 171.

12. Ralph Gray, The Coronation Ballad (1689), Add. Mss. 29497, fol. 101, BL; quoted in O'Neill, "Sexuality, Deviance, and Moral Character," *Eighteenth-Century Life*, II (1975–1976), 17. Satiricial writers of this time, imbued with anti-Catholic bias, frequently associated Italy with sodomy.

13. Charles E. Clark, *The Public Prints: The Newspaper in Anglo-American Culture, 1665–1740* (New York, 1994), 15; Harris, *Politics under the Later Stuarts*, 186–188. For printed satire, see Lord et al., eds., *Poems on Affairs of State*, I, xxxii–xxxiii. (The imposition of a tax on printed papers in August 1712 did little to slow the presses; see VI, xxvii, xxxv, VII, xxvii–xxviii.) For Grub Street, see Clark, *Public Prints*, 42, 47–50; Leonard W. Levy, *Legacy of Suppression: Freedom of Speech and Press in Early American History* (New York, 1960), 8–11, Blackstone quotation on 14; Frederick Seaton Siebert, *Freedom of the Press in England, 1476–1776* (Urbana, Ill., 1952), 261, 301. Seditious libel was a criminal offense, libel a civil offense.

14. *The Conference on Gregg's Ghost* (London, 1711), 11, quoted in Isaac Kramnick, *Bolingbroke and His Circle: The Politics of Nostalgia in the Age of Walpole* (Cambridge, Mass., 1968), 271, n. 11. Swift's sentence concludes, "though I have been of late but a small contributor." That Swift acknowledged his contributions to Grub Street shows how thin was the line between the hacks and the wits. Swift to Robert Hunter, London, Mar. 22, 1709, in F. Elrington Ball, ed., *The Correspondence of Jonathan Swift, D.D.*, 6 vols. (London, 1910–1914), I, 143.

15. Located near the present-day Barbican Center, Grub Street was in 1830 renamed Milton Street; Pat Rogers, *Grub Street: Studies in a Subculture* (London, 1972), 1. Clark, *Public Prints*, 42, places Milton Street near Moorgate. For French Grub Street writing, see Robert Darnton, *The Literary Underground of the Old Regime* (Cambridge, Mass., 1982). And see Hunt, ed., *Invention of Pornography*.

16. The quotation is from David S. Shields, *Civil Tongues and Polite Letters in British America* (Chapel Hill, N.C., 1997), 47. According to Philip Pinkus, *Grub St. Stripped Bare: The Scandalous Lives and Pornographic Works of the Original Grub St. Writers . . .* (Hamden, Conn., 1968), Grub Street "came into its own" at the end of the 17th century (13n).

On scatology see, e.g., *The Wandering Spy: or, The Way of the World Inquired into; with Reflections on the Humours of the Town*, I, nos. 5–27 (July 7, 1705–Dec. 1, 1705), Boston Public Library; [John Dunton], "The Best Perfume, or a Paradox in Praise of Farting," in *Athenian Sport . . .* (London, 1707), 114. According to one scholar, Jonathan Swift used more scatology "than any other major author in English literature," though it was of a "moral and humanistic character"; see Jae Num Lee, *Swift and Scatological Satire* (Albuquerque, N.Mex., 1971), 1, 121.

17. John Tutchin, *The Foreigners: A Poem*, part I (London, 1700); Defoe's *True*

*Born Englishman* (1701) was in answer to Tutchin's piece. Brown was criticized in [Richard Kingston], *Impudence, Lying, and Forgery Detected and Chastiz'd etc.* (London, 1700), as cited in Pinkus, *Grub St. Stripped Bare*, 27. For more on political pamphlets, see ibid., chap. 5; and *The Works of Mr. Thomas Brown . . .* , 4 vols. (London, 1730), e.g., *Laconics; or, New Maxims of State and Conversation* (1701), IV, 100–119. David S. Shields notes that Tom Brown's autobiographical poem of 1703, "The Mourning Poet; or, The Unknown Comforts of Imprisonment," "is the most searching condemnation of the civic and political life of 1690s–1703" England (Shields to author, Feb. 16, 1996). I am much in Shields's debt for valuable discussions about Grub Street writers.

On Ward, see *Hudibras Redivivus; or, A Burlesque Poem on the Times* (London, 1705); Howard William Troyer, *Ned Ward of Grubstreet: A Study of Sub-Literary London in the Eighteenth Century* (Cambridge, Mass., 1946), 95; for Tutchin, Pinkus, *Grub St. Stripped Bare*, 245–250, quotation on 248.

18. R. O. Bucholz, *The Augustan Court: Queen Anne and the Decline of Court Culture* (Stanford, Calif., 1993), 206, 210–212, 224–225; Edward Gregg, *Queen Anne* (London, 1980), 137–138. Even her miserable, and very public, sufferings from the gout seem not to have undermined Anne's authority; on ceremonial occasions and royal progresses throughout her reign, even when visibly ill, she enjoyed steady popularity with her subjects (150). The few challenges to the legitimacy of Anne's reign came from Jacobites loyal to the Stuart Pretender; see Paul Kléber Monod, *Jacobitism and the English People, 1688–1788* (Cambridge, 1989), 139–140, 180, 292. True, in 1706, Sir John Clerk, appalled at Anne's gouty physical condition during an interview at Kensington Palace, was moved to write, "Nature seems to be inverted when a poor infirm Woman becomes one of the Rulers of the World." Yet he immediately added that women had governed in England before, "and indeed they have sometimes done this to better purpose than Men"; see John M. Gray, ed., *Memoirs of the Life of Sir John Clerk . . .* , (Edinburgh, 1892), 62.

19. Frances Harris, *A Passion for Government: The Life of Sarah, Duchess of Marlborough* (Oxford, 1991), intro., 90–91, 101–102, chap. 8; Gregg, *Queen Anne,* esp. 28, 192–193, 328. Bucholz observes that the influence of Anne's bedchamber attendants was "vastly overrated by contemporaries" as well as by historians until recently (*Augustan Court,* 168).

20. *An Answer* [1708]. Though the piece apparently was published, it survives today mainly in manuscript; Lansdowne Mss. 852, fols. 39b–40, BL. See also Add. Mss. 40060, fols. 70b–71, BL; and Lord et al., eds., *Poems on Affairs of State,* VII, 317.

For a sampling of attacks on Sarah Marlborough, see William Shippen, *Moderation Display'd* (1704), in Lord et al., eds., *Poems on Affairs of State,* VII, 35, n. 267, 36, VI, 526, 610, 649–650, 670; [Mary de la Rivière Manley], *The Secret*

*History of Queen Zarah, and the Zarazians* . . . , 2 vols. (London, 1705), I, 86–94, II, 13–14, 24–25; [Mary de la Rivière Manley?], *Secret Memoirs and Manners of Several Persons of Quality of Both Sexes from the New Atalantis* . . . (1709), 4 vols. (London, 1736), II, 134–140.

21. [Arthur Mainwaring?], *Masham Display'd* (1708), in Lord et al., eds., *Poems on Affairs of State*, VII, 320.

22. [Arthur Mainwaring?], "A New Ballad: To the Tune of 'Fair Rosamond'" [February–July 1708], ibid., 309–316. The duchess of Marlborough not only showed this ballad to the queen but in a rage of jealous pique wrote Anne a letter accusing her, according to some historians, of lesbian tendencies. If such was Sarah's intent (and her oblique language contains a number of ambiguities), the charge was indeed "ludicrous even within the context of their [Sarah and Anne's] bitter quarrel"; see Bucholz, *Augustan Court*, 331, n. 110. See also Gregg, *Queen Anne*, 272–278. Anne received a few other mild criticisms (Lord et al., eds., *Poems on Affairs of State*, VII, 147–148, 592; and note 18, above), but on the whole she was cast, even in satiric doggerel pointed at her court, as "Our Good and Gracious Queen" (315).

23. [Arthur Mainwaring?], *A New Protestant Litany* [1712?], and anon., *The British Embassadress's Speech to the French King* (1713), in Lord et al., eds., *Poems on Affairs of State*, VII, 549, 595–596. In the latter satire Queen Anne is painted as a Jacobite and her chief minister Harley as a bribe-taker (593, 594).

Whether the "*Italian* Dame" reference hinted that the duchess was a lesbian (see note 12, above) is unclear. She was tagged as the "Masculine Duchess" in another satirical offering, and the comte de Saint-Simon described her as "une grande créature et grosse, hommasse." However, Adelhida Paleotti, duchess of Shrewsbury, actually was of Italian descent. See Lord et al., eds., *Poems on Affairs of State*, VII, 549 and n. 13.

24. Manley's satire was republished as Mary de la Rivière Manley, *Secret Memoirs from the New Atlantis* (New York, 1972), 5–9. For Manley's earlier attack on Sarah Marlborough, see note 20, above. For the duke, see Jonathan Swift, *The Fable of Midas* (1712), in Lord et al., eds., *Poems on Affairs of State*, VII, 552–558; [Manley], *Secret History of Queen Zarah*; and the early chapters of Robert D. Horn, *Marlborough: A Survey: Panegyrics, Satires, and Biographical Writings, 1688–1788* (New York, 1975). The quotation is from Lord Mahon [Philip H. Stanhope], *History of England, Comprising the Reign of Queen Anne until the Peace of Utrecht*, 2d ed. (London, 1870), 553. For Harley and Walpole, see *The British Embassadress's Speech to the French King* (1713), in Lord et al., eds., *Poems on Affairs of State*, VII, 594; James O. Richards, *Party Propaganda under Queen Anne: The General Elections of 1703–1713* (Athens, Ga., 1972), 183; and J. H. Plumb, *Sir Robert Walpole: The Making of a Statesman* (Boston, 1956), 183.

25. Jeremy Black, *The English Press in the Eighteenth Century* (London, 1987), 10; Siebert, *Freedom of the Press in England,* 309–312. The Revenue Act of 1710 had also imposed a tax on printed matter. And see the discussion in Lord et al., eds., *Poems on Affairs of State,* VII, 570–571. The last quotation is from W. A. Speck, "Political Propaganda in Augustan England," Royal Historical Society, *Transactions,* 5th Ser., XXII (1972), 21. And see J. A. Downie, "The Development of the Political Press," in Clyve Jones, ed., *Britain in the First Age of Party, 1680–1750: Essays Presented to Geoffrey Holmes* (London, 1987), 111–128.

26. Some examples are HMC, *Report on the Manuscripts of the Duke of Portland . . .* , 10 vols. (London, 1891–1931); Gilbert Parke, ed., *Letters and Correspondence, Public and Private, of the Right Honourable Henry St. John, Lord Vis. Bolingbroke; During the Time He Was Secretary of State to Queen Anne,* 4 vols. (London, 1798); *Private Correspondence of Sarah, Duchess of Marlborough, Illustrative of the Court and Times of Queen Anne,* 2d ed., 2 vols. (London, 1838); Hon. Spencer Cowper, ed., *Diary of Mary Countess Cowper . . . 1714–1720* (London, 1864). And see John Beresford, *Gossip of the Seventeenth and Eighteenth Centuries* (London, 1923).

27. Lord Berkeley to Lord Strafford, Apr. 15, 1712, Jan. 9, 1713, Add. Mss. 22220, fols. 23, 46, BL; James J. Cartwright, ed., *Wentworth Papers, 1705–1739 . . . Private and Family Correspondence of Thomas Wentworth . . . Earl of Strafford* (London, 1883), 406. First and second quotations: Berkeley to Strafford, May 2, 1713, July 27, 1714, ibid., 331, 406; third quotation: Berkeley to Strafford, Jan. 27, 1713, Add. Mss. 22220, fol. 48, BL; on Mrs. Dormer: Berkeley to Strafford, Apr. 24, 1713, Cartwright, ed., *Wentworth Papers,* 329–330, Lady Berkeley to Lord Berkeley, Nov. 20, 1711, 208. John, Lord Berkeley of Stratton, had been a colonel of Queen Anne's dragoons and was a longtime member of Anne's intimate circle.

28. Newsletters examined include those for 1688 and selected numbers from 1706 to 1714 in the Newdigate Collection at the Folger Library, Washington, D.C., newsletter collections at the Huntington Library, San Marino, Calif., and at the British Library, and scattered numbers at several other locations. The items of gossip cited in the text are from the Newdigate newsletters of 1706. For more information, see Henry L. Snyder, "Newsletters in England, 1689–1715, with Special Reference to John Dyer — A Byway in the History of England," in Donovan H. Bond and W. Reynolds McLeod, eds., *Newsletters to Newspapers: Eighteenth-Century Journalism* (Morgantown, W.Va., 1977), 3–19. On the importance of coffeehouses, see Shields, *Civil Tongues,* chap. 3.

29. Richard Ollard, *Clarendon and His Friends* (New York, 1988), 226–228.

30. For the late 17th century, see Lord et al., eds., *Poems on Affairs of State,* V, 81, 59. The editors note that military figures, especially those who defected after Torbay, "earned most attention from the [Jacobite] satirists" (62–63). Periodic

reports about Cornbury's activities can best be followed in Narcissus Luttrell, *A Brief Historical Relation of State Affairs from September 1678 to April 1714*, 6 vols. (Oxford, 1857), which is based on the newsletters.

31. Isaac Norris, Sr., to James Logan, London, Mar. 10. 1707, Norris Papers, VII, 38, HSP.

32. [Cotton Mather?], *A Memorial of the Present Deplorable State of New-England* ([Boston] London, 1707), in MHS, *Colls.*, 5th Ser., VI (1879), 37, 36, 43. The pamphlet included a number of "Affidavits of People of Worth." For more on this publication, see Clark, *Public Prints*, 94.

Sir Henry Ashurst, agent for Connecticut, labeled Joseph Dudley and Cornbury "the two hammonds [Hamans]," drawing on the Book of Esther, for attempting to force the colonies into English paths. Ashurst to governor and Council of Connecticut, London, Apr. 24, 1707, MHS, *Colls.*, 6th Ser., III (1889), 379. For a fuller look at the satire directed against Dudley, see David S. Shields, *Oracles of Empire: Poetry, Politics, and Commerce in British America, 1690–1750* (Chicago, 1990), 110–117. For more on Dudley's career, see Richard R. Johnson, *Adjustment to Empire: The New England Colonies, 1675–1715* (New Brunswick, N.J., 1981), chaps. 6–7.

33. Mr. James Blair's Affidavit Relating to the Mal-administration of Col. Nicholson, Governor of Virginia, Apr. 25, 1704, in William S. Perry, ed., *Historical Collections Relating to the American Colonial Church*, 4 vols. (Hartford, Conn., 1870), I, 103; Colonel Robert Quary to Board of Trade, Virginia, Oct. 15, 1703, *CSPC*, XXI, 1150. For more on Francis Nicholson's opposition in Virginia, see NY Col. Mss., LI, 1–67, NYSL; Stephen Saunders Webb, "The Strange Career of Francis Nicholson," *WMQ*, 3d Ser., XXIII (1966), 513–548; and Edmund S. Morgan, *American Slavery, American Freedom: The Ordeal of Colonial Virginia* (New York, 1975), 351–357.

Historians have usually accepted at face value that Nicholson was smitten by the Virginian Lucy Burwell and on being rejected made threats against her family. But the evidence is, at the least, ambiguous, consisting largely of affidavits by James Blair, Nicholson's most inveterate enemy, and an anonymous satirical letter from a "friend." Some of this material is printed in Perry, ed., *Historical Collections*, I, esp. 69–75, 87–93, 102, 131–138. And see Parke Rouse, Jr., *James Blair of Virginia* (Chapel Hill, N.C., 1971), 135. Quary clearly thinks the whole affair was a fabrication.

34. "Commissioner Peter Fauconnier's Reply and Petition . . . [burned] the Admiralty's further petition to your Excellency against Him," Jan. 26, 1708, NY Col. Mss., LII, 94.

35. To His Excellency John Lord Lovelace . . . The humble Address of the Representatives of . . . New Jersey, Mar. 18, 1708/9, *NJA*, III, 374–378, quotation on 377–378; To His Excellency John Lord Lovelace . . . The Answer of Peter

Sonmans, Apr. 14, 1709, 416–444, quotations on 434, 439, 440. As was customary, each side in this dispute supported its charges with sworn depositions; see 445–460.

36. Daniel Coxe to [William Dockwra], Burlington, N.J., Jan. 17, 1709, HM 22302, HL. Dockwra, London secretary to the East Jersey Proprietors, noted on the cover of this letter that Colonel Coxe was a man of good parts who knew well "the Seditious turbulent Knaves of the faction."

37. For Hunter: Deposition of Robert Drummond, *DHNY*, III, 273, and see the deposition of Anne Drummond. For Morris: Jacob Henderson to SPG, London, July 1, 1712, SPG, Letterbook C, I, n.p. (microfilm).

For the Anglican clergy: Morris to the secretary, May 30, 1709, SPG, Letterbook A, IV, 499–504 (microfilm); Quary to the bishop of London, Philadelphia, Jan. 20, 1708, 90–110 (microfilm). This case spreads across the SPG records in the first decade of the 18th century; see esp. SPG, Letterbook A, I, 171, where Lewis Morris calls the Reverend Mr. Honeyman's accuser an "Infamous Prostitute" (II, 51); and American Papers of the SPG, Lambeth Palace, I, 247–254 (microfilm).

38. In Virginia and Massachusetts, slander was the second most common cause of legal action (second only to debt in Virginia and fornication in Massachusetts); Helena M. Wall, *Fierce Communion: Family and Community in Early America* (Cambridge, Mass., 1990), 31. And see Mary Beth Norton, "Gender and Defamation in Seventeenth-Century Maryland," *WMQ*, 3d Ser., XLIV (1987), 3–39. Opposition attacks on the Church of England were equivalent to attacks on the state; see J. C. D. Clark, *The Language of Liberty, 1660–1832: Political Discourse and Social Dynamics in the Anglo-American World* (Cambridge, 1994), 46–62.

39. 1702, Livingston-Redmond Mss., reel 2 (microfilm). Probably few manuscript satires are extant today. The earliest doggerel found in New York is in Dutch; see, e.g., Robert Livingston's lampoon of Jacob Leisler, reprinted in translation by David William Voorhees in "'Rhyme Weg': Leyslers Regeerds': The New York City Election of October 1689," *De Halve Maen*, LXIV (1991), 46–48.

Provincial manuscript newsletters also circulated in the colonies, though how extensively is difficult to discern. "Sharpe's newsletter" is mentioned in a missive from Johannes DePeyster to Abraham DePeyster, Boston, Jan. 5, 1703, DePeyster Papers, NYHS; for nine of Duncan and John Campbell's Boston newsletters of 1703, which include brief mention of Cornbury, see MHS, *Procs.*, 1st Ser., IX (1867), 485–501. Other references to colonial newsletters are in Lyman Horace Weeks and Edwin M. Bacon, *An Historical Digest of the Provincial Press* (Boston, 1911). For the rise of pasquinades and parody speech directed against colonial executive power after the Glorious Revolution, see Shields, *Oracles of Empire*, esp. 99–100. For the reaction against such attacks and growing concern in the colonies after 1720 for civility of speech and manners, see Shields, *Civil Tongues and Polite Letters in British America.*

40. *NJA*, III, 382–383, 384. The relative civility of this exchange suggests that the Middle Colonies politicians were trying, at least for the moment, to rein in their rhetorical excesses.

41. Clark, *Public Prints*, esp. 178–188 on New York; Shields, *Oracles of Empire*, 100–101. Only two presses were known to exist in the Middle Colonies by the late 17th century, one in Philadelphia and another after 1693 in New York City (Lawrence C. Wroth, *The Colonial Printer*, 2d ed. [Charlottesville, Va., 1938; rpt. 1964], 15, 29–36). The number of colonial presses grew after the Licensing Act expired in 1695, though strong if informal pressure from provincial governments restrained many printers until the 1730s (13). That a major part of any printer's business was publishing government documents and proclamations certainly checked the colonial press. Further, colonial assemblies did not hesitate to arrest printers who infringed parliamentary privilege; see Leonard W. Levy, *Emergence of a Free Press* (New York, 1985), 82; Richard Buel, Jr., "Freedom of the Press in Revolutionary America: The Evolution of Libertarianism, 1760–1820," in Bernard Bailyn and John B. Hench, eds., *The Press and the American Revolution* (Worcester, Mass., 1981), 59–97.

42. [Francis Makemie?], *An Answer to George Keith's Libel* (Boston, 1694), 88–89. For a representative sampling of pamphlets published during this controversy, see Thomas Budd, *A Just Rebuke to Several Calumnies, Lyes, and Slanders Reported against Thomas Budd* (Philadelphia, 1692); [John Philly], *A Paraphrastical Exposition on a Letter from a Gentleman in Philadelphia to His Friend in Boston* (New York, 1693); Samuel Jennings, *Truth Rescued from Forgery and Falsehood* (Philadelphia, 1699). For more on the Keithian Schism, see Jon Butler, "Into Pennsylvania's Spiritual Abyss: The Rise and Fall of the Later Keithians, 1693–1703," *Pennsylvania Magazine of History and Biography*, CI (1977), 151–170.

43. [Daniel Leeds], *The Great Mistery of Fox-Craft Discovered and the Quaker Plainness and Sincerity Demonstrated . . .* (New York, 1705), 6. Leeds's broadside struck directly at a signal part of the Quakers' faith — literacy. Burlington's Anglican minister, the virulently anti-Quaker Reverend John Talbot, may have collaborated with Leeds on this pamphlet, for Talbot claimed to possess the Fox letters. For more on Leeds, see Valerie G. Gladfelter, "Power Challenged: Rising Individualism in the Burlington, New Jersey, Friends Meeting, 1678–1720," in Michael Zuckerman, ed., *Friends and Neighbors: Group Life in America's First Plural Society* (Philadelphia, 1982), 116–144.

44. Leeds claimed that he made this correction "in point of justice, to prevent mistakes," for he would wrong no person. [Leeds], *Great Mistery of Fox-Craft Discovered*, 4; Daniel Leeds, *The American Almanack . . . 1707* (New York, 1706), 11. Caleb Pusey's *Some Remarks upon a Late Pamphlet* (Philadelphia, 1705) in-

cluded a signed statement by the sister of the now-deceased Mary Andrews denying that the baby born in Barbados was any but the husband's child, as well as lengthy statements to the same effect by three Barbadians.

45. Quary to Lords of Trade, Philadelphia, June 28, 1707, *NYCD*, V, 18; Cornbury to Dudley, New York, Feb. 11, 1707, HL. Makemie's letter, dated July 28, 1707, is printed in *A Narrative of a New and Unusual American Imprisonment of Two Presbyterian Ministers: And Prosecution of Mr. Francis Makemie, One of Them, for Preaching One Sermon at the City of New-York* (London, 1707), in Peter Force, *Tracts and Other Papers, Relating Principally to the Origins, Settlement, and Progress of the Colonies of North America*, IV (1847; rpt. New York, 1947), no. 4.

46. Morris to [the Reverend Thoroughgood] Moore and [John] Brooke, Morrisania, Dec. 26, 1707, American Papers of the SPG, Lambeth Palace, XIV (microfilm). Unfortunately, the Information, in which Morris says that *Forget and Forgive* "was writ at length in Parchment," seems not to have survived. It named John Pike, John Barclay, George and Margaret Willocks, and David and Mary Johnson. The cases were postponed several times and finally dismissed in 1709, though some or all of the defendants were ordered to pay court costs. See Minutes and Rules of the [New Jersey] Supreme Court, 1704–1715, 47–49, 57, 62, 69, New Jersey State Archives, New Jersey State Library, Trenton.

47. Minutes and Rules of the [New Jersey] Supreme Court, 1704–1715, 36, 45, 49, 54. For similar actions in the French colonies, see Peter N. Moogk, "'Thieving Buggers' and 'Stupid Sluts': Insults and Popular Culture in New France," *WMQ*, 3d Ser., XXXVI (1979), 524–547.

48. James Logan to [Mr. Williams?], Philadelphia, July 6, 1705, Logan Letterbook II, 58, HSP. Cornbury also instituted suits against a number of the New Jerseyans who had accused him of accepting bribes as well as others who disputed his authority to dismiss Lewis Morris from the council and such; Minutes and Rules of the [New Jersey] Supreme Court, 1704–1715, 7–9, 13, 28.

For more on the use of colonial courts to redeem reputations, see Peter Charles Hoffer, "Honor and the Roots of American Litigiousness," *American Journal of Legal History*, XXXIII (1989), 297–319; and see note 38, above.

49. For the Hunter-Morris alliance, see Eugene R. Sheridan, *Lewis Morris, 1671–1746: A Study in Early American Politics* (Syracuse, N.Y., 1981), esp. 94. Cornbury left office at the end of 1708 (and New York in mid-1710); not until 1714 did Hunter gain a majority in the assembly.

50. This anti-Anglican incident may have been particularly directed against William Vesey, rector of Trinity Church. Hunter was a friend and correspondent of Swift and other of the wits; Lustig, *Robert Hunter*, 51–54, 115–116, 133–134. For an evaluation of *Androboros* as Anglo-American satiric literature, see Shields, *Oracles of Empire*, 139–149.

Apparently only one copy of *Androboros* now exists, which suggests that few copies were printed and its circulation was limited. For a modern annotated version, based on the original in the Huntington Library, see Lawrence H. Leder, "Robert Hunter's *Androboros*," *Bulletin of the New York Public Library*, LXVIII (1964), 153–190. See also Lustig, *Robert Hunter*, 116–117, 135–140, for astute commentary on the play and its characters.

51. [Robert Hunter], *Androboros: A Bographical Farce in Three Acts, Viz. The Senate, The Consistory, and The Apotheosis* (Moropolis [New York], 1714), 10, 12–13, 13–14, HL. Lustig states that the names of colonials written next to the cast of characters on this copy of the play are in Hunter's hand (*Robert Hunter*, 137). This is the first, and so far as is known the only, contemporary printed reference to Cornbury's alleged cross dressing.

CHAPTER SIX

1. Others accused of cross dressing in the 17th and 18th centuries include Emil August, duke of Saxe Gotha and Altenburg (d. 1680?), the second earl of Sunderland (1641–1702), the abbé de Choisy (1664–1724), and the Chevalier d'Eon de Beaumont (1728–1810). See *Love-Letters between a Certain Late Nobleman and the Famous Mr. Wilson* (London, n.d. [1712]); Harry Brierley, *Transvestism: A Handbook with Case Studies for Psychologists, Psychiatrists, and Counsellors* (Oxford, 1979), 5; and Ralph Henry Forster Scott, ed. and trans., *The Transvestite Memoirs of the Abbé de Choisy* (London, 1973). D'Eon is discussed in chap. 1.

2. Jean E. Howard, "Crossdressing, the Theatre, and Gender Struggle in Early Modern England," *Shakespeare Quarterly*, XXXIX (1988), 421–423. Concern about cross dressing, especially by females, flared early in the 17th century, possibly in reaction to the emboldening of women in the reign of Elizabeth I. See *Hic Mulier; or, The Man-Woman* (London, 1620), in Barbara J. Baines, ed., *Three Pamphlets on the Jacobean Antifeminist Controversy* (Delmar, N.Y., 1978).

3. Natalie Zemon Davis, "Women on Top," in Davis, *Society and Culture in Early Modern France* (Stanford, Calif., 1975), 124–151, quotation on 132. For English practice, see Terry Castle, "The Culture of Travesty: Sexuality and Masquerade in Eighteenth-Century England," in G. S. Rousseau and Roy Porter, eds., *Sexual Underworlds of the Enlightenment* (Chapel Hill, N.C., 1988), 156–180. A recent study of cross dressing among Dutch women is Rudolf M. Dekker and Lotte C. van de Pol, *The Tradition of Female Transvestism in Early Modern Europe* (London, 1989).

4. Kenneth Fraser Easton, "Bad Habits: Cross-Dressing and the Regulation of Gender in Eighteenth-Century British Literature and Society" (Ph.D. diss., Princeton University, 1990), quotation on 60. For the importance of the theater to gender definition, see Kristina Straub, *Sexual Suspects: Eighteenth-Century Play-*

*ers and Sexual Ideology* (Princeton, N.J., 1992), esp. chap. 1; Howard, "Crossdressing," *Shakespeare Qtly.*, XXXIX (1988); Peter Ackroyd, *Dressing Up, Transvestism, and Drag: The History of an Obsession* (New York, 1979), 57; Richard Davenport-Hines, *Sex, Death, and Punishment: Attitudes to Sex and Sexuality in Britain since the Renaissance* (London, 1990), 55–70. Michael S. Kimmel, ed., *"Mundus Foppensis" ([London], 1691), and "The Levellers" ([1703]; 1745),* Augustan Reprint Society, Publication no. 248 (Los Angeles, Calif., 1988), x, 419–420.

The fop, a familiar figure in Restoration and early 18th-century literature, was known to be of delicate sensibilities, most content in the company of women, attentive to his wardrobe, and sensitive to odors. Susan Staves, "A Few Kind Words for the Fop," *Studies in English Literature*, XXII (1982), 413–428.

5. Kimmel, ed., *"The Levellers,"* viii. Michael McKeon, "Historicizing Patriarchy: The Emergence of Gender Difference in England, 1660–1760," *Eighteenth-Century Studies*, XXVIII (1995), 295–322. James Peller Malcolm, *Anecdotes of the Manners and Customs of London, during the Eighteenth Century . . .* , 2 vols. (London, 1808), I, 62; Dudley W. R. Bahlman, *The Moral Revolution of 1688* (New Haven, Conn., 1957). One of the most visible manifestations of the impulse for reform and greater civility is the changing language of court reports from the Old Bailey. In contrast with the explicit descriptions of sexual behavior in earlier years, the trial reports of the later-1720s and after regularly suppress such details, substituting euphemistic generalities; see *Select Trials . . . at the Sessions-House in the Old-Bailey*, 2d ed., 4 vols. (London, 1742), II, III.

6. Mar. 9, 16, 1711, in Donald F. Bond, ed., *The Spectator*, 5 vols. (Oxford, 1965), I, 36, n. 3, 62, n. 1. For Samuel Pepys, see Brierley, *Transvestism*, 5.

7. Castle, "Culture of Travesty," in Rousseau and Porter, eds., *Sexual Underworlds*, 163; June 29, Mar. 9, 1711, in Bond, ed., *Spectator*, I, 435, 36–37; C. R., *The Danger of Masquerades and Raree-Shows . . .* (London, 1718).

8. Castle, "Culture of Travesty," in Rousseau and Porter, eds., *Sexual Underworlds*, 158–159, 156–157; *Weekly Journal*, Jan. 25, 1724, cited ibid., 159. The characterization of the pamphlet is Castle's, in "Culture of Travesty," ibid., 170. The 1721 work, titled *The Conduct of the Stage Consider'd*, is quoted on 161. See also C. R., *Danger of Masquerades and Raree-Shows*, 13–14. Whereas Castle depicts the masquerade as blurring gender boundaries, my emphasis in the paragraphs to follow falls on the ways discussion about the masquerade's corrupting influence sharpened gender stereotypes in the early 18th century.

9. Thus did nature rebel against those "occasional Perplexities and Mixtures of Dress" (June 29, 1711, in Bond, ed., *The Spectator*, I, 435).

10. Randolph Trumbach, "The Birth of the Queen: Sodomy and the Emergence of Gender Equality in Modern Culture, 1660–1750," in Martin Bauml Duberman et al., eds., *Hidden from History: Reclaiming the Gay and Lesbian Past*

(New York, 1989), 129–140; Mary McIntosh, "The Homosexual Role," *Social Problems*, XVI (1968), 182–192, reprinted with comments and additions in Kenneth Plummer, ed., *The Making of the Modern Homosexual* (London, 1981).

11. Homosexual activity, of course, has a long history in Western society. Scholars disagree about when its association with an indeterminate kind of sexual debauchery — in which "the young man about town . . . was to be found with his mistress on one arm and his catamite on the other" — shifted to its modern association with communities of men attracted only to other men. Randolph Trumbach, "Sodomitical Subcultures, Sodomitical Roles, and the Gender Revolution of the Eighteenth Century: The Recent Historiography," *Eighteenth-Century Life*, IX (1985), 109–121; Trumbach, "London's Sodomites: Homosexual Behavior and Western Culture in the Eighteenth Century," *Journal of Social History*, XI (1977–1978), 1–11; Alan Bray, *Homosexuality in Renaissance England* (1982; rpt. New York, 1995); Mary McIntosh, "The Homosexual Role," *Social Problems*, XVI (1968). Also see Keith Thomas, "As You Like It," *New York Review of Books*, XLI, no. 15 (Sept. 22, 1994), 9–12.

12. For more on London locations, see Trumbach, "London's Sodomites," *Jour. Soc. Hist.*, XI (1977–1978), 15–16; Bray, *Homosexuality*, 84–85.

13. Gerald Howson, *Thief-Taker General: The Rise and Fall of Jonathan Wild* (London, 1970), 62; original documents from the first two decades of the 18th century are cited at length in this book.

14. Edward Chamberlayne, *Angliae Notitia; or, The Present State of England* (London, 1700), 319. (It might be noted that the men tried for sodomy in the first third of the 18th century had resoundingly English names; see *Select Trials*.) "The Bawdy House," in Arthur L. Hayward, ed., *Amusements Serious and Comical, and Other Works, by Tom Brown* (New York, 1927), 99; *Wandering Spy*, Aug. 25, 1705, I, no. 12. *He-Strumpets*, reprinted in John Dunton's periodical *Athenianism* (London, 1710), II, 93–99, cited in Rictor Norton, *Mother Clap's Molly Home: The Gay Subculture in England, 1700–1830* (London, 1992), 51, and listed in Stephen Parks, *John Dunton and the English Book Trade . . .* (New York, 1976), 348; *The Women-Hater's Lamentation . . .* (London, 1707).

15. [Edward Ward], *A Compleat and Humorous Account of All the Remarkable Clubs and Societies in the Cities of London and Westminster . . .* (1709; London, 1745), 265, 268. Though Ward's account was offered as fiction, it was evidently based, at least in part, on actual places and incidents.

16. J. Ellis to Ambassador Williamson, Dec. 3, 20, 1698, *CSPD, William III*, IV, 427, 430; Warrant to recorder, City of London, June 7, 1701, VI, 357. Rigby had been sentenced to one year in prison; unable to pay his £1,000 fine, he actually served nearly three years. Dunton, *He-Strumpets*; for 1699, see Bray, *Homosexuality*, 91.

17. Howson, *Thief-Taker General,* 62–65; *Select Trials,* II, 363, 368, III, 37; Trumbach, "London's Sodomites," *Jour. Soc. Hist.,* XI (1977–1978), 16.

18. Bray, *Homosexuality,* 88–89 (for a balanced evaluation of the accuracy of the published trials, see 132–133, n. 1); *A Genuine Narrative of All the Street-Robberies Committed since October Last, by James Dalton and His Accomplices . . . from the Mouth of James Dalton* (London, 1728), 37, 40.

19. Bahlman, *Moral Revolution,* chap. 1; Peter Fryer, *Mrs. Grundy: Studies in English Prudery* (London, 1963), 337; Dennis Rubini, "Sexuality and Augustan England: Sodomy, Politics, Elite Circles, and Society," *Journal of Homosexuality,* XVI (1988), 357; Bray, *Homosexuality,* 91.

20. Dekker and van de Pol, *Female Transvestism,* 48, 56, and nn.; Trumbach, "Sodomitical Subcultures," *Eighteenth-Century Life,* IX (1985), 118–119, 113, 120, n. 10. Most of those prosecuted in the Netherlands were convicted, and approximately 10% were executed; see Simon Schama, *The Embarrassment of Riches: An Interpretation of Dutch Culture in the Golden Age* (New York, 1987), 602. For more on early-18th-century Dutch urban homosexual networks, including public cross dressing, see ibid., 601–605.

On England, see Arthur N. Gilbert, "Buggery and the British Navy, 1700–1861," *Jour. Soc. Hist.,* X (1976–1977), 72–98. Between 1703 and 1710, 12 seamen in the Royal Navy were found guilty of buggery, 6 of whom were sentenced to death; this constituted 27% of naval courts-martial death sentences in those years (79). See also Trumbach, "Sodomitical Subcultures," *Eighteenth-Century Life,* IX (1985), 112–113.

21. Mollies sometimes took their nicknames from their occupations, as in the case of the tallow chandler "dip-Candle-Mary," or the barber known as "Nurse Mitchell." Dalton, *Narrative of Street-Robberies,* 38, 39. For an explanation of the "longstanding misapprehension" that sodomy was associated with an enervated aristocracy, see McKeon, "Historicizing Patriarchy," *Eighteenth-Century Studies,* XXVIII (1995), 309–312.

22. Trumbach, "London's Sodomites," *Jour. Soc. Hist.,* XI (1977–1978), 19–20, quotation on 23; and Trumbach, "Sodomy Transformed: Aristocratic Libertinage, Public Reputation, and the Gender Revolution of the Eighteenth Century," *Jour. Homosexuality,* XIX (1990), 105–124; G. S. Rousseau, *Perilous Enlightenment: Pre- and Post-Modern Discourses* (Manchester, 1991), 156–161; Peter Wagner, *Eros Revived: Erotica of the Enlightenment in England and America* (London, 1988), 101; Robert Halsband, *Lord Hervey, Eighteenth-Century Courtier* (New York, 1974), chap. 9.

Dennis Rubini alleges that 35 reputed sodomites were attached to the court or Whitehall in 1692, in "Sexuality and Augustan England," *Jour. Homosexuality,* XVI (1988), 366–369. There was, one might note, no Hyde among them.

23. Abraham Crabaat was arrested in 1654 for "having last Shrove Tuesday walked along the street in woman's clothes"; after pleading that he "did not know that he was doing wrong," Crabaat paid a fine of six guilders and court costs (A. J. F. van Laer, ed., *Minutes of the Court of Fort Orange and Beverwyck, 1652–1656*, 2 vols. [Albany, N.Y., 1920–1923], I, 118). In 1661, Pieter Maertensz of Flatbush, according to the sheriff, "on Shrove-Tuesday clothed himself in woman's clothing, which is against the commands of God." The defendant acknowledged that he "committed the aforesaid misdeed" (Flatbush Town Records, Liber B., Court Minutes, 1659–1664, vol. 10003, no. 57, Municipal Archives, New York City). New Yorkers apparently dressed up on the day before the start of Lent, sometimes in the clothing of the opposite sex. (I wish to thank Eric Nooter for bringing the Flatbush documents to my attention.) For the Massachusetts law, see L. Kinvin Wroth and Hiller B. Zobel, eds., *Legal Papers of John Adams*, 3 vols. (Cambridge, Mass., 1965), I, 161, n. 17. A Virginia case of cross dressing in 1629 is that of the supposed hermaphrodite Thomas, or Thomasine, Hall; see Mary Beth Norton, *Founding Mothers and Fathers: Gendered Power and the Forming of American Society* (New York, 1996), 183–197.

In the Philadelphia episode a second man was charged with being masked, two women were charged with being "masked or disguised" in men's clothes, and a tavernkeeper was accused of "sufering Masqueraded persons in the house, to dance and Revell . . . to the Greef of and Disturbance of peaceable minds and propigating the Throne of wickedness amongst us" (Feb. 4, 1703, Ancient Records of Philadelphia [the Wallace Collection], HSP). Because the revels had taken place on the previous December 26 or 28, during a Christmas season that in those days ran from Christmas Eve to Twelfth Night, this may be another case of a holiday frolic; see David Cressy, *Bonfires and Bells: National Memory and the Protestant Calendar in Elizabethan and Stuart England* (Berkeley, Calif., 1989), 7, 31–32, 46–49. I wish to thank Peter Thompson and Craig W. Horle for providing the text of this case. Thompson speculates that the magistrates might have been looking for an excuse to shut down the tavernkeeper's raucous establishment, which the cross-dressing incident supplied (Thompson to author, Oct. 21, 1991).

24. Samuel Sewall to Thomas Cockerill, Feb. 21, 1709, MHS, *Colls.*, 6th Ser., I (1886), 380–381. Deuteronomy declares: "A woman shall not wear anything that pertains to a man, nor shall a man put on a woman's garment; for whoever does these things is an abomination to the Lord your God."

In 1771, John Adams defended one Pitts, who had innocently "gallanted" a transvestite named Gray, against a charge of assault and battery. On realizing Gray's true sex, Pitts had struck him on the head with his cane, bringing blood. According to one witness, Gray "had the outward Appearance of a Woman, a Gown and Womens Cloaths"; see Wroth and Zobel, eds., *Legal Papers of John*

*Adams,* I, 157–161. (I am grateful to Edward Countryman for bringing this case to my attention.)

25. David Underdown, *Revel, Riot and Rebellion: Popular Politics and Culture in England, 1603–1660* (Oxford, 1985), 111, n. 20; Philip Vickers Fithian, *Journal, 1775–1776, Written on the Virginia-Pennsylvania Frontier and in the Army around New York,* ed. Robert Greenhalgh Albion and Leonidas Dodson (Princeton, N.J., 1934), 238, n. 26. The Virginia court that sentenced Thomas (Thomasine) Hall (see note 23, above) to wear male clothing topped by a woman's apron and headdress may have intended not only to mark him out as deviant but to shame him; see Kathleen Brown, "'Changed into the Fashion of a Man': The Politics of Sexual Difference in a Seventeenth-Century Anglo-American Settlement," *Journal of the History of Sexuality,* VI (1995), 188–189.

26. Brierley, *Transvestism;* Robert J. Stoller, *Sex and Gender: The Transsexual Experiment,* 2 vols. (New York, 1975), II, 142–155; Richard F. Docter, *Transvestites and Transsexuals: Toward a Theory of Cross-Gender Behavior* (New York, 1988), chap. 2. Specialists in the study of transvestism would be the first to acknowledge that the boundaries between categories are ill defined and that much remains to be learned about the subject.

27. Ron Langevin, "The Meanings of Cross-Dressing," in Betty W. Steiner, ed., *Gender Dysphoria: Development, Research, Management* (New York, 1985), 207–225; Stoller, *Sex and Gender,* II, 148–149; Brierley, *Transvestism,* 11, 12; Docter, *Transvestites and Transsexuals,* 24–37. In a very few cases, the use of female attire expresses social defiance or an attitude of hostility toward women (ibid.).

28. Stoller, *Sex and Gender,* II, 143–144, quotation on 144; Docter, *Transvestites and Transsexuals,* 11–16, 19–21; P. M. Bentler and Charles Prince, "Psychiatric Symptomatology in Transvestites," *Journal of Clinical Psychology,* XXVI (1970), 434–436.

Psychologists differ somewhat on the last point. In contradistinction to the "fetishist," whose cross dressing is only partial and always private, a category of "fetishistic transvestites" who try to pass in public dressed in complete female habit is described by Docter (10–12). See also Neil Buhrich and Neil McConaghy, "Three Clinically Discrete Categories of Fetishistic Transvestism," *Archives of Sexual Behavior,* VIII (1979), 151–157. In my discussion, fetishistic transvestites are included in the category of cross dressers falling between the homosexual and heterosexual types.

29. Docter, *Transvestites and Transsexuals,* 11–27. For a detailed case history of a transvestite who thought he was deceiving the public, see the classic study by Magnus Hirschfeld, *Transvestites: The Erotic Drive to Cross-Dress* (1910; rpt. Buffalo, N.Y., 1991), chap. 15.

30. Docter, *Transvestites and Transsexuals,* 10, 14, 22, 54–57; Philippe Ariès, *Centuries of Childhood: A Social History of Family Life* (New York, 1962), 52–53.

31. According to Esther Newton, "All female impersonators are thought to be members of the homosexual subculture or gay world"; see *Mother Camp: Female Impersonators in America* (Englewood Cliffs, N.J., 1972), 4; see also Docter, *Transvestites and Transsexuals*, 34–36, 98–99, 208–209.

Jonathan Ned Katz suggests that the association of transvestism with homosexuality would not have occurred to the colonials this early, in *Gay-Lesbian Almanac: A New Documentary* (New York, 1983), 49–51. Yet we have seen that Lewis Morris, for example, was familiar with turn-of-the-century satirical writing in which such connections were made. Moreover, the three accusers of Cornbury — Morris, Robert Livingston, and Elias Neau — were in all likelihood exposed to such material while resident in England or France before 1707. According to Peter Wagner, salacious works including "the Earl of Rochester's obscene poems were on sale in Boston before 1700"; other erotica could be found in the libraries of clergymen and colonial gentlemen, in *Eros Revived: Erotica of the Enlightenment in England and America* (London, 1988), 293–294. For the rapid transmission of English satire to the colonies, see David S. Shields, *Oracles of Empire: Poetry, Politics, and Commerce in British America, 1690–1750* (Chicago, 1990), 95–102. I, too, have been struck by how quickly satire and other sorts of news reached North American shores.

Cornbury was first associated with "contrary sexual sensation," as it was then called, in a medical treatise in 1881; see E. C. Spitzka, "A Historical Case of Sexual Perversion," *Chicago Medical Review*, IV (August 1881), 378–379. Yet even popular historians have trod cautiously here, making sport of Cornbury's cross dressing but rarely suggesting that he was homosexual. (For a recent though unsupported exception, see Louis Auchincloss, ed., *The Hone and Strong Diaries of Old Manhattan* [New York, 1989], 77.) For a clever retelling of the Cornbury legend, see Marjorie Garber, *Vested Interests: Cross-Dressing and Cultural Anxiety* (New York, 1992), 52–53, 395, nn. 18–23.

32. Stoller, *Sex and Gender*, II, 143–144; Docter, *Transvestites and Transsexuals*, 10–11.

33. Neau to the secretary, Feb. 27, 1709, SPG, Letterbook A, IV, 402–413 (microfilm). True, Cornbury never mentioned the rumor of cross dressing, though he must have known that any written comment would only reinforce it.

CHAPTER SEVEN

1. Patricia Meyer Spacks, *Gossip* (New York, 1985), 4–6, 48. This book, especially the early chapters, has clarified my understanding of how gossip might have shaped the Cornbury legend. See also Robert Paine, "What Is Gossip About? An Alternative Hypothesis," *MAN*, N.S., II (1967), 278–285; and Jörg

R. Bergmann, *Discreet Indiscretions: The Social Organization of Gossip* (1987; rpt. New York, 1993).

2. Spacks, *Gossip*, 5, 45, 121–122. As Spacks notes, gossip "often partakes of fiction (some people would say *lies*), less because of the inevitable distortions of its passage from mouth to mouth than because of the purposes it serves for the retailer" (50).

3. For delayed and lost mail, see, e.g., Cornbury to Board of Trade, New York, Dec. 12, 1702, July 20, 1707, *NYCD*, IV, 1017, V, 20–21; Board of Trade to Cornbury, May 7, 1707, V, 5–7. Whenever the governor chanced on a ship going directly from New York or New Jersey to England, he always grasped the opportunity to write hasty dispatches home; e.g., Cornbury to Board of Trade, New York, June 30, 1703, IV, 1060–1062. For Cornbury's statement that he had received not one line from the Board of Trade in 15 months, see Cornbury to Board of Trade, New York, July 1, 1708, V, 55–56.

For more on early postal service across the Atlantic, see Ian K. Steele, *The English Atlantic, 1675–1740: An Exploration of Communication and Community* (New York, 1986). As an important royal colony, New York enjoyed better communications than some other colonies. According to Steele, letters were sent out approximately every two months and replies from the board received about twice a year (237–238), though other less formal communications supplemented these exchanges.

4. Board of Trade to Cornbury, Apr. 7, 1703, *CSPC*, XXI, 554. Governors sent duplicates and even triplicates of their correspondence by different routes, putting historians forever in debt to the amanuenses who had to copy out everything by hand. The difficulty of maintaining confidentiality is discussed in Cornbury to Lord Clarendon, New York, Jan. 25, 1709, and Cornbury to Lord Rochester, New York, Feb. 21, 1709, A Collection of Original Letters, JCBL.

5. During the Glorious Revolution, critical weeks of uncertainty about whether William of Orange had succeeded in displacing James II or had suffered Monmouth's fate plunged the colony into the civil war of Leisler's Rebellion. A crucial letter from Leisler to the crown was captured by a French privateer in June 1689. In 1691, Leisler's refusal to turn over New York's fort to a subordinate of the newly appointed governor — whose ship was being held in Bermuda by bad weather — led to charges of treason that sealed his fate. See David William Voorhees, "'In Behalf of the True Protestants Religion': The Glorious Revolution in New York" (Ph.D. diss., New York University, 1988), chap. 8.

The only official censure of Cornbury's governorship may similarly be attributed to a failure of communication. It involved the Vice Admiralty Court's condemnation of a cargo of logwood in 1702, a decision subsequently reversed by the High Court of Admiralty in England. A dispute arose over the shipowner's demand that Cornbury return his "third" of the condemned cargo, which had already been sold at auction. Cornbury's letter explaining his attempt to reimburse the owner apparently never reached his London agent; as a consequence, the Board of Trade censured him without hearing his side of the story. Cornbury to Secretary Hedges, New York, Oct. 16, 1706, *CSPC*, XXIII, 541; Board of Trade to Lord Sunderland, Oct. 23, 1707, *NYCD*, V, 27–28.

6. Mr. Fauconnier's Deposition in Justification of the Earle of Clarendon, Jan. 19, 1712, SPG, Letterbook A, VII, 342–347 (microfilm). This type of graphic description may have originated in diplomatic correspondence; since the formalities of time, space, and body language at foreign courts were laden with meaning (as we saw in Cornbury's dispatches from Hanover), diplomats wrote minutely detailed reports to their superiors.

7. Colonel Robert Quary to the bishop of London, Philadelphia, Jan. 20, 1708, SPG, Letterbook A, IV, 90–110 (microfilm). See also Quary's letter to the secretary of the SPG, Feb. 12, 1708, III, 501–506 (microfilm). Quary's reading of the episode is confirmed by Chaplain Sharpe, who also was in an excellent position to judge events. According to Lewis Morris, following Thoroughgood Moore's escape from the fort, John Sharpe became "a Violent advocate for his Lordship." Sharpe believed Cornbury "designed no harm" to either Moore or Brooke. See Morris to Moore and John Brooke, Morrisania, Dec. 26, 1707, American Papers of the SPG, Lambeth Palace, XIV, n.p. (microfilm), Lambeth Palace Library, London. For the bishop of London's verdict, see his letter to the secretary, June 11, 1708, X, n.p., and Secretary Chamberlayne to Quary, Windsor Castle, Aug. 6, 1708, XV, 127 (microfilm).

8. Morris to the secretary, Feb. 20, 1712, SPG, Letterbook A, VII, 162 (microfilm).

9. The statements include Affadavit of [Lt.] John Rigg, Esp. relating to Mr. Moor, Jan. 3, 1712, and Affidavit of James Walters, Affidavit of Francis Sheirman, and Affidavit of John Grimes, all Jan. 2, 1712, ibid., 248–251; Affidavit of Peter Fauconnier, Jan. 19, 1712, ibid., 342–347; Affidavits of William Anderson and Ebenezer Wilson, Jan. 19, 1712, SPG, Letterbook C, I (microfilm). Cornbury had threatened from London to sue certain colonials, though it is not clear that any suit was ever filed.

10. Cornbury to Board of Trade, Nov. 26, 1705, CO 5/1049, fol. 10, LOC Transcripts. When Connecticut and Rhode Island failed to pay their quotas for defense of the northern frontier, Cornbury notified the Board of Trade that the two colonies had pleaded impoverishment as an excuse: "This is a truth, which if they deny, I will make Oath of whenever your Lordshipps will please to command me."

11. Governor Bellomont to Board of Trade, Boston, July 22, 1699, *NYCD*, IV, 534.

12. For examples of character description, see Morris to the secretary, May 30, 1709, SPG Journals, App. B, 411 (East Ardsley, England: Micro Methods, 1964); William Penn to James Logan, Mar. 2, 1706, and Penn to Logan, May 31, 1708, in Papers of William Penn, XII, 647, XIII, 421 (microfilm). For Fauconnier, see George Clarke and Thomas Byerly to William Blathwayt, New York, Feb. 16, 1707, William Blathwayt Papers, X, Colonial Williamsburg Foundation, Williamsburg, Va. (microfilm); Cornbury to Board of Trade, n.d., T 1/94 fol. 390, PRO. For more on Fauconnier, consult Abraham Ernest Helffenstein, *Pierre Fauconnier and His Descendants . . .* (Philadelphia, 1911).

13. John Champante to Roger Mompesson, Oct. 16, 18, 1707, Champante Letterbook, Rawlinson Mss., fols. 239–240, Bodl. Lib.; Champante to Colonel Abraham DePeyster, Oct. 10, 1707, fols. 238–239. In urging New Yorkers to oppose Cornbury, Champante also dropped hints about the offices they might obtain in the administration of a successor; Champante to Mompesson, Oct. 18, 1707, fol. 240.

14. Cornbury to Board of Trade, n.d., T 1/94, fols. 389–391, PRO. When the informant did supply proof of his charge, including bills of store, Cornbury consulted with lawyers and then suspended the receiver, Thomas Byerly, from office.

15. William Anderson to Clarendon, New York, May 31, 1711, Misc. Mss., NYHS. Jacob Regnier, in any case, was described by Anderson as "a Common Incendiary wherever he goes." Good examples of hearsay ignored can be found in official correspondence at the Public Record Office as well as in the letterbooks and journals of the SPG.

This response and the three categories of communication suggested here had become "part of the stock of social knowledge" absorbed by early modern bureaucrats. For more on "genres of communication," see Bergmann, *Discreet Indiscretions*, 26–32, quotations on 29.

16. Board of Trade to Cornbury, Feb. 4, 1706, *CSPC*, XXIII, 80; Cornbury to Board of Trade, New York, Sept. 10, 1706, ibid., 488. Chamberlayne to Mr. John Bartow, Westminster, July 26, 1708, American Papers of the SPG, Lambeth Palace, XIV, 110. For the double set of instructions, see Board of Trade to Cornbury, Whitehall, Mar. 16, 1704, *NYCD*, IV, 1050.

17. Bellomont to the bishop of London, Boston, Sept. 11, 1699, *NYCD*, IV, 580–582. For more on this case, see Bellomont to Board of Trade, July 22, 1699, 531–537.

18. For the bishop of London's defense of Godfriedus Dellius, whom he hoped to bring into the Anglican fold, see his letter to the Lords of Trade, Nov. 1, 1700, ibid., 774.

19. Chamberlayne to William Urquhart, Windsor Castle, Aug. 7, 1708, American Papers of the SPG, Lambeth Palace, XIV, 117; Chamberlayne to Vesey, Windsor Castle, Aug. 10, 1708, 118; Chamberlayne to Quary, Windsor Castle,

Aug. 6, 1708, XV, 128 (microfilm). See my discussion of Quary's letter to the bishop in chap. 3; for the bishop's subsequent evaluation of the affair, see his letter to Chamberlayne, June 11, 1708, XX, n.p. (microfilm). Chamberlayne also wrote to Elias Neau on Aug. 5, 1708 (XIV, 112), asking: "Why did Brooks voluntarily abandon his Charge? and why did Moore steal out of his prison?" Neau's letter to the secretary of February 1709, in which he defended the two missionaries and accused Cornbury of cross dressing, was very likely in response to this request for information.

The SPG secretary's instruction is in Chamberlayne to John Bartow, Westminster, July 26, 1708, ibid., XIV, 110 (microfilm).

20. Evan Evans to the secretary, Burlington, N.J., Feb. 19, 1712, SPG, Letterbook A, VII, 139 (microfilm), is one such letter; similar sentiments are expressed repeatedly in the SPG correspondence.

21. William Vesey to Mr. Gibbon, New York, Dec. 18, 1718, Rawlinson Papers, C 933, fol. 130 (microfilm), HHV; Cornbury to Board of Trade, New York, June 24, 1704, *NYCD*, IV, 1108; Samuel Vetch to Sunderland, New York, June 28, 1709, HM 22283, HL; Morris to the Secretary of State [Robert Harley], New York, Feb. 9, 1708, Eugene R. Sheridan, ed., *The Papers of Lewis Morris*, 3 vols. (Newark, N.J., 1991–1993), I, 72.

22. Cornbury to Clarendon, New York, Jan. 25, 1709, and Cornbury to Rochester, New York, Feb. 21, 1709, Collection of Original Letters; Robert Hunter to Jonathan Swift, New York, Nov. 1, 1712, F. Elrington Ball, ed., *The Correspondence of Jonathan Swift, D.D.*, 6 vols. (London, 1910–1914), II, 11; Hunter to the Lords of Trade, New York, July 7, 1718, *NYCD*, V, 510. Yet Hunter, like his predecessors, continued to defend himself against the aspersions of his critics; see, e.g., Mary Lou Lustig, *Robert Hunter, 1666–1734: New York's Augustan Statesman* (Syracuse, N.Y., 1983), chap. 6.

23. Robert Livingston to [William] Lowndes, New London, June 2, 1707, T 1/102, fol. 130–131, PRO (microfilm), HHV. It was around this time, of course, that Champante launched his campaign for Cornbury's recall. For Livingston's activities in 1706–1707, see Lawrence H. Leder, *Robert Livingston, 1654–1728, and the Politics of Colonial New York* (Chapel Hill, N.C., 1961), 199–203. Leder asserts that Livingston's earlier falling out with Cornbury over repayment of his accounts was now exacerbated by Cornbury's reluctance to recognize Livingston's royal commissions for New York offices, including secretary of Indian affairs (201).

24. Both the passion of Morris's letter and its reference to Moore and Brooke being on their way to England suggest that the letter was written about the time of the two men's "escape," as Morris calls it, from New York. Sheridan dates it September 1707 in *Papers of Lewis Morris*, I, 59, 62. In SPG, Letterbook C, I, no. 2 (microfilm), the letter is endorsed "Colonel Morris to the Secretary concerning

the State of the Church in New York and the Jerseys supposed to be writ about the end of the year 1707 or beginning of 1708." It also appears with the same endorsement in the SPG Journals, App. B, 121 (microfilm). I am inclined to agree with Sheridan's date.

25. Morris to Secretary of State [Harley], New York, Feb. 9, 1708, Sheridan, ed., *Papers of Lewis Morris*, I, 78.

26. The only subsequent description of Lord Cornbury by Morris, offered in an essay in the *New-York Weekly Journal* of Dec. 24, 1733, that aspersed all New York governors whose names began with *C*, balanced Cornbury's bad qualities with a few good ones, and said nothing at all about cross dressing.

27. Neau to the secretary, New York, Feb. 27, 1709, SPG, Letterbook A, IV, 402–413. The original letter in French (and accurately translated into English by the SPG clerk) is in the American Papers of the SPG, Lambeth Palace, XIV, 121 (microfilm).

28. What being garbed in the Dutch manner means is unclear (though it could suggest a form of country as opposed to city dress). Moreover, the whimsical tone of the comment makes one wonder whether Neau's correspondent was supposed to take any of this seriously. During Neau's visit to Cornbury at his house, noted in the letter, he apparently found nothing amiss in the former governor's attire. The location of the fort, ca. 1717, is shown in some detail in John A. Kouwenhoven, *The Columbia Historical Portrait of New York* (Garden City, N.Y., 1953), 52–53, 55. Chaplain Sharpe, who visited Cornbury about twice a month in this period, said nothing regarding cross dressing and emerged as one of Cornbury's strong defenders; "Journal of Rev. John Sharpe," *Pennsylvania Magazine of History and Biography*, XL (1916), 257–297, 412–425, the years 1709–1710.

29. Livingston to Lowndes, New London, June 2, 1707, T 1/102, fol. 130–131, PRO (microfilm), HHV (emphasis added). The anthropologist F. G. Bailey proposes six categories by which private news is communicated from a sender to a receiver — "chat, scandal, rumour, confidence, gossip, open criticism" — and notes the sender's strategies as well as the responsibility he or she assumes for each category of news; Bailey, ed., *Gifts and Poison: The Politics of Reputation* (New York, 1971), 281–301.

30. One study of early modern English cross dressing concludes that by the turn of the 17th century a man actually wearing women's clothes in public would have been seen as "monstrous"; see Jean E. Howard, "Crossdressing, the Theatre, and Gender Struggle in Early Modern England," *Shakespeare Quarterly*, XXXIX (1988), 424. See also Kenneth Fraser Easton, "Bad Habits: Cross-Dressing and the Regulation of Gender in Eighteenth-Century British Literature and Society" (Ph.D. diss., Princeton University, 1990).

31. Viscount Bolingbroke "despised him [Bothmer] as a tool of the whigs"; see J. R. Jones, *Country and Court; England, 1658–1714* (Cambridge, Mass., 1978),

298. For more on Bothmer, see chap. 2. As one Tory diplomat of the time wrote, Bothmer "understands no more of affairs of England than a horse"; see earl of Strafford to the earl of Oxford, The Hague, May 28, 1714, HMC, *[Fifteenth Report]*, *Report on the Manuscripts of His Grace the Duke of Portland* . . . , IX (London, 1923), 398.

Though the cross-dressing story was not, so far as I can ascertain, recorded again in England until 1796, it apparently never completely died in 18th-century Whig circles, being part of the lore retailed by such as Horace Walpole and his friends, as well as by Lord North, fifth earl of Guilford; see Francis Bickley, ed., *The Diaries of Sylvester Douglas (Lord Glenbervie)*, 2 vols. (London, 1928), I, 76–77.

32. Samuel Sewall to Thomas Cockerill, Feb. 21, 1709, MHS, *Colls.*, 6th Ser., I (1886), 380–381. As Morris reported to Moore and Brooke, "Your friend Sharpe is become a Violent advocate for his Lordship" (Dec. 26, 1707, American Papers of the SPG, Lambeth Palace, XIV, n.p. [microfilm]). See also "Sharpe's Journal," *PMHB*, XL (1916).

33. Late-18th- and 19th-century writers most commonly explained Cornbury's supposed cross dressing by noting his connection to the queen. These authors may have had access only to H. C. von Bothmer's letter of 1714, which passed on the rumor that Cornbury dressed as a woman "in order to represent her Majesty" in the colonies (see chap. 2).

Lynn Hunt discusses negative images applied to political women in revolutionary France in *The Family Romance of the French Revolution* (Berkeley, Calif., 1992), chap. 4. As noted in chap. 5 (above), such imagery may have been less viable in England, where, contrary to practice in France, women could inherit the throne. There can be little doubt that the high esteem in which Queen Elizabeth was held by the 18th century helped clear the path for Anne.

34. Livingston to Lowndes, New London, June 2, 1707, T 1/102, fols. 130–131, PRO (microfilm), HHV; Morris, State of the Church, [late 1707?], and Morris to the Secretary of State [Harley], Feb. 9, 1708, in Sheridan, ed., *Papers of Lewis Morris*, I, 59, 78; Sewall to Cockerill, Feb. 21, 1709, MHS, *Colls.*, 6th Ser., I (1886), 380–381; Neau to the secretary, New York, Feb. 27, 1709, SPG, Letterbook A, IV, 402–413 (microfilm).

35. Rebecca W. Bushnell, *Tragedies of Tyrants: Political Thought and Theater in the English Renaissance* (Ithaca, N.Y., 1990), 9, 13, 20–25, and chap. 5. (I thank my colleague Antonio Feros for bringing this book to my attention.)

Early modern Dutch political satire drew heavily on the classical tradition, especially the works of Juvenal (Maria A. Schenkeveld, *Dutch Literature in the Age of Rembrandt: Themes and Ideas* [Amsterdam, 1991], 146), where gender confusion, masquerade, and depictions of cross dressing were legion. The historian Lotte van de Pol says Dutch satire had a "long tradition of symbolic gender reverse, women 'wearing breeches' and men depicted as spinning and wearing pinafores. A woman's role and therefore also women's clothes were considered to debase a man" (van de Pol to author, Aug. 15, 1995); and see Rudolf M. Dekker and Lotte C. van de Pol, *The Tradition of Female Transvestism in Early Modern Europe* (London, 1989).

36. Byerly, Journal or Particular . . . transactions, June 10, 1704–1707/8, CO 5/1084, fol. 62, PRO (microfilm), HHV. The words Byerly puts in Cornbury's mouth bear an uncanny resemblance to those attributed to a governor of New Netherland, Willem Kieft (1638–1647), more than 50 years earlier; as one political opponent asserted, Kieft claimed "he was sovereign in [New Netherland], or the same as the Prince in the Netherlands"; "The Representation of New Netherland, 1650," in J. Franklin Jameson, ed., *Narratives of New Netherland, 1609–1664* (New York, 1909), 324.

The final fictitious comment might have been in character for Byerly, who was said to have a nasty tongue. Cornbury complained about the "very abusive language he has bellowed upon me behind my back in the taverns of this towne." Attorney General Samuel Broughton similarly protested that Byerly "takes upon him to . . . defame me publickly to the people . . . [and] gave me very base and scurvey language." Peter Fauconnier reported the same. Cornbury to the lord treasurer, New York, Sept. 24, 1707, CO 5/103, fol. 72, PRO; Broughton to Board of Trade, New York, June 27, 1704, *NYCD*, IV, 1109; Peter Fauconnier's Reply and Petition, New York, Jan. 26, 1708, NY Col. Mss., LII, fol. 94, NYSL.

CHAPTER EIGHT

1. When John Nanfan, who had taken over the government at Governor Bellomont's death, heard that Cornbury's ship had been spotted off Sandy Hook, he supposedly rushed through the assembly a series of acts directed against the anti-Leislerian opposition; see "Abstract of Some Letters from New York, May 4, 1702," *CSPC*, XX, 412.

The "English party" label for the anti-Leislerians, like the occasional designation of "Dutch party" for the Leislerians, should not be taken as a literal description of the two groups' ethnic composition. Bellomont once noted how his opposition manipulated such terms: the anti-Leislerian faction, "as an artifice to draw all the English to vote for their friends, call'd themselves the English party, but what is observable and very rediculous besides is, that three of the four Candidates they set up [in New York County] were as meer Dutch as any are in this town" (Bellomont to Board of Trade, New York, Apr. 27, 1699, *NYCD*, IV, 508). And Cornbury observed that some adherents of the so-called Dutch faction were Dutch not so much by nation as by "inclination," by which he meant former New Englanders and other local Dissenters whose loyalty to the English crown, especially after the death of their coreligionist William III, was suspect. Both labels had thus taken on wider political-religious meanings. Cornbury to Sir Charles Hedges, New York, July 15, 1705, *NYCD*, IV, 1155.

2. Cornbury to Board of Trade, N.Y., June 16, 1702, *NYCD*, IV, 959–960; "Lord Cornbury's Reasons for Suspending Chief Justice Atwood," copy, Oct. 2, 1702, 1010–1012; Board of Trade to the Queen, Oct. 31, 1702, *CSPC*, XXI, 100. On the New York Council, see Jessica Kross, "'Patronage Most Ardently Sought': The New York Council, 1665–1775," in Bruce C. Daniels, ed., *Power and Status: Office-holding in Colonial America* (Middletown, Conn., 1986).

3. For an exchange in 1709 between two of the dismissed councilmen, Samuel Staats and Robert Walters, and Lord Cornbury, see NY Col. Mss., LIII, fols. 14, 16, 37, NYSL. See also Nanfan to John Champante, New York, May 27, 1703, Rawlinson Mss., A272, fols. 208–213, Bodl. Lib. Mr. Fauconnier's Deposition, Feb. 25, 1712, SPG, Letterbook A, VII, 327–333 (microfilm) (first quotation); Robert Livingston to Fitz-John Winthrop, New York, Dec. 29, 1702, MHS, *Colls.*, 6th Ser., III (1889), 115–117 (second quotation). Livingston seems to have had interests of his own. He criticized Cornbury for delaying reimbursement of money he had loaned to previous administrations, though Cornbury appointed commissions that eventually offered Livingston some relief. For a somewhat different reading, see Lawrence H. Leder, *Robert Livingston, 1654–1728, and the Politics of Colonial New York* (Chapel Hill, N.C., 1961), 181–185.

4. Winthrop to Cornbury, Aug. 8, 1705, MHS, *Colls.*, 6th Ser., III (1889), 302; see also 307, 356, 359. True, Cornbury sent Whitehall some 30 sworn depositions from critics of Connecticut. Yet even Sir Henry Ashurst, Connecticut's agent in London, blamed the colony's troubles largely on "one man," Governor Dudley of Massachusetts (Sir Henry Ashurst to the Connecticut governor and Council, London, May 21, 1706, ibid., 325–327). See also Richard S. Dunn, *Puritans and Yankees: The Winthrop Dynasty of New England, 1630–1717* (1962; rpt. New York, 1971), esp. 335.

5. Memorial from Mr. [Robert] Livingston about New York, n.d. [late 1702], *NYCD*, IV, 1067–1068; Cornbury to Board of Trade, Orange County, N.Y., Sept. 24, 1702, 969; Conference of Lord Cornbury with the Indians, July 1702, 983; Cornbury to Board of Trade, Sept. 29, 1702, 977–978.

Daniel K. Richter offers a nuanced reading of the so-called neutrality pact of 1701 between certain of the Iroquois and French Canada in *The Ordeal of the Longhouse: The Peoples of the Iroquois League in the Era of European Colonization* (Chapel Hill, N.C., 1992), chap. 8. He shows the Five Nations as subject to extreme factionalism, dividing both within and between nations into "anglophiles" and "francophiles." This made it impossible for the Iroquois League to pursue a single united policy toward either France or England. Richard Haan suggests that such neutrality was in part a "device" by which the Iroquois hoped to divert the Great Lakes Indian trade from Montreal to Albany; see "The Problem of Iroquois Neutrality: Suggestions for Revision," *Ethnohistory*, XXVII (1980), 318–322.

6. Conference of Lord Cornbury with the Indians, July 1702, *NYCD*, IV, 983; Cornbury to Board of Trade, Sept. 24, 1702, 970. For praise of Cornbury, see 988, 992, 998. Colonel Robert Quary to Board of Trade, New York, June 16, 1703, 1053; Memorial from Mr. Livingston about New York, n.d. [late 1702], 1068.

Daniel Richter's belief that Cornbury had no Indian policy, and even ignored the Five Iroquois Nations, appears to stem from his reliance on the opinions of Cadwallader Colden and Peter Wraxall (*Ordeal of the Longhouse*, 215–216). Colden arrived in New York in 1718 and thus was not a witness to Cornbury's dealings with the Indians. For Wraxall's bias, including his disdain for the Albany Dutch, see note 9, below.

7. Cornbury to Board of Trade, Nov. 6, 1704, *NYCD*, IV, 1120–1121. Howard H. Peckham, *The Colonial Wars, 1689–1762* (Chicago, 1964), 60; Michael Kammen, *Colonial New York: A History* (New York, 1975), 144.

8. Cornbury to the earl of Nottingham, New York, June 22, 1704, *NYCD*, IV, 1099–1100. Governor Dudley apparently received Cornbury's message, for on Feb. 16, 1704, he notified officials in western Massachusetts that 300 Indians might be on the march from Albany (Dudley to ?, Feb. 16, 1704, no. 1727, Emmet Collection, NYPL). Cornbury had also sent warnings some months earlier; see his letter to the Lords of Trade, New York, June 30, 1703, *NYCD*, IV, 1061, and that of May 27, 1703, *CSPC*, XXI, 739.

In addition to those killed outright at Deerfield, 109 persons were taken captive, a number of whom died on the subsequent trek to Canada. Evan Haefeli and Kevin Sweeney, "Revisiting *The Redeemed Captive:* New Perspectives on the 1704 Attack on Deerfield," *WMQ*, 3d Ser., LII (1995), 3–46.

9. Cornbury to Board of Trade, New York, Nov. 6, 1704, *NYCD*, IV, 1121; Peckham, *Colonial Wars*, 60. Robert Quary had finally despaired of persuading the Board of Trade to move against Canada, having "so often troubled your Lordships on this subject" without success, as had New York governors going back at least to Fletcher; see Quary to Board of Trade, May 30, 1704, *NYCD*, IV, 1083.

On the New Englanders' position after Deerfield, see Winthrop to Cornbury, New London, Apr. 11, 1704, Governor Dudley to Winthrop, Aug. 28, 1704, Winthrop to Peter Schuyler, New London, Sept. 10, 1704, and Cornbury to Winthrop, Burlington, N.J., Sept. 25, 1704, all in MHS, *Colls.*, 6th Ser., III (1889), 192–193, 261, 263, 267. In May 1708, Cornbury's government sent a belt of wampum to the Caughnawaga Indians in Canada as a seal on the Indians' promise never again to attack New England; see Peter Wraxall, *An Abridgement of the*

*Indian Affairs . . . in the Colony of New York . . . 1678 to . . . 1751*, ed. Charles Howard McIlwain (Cambridge, Mass., 1915), 53.

The charge, often repeated by historians, that Cornbury advocated neutrality with Canada, or that he was somehow responsible for French and Indian attacks on New England, is without foundation. Wraxall's *Abridgement*, ed. McIlwain, a frequently consulted 18th-century source on English dealings with the Iroquois, entirely omits from the record Cornbury's important conference of 1702 with the Indians at Albany. Wraxall himself — who detested the Albanians — is the likely author of an unattributed passage smuggled into the *Abridgement* that blames New York for the Indians' alleged neutrality and castigates Albany's leaders as "a set of Weak, Mercenary, mean Spirited People" (59).

Indeed, Wraxall may be the originator of the myth that New York's government supported a neutral position in Queen Anne's War (see his *Abridgement*, ed. McIlwain, 48). As Campbell wrote in his newsletter, the Indians did propose a neutrality with the French, "which his Lordship would not admitt of." That some of the tribes may have been on "both sydes, and receive presents from both," was a fait accompli by the time Cornbury arrived. Cornbury's commitment to strengthening the Iroquois alliance, as shown in his repeated pleas to England and the New York Assembly for aid, cannot be doubted. See Campbell's Newsletter, October 1703, MHS, *Procs.*, 1st Ser., IX (1867), 500; Cornbury's Speech to the Assembly, Aug. 20, 1708, *Journal of the Votes and Proceedings of the General Assembly of the Colony of New York, 1691–1765*, 2 vols. (New York, 1764–1766), I, 219. For further discussion of Wraxall's railings against the "Albany Spirit" in Indian affairs, see Patricia U. Bonomi, *A Factious People: Politics and Society in Colonial New York* (New York, 1971), 48–53.

10. For Cornbury's final effort to gain support for an attack on Quebec, his remarks on the Albany trade, and his persistent urging that presents be sent to the Indians, see Cornbury to Board of Trade, New York, Aug. 20, 1708, *NYCD*, IV, 977–978, 1061, 1123, 1166, V, 64–66. Haan, "Iroquois Neutrality," *Ethnohistory*, XXVII (1980), 322–323; Bonomi, *A Factious People*, 43–45.

On 1709, see G. M. Waller, *Samuel Vetch, Colonial Enterpriser* (Chapel Hill, N.C., 1960). In preparing for the invasion of Canada, Vetch noted that the New Jersey Assembly, whose membership he estimated at about half-Quaker, was reluctant to supply money or men for the attack; Vetch to the earl of Sunderland, June 29, 1709, copy, Special Collections, Columbia University, New York. This sort of report, which served to validate Cornbury's estimation of his New Jersey opponents, could only have strengthened his position at Whitehall.

11. Quary to Board of Trade, New York, June 16, 1703, *NYCD*, IV, 1054; Julius M. Block et al., eds., *An Account of Her Majesty's Revenue in the Province of New York, 1701–09: The Customs Records of Early Colonial New York* (Ridgewood, N.J., 1966).

For the shift of defense costs, see, e.g., Board of Trade to Cornbury, Mar. 26, 1705, *NYCD*, IV, 1139. Some two-thirds of England's budget was committed to military expenditures during Queen Anne's reign; see John Brewer, *The Sinews of Power: War, Money, and the English State, 1688–1783* (New York, 1989), 40.

12. The historian quoted is Oliver Morton Dickerson, *American Colonial Government: 1696–1765 . . .* (Cleveland, Ohio, 1912), 160; and see Evarts Boutell Greene, *The Provincial Governor in the English Colonies of North America* (1898; rpt. New York, 1966), 184. *Journal of the Assembly of New York,* I, 171 (second quotation, emphasis added); the language unambiguously points to Bellomont and Nanfan. See also 156–157, 166, 170; *Journal of the Legislative Council of the Colony of New York . . . April 9, 1691–September 27, 1743* (Albany, N.Y., 1861), 183; NY Col. Mss., XLVII, fols. 141–143; [Robert Hunter], *To All Whom These Presents May Concern* (New York, 1713), 5–6; May 27, 1703, *CSPC*, XXI, 748; and *Journal of the Assembly of New York,* I, 206 (third quotation). It might be recalled that Cornbury initiated the assembly's discussion of the £1,500 fund for placing cannon at the Narrows (discussed above). For complaints about the receivers Thomas Byerly and Peter Fauconnier during Cornbury's governorship, see, e.g., *Journal of the Assembly of New York,* I, 227, 238.

13. Cornbury to Board of Trade, Nov. 6, 1704, July 8, 1705, *NYCD*, IV, 1121–1122, 1145–1146.

14. Ibid., July 8, 1705, 1145–1146; Cornbury to Secretary Hedges, New York, July 15, 1705, 1151, 1155. To strengthen his case against the assembly, Cornbury showed the pertinent passages of his Instructions to the Council, which backed his position (1145).

15. Board of Trade to Cornbury, Feb. 4, 1706, ibid., 1171–1172; *Journal of the Assembly of New York,* I, 213. Clearly this concession was made to encourage New Yorkers to provide for their own defense rather than rely on England for arms and ammunition. For council discussions of this controversy, see *Journal of the Legislative Council of New York,* 183, 273. For additional details, consult Philip L. White, *The Beekmans of New York in Politics and Commerce, 1647–1877* (New York, 1956), 99–104.

Abraham DePeyster, whom Cornbury had dismissed from the council in 1702 for Leislerian leanings, was appointed treasurer. When critics admonished the governor for reversing his position on DePeyster by approving the assembly's choice, Cornbury observed that DePeyster was "not the first honest Man" to fall into bad company. And if some thought that "whoever [erred] once ought never to be forgiven," that was a doctrine Cornbury could not live by. *Journal of the Assembly of New York,* I, 223–225; NY Col. Mss., LIII, fol. 37.

16. Cornbury to Hedges, New York, July 15, 1705, *NYCD*, IV, 1154–1155. Compare *Journal of the Assembly of New York,* I, 206, with Morris's undated notes in the Robert Morris Papers, box I, Special Collections, Rutgers University, New

Brunswick, N.J. Cornbury's comment on colonial assemblies is in his letter to the Board of Trade, Feb. 19, 1705, *CSPC*, XXII, 878. The three assemblymen opposing Cornbury were Philip French and Thomas Codrington of New York Co. and Thomas Garton of Ulster Co.; *NYCD*, IV, 1150.

17. For Morris's role as Hunter's legislative adviser on these matters, see Eugene R. Sheridan, *Lewis Morris, 1671–1746: A Study in Early American Politics* (Syracuse, N.Y., 1981), 101–103, 111–113.

18. To be sure, Cornbury had private reasons for protesting Hunter's program, specifically that it did not repay money he believed was owed him when governor, the withholding of which had forced him into debt. See An Account of money due to me in the Provinces of New York and New Jersey for which I have not yet any Warrants, New York, Feb. 24, 1709, Cornbury Papers, NYHS; Sheridan, *Lewis Morris*, chap. 6, esp. 113. We have already seen that Cornbury also deplored such legislation because it drained power from metropolis to colonies.

19. The best modern study of this period of New Jersey history is Sheridan, *Lewis Morris*. For a draft of Cornbury's Instructions as royal governor of New Jersey, see Board of Trade to the queen, Aug. 21, 1702, *CSPC*, XX, 887.

20. Quary to Board of Trade, Aug. 14, Dec. 20, 1703, and Sir Thomas Laurence to Board of Trade, Virginia, Oct. 25, 1703, both in *CSPC*, XXI, 1033, 1190, 1400. James Logan reported to William Penn that Cornbury was "Exceedingly beloved" in the Jerseys (July 29, 1702, James Logan Letterbook I, 41, HSP). For Cornbury's assessment of his first days as governor of New Jersey, see his letter to the Board of Trade, New York, Sept. 9, 1703, *NJA*, III, 1–6.

21. Quotation in Sheridan, *Lewis Morris*, 53. For divisions in the New Jersey colonial assembly, see Thomas L. Purvis, *Proprietors, Patronage, and Paper Money: Legislative Politics in New Jersey, 1703–1776* (New Brunswick, N.J., 1986), esp. chap. 4.

22. *NJA*, II, 452–462. Under the royal charter, East and West Jersey Proprietors retained significant authority over the distribution of lands from their patents. And see John Strassburger, "'Our Unhappy Purchase': The West Jersey Society, Lewis Morris, and Jersey Lands, 1703–36," *New Jersey History*, XLVIII (1980), 97–113; Sheridan, *Lewis Morris*, 50–51, 54–55.

23. With proprietary rights under attack in these years, William Penn, for example, had no doubt that London was trying to force the surrender of his charter for Pennsylvania. Ian K. Steele, "The Board of Trade, the Quakers, and Resumption of Colonial Charters, 1699–1702," *WMQ*, 3d Ser., XXIII (1966), 596–619; and Alison Gilbert Olson, "William Penn, Parliament, and Proprietary Government," *WMQ*, 3d Ser., XVIII (1961), 176–195.

Regarding the land tax, see The Humble Memoriall of the Proprietors of the Western Division of the Province of New Jersey in America, Apr. 17, 1705, *NJA*, III, 91. As for the Quakers, though it is unlikely Cornbury took the lead in punitive actions against them, as a military man he probably shared the opinion of some of his supporters that the Quaker presence in New Jersey weakened the colony militarily. By 1707 he was convinced that as long as the Quakers, who he claimed composed two-thirds of the colony's population, were allowed to participate in government no revenue would be settled to support royal authority. Memorial of Mr. Cox[e], Mr. Dockwra, and Mr. Sonmans to the Board of Trade, 1705, *NJA*, III, 83; Cornbury to Sunderland, New York, Nov. 29, 1707, Sunderland Papers, HM 22032, HL.

For Lewis Morris's perspective on these issues, see his letter to Secretary of State [Robert Harley], Feb. 9, 1708, *NYCD*, V, 33–38; and Sheridan, *Lewis Morris*, 64–67.

24. Cornbury was praised for resisting attempts by Morris and other New Jerseyans to limit the surrender of proprietary rights under the royal charter; see Board of Trade to Cornbury, Feb. 4, 1706, *CSPC*, XXIII, 80. On political machinations in England, see Earl Godolphin to the duke of Marlborough, May 14, 1706, in Henry L. Snyder, ed., *The Marlborough-Godolphin Correspondence*, 3 vols. (Oxford, 1975), I, 548, June 9, 1707, II, 801. See also 695, 699; J. R. Jones, *Country and Court: England, 1658–1714* (Cambridge, Mass., 1978), 320–327; Stephen Saunders Webb, "William Blathwayt, Imperial Fixer: Muddling through to Empire, 1689–1717," *WMQ*, 3d Ser., XXVI (1969), 412–414; Geoffrey Holmes, *British Politics in the Age of Anne*, rev. ed. (London, 1987), esp. 449–457. For the effect of shifting parties in England on provincial governors, see Alison Gilbert Olson, *Anglo-American Politics, 1660–1775: The Relationship between Parties in England and Colonial America* (New York, 1973), esp. 84–93.

25. Champante to Roger Mompesson, Oct. 18, 1707, Champante to Colonel Abraham DePeyster, Oct. 10, 1707, and Champante to Mompesson, Oct. 16, 1707, all in Rawlinson Mss., fols. 238, 239, 240. Though Champante addressed these remarks to New Yorkers, his involvement in furthering New Jersey's *Remonstrance* is also suggested in his letter to Mompesson, Oct. 18, 1707. One of the advantages of Cornbury's removal would be Champante's own reappointment as London agent for the two colonies, which, as he observed, "would be very acceptable to me."

26. Champante to Mompesson, Oct. 18, 1707, ibid., fol. 240. Some writers assert that the New York Assembly submitted a list of charges against Cornbury, citing a Sept. 11, 1708, report of the assembly's Committee of Grievances. This report urges that coroners be elected rather than appointed, taxes and fees be levied only with the consent of the assembly, no duties be laid on imports or port charges on vessels, no Court of Equity be erected, and so on. These, however, were already familiar grievances and would be almost ritually pressed on imperial authorities through the 18th century. The only item on the committee's list that may have been directed specifically at Cornbury urged that no defendant

adjudged innocent be forced to pay the fees for his own prosecution, a seeming reference to the Makemie case (see chap. 3). *Journal of the Assembly of New York*, I, 223–224.

27. Morris and Jennings may have been the first colonials deliberately to employ the assembly as a forum from which to concert opposition to a sitting governor. When some 20 years later James Alexander of New York described the opposition politics of his day — wherein the governor's opponents told the people they were oppressed "and Set up for . . . patriot[s] defend[ing] the Country Liberties and priviledges" — he used the Morris-Cornbury dispute as a first instance in which the assembly had undertaken to manipulate public opinion. At that time, New Jerseyans were "inraged against" Morris so long as he was a member of the New Jersey Council. But, Alexander sardonically noted, once Morris resigned his council seat and took up leadership of the opposition to Cornbury (thereby deflecting hostility from himself to the governor), Morris could have "come representative for most Counties of Jersey[;] and Soon after carried his point so far as to get Lord Cornbury turned out with disgrace"; James Alexander to Hunter, draft, New York, Nov. 20, 1728, Rutherfurd Collection, vols. I–III (microfilm), NYHS. (Alexander arrived in the colonies from Scotland in 1715 and thus had only secondhand information on Morris's campaign against Cornbury.)

Alexander's candid description of the machinations of Country politics suggests how familiar such an opposition style had become by the late 1720s. As John Brewer observes, by that time, rather than Country ideology's being the victim of manipulative politicians, it may be that "manipulative politicians were held in thrall by country ideology" (*Sinews of Power*, 157). Alexander's comment also offers a valuable perspective on the more balanced way in which the Cornbury episode was perceived some 20 years after the fact.

28. Cornbury to Sunderland, New York, Nov. 29, 1707, Sunderland Papers, HM 22032. The petition, the *Remonstrance*, and Cornbury's extensive answer thereto, dated respectively May 5 and May 12, 1707, are in CO 5/970, fol. 49ii, PRO, reprinted in *NJA*, III, 171–198. A note at the bottom of the address to Queen Anne reads: "Divers of the Members of this Assembly being of the people Called *Quakers* do all assent to the matter and substance of the above written but make some Exceptions to the Stile." See also Sheridan, *Lewis Morris*, 69–77.

Regarding the courts, Cornbury established the first colonywide judicial system in New Jersey. According to a 19th-century legal scholar, he laid the system well, giving it "shape, and beauty, and proportion" (Richard S. Field, *The Provincial Courts of New Jersey* [New York, 1849], 42).

29. Livingston to William Lowndes, New London, June 2, 1707, T 1/102, fols. 130–131 (microfilm), HHV. Lowndes is described as "Oxford's [Harley's]

chief civil servant in the Treasury" by Edward Gregg in *Queen Anne* (London, 1980), 364.

30. Quary to Board of Trade, Philadelphia, June 28, 1707, *NJA*, III, 237; Quary to Lord Rochester, New York, June 28, 1709, A Collection of Original Letters, JCBL; Mompesson to Board of Trade, New York, Oct. 8, 1706, CO 5/ 1049, fol. 27, PRO. (In addition to his membership on the New Jersey Council, Mompesson was chief justice of the New York Supreme Court.) The final quotation is from To the Queen's Most Excellent Majesty, n.d. [late 1707], *NJA*, III, 287–290.

31. At a Council held at Fort Anne in New York on the 26th day of October 1708 . . . [and] on the 27th day of October 1708, Collection of Original Letters. Signing the documents were John Barbarie, Roger Mompesson, Adolph Philipse, Peter Schuyler, Gerardus Beekman, Rip Van Dam, and Thomas Wenham. By this date, of course, the councilmen knew that Cornbury had been recalled.

Roger Mompesson's relationship with Cornbury is difficult to sort out. Cornbury appointed Mompesson to high office in both New York and New Jersey, and their association generally appears to have been cordial. At the same time, Mompesson was a friend of Thomas Byerly, New York's irascible receiver, and was one of those John Champante wrote to when plotting Cornbury's recall. In 1709, Cornbury wrote his father denouncing Mompesson (along with Clarke, Byerly, and Councilman Adolph Philipse) as a "most ungratefull rascall" for not supporting his efforts to repay his debts. Yet in a letter to Cornbury in 1714, Mompesson described himself as a lifelong ally and beneficiary of "the Noble House of Clarendon." See Cornbury to the earl of Clarendon, Mar. 9, 1709, Add. Mss. 15895, fol. 339, BL; Mompesson to Clarendon, New York, Nov. 13, 1714, Collection of Original Letters.

Roger Brett allowed Cornbury the use of his New York City house while Cornbury was detained for debt. Bidding Cornbury farewell at his departure for England in July 1710, Brett wrote: "The sincere wishes of a true hearted man go along with you wheresoever you go. As for your Lordshipp's Living in my house I am glad that I have any thing that could in any wise be serviceable to you and there is nothing to pay my Lord upon that skore." Brett to Cornbury, July 12, 1710, and Cornbury to Clarendon, New York, Jan. 25, 1709, both in Collection of Original Letters.

32. Memorial of the Clergy Relating to Mr. Poyer and the Church of Jamaica, Nov. 13, 1711, SPG, Letterbook A, VII, 295–304 (microfilm). (The Memorial was signed by the Reverends Poyer, Vesey, Bartow, Evans, Talbot, McKenzie, Henderson, and Thomas.) Mr. Halliday to the secretary, Burlington, N.J., May 11, 1713, VIII, 151; Jeremiah Basse to the secretary [1710], VI, 94; Mr. Fauconier's Deposition, Feb. 25, 1712, VII, 327–333; churchwardens of St. Mary's, Bur-

lington, N.J., to the bishop of London, Mar. 25, 1714, IX, 98–101 (microfilm). This is but a sampling of a large volume of letters of similar tenor in the SPG records.

Considering that two of the four letters charging Cornbury with dressing as a woman were sent to the SPG, it is of interest that the society's annual sermons spoke warmly of him throughout these years, in 1713, for example, commending him as one "who has ever been no less zealous than capable of assisting the Society in Affairs of Importance." *An Abstract of the Most Remarkable Proceedings . . . of the Society for the Propagation of the Gospel . . . Feb. 15, 1712–Feb. 20, 1713* (London, 1713), 59.

33. Francis Harison to Champante, New York, Oct. 5, 1710, Rawlinson Mss., fol. 255. A year earlier when Cornbury was still under detention for debt, another critic had declared that he "governs his party more absolutely while in custody of a Sherif of his making" than he did when governor (William Atwood to Board of Trade, Oct. 26, 1709, *NYCD*, V, 106).

34. Benjamin Ashe to Cornbury, New York, May 31, July 6, 1711, Clarendon Mss., CVI–CVII, fols. 209, 210, Bodl. Lib.; William Carter to Clarendon, New York, Jan. 10, 1714, Collection of Original Letters.

In England, Cornbury was deeply engaged in trying to straighten out New York's tangled accounts, including his own debts, so that Anderson would not be held liable for releasing him from detention; see Cornbury to Treasury Office, Somerset House, London, Mar. 26, 1711, T 1/146, fols. 83, 85; Petition to the Queen, n.d. [March 1711?], SP 44/245, fol. 268–271, PRO. For more on the efforts to charge Anderson, see NY Col. Mss., LIII, fols. 179, 185, 186.

35. Deposition of George Ewbanck of Woodbridge, sworn before Peter Sonmans, Nov. 25, 1710, Add. Mss. 14034, fol. 130, BL. Neither George Ewbanck nor Beyer Schermerhorn has been further identified in a search of New Jersey records. The Schermerhorn family of New York did include a Ryer (or Reyer) (Bonomi, *A Factious People*, Append. C).

36. Sonmans to [Clarendon], Burlington, N.J., Feb. 12, 1711, Add. Mss. 14034, fol. 118, BL. Sonmans himself was officially accused of adultery by the New Jersey Assembly; see chap. 5. *The Humble Representation of the General Assembly . . . of New Jersey to His Excellency Robert Hunter* (New York, 1710); Sheridan, *Lewis Morris*, 82–87.

The executive sequence was: Cornbury turned the seals of office over to Lovelace on Dec. 18, 1708, and promptly moved out of Fort Anne (Cornbury to Clarendon, New York, Jan. 25, 1709, Collection of Original Letters); Lovelace died in May 1709; Hunter arrived June 14, 1710.

37. Extracts from the Minutes of Council of New Jersey, Aug. 14, 1703–Nov. 7, 1715, Peter Force Collection, Ser. 8B, no. 115, (microfilm), LOC. Earlier the council had declared that "the rude and unmannerly treatment of the then Gov-

ernour my Lord Cornbury . . . is such as we presume no age can parallel . . . such daring chardges without any proof . . . that we can deem them no less than Scandalous and Infamous Libells" (To His Excellency John Lord Lovelace, April 1709, *NJA*, III, 405). For Lovelace's sympathetic view of Cornbury's dilemma, see Lovelace to Sunderland, Perth Amboy, N.J., Mar. 4, 1709, Sunderland Papers, HM 22264.

38. Such control may have been reinforced by the rumor that Cornbury might return as governor, or even as "vice Roy or Generall Governour of all her Majesties plantations in America"; The hard Case of Brigadier Hunter Governor of New York and the Jerseys in North America, n.d. [1710–1714], 5, LO 11, HL, quotation on 5.

39. Ibid. Hunter asserted that an opposition faction loyal to Cornbury won the first two elections of his administration in New York. For evidence that a number of Cornbury loyalists continued to torment Hunter well into 1717, see Henry Stevens, comp., *An Analytical Index to the Colonial Documents of New Jersey, in the State Paper Offices of England*, 5 vols. (New York, 1858), V, 89–108. The Morrisites expressed their views in Representation of the New Jersey Assembly, Feb. 8, 1711, in Eugene R. Sheridan, ed., *The Papers of Lewis Morris*, 3 vols. (Newark, N.J., 1991–1993), I, 130. Daniel Coxe to William Dockwra, Burlington, N.J., Jan. 17, 1709, copy, Sunderland Papers, HM 22302.

40. Frederick B. Tolles, *James Logan and the Culture of Provincial America* (Boston, 1957), 16–17, 22, 75–77; Gary B. Nash, *The Urban Crucible: Social Change, Political Consciousness, and the Origins of the American Revolution* (Cambridge, Mass., 1979), 95–98.

41. Logan to Penn, June 18, 25, 1702, Jan. ?, July 9, 1703, Logan Letterbook I, 30, 31–32, 60, 71, 103–104.

42. Logan to Penn, Sept. 2, 1703, Sept. 28, 1704, ibid., 109–111, 161. In the second letter Logan also noted that Cornbury was "jealous" that the Pennsylvanians should treat, as they had recently done, with the Five Nations (163).

43. Logan to Penn, May 20, 1707, ibid., 290. Logan to Charles Eden, Sept. 22, 1708, and Logan to Penn, Feb. 24, 1709, Logan Letterbook II, 115, 321–322.

44. Logan to Penn, Feb. 24, 1709, Logan Letterbook II, 321–322.

CHAPTER NINE

1. Michael Ayon to Board of Trade, Antigua, Sept. 20, 1709, *CSPC*, XXIV, no. 741; Daniel Parke to Board of Trade, Antigua, May 11, 1710, XXV, no. 229; lieutenant governor and council to the queen, Jan. 26, 1711, XXV, no. 674ii. See also XXV, nos. 677i, 683, and 809; and Helen Hill Miller, *Colonel Parke of Virginia: The Greatest Hector in Town: A Biography* (Chapel Hill, N.C., 1989), chaps. 15–16. The Parke and Cornbury stories, despite different endings, display a number

of similarities. Parke, like Cornbury, was a target of sexual innuendo; both men had staunch defenders as well as bitter opponents; the affidavits describing Parke's administrative policies and the events leading to his death vary widely (*CSPC*, XXV, nos. 161, 386–401, 626, 674–678, 783iv, 852). Moreover, Parke was accused of rambling abroad at night "in different disguises" to eavesdrop on his political enemies (XXIV, nos. 443, 597).

2. As its elements stabilized after 1714, the Country outlook would become "virtually the only larger ideological context in which . . . opponents could place their hostility to government policy"; see John Brewer, *The Sinews of Power: War, Money, and the English State, 1688–1783* (New York, 1989), 155–157, quotation on 157.

3. Our understanding of this larger Atlantic perspective — to which this book hopes to contribute — has been clarified by such studies as Ian K. Steele, *The English Atlantic, 1675–1740: An Exploration of Communication and Community* (New York, 1986); Alison Gilbert Olson, *Making the Empire Work: London and American Interest Groups, 1690–1790* (Cambridge, Mass., 1992); and David S. Shields, *Oracles of Empire: Poetry, Politics, and Commerce in British America, 1690–1750* (Chicago, 1990).

4. J. G. A. Pocock has suggested that in colonial America there existed "a Country without a Court" (*The Machiavellian Moment: Florentine Political Thought and the Atlantic Republican Tradition* [Princeton, N.J., 1975], 509). For the attenuation of the governors' powers, see Bernard Bailyn, *The Origins of American Politics* (1967; rpt. New York, 1970).

5. Gordon S. Wood, *The Radicalism of the American Revolution* (New York, 1992), pt. I.

6. A striking example of such an Anglo-American in the 1750s is the New Yorker James DeLancey; see Patricia U. Bonomi, *A Factious People: Politics and Society in Colonial New York* (New York, 1971), chap. 5.

7. C. R., *The Dangers of Masquerades and Raree-Shows . . .* (London, 1718), 29.

# Bibliography

MANUSCRIPT SOURCES

Albany Institute of History and Art, Albany, N.Y.
  Mss. Documents
Bodleian Library, Oxford
  Clarendon Papers
  Rawlinson Mss.
British Library, London
  Additional Mss.
  Egerton Mss.
  Stowe Mss.
Colonial Williamsburg Foundation, Williamsburg, Va.
  William Blathwayt Papers (microfilm)
Columbia University
  Special Collections
Folger Library, Washington, D.C.
  Newdigate Newsletters
Historical Society of Pennsylvania, Philadelphia
  James Logan Letterbook
  Norris Papers
  Wallace Collection
Huntington Library, San Marino, Calif.
  Blathwayt Papers
  Miscellaneous Manuscripts
  Sunderland Collection
John Carter Brown Library, Providence, R.I.
  A Collection of Original Letters
Lambeth Palace Library, London
  American Papers of the Society for the Propagation of the Gospel in
  Foreign Parts
Library of Congress, Washington, D.C.
  Bancroft Transcripts
  Peter Force Collection
Morgan Library, New York
  Livingston-Redmond Mss. (microfilm)
Municipal Archives, New York City
  Flatbush Town Records, Liber B., Court Minutes, 1659–1664
Musée d'Art et d'Histoire, Geneva
  Musée de l'Horlogerie et de l'Emaillerie

New Jersey State Archives, Trenton
Minutes and Rules of the [New Jersey] Supreme Court, 1704–1715
New-York Historical Society, New York City
George Clarke Mss.
Cornbury Mss.
DePeyster Papers
Miscellaneous Mss.
New Netherland Papers
Rutherfurd Collection
New York Public Library
Emmet Collection
New York State Library, Albany
New York Colonial Manuscripts
Princeton University Library, Rare Book Room
Edward Livingston Papers
Public Record Office, London
Admiralty Papers
Colonial Office Papers 5
Privy Council Papers
State Papers (Domestic)
Treasury Papers
Rutgers University, Special Collections
Robert Morris Papers
Society for the Propagation of the Gospel in Foreign Parts
Letterbook Series A, C
Journals
Worcestershire Records Office, Worcester, England
Hampton Collection (microfilm)

NEWSPAPERS

*The Daily Advertiser* (London)
*New York Mercury*
*New-York Weekly Journal*
*Pennsylvania Gazette*
*The Wandering Spy; or, The Way of the World Inquired Into; with Reflections on the Humours of the Town* (London, July 7, 1705–Dec. 1, 1705)
*Weekly Journal* (London)

PRINTED PRIMARY SOURCES

*Abstract of the Most Remarkable Proceedings . . . of the Society for the Propagation of the Gospel . . . Feb. 15, 1712–Feb. 20, 1713, An.* London, 1713.

Adams, John. *Legal Papers of John Adams.* Ed. L. Kinvin Wroth and Hiller B. Zobel. 3 vols. Cambridge, Mass., 1965.

American Antiquarian Society, *Proceedings,* N.S., XIX (Worcester, Mass., 1908–1909), 151–181.

Berwick, James Fitz-James. *Memoirs of the Marshal Duke of Berwick.* 2 vols. London, 1779.

Block, Julius M., et al., eds. *An Account of Her Majesty's Revenue in the Province of New York, 1701–09: The Customs Records of Early Colonial New York.* Ridgewood, N.J., 1966.

[Bohun, Edmund]. *The History of the Desertion. . . .* 1688. In *A Collection of State Tracts, Publish'd on Occasion of the Late Revolution in 1688, and during the Reign of King William III,* I. London, 1705.

Bolingbroke, Henry St. John, Viscount. *Letters and Correspondence, Public and Private, of the Right Honourable Henry St. John, Lord Vis. Bolingbroke; During the Time He Was Secretary of State to Queen Anne.* Ed. Gilbert Parke. 4 vols. London, 1798.

Bond, Donald F., ed. *The Spectator.* 5 vols. Oxford, 1965.

Brown, Tom. *Amusements Serious and Comical, and Other Works, by Tom Brown.* Ed. Arthur L. Hayward. New York, 1927.

———. *The Works of Mr. Thomas Brown. . . .* 4 vols. London, 1730.

Budd, Thomas. *A Just Rebuke to Several Calumnies, Lyes, and Slanders Reported against Thomas Budd.* Philadelphia, 1692.

Burnet, Gilbert. *Burnet's History of His Own Time. . . .* 1724–1734. London, 1883.

———. *A Supplement to Burnet's History of My Own Time.* Ed. H. C. Foxcroft. Oxford, 1902.

Byrd, William. *The Secret Diary of William Byrd of Westover, 1709–1712.* Ed. Louis B. Wright and Marion Tinling. Richmond, Va., 1941.

*Calendar of Treasury Papers, 1697–1702.* London, 1871.

*Catalogue of the Second Special Exhibition of National Portraits, Commencing with the Reign of William and Mary and Ending with the Year MDCCC, on Loan to the South Kensington Museum, May 1, 1867.* London, 1867.

Chamberlayne, Edward. *Angliae Notitia; or, The Present State of England.* London, 1700.

Choisy, Abbé de. *The Transvestite Memoirs of the Abbé de Choisy.* Ed. and trans. Ralph Henry Forster Scott. London, 1973.

Clarendon, Earl of [Edward Hyde]. *History of the Rebellion and Civil Wars in England.* 1702–1704. 31 vols. Oxford, 1837.

Clarke, George. *Voyage of George Clarke, Esq., to America.* Ed. E. B. O'Callaghan. Albany, N.Y., 1867.

Cobbett, William, ed. *Parliamentary History of England, from the Norman Conquest in 1066, to the Year 1803,* VI. London, 1810.

"Colden Letters on Smith's History, The." New-York Historical Society, *Collections,* I (1868), 181–235.

Corwin, E. T., ed. *Ecclesiastical Records of the State of New York.* 7 vols. Albany, N.Y., 1901–1916.

Cowper, Hon. Spencer, ed. *Diary of Mary Countess Cowper . . . 1714–1720.* London, 1864.

Dalton, James. *A Genuine Narrative of All the Street-Robberies Committed since October Last, by James Dalton and His Accomplices . . . from the Mouth of James Dalton.* London, 1728.

Douglas, Sylvester. *The Diaries of Sylvester Douglas (Lord Glenbervie).* Ed. Francis Bickley. 2 vols. London, 1928.

[Dunton, John]. "The Best Perfume, or a Paradox in Praise of Farting." In *Athenian Sport. . . .* London, 1707.

Evelyn, John. *The Diary of John Evelyn.* Ed. E. S. de Beer. 6 vols. Oxford, 1955.

———. ———. Ed. Austin Dobson. 3 vols. London, 1906–1908.

Fithian, Philip Vickers. *Journal, 1775–1776, Written on the Virginia-Pennsylvania Frontier and in the Army around New York.* Ed. Robert Greenhalgh Albion and Leonidas Dodson. Princeton, N.J., 1934.

Gray, John M. *Memoirs of the Life of Sir John Clerk. . . .* Edinburgh, 1892.

Green, Mary Anne Everett, F. H. Blackburne Daniell, et al., eds. *Calendar of State Papers.* Domestic Series. London, 1860–1938.

Hall, Michael G., et al., eds. *The Glorious Revolution in America: Documents on the Colonial Crisis of 1689.* Chapel Hill, N.C., 1964.

Hamilton, Anthony. *Memoirs of the Comte de Gramont.* London, 1930.

Hearne, Thomas. *Reliquiae Hearnianae: The Remains of Thomas Hearne . . . Being Extracts from his MS. Diaries.* Comp. Philip Bliss. Oxford, 1857.

———. *Remarks and Collections of Thomas Hearne.* Ed. C. E. Doble et al. Vol. VIII. Oxford, 1907.

*Hic Mulier; or, The Man-Woman.* London, 1620. In Barbara J. Baines, ed., *Three Pamphlets on the Jacobean Antifeminist Controversy.* Delmar, N.Y., 1978.

Historical Manuscripts Commission. *Seventh Report.* London, 1879. Rpt. London, 1979.

———. *Eleventh Report,* Appendix, Part VII. *The Manuscripts of the Duke of Leeds. . . .* London, 1888.

———. *Twelfth Report,* Appendix, Part V. *The Manuscripts of His Grace the Duke of Rutland . . . ,* II. London, 1889.

————. *Fourteenth Report*, Appendix, Part II. *The Manuscripts of His Grace the Duke of Portland Preserved at Welbeck Abbey*, II. London, 1894.

————. *Fifteenth Report*, Appendix, Part IV. *The Manuscripts of His Grace the Duke of Portland, Preserved at Welbeck Abbey*, IV. *Harley Letters and Papers*, II. London, 1897.

————. *[Eighteenth Report]*, *Report of the Manuscripts of the Marquess of Downshire*, I. *Papers of Sir William Trumbull*, Part II. London, 1924.

*Humble Representation of the General Assembly . . . of New Jersey to His Excellency Robert Hunter, The*. New York, 1710.

[Hunter, Robert]. *Androboros: A Bographical Farce in Three Acts, Viz. The Senate, The Consistory, and The Apotheosis*. Moropolis [New York], 1714.

[————]. *To All Whom These Presents May Concern*. New York, 1713.

Hutchinson, Thomas. *History of the Colony and Province of Massachusetts-Bay*. 1760–1768. Ed. Lawrence Shaw Mayo. 3 vols. 1936. Rpt. New York, 1970.

Jameson, J. Franklin, ed. *Narratives of New Netherland, 1609–1664*. New York, 1909.

Jennings, Samuel. *Truth Rescued from Forgery and Falsehood*. Philadelphia, 1699.

*Journal of the Legislative Council of the Colony of New York . . . April 9, 1691– September 27, 1743*. Albany, N.Y., 1861.

*Journal of the Votes and Proceedings of the General Assembly of the Colony of New York, 1691–1765*. 2 vols. New York, 1764–1766.

Keith, George. *A Journal of Travels from New-Hampshire to Caratuck. . . .* London, 1706.

Kimmel, Michael S., ed. *"Mundus Foppensis" ([London], 1691), and "The Levellers" ([1703]; 1745)*. Augustan Reprint Society, Publication no. 248. Los Angeles, Calif., 1988.

Leeds, Daniel. *The American Almanack . . . 1707*. New York, 1706.

[————]. *The Great Mistery of Fox-Craft Discovered and the Quaker Plainness and Sincerity Demonstrated. . . .* New York, 1705.

Lord, George deF., et al., eds. *Poems on Affairs of State: Augustan Satirical Verse, 1660–1714*. 7 vols. New Haven, Conn., 1963–1975.

*Love-Letters between a Certain Late Nobleman and the Famous Mr. Wilson*. London, [1712].

Luttrell, Narcissus. *A Brief Historical Relation of State Affairs from September 1678 to April 1714*. 6 vols. Oxford, 1857.

Macpherson, James, comp. *Original Papers: Containing the Secret History of Great Britain, from the Restoration to the Accession of the House of Hannover*. 2 vols. London, 1775.

[Makemie, Francis]. *An Answer to George Keith's Libel*. Boston, 1694.

[————]. *A Narrative of a New and Unusual American Imprisonment of Two*

*Presbyterian Ministers: And Prosecution of Mr. Francis Makemie, One of Them, for Preaching One Sermon at the City of New-York.* London, 1707. In Peter Force, comp., *Tracts and Other Papers, Relating Principally to the Origins, Settlement, and Progress of the Colonies of North America,* IV, no. 4. 1847. Rpt. New York, 1947.

Malcolm, James Peller. *Anecdotes of the Manners and Customs of London, during the Eighteenth Century.* . . . 2 vols. London, 1808.

[Manley, Mary de la Rivière]. *The Secret History of Queen Zarah, and the Zarazians.* . . . 2 vols. London, 1705.

[———?]. *Secret Memoirs and Manners of Several Persons of Quality of Both Sexes from the New Atalantis.* . . . 1709. 4 vols. London, 1736.

———. *Secret Memoirs from the New Atlantis.* New York, 1972.

Marlborough, Sarah, Duchess of. *Private Correspondence of Sarah, Duchess of Marlborough, Illustrative of the Court and Times of Queen Anne.* 2d ed. 2 vols. London, 1838.

Morris, Lewis. *The Papers of Lewis Morris.* Ed. Eugene R. Sheridan. 3 vols. Newark, N.J., 1991–1993.

Munsell, Joel. *The Annals of Albany.* 10 vols. Albany, N.Y., 1850–1859.

Nicolson, William. *The London Diaries of William Nicolson, Bishop of Carlisle, 1702–1718.* Ed. Clyve Jones and Geoffrey Holmes. Oxford, 1985.

O'Callaghan, E. B., ed. *The Documentary History of the State of New-York.* 4 vols. Albany, N.Y., 1849–1851.

———. *Documents Relative to the Colonial History of the State of New York.* 15 vols. Albany, N.Y., 1853–1887.

Penn, William. *The Papers of William Penn.* Ed. Mary Maples Dunn, Richard S. Dunn, et al. 5 vols. Philadelphia, 1981–1987.

Perry, William S., ed. *Historical Collections Relating to the American Colonial Church.* 4 vols. Hartford, Conn., 1870.

[Philly, John]. *A Paraphrastical Exposition on a Letter from a Gentleman in Philadelphia to His Friend in Boston.* New York, 1693.

*Playing Cards of Various Ages and Countries, Selected from the Collection of Lady Charlotte Schreiber.* 3 vols. London, 1892.

Pusey, Caleb. *Some Remarks upon a Late Pamphlet.* Philadelphia, 1705.

R., C. *The Danger of Masquerades and Raree-Shows.* . . . London, 1718.

Sainsbury, W. Noel, et al., eds. *Calendar of State Papers.* Colonial Series. *America and West Indies.* 35 vols. London, 1860–1939.

*Select Trials . . . at the Sessions-House in the Old-Bailey.* 2d ed. 4 vols. London, 1742.

Sewall, Samuel. *The Diary of Samuel Sewall, 1674–1729.* Ed. M. Halsey Thomas. 2 vols. New York, 1973.

Sharpe, John. "Journal of Rev. John Sharpe." *Pennsylvania Magazine of History and Biography*, XL (1916), 257–297.

————. *A Sermon Preached at the Funeral of the Right Honorable Katherine Lady Cornbury, the Thirteenth of August, 1706*. New York, 1706.

Shaw, William A., ed. *Calendar of Treasury Books*. Vol. XVI. *1 October 1700 to 31 December 1701*. London, 1938.

Singer, Samuel Weller, ed. *The Correspondence of Henry Hyde, Earl of Clarendon, and of His Brother Laurence Hyde, Earl of Rochester; with the Diary of Lord Clarendon from 1687 to 1690. . . .* 2 vols. London, 1828.

Smith, William, Jr. *The History of the Province of New-York: From the First Discovery to the Year 1732*. 1757. Ed. Michael Kammen. 2 vols. Cambridge, Mass., 1972.

Snyder, Henry L., ed. *The Marlborough-Godolphin Correspondence*. 3 vols. Oxford, 1975.

Stock, Leo Francis, ed. *Proceedings and Debates of the British Parliaments respecting North America*. 5 vols. Washington, D.C., 1924–1941.

Swift, Jonathan. *The Correspondence of Jonathan Swift, D.D*. Ed. F. Elrington Ball. 6 vols. London, 1910–1914.

[Timberland, Ebenezer]. *The History and Proceedings of the House of Lords. . . .* London, 1742.

Tutchin, John. *The Foreigners: A Poem*. Part I. London, 1700.

van Laer, A. J. F., ed. *Minutes of the Court of Fort Orange and Beverwyck, 1652–1660*. 2 vols. Albany, N.Y., 1920–1923.

Walpole, Horace. *Horace Walpole's Correspondence*. Vol. XXXIII. Ed. W. S. Lewis et al. New Haven, Conn., 1965.

————. "Horace Walpole's Journals of Visits to Country Seats etc." Ed. Paget Toynbee. *Walpole Society*, XVI (1927–1928), 9–80.

[Ward, Edward]. *A Compleat and Humorous Account of All the Remarkable Clubs and Societies in the Cities of London and Westminster. . . .* 1709. London, 1745.

[————]. *Hudibras Redivivus; or, A Burlesque Poem on the Times*. London, 1705.

Wentworth, Thomas. *The Wentworth Papers, 1705–1739 . . . Private and Family Correspondence of Thomas Wentworth . . . Earl of Strafford*. Ed. James J. Cartwright. London, 1883.

White, Antonia, trans., and Robert Baldick, intro. *Memoirs of Chevalier d'Eon*. London, 1970.

Whitehead, William A., et al., eds. *New Jersey Archives: Documents Relating to the Colonial History of the State of New Jersey*. 43 vols. Newark, N.J., 1880–1949.

*Women-Hater's Lamentation, The. . . .* London, 1707.

Wood, Anthony. *The Life and Times of Anthony Wood, Antiquary, of Oxford, 1632–1695, Described by Himself*. Ed. Andrew Clark. 5 vols. Oxford, 1891–1900.

Wraxall, Peter. *An Abridgement of the Indian Affairs . . . in the Colony of New York . . . 1678 to . . . 1751.* Ed. Charles Howard McIlwain. Cambridge, Mass., 1915.


SECONDARY SOURCES

Ackroyd, Peter. *Dressing Up, Transvestism, and Drag: The History of an Obsession.* New York, 1979.

Andrew, Donna T. "The Code of Honour and Its Critics: The Opposition to Duelling in England, 1700–1850." *Social History,* V (1980), 409–434.

Ariès, Philippe. *Centuries of Childhood: A Social History of Family Life.* New York, 1962.

Atkinson, C. T. *History of the Royal Dragoons, 1661–1934.* Glasgow, 1934.

Auchincloss, Louis, ed. *The Hone and Strong Diaries of Old Manhattan.* New York, 1989.

Bahlman, Dudley W. R. *The Moral Revolution of 1688.* New Haven, Conn., 1957.

Bailey, F. G., ed. *Gifts and Poison: The Politics of Reputation.* New York, 1971.

Bailyn, Bernard. *The Ideological Origins of the American Revolution.* Cambridge, Mass., 1967.

———. *The Origins of American Politics.* 1967. Rpt. New York, 1970.

Balmer, Randall. *A Perfect Babel of Confusion: Dutch Religion and English Culture in the Middle Colonies.* New York, 1989.

Bancroft, George. *History of the United States from the Discovery of the American Continent.* 19th ed. Vol. III. Boston, 1866.

Barnard, E. A. B. "The Pakingtons of Westwood." Worcestershire Archeological Society, *Transactions,* N.S., XIII (1937), 28–47.

Barrow, Thomas C. *Trade and Empire: The British Customs Service in Colonial America, 1660–1775.* Cambridge, Mass., 1967.

Baxter, Stephen B. *William III and the Defense of European Liberty, 1650–1702.* London, 1966.

Beckett, J. V. *The Aristocracy in England, 1660–1914.* Oxford, 1986.

Belknap, Waldron Phoenix, Jr. *American Colonial Painting: Materials for a History.* Cambridge, Mass., 1959.

Bentler, P. M., and Charles Prince. "Psychiatric Symptomatology in Transvestites." *Journal of Clinical Psychology,* XXVI (1970), 434–436.

Beresford, John. *Gossip of the Seventeenth and Eighteenth Centuries.* London, 1923.

Bergmann, Jörg R. *Discreet Indiscretions: The Social Organization of Gossip.* 1987. Trans. John Bednarz, Jr. New York, 1993.

Bill, E. G. W. *Education at Christ Church, Oxford, 1660–1800.* Oxford, 1988.

Black, Jeremy. *The English Press in the Eighteenth Century.* London, 1987.

Black, Mary. "Contributions toward a History of Early Eighteenth-Century New York Portraiture: Identification of the Aetatis Suae and Wendell Limners." *American Art Journal,* XII, no. 4 (Autumn 1980), 4–31.

Bonomi, Patricia U. *A Factious People: Politics and Society in Colonial New York.* New York, 1971.

Borgeaud, Charles. *Histoire de l'Université de Genève.* I. *L'Académie de Calvin, 1559–1796.* Geneva, 1900.

Braverman, Richard. *Plots and Counterplots: Sexual Politics and the Body Politic in English Literature, 1660–1730.* Cambridge, 1993.

Bray, Alan. *Homosexuality in Renaissance England.* London, 1982; New York, 1995.

Breen, Timothy H. "The Meaning of 'Likeness': American Portrait Painting in an Eighteenth-Century Consumer Society." *Word and Image,* VI (1990), 325–350.

Brewer, John. *The Sinews of Power: War, Money, and the English State, 1688–1783.* New York, 1989.

Bridenbaugh, Carl. *Mitre and Sceptre: Transatlantic Faiths, Ideas, Personalities, and Politics, 1689–1775.* New York, 1962.

Brierley, Harry. *Transvestism: A Handbook with Case Studies for Psychologists, Psychiatrists, and Counsellors.* Oxford, 1979.

Brodhead, J. Romeyn. "Lord Cornbury." *Historical Magazine* [Morrisania, N.Y.], N.S., III (January 1868), 71–72.

Brooks, Colin. "The Country Persuasion and Political Responsibility in England in the 1690s." *Parliaments, Estates, and Representation,* IV, no. 2 (December 1984), 135–146.

Brown, Kathleen. "'Changed . . . into the Fashion of a Man': The Politics of Sexual Difference in a Seventeenth-Century Anglo-American Settlement." *Journal of the History of Sexuality,* VI (1995), 171–193.

Bucholz, R. O. *The Augustan Court: Queen Anne and the Decline of Court Culture.* Stanford, Calif., 1993.

Buel, Richard, Jr. "Freedom of the Press in Revolutionary America: The Evolution of Libertarianism, 1760–1820." In Bernard Bailyn and John B. Hench, eds., *The Press and the American Revolution,* 59–97. Worcester, Mass., 1981.

Buhrich, Neil, and Neil McConaghy. "Three Clinically Discrete Categories of Fetishistic Transvestism." *Archives of Sexual Behavior,* VIII (1979), 151–157.

Bushman, Richard L. *The Refinement of America: Persons, Houses, Cities.* New York, 1992.

Bushnell, Rebecca W. *Tragedies of Tyrants: Political Thought and Theater in the English Renaissance.* Ithaca, N.Y., 1990.

Butler, Jon. "Into Pennsylvania's Spiritual Abyss: The Rise and Fall of the Later Keithians, 1693–1703." *Pennsylvania Magazine of History and Biography,* CI (1977), 151–170.

Castle, Terry. "The Culture of Travesty: Sexuality and Masquerade in Eighteenth-Century England." In G. S. Rousseau and Roy Porter, eds., *Sexual Underworlds of the Enlightenment,* 156–180. Chapel Hill, N.C., 1988.

Childs, John. *The Army, James II, and the Glorious Revolution.* New York, 1980.

Clark, Charles E. *The Public Prints: The Newspaper in Anglo-American Culture, 1665–1740.* New York, 1994.

Clark, Dora Mae. *The Rise of the British Treasury: Colonial Administration in the Eighteenth Century.* New Haven, Conn., 1960.

Clark, J. C. D. *English Society, 1688–1832: Ideology, Social Structure, and Political Practice during the Ancien Regime.* New York, 1985.

———. *The Language of Liberty, 1660–1832: Political Discourse and Social Dynamics in the Anglo-American World.* Cambridge, 1994.

Colley, Linda. *In Defiance of Oligarchy: The Tory Party, 1714–60.* Cambridge, 1982.

Cos, Cynthia. *The Enigma of the Age: The Strange Story of the Chevalier d'Eon.* London, 1966.

Cressy, David. *Bonfires and Bells: National Memory and the Protestant Calendar in Elizabethan and Stuart England.* Berkeley, Calif., 1989.

Darnton, Robert. *The Literary Underground of the Old Regime.* Cambridge, Mass., 1982.

Davenport-Hines, Richard. *Sex, Death, and Punishment: Attitudes to Sex and Sexuality in Britain since the Renaissance.* London, 1990.

Davis, Natalie Zemon. "Women on Top." In Davis, *Society and Culture in Early Modern France,* 124–151. Stanford, Calif., 1975.

de Kay, Ormonde, Jr. "His Most Detestable High Mightiness." *American Heritage,* XXVII, no. 3 (April 1976), 60–61, 89.

Dekker, Rudolf M., and Lotte C. van de Pol. *The Tradition of Female Transvestism in Early Modern Europe.* London, 1989.

De Krey, Gary Stuart. *A Fractured Society: The Politics of London in the First Age of Party, 1688–1715.* Oxford, 1985.

Delafield, Julia. *Biographies of Francis Lewis and Morgan Lewis.* 2 vols. New York, 1877.

Dickerson, Oliver Morton. *American Colonial Government, 1696–1765....* Cleveland, Ohio, 1912.

Dickinson, H. T. *Liberty and Property: Political Ideology in Eighteenth-Century Britain.* London, 1977.

———. "The Precursors of Political Radicalism in Augustan Britain." In Clyve Jones, ed., *Britain in the First Age of Party, 1680–1750,* 63–84. London, 1987.

Dickson, P. G. M. *The Financial Revolution in England: A Study in the Development in Public Credit, 1688–1756.* 2d ed. Aldershot, Hampshire, 1993.

Docter, Richard F. *Transvestites and Transsexuals: Toward a Theory of Cross-Gender Behavior.* New York, 1988.

Downie, J. A. "The Development of the Political Press." In Clyve Jones, ed., *Britain in the First Age of Party, 1680–1750: Essays Presented to Geoffrey Holmes,* 111–128. London, 1987.

Dumont, Eugène-Louis. *Exercices de l'arquebuze et de la navagation.* Geneva, 1979.

Dunn, Richard S. *Puritans and Yankees: The Winthrop Dynasty of New England, 1630–1717.* 1962. New York, 1971.

Easton, Kenneth Fraser. "Bad Habits: Cross-Dressing and the Regulation of Gender in Eighteenth-Century British Literature and Society." Ph.D. diss., Princeton University, 1990.

Egerton, Hugh Edward. *A Short History of British Colonial Policy.* London, 1897.

Elkins, Stanley, and Eric McKitrick. *The Age of Federalism.* New York, 1993.

Field, Richard S. *The Provincial Courts of New Jersey.* New York, 1849.

Fletcher, Anthony. *Gender, Sex, and Subordination in England, 1500–1800.* New Haven, Conn., 1995.

Foster, Joseph, comp. *Alumni Oxonienses . . . 1500–1714.* Oxford, 1888. Rpt. Nendeln, Liechtenstein, 1968.

Fox, Adam. "Ballads, Libels, and Popular Ridicule in Jacobean England." *Past and Present,* no. 145 (November 1994), 47–83.

Foxon, David. *Libertine Literature in England, 1660–1745.* New Hyde Park, N.Y., 1965.

Friedli, Lynne. "'Passing Women' — A Study of Gender Boundaries in the Eighteenth Century." In G. S. Rousseau and Roy Porter, eds., *Sexual Underworlds of the Enlightenment,* 234–260. Chapel Hill, N.C., 1988.

Fryer, Peter. *Mrs. Grundy: Studies in English Prudery.* London, 1963.

Garber, Marjorie. *Vested Interests: Cross-Dressing and Cultural Anxiety.* New York, 1992.

Gerard, James W. "The Dongan Charter of the City of New York." *Magazine of American History,* XVI (July 1886), 30–49.

Gibbs, Vicary, ed. *The Complete Peerage. . . .* New ed. London, 1913.

Gibson, Robin, comp. *Catalogue of Portraits in the Collection of the Earl of Clarendon.* Wallop, Hampshire, 1977.

Gilbert, Arthur N. "Buggery and the British Navy, 1700–1861." *Journal of Social History,* X (1976–1977), 72–98.

Gladfelter, Valerie G. "Power Challenged: Rising Individualism in the Burlington, New Jersey, Friends Meeting, 1678–1720." In Michael Zuckerman, ed., *Friends and Neighbors: Group Life in America's First Plural Society,* 116–144. Philadelphia, 1982.

Goldman, Paul. *Sporting Life: An Anthology of British Sporting Prints.* London, 1983.

"Governor in Petticoats, A." *Historical Magazine* (Morrisania, N.Y.), 2d Ser., II (1867), 169.

Grahame, James. *The History of the United States of North America.* 4 vols. Boston, 1845.

Greene, Evarts Boutell. *The Provincial Governor in the English Colonies of North America.* 1898. Rpt. New York, 1966.

Greene, Jack P. *Peripheries and Center: Constitutional Development in the Extended Polities of the British Empire and the United States, 1607–1788.* Athens, Ga., 1986.

———. *The Quest for Power: The Lower Houses of Assembly in the Southern Royal Colonies, 1689–1776.* 1963. Rpt. New York, 1972.

Gregg, Edward. *Queen Anne.* London, 1980.

Griffin, Dustin. *Satire: A Critical Reintroduction.* Lexington, Ky., 1994.

Haan, Richard. "The Problem of Iroquois Neutrality: Suggestions for Revision." *Ethnohistory,* XXVII (1980), 318–330.

Haefeli, Evan, and Kevin Sweeney. "Revisiting *The Redeemed Captive:* New Perspectives on the 1704 Attack on Deerfield." *William and Mary Quarterly,* 3d Ser., LII (1995), 3–46.

Halsband, Robert. *Lord Hervey, Eighteenth-Century Courtier.* New York, 1974.

Harris, Frances. *A Passion for Government: The Life of Sarah, Duchess of Marlborough.* Oxford, 1991.

Harris, Tim. *Politics under the Later Stuarts: Party Conflict in a Divided Society, 1660–1715.* New York, 1993.

Hatfield, Edwin F. *History of Elizabeth, New Jersey.* New York, 1868.

Hayton, David. "Moral Reform and Country Politics in the Late Seventeenth-Century House of Commons." *Past and Present,* no. 128 (August 1990), 48–91.

Helffenstein, Abraham Ernest. *Pierre Fauconnier and His Descendants. . . .* Philadelphia, 1911.

Hills, George Morgan. *History of the Church in Burlington, New Jersey.* Trenton, N.J., 1876.

Hirschfeld, Magnus. *Transvestites: The Erotic Drive to Cross-Dress.* 1910. Rpt. Buffalo, N.Y., 1991.

Hoffer, Peter Charles. "Honor and the Roots of American Litigiousness." *American Journal of Legal History,* XXIII (1989), 297–319.

Hofstadter, Richard. *The Idea of a Party System: The Rise of Legitimate Opposition in the United States, 1780–1840.* Berkeley, Calif., 1969.

Holmes, Geoffrey. *British Politics in the Age of Anne.* 1967. Rev. ed. London, 1987.

Horn, Robert D. *Marlborough: A Survey: Panegyrics, Satires, and Biographical Writings, 1688–1788.* New York, 1975.

Horwitz, Henry. *Parliament, Policy, and Politics in the Reign of William III.* Manchester, 1977.

———. *Revolution Politicks: The Career of Daniel Finch, Second Earl of Nottingham, 1647–1730.* Cambridge, 1968.

Howard, Jean E. "Crossdressing, the Theatre, and Gender Struggle in Early Modern England." *Shakespeare Quarterly,* XXXIX (1988), 418–440.

Howe, Adrian. "The Bayard Treason Trial: Dramatizing Anglo-Dutch Politics in Early Eighteenth-Century New York City." *William and Mary Quarterly,* 3d Ser., XLVII (1990), 57–89.

Howson, Gerald. *Thief-Taker General: The Rise and Fall of Jonathan Wild.* London, 1970.

Humphreys, David. *An Historical Account of the Incorporated Society for the Propagation of the Gospel in Foreign Parts. . . .* London, 1730.

Hunt, Lynn. *The Family Romance of the French Revolution.* Berkeley, Calif., 1992.

Jesse, John Heneage. *Memoirs of the Court of England: George Selwyn and His Contemporaries.* Boston, 1843.

Johnson, Richard R. *Adjustment to Empire: The New England Colonies, 1675– 1715.* New Brunswick, N.J., 1981.

———. "Politics Redefined: An Assessment of Recent Writings on the Late Stuart Period of English History, 1660–1714." *William and Mary Quarterly,* 3d Ser., XXXV (1978), 691–732.

Jones, Clyve. "The House of Lords and the Growth of Parliamentary Stability, 1704–1742." In Jones, ed., *Britain in the First Age of Party, 1680–1750: Essays Presented to Geoffrey Holmes,* 85–110. London, 1987.

Jones, J. R. *Country and Court: England, 1658–1714.* Cambridge, Mass., 1978.

Kammen, Michael. *Colonial New York: A History.* New York, 1975.

Kates, Gary. "D'Eon Returns to France: Gender and Power in 1777." In Julia Epstein and Kristina Straub, eds., *Body Guards: The Cultural Politics of Gender Ambiguity,* 167–194. New York, 1991.

———. *Monsieur d'Eon Is a Woman: A Tale of Political Intrigue and Sexual Masquerade.* New York, 1995.

Katz, Jonathan Ned. *Gay-Lesbian Almanac: A New Documentary.* New York, 1983.

Katz, Stanley Nider. *Newcastle's New York: Anglo-American Politics, 1732–1753.* Cambridge, Mass., 1968.

Kenyon, J. P. *Revolution Principles: The Politics of Party, 1689–1720.* Cambridge, 1977.

———. *Robert Spencer, Earl of Sunderland, 1641–1702.* London, 1958.

Kishlansky, Mark A. *Parliamentary Selection: Social and Political Choice in Early Modern England.* Cambridge, 1986.

Klein, Lawrence E. *Shaftesbury and the Culture of Politeness: Moral Discourse and Cultural Politics in Early Eighteenth-Century England.* Cambridge, 1994.

Kouwenhoven, John A. *The Columbia Historical Portrait of New York.* Garden City, N.Y., 1953.

Kramnick, Isaac. *Bolingbroke and His Circle: The Politics of Nostalgia in the Age of Walpole.* Cambridge, Mass., 1968.

Kross, Jessica. "'Patronage Most Ardently Sought': The New York Council, 1665–1775." In Bruce C. Daniels, ed., *Power and Status: Officeholding in Colonial America.* Middletown, Conn., 1986.

Labaree, Leonard Woods. *Royal Government in America: A Study of the British Colonial System before 1783.* New York, 1958.

Langevin, Ron. "The Meanings of Cross-Dressing." In Betty W. Steiner, ed., *Gender Dysphoria: Development, Research, Management,* 207–225. New York, 1985.

Leamon, James S. "Governor Fletcher's Recall." *William and Mary Quarterly,* 3d Ser., XX (1963), 527–542.

Leder, Lawrence H. "Robert Hunter's *Androboros*." *Bulletin of the New York Public Library,* LXVIII (1964), 153–190.

———. *Robert Livingston, 1654–1728, and the Politics of Colonial New York.* Chapel Hill, N.C., 1961.

Lee, Francis Bazley. *New Jersey as a Colony and as a State.* 4 vols. New York, 1902.

Lee, Jae Num. *Swift and Scatological Satire.* Albuquerque, N.M., 1971.

Levin, Carole. *"The Heart and Stomach of a King": Elizabeth I and the Politics of Sex and Power.* Philadelphia, 1994.

Levy, Leonard W. *Emergence of a Free Press.* New York, 1985.

———. *Legacy of Suppression: Freedom of Speech and Press in Early American History.* New York, 1960.

Lewis, Lady Theresa. *Lives of the Friends and Contemporaries of Lord Chancellor Clarendon: Illustrative of Portraits in His Gallery.* 3 vols. London, 1852.

Lockard, Duane. *The New Jersey Governor: A Study in Political Power.* Princeton, N.J., 1964.

Love, Harold. "Rochester and the Traditions of Satire." In Love, ed., *Restoration Literature: Critical Approaches,* 145–175. London, 1972.

Lustig, Mary Lou. *Robert Hunter, 1666–1734: New York's Augustan Statesman.* Syracuse, N.Y., 1983.

Macaulay, Thomas Babington. *The History of England from the Accession of James II.* Ed. Charles Harding Firth. 6 vols. 1914. Rpt. New York, 1968.

Maccubbin, Robert Purks, ed. *'Tis Nature's Fault: Unauthorized Sexuality during the Enlightenment.* Cambridge, 1987.

McIntosh, Mary. "The Homosexual Role." *Social Problems,* XVI (1968), 182–192.

McKeon, Michael. "Historicizing Patriarchy: The Emergence of Gender Difference in England, 1660–1760." *Eighteenth-Century Studies,* XXVIII (1995), 295–322.

Mahon, Lord [Philip H. Stanhope]. *History of England, Comprising the Reign of Queen Anne until the Peace of Utrecht.* 2d ed. London, 1870.

————. *History of England from the Peace of Utrecht to the Peace of Versailles, 1713–1783.* 3d ed. London, 1853.

Manross, William Wilson. *A History of the American Episcopal Church.* New York, 1935.

Melville, Lewis [pseud. of Lewis Saul Benjamin]. *Life and Letters of John Gay.* . . . London, 1921.

Miller, Helen Hill. *Colonel Parke of Virginia: The Greatest Hector in Town: A Biography.* Chapel Hill, N.C., 1989.

Monod, Paul Kléber. *Jacobitism and the English People, 1688–1788.* Cambridge, 1989.

Moogk, Peter N. "'Thieving Buggers' and 'Stupid Sluts': Insults and Popular Culture in New France." *William and Mary Quarterly,* 3d Ser., XXXVI (1979), 524–547.

Morgan, Edmund S. *American Slavery, American Freedom: The Ordeal of Colonial Virginia.* New York, 1975.

Morgan, John Hill. *John Watson, Painter, Merchant, and Capitalist of New Jersey, 1685–1768.* Worcester, Mass., 1941. Orig. publ. as American Antiquarian Society, *Proceedings,* L, pt. 1 (1940), 225–317.

Naef, Ernest. "Les exercices militaire à Genève." *Genava: Bulletin du Musée d'Art et d'Histoire de Genève,* XI (1933), 110–120.

Needham, Raymond, and Alexander Webster. *Somerset House, Past and Present.* London, 1905.

Newton, Esther. *Mother Camp: Female Impersonators in America.* Englewood Cliffs, N.J., 1972.

Norton, Mary Beth. *Founding Mothers and Fathers: Gendered Power and the Forming of American Society.* New York, 1996.

————. "Gender and Defamation in Seventeenth-Century Maryland." *William and Mary Quarterly,* 3d Ser., XLIV (1987), 3–39.

Norton, Rictor. *Mother Clap's Molly Home: The Gay Subculture in England, 1700–1830.* London, 1992.

Ollard, Richard. *Clarendon and His Friends.* New York, 1988.

Olson, Alison Gilbert. *Anglo-American Politics, 1660–1775: The Relationship between Parties in England and Colonial America.* New York, 1973.

————. *Making the Empire Work: London and American Interest Groups, 1690–1790.* Cambridge, Mass., 1992.

————. "William Penn, Parliament, and Proprietary Government." *William and Mary Quarterly,* 3d Ser., XVIII (1961), 176–195.

O'Neill, John H. "Sexuality, Deviance, and Moral Character in the Personal Satire of the Restoration." *Eighteenth-Century Life,* II (1975–1976), 16–19.

Osgood, Herbert L. *The American Colonies in the Eighteenth Century.* 4 vols. New York, 1924–1925.

Paine, Robert. "What is Gossip About? An Alternative Hypothesis." *MAN,* N.S., II (1967), 278–285.

Pargellis, Stanley McCrory. "The Four Independent Companies of New York." In *Essays in Colonial History Presented to Charles McLean Andrews by His Students,* 96–123. 1931. Rpt. Freeport, N.Y., 1966.

Parks, Stephen. *John Dunton and the English Book Trade. . . .* New York, 1976.

Peckham, Howard H. *The Colonial Wars, 1689–1762.* Chicago, 1964.

Pierce, Arthur D. "A Governor in Skirts." New Jersey Historical Society, *Proceedings,* LXXXVIII (1965), 1–9.

Pinkus, Philip. *Grub St. Stripped Bare: The Scandalous Lives and Pornographic Works of the Original Grub St. Writers. . . .* Hamden, Conn., 1968.

Piper, David, comp. *Catalogue of Seventeenth-Century Portraits in the National Portrait Gallery, 1625–1714.* Cambridge, 1963.

Plumb, J. H. *The Growth of Political Stability in England, 1675–1725.* London, 1967.

————. *Sir Robert Walpole: The Making of a Statesman.* Boston, 1956.

Plummer, Kenneth, ed. *The Making of the Modern Homosexual.* London, 1981.

Pocock, J. G. A. *The Machiavellian Moment: Florentine Political Thought and the Atlantic Republican Tradition.* Princeton, N.J., 1975.

Purvis, Thomas L. *Proprietors, Patronage, and Paper Money: Legislative Politics in New Jersey, 1703–1776.* New Brunswick, N.J., 1986.

Quimby, Ian M. G., ed. *American Painting to 1776: A Reappraisal.* Charlottesville, Va., 1971.

Reynolds, Patrick M. *Big Apple Almanac.* Willow Street, Pa., 1989–.

Richards, James O. *Party Propaganda under Queen Anne: The General Elections of 1702–1713.* Athens, Ga., 1972.

Richter, Daniel K. *The Ordeal of the Longhouse: The Peoples of the Iroquois League in the Era of European Colonization.* Chapel Hill, N.C., 1992.

Ritchie, Robert C. *Captain Kidd and the War against the Pirates.* Cambridge, Mass., 1986.

Rogers, Pat. *Grub Street: Studies in a Subculture.* London, 1972.

Ross, Shelley. *Fall from Grace: Sex, Scandal, and Corruption in American Politics, from 1702 to the Present.* New York, 1988.

Rouse, Parke, Jr. *James Blair of Virginia*. Chapel Hill, N.C., 1971.

Rousseau, G. S. *Perilous Enlightenment: Pre- and Post-Modern Discourses*. Manchester, 1991.

Rubincam, Milton. "The Formative Years of Lord Cornbury, the First Royal Governor of New York and New Jersey." *New York Genealogical and Biographical Record*, LXXI (1940), 106–116.

Rubini, Dennis. "Sexuality and Augustan England: Sodomy, Politics, Elite Circles, and Society." *Journal of Homosexuality*, XVI (1988), 349–381.

Runcie, John D. "The Problem of Anglo-American Politics in Bellomont's New York." *William and Mary Quarterly*, 3d Ser., XXVI (1969), 191–217.

Russell, Lady Charlotte C. *Swallowfield and Its Owners*. London, 1901.

Sabor, Peter. "Horace Walpole as a Historian." *Eighteenth-Century Life*, XI (1987), 5–17.

Sacks, David Harris. "Searching for 'Culture' in the English Renaissance." *Shakespeare Quarterly*, XXXIX (1988), 465–488.

Saunders, Richard H., and Ellen G. Miles. *American Colonial Portraits, 1700–1776*. Washington, D.C., 1987.

Schama, Simon. *The Embarrassment of Riches: An Interpretation of Dutch Culture in the Golden Age*. New York, 1987.

Schenkeveld, Maria A. *Dutch Literature in the Age of Rembrandt: Themes and Ideas*. Amsterdam, 1991.

Schidlof, Leo R. *La miniature en Europe. . . .* Graz, 1964.

Seaward, Paul. *The Cavalier Parliament and the Reconstruction of the Old Regime, 1661–1667*. Cambridge, 1989.

Sellers, Charles Coleman. "Mezzotint Prototypes of Colonial Portraiture. . . ." *Art Quarterly*, XX (1957), 407–468.

Sheridan, Eugene R. *Lewis Morris, 1671–1746: A Study in Early American Politics*. Syracuse, N.Y., 1981.

Shields, David S. *Civil Tongues and Polite Letters in British America*. Chapel Hill, N.C., 1997.

———. *Oracles of Empire: Poetry, Politics, and Commerce in British America, 1690–1750*. Chicago, 1990.

Siebert, Frederick Seaton. *Freedom of the Press in England, 1476–1776*. Urbana, Ill., 1952.

Snyder, Henry L. "Newsletters in England, 1689–1715, with Special Reference to John Dyer — A Byway in the History of England." In Donovan H. Bond and W. Reynolds McLeod, eds., *Newsletters to Newspapers: Eighteenth-Century Journalism*, 3–19. Morgantown, W. Va., 1977.

Sosin, J. M. *English America and Imperial Inconstancy: The Rise of Provincial Autonomy, 1696–1715*. Lincoln, Nebr., 1985.

Spacks, Patricia Meyer. *Gossip*. New York, 1985.

Speck, W. A. *The Birth of Britain: A New Nation, 1700–1710.* Oxford, 1994.

———. "The International and Imperial Context." In Jack P. Greene and J. R. Pole, eds., *Colonial British America: Essays in the New History of the Early Modern Era,* 384–407. Baltimore, 1984.

———. "Political Propaganda in Augustan England." Royal Historical Society, *Transactions,* 5th Ser., XXII (1972), 17–32.

———. *Reluctant Revolutionaries: Englishmen and the Revolution of 1688.* Oxford, 1988.

Spencer, Charles Worthen. "The Cornbury Legend." New York State Historical Association, *Proceedings,* XIII (1914), 309–320.

Spielmann, M. H. *British Portrait Painting to the Opening of the Nineteenth Century.* 2 vols. London, 1910.

Spitzka, E. C. "A Historical Case of Sexual Perversion." *Chicago Medical Review,* IV (August 1881), 378–379.

Staves, Susan. "A Few Kind Words for the Fop." *Studies in English Literature,* XXII (1982), 413–428.

Steele, Ian K. "The Board of Trade, the Quakers, and Resumption of Colonial Charters, 1699–1702." *William and Mary Quarterly,* 3d Ser., XXIII (1966), 596–619.

———. *The English Atlantic, 1675–1740: An Exploration of Communication and Community.* New York, 1986.

———. *Politics of Colonial Policy: The Board of Trade in Colonial Administration, 1696–1720.* Oxford, 1968.

Stevens, Henry, comp. *An Analytical Index to the Colonial Documents of New Jersey, in the State Paper Offices of England.* 5 vols. New York, 1858.

Stoller, Robert J. *Sex and Gender: The Transsexual Experiment.* 2 vols. New York, 1975.

Stone, Lawrence, and Jeanne Fawtier Stone. *An Open Elite? England, 1540–1880.* Oxford, 1984.

Strassburger, John. "'Our Unhappy Purchase': The West Jersey Society, Lewis Morris, and Jersey Lands, 1703–36." *New Jersey History,* XLVIII (1980), 97–113.

Straub, Kristina. *Sexual Suspects: Eighteenth-Century Players and Sexual Ideology.* Princeton, N.J., 1992.

Strickland, Agnes. *Lives of the Queens of England.* 12 vols. London, 1842–1847.

Sweet, Frederick A. "Mezzotint Sources of American Colonial Portraits." *Art Quarterly,* XIV (1951), 148–157.

Telfer, J. Buchan. *The Strange Career of the Chevalier D'Eon de Beaumont. . . .* London, 1885.

Thomas, Keith. "As You Like It." *New York Review of Books,* XLI, no. 15 (Sept. 22, 1994), 9–12.

Tolles, Frederick B. *James Logan and the Culture of Provincial America*. Boston, 1957.

Troyer, Howard William. *Ned Ward of Grubstreet: A Study of Sub-Literary London in the Eighteenth Century*. Cambridge, Mass., 1946.

Trumbach, Randolph. "The Birth of the Queen: Sodomy and the Emergence of Gender Equality in Modern Culture, 1660–1750." In Martin Bauml Duberman et al., eds., *Hidden From History: Reclaiming the Gay and Lesbian Past*, 129–140. New York, 1989.

———. "London's Sodomites: Homosexual Behavior and Western Culture in the Eighteenth Century." *Journal of Social History*, XI (1977–1978), 1–33.

———. "Sodomitical Subcultures, Sodomitical Roles, and the Gender Revolution of the Eighteenth Century: The Recent Historiography." *Eighteenth-Century Life*, IX (1985), 109–121.

———. "Sodomy Transformed: Aristocratic Libertinage, Public Reputation, and the Gender Revolution of the Eighteenth Century." *Journal of Homosexuality*, XIX, (1990), 105–124.

Underdown, David. *Revel, Riot, and Rebellion: Popular Politics and Culture in England, 1603–1660*. Oxford, 1985.

Voorhees, David William. "'In Behalf of the True Protestants Religion': The Glorious Revolution in New York." Ph.D. diss., New York University, 1988.

———. "'Rhyme Weg: Leyslers Regeerds': The New York City Election of October 1689." *De Halve Maen*, LXIV (1991), 46–48.

Wagner, Peter. *Eros Revived: Erotica of the Enlightenment in England and America*. London, 1988.

Wall, Helena M. *Fierce Communion: Family and Community in Early America*. Cambridge, Mass., 1990.

Waller, G. M. *Samuel Vetch, Colonial Enterpriser*. Chapel Hill, N.C., 1960.

Watney, Vernon J. *Cornbury and the Forest of Wychwood*. London, 1910.

Webb, Stephen Saunders. *The Governors-General: The English Army and the Definition of the Empire, 1569–1681*. Chapel Hill, N.C., 1979.

———. *Lord Churchill's Coup: The Anglo-American Empire and the Glorious Revolution Reconsidered*. New York, 1995.

———. "The Strange Career of Francis Nicholson." *William and Mary Quarterly*, 3d Ser., XXIII (1966), 513–548.

———. "William Blathwayt, Imperial Fixer: Muddling through to Empire, 1689–1717." *William and Mary Quarterly*, 3d Ser., XXVI (1969), 373–415.

Weeks, Lyman Horace, and Edwin M. Bacon. *An Historical Digest of the Provincial Press*. Boston, 1911.

Weil, Rachel. "Sometimes a Scepter Is Only a Scepter: Pornography and Politics in Restoration England." In Lynn Hunt, ed., *The Invention of*

*Pornography: Obscenity and the Origins of Modernity, 1500—1800*, 125—153. New York, 1993.

Weis, Frederick Lewis. *The Colonial Clergy of the Middle Colonies: New York, New Jersey, and Pennsylvania, 1628—1776*. 1957. Rpt. Baltimore, 1978.

White, Philip L. *The Beekmans of New York in Politics and Commerce, 1647—1877*. New York, 1956.

Wilson, James Grant. *The Memorial History of the City of New York*. 4 vols. New York, 1892—1893.

Wood, Gordon S. "Conspiracy and the Paranoid Style: Causality and Deceit in the Eighteenth Century." *William and Mary Quarterly*, 3d Ser., XXXIX. 1982), 401—441.

———. *The Creation of the American Republic, 1776—1787*. Chapel Hill, N.C., 1969.

———. *The Radicalism of the American Revolution*. New York, 1992.

Wroth, Lawrence C. *The Colonial Printer*. 2d ed. Charlottesville, Va., 1938. Rpt. 1964.

Zwicker, Steven N. *Politics and Language in Dryden's Poetry*. Princeton, N.J., 1984.

———. "Virgins and Whores: The Politics of Sexual Misconduct in the 1660s." In Conal Condren and A. D. Cousins, eds., *The Political Identity of Andrew Marvell*, 85—110. Aldershot, England, 1990.

# Index